Culture and Conquest in Mongol Eurasia

In the thirteenth century the Mongols created a vast transcontinental empire that functioned as a cultural "clearing house" for the Old World. Under Mongol auspices various commodities, ideologies, and technologies were disseminated and displayed across Eurasia. The focus of this path-breaking study is the extensive exchanges between Iran and China. The Mongol rulers of these two ancient civilizations "shared" the cultural resources of their realms with one another. The result was lively traffic in specialist personnel and scholarly literature between East and West. These exchanges ranged from cartography to printing, and from agriculture to astronomy. Unexpectedly, the principal conduit of this transmission was an obscure Mongol tribesman, Bolad Aqa, who first served Chinggisid rulers of China and was then posted to Iran where he entered into a close and productive collaboration with the famed Persian statesman and historian, Rashīd al-Dīn. The conclusion of the work examines why the Mongols made such heavy use of sedentary scholars and specialists in the elaboration of their court culture and why they initiated so many exchanges across Eurasia. The book is informative and erudite. It crosses new scholarly boundaries in its analysis of communication and culture in the Mongol Empire and promises to become a classic in the field.

THOMAS T. ALLSEN is Professor in the Department of History, The College of New Jersey, Ewing. His publications include *Commodity and Exchange in the Mongol Empire: A Cultural History of Islamic Textiles* (1997).

CAMBRIDGE STUDIES IN ISLAMIC CIVILIZATION

Published titles in the series are listed at the back of the book

Culture and Conquest in Mongol Eurasia

THOMAS T. ALLSEN

The College of New Jersey, Ewing

CAMBRIDGE
UNIVERSITY PRESS

PUBLISHED BY THE PRESS SYNDICATE OF THE UNIVERSITY OF CAMBRIDGE
The Pitt Building, Trumpington Street, Cambridge, United Kingdom

CAMBRIDGE UNIVERSITY PRESS
The Edinburgh Building, Cambridge CB2 2RU, UK
40 West 20th Street, New York, NY 10011–4211, USA
477 Williamstown Road, Port Melbourne, VIC 3207, Australia
Ruiz de Alarcón 13, 28014 Madrid, Spain
Dock House, The Waterfront, Cape Town 8001, South Africa

http://www.cambridge.org

First published 2001
Reprinted 2003

Printed in the United Kingdom at the University Press, Cambridge

Typeface Times NR MT 10/12pt *System* QuarkXPress™ [SE]

A catalogue record for this book is available from the British Library

Library of Congress Cataloguing in Publication data

Allsen, Thomas T.
Conquest and Culture in Mongol Eurasia / Thomas T. Allsen.
p. cm. – (Cambridge Studies in Islamic Civilization)
Includes bibliographical references and index.
ISBN 0 521 80335 7
1. China – Relations – Iran. 2. Iran – Relations – China. 3. Mongols – Eurasia.
4. China – Civilization – 13th century. 5. Iran – Civilization – 13th Century. I. Title.
II. Series.

DS740.5.I7 A45 2001
303.48′255051′09022 – dc21 00-054700

ISBN 0 521 80335 7 hardback

Contents

Preface

The present study originated some twenty-five years ago with a chance discovery that the Mongolian courts in China and Iran both sponsored the compilation of agricultural manuals in the course of the late thirteenth and early fourteenth centuries. A few years later I discovered, again quite by accident, that this was not mere coincidence, and that there were indeed "agronomical relations" between these two courts. This in turn led to an interest in other types of cultural exchange between the Il-qans and the Yuan, an exchange that became the focal point of my research over the last decade.

My initial intention was to cover all facets of the interchange in one large monograph but this was clearly impractical. Consequently, I have concentrated here on cultural exchanges in the fields of historiography, geography, cartography, agronomy, cuisine, medicine, astronomy, and printing technology. My investigations into other areas of their contact – language study, popular entertainments, and economic thought, as well as the transfer of military technology and the transcontinental resettlement of artisans of varied specialties – will appear as separate studies.

I have had the opportunity to present my preliminary findings in the form of lectures at a number of academic institutions and the response has always been welcoming and the questions and comments from these audiences most helpful in shaping the direction of my subsequent research. To these various students and scholars I offer my thanks for their guidance and encouragement. I must also record my gratitude to the National Endowment for the Humanities which awarded me a Fellowship for the academic year 1998–99 that permitted me to complete research and prepare a first draft of the manuscript.

Peter Golden and Stephen Dale read and commented on this manuscript and helped to improve it in many substantial ways. So too did the many suggestions and corrections of the anonymous reviewers of the Press. I am deeply indebted to all of these scholars.

I must also offer special thanks to my current department chair, Daniel Crofts, who has supported and facilitated my research over the last several years.

Finally, I again express my profound gratitude to my wife, Lucille Helen Allsen, whose enthusiasm, patience, and editorial and word-processing skills are essential ingredients in all my scholarly endeavors.

Note on transliteration

For Persian, Arabic, and Russian I have used the Library of Congress system. Chinese is in Wade-Giles, and for Mongolian I have used the system found in Cleaves' translation of the *Secret History*. Lastly, for Turkic, I have followed Nadeliaev *et al.*, *Drevnetiurkskii slovar*.

Abbreviations

AEMA	*Archivum Eurasiae Medii Aevi.*
AOASH	*Acta Orientalia Academiae Scientiarum Hungaricae.*
Bar Hebraeus	Bar Hebraeus, *The Chronography of Gregory Abū'l-Faraj . . . commonly known as Bar Hebraeus*, trans. by Ernest A. Wallis Budge, London: Oxford University Press, 1932, vol. I.
BSOAS	*Bulletin of the School of Oriental and African Studies.*
CAJ	*Central Asiatic Journal.*
DTS	Nadeliaev, V. M. *et al.*, eds., *Drevnetiurkskii slovar*, Leningrad: Nauka, 1969.
EI, 2nd edn	*Encyclopedia of Islam*, 2nd edn, Leiden: E. J. Brill, 1960–97, 9 vols. to date.
Farquhar, *Government*	Farquhar, David M., *The Government of China under Mongolian Rule: A Reference Guide*, Stuttgart: Franz Steiner, 1990.
Golden, *Hexaglot*	Golden, Peter B., ed., *The King's Dictionary: The Rasūlid Hexaglot, Fourteenth Century Vocabularies in Arabic, Persian, Turkic, Greek, Armenian and Mongol*, Leiden: Brill, 2000.
HJAS	*Harvard Journal of Asiatic Studies.*
Hsiao, *Military*	Hsiao Ch'i-ch'ing, *The Military Establishment of the Yuan Dynasty*, Cambridge, Mass.: Harvard University Press, 1978.
Ibn Baṭṭuṭah/Gibb	Ibn Baṭṭuṭah, *The Travels of Ibn Baṭṭuṭah*, trans. by H. A. R. Gibb, Cambridge University Press for the Hakluyt Society, 1958–94, 4 vols.
JAOS	*Journal of the American Oriental Society.*
JRAS	*Journal of the Royal Asiatic Society.*
Juvaynī/Boyle	Juvaynī, ʿAtā-Malik, *The History of the World Conqueror*, trans. by John A. Boyle, Cambridge, Mass.: Harvard University Press, 1958, 2 vols.
Juvaynī/Qazvīnī	Juvaynī, ʿAtā-Malik, *Ta'rīkh-i Jahāngushā*, ed. by

	Mīrza Muḥammad Qazvīnī, E. J. W. Gibb Memorial Series, vol. XVI; London: Luzac, 1912–37, 3 vols.
Jūzjānī/Lees	Jūzjānī, *Ṭabaqāt-i nāṣirī*, ed. by W. Nassau Lees, Bibliotheca Indica, vol. XLIV; Calcutta: College Press, 1864.
Jūzjānī/Raverty	Jūzjānī, *Ṭabaqāt-i nāṣirī*, trans. by H. G. Raverty, repr., New Delhi: Oriental Books Reprint Corp., 1970, 2 vols.
Kirakos, *Istoriia*	Kirakos Gandzaketsi, *Istoriia Armenii*, trans. by L. A. Khanlarian, Moscow: Nauka, 1976.
Kōdō Tasaka	Tasaka Kōdō, "An Aspect of Islam[ic] Culture Introduced into China," *Memoirs of the Research Department of Toyo Bunko* 16 (1957), 75–160.
Laufer, *Sino-Iranica*	Laufer, Bertold, *Sino-Iranica: Chinese Contributions to the History of Civilization in Ancient Iran*, repr., Taipei: Ch'eng-wen, 1967.
Marco Polo	Marco Polo, *The Description of the World*, trans. by A. C. Moule and Paul Pelliot, London: Routledge, 1938, vol. I.
Mongol Mission	Dawson, Christopher, ed., *The Mongol Mission: Narratives and Letters of the Franciscan Missionaries in Mongolia and China in the Thirteenth and Fourteenth Centuries*, New York: Sheed and Ward, 1955.
MS	*Monumenta Serica.*
MSC	Wang Shih-tien, *Mi-shu chih*, Taipei: Wei-wen tu-shu pan-she, 1976.
Needham, *SCC*	Needham, Joseph *et al.*, *Science and Civilization in China*, Cambridge University Press, 1954–.
Pelliot, *Notes*	Pelliot, Paul, *Notes on Marco Polo*, Paris: Adrien-Maissoneuve, 1959–61, 2 vols.
Qāshānī/Hambly	Al-Qāshānī, Abū al-Qasīm, *Ta'rīkh-i Ūljaytū*, ed. by Mahin Hambly, Tehran: BTNK, 1969.
Rashīd/Alizade	Rashīd al-Dīn, *Jāmiʿ al-tavārīkh*, ed. by A. A. Alizade, A. A. Romaskevich, and A. A. Khetagurov, Moscow: Nauka, 1968–80, vols. I and II.
Rashīd/Boyle	Rashīd al-Dīn, *The Successors of Genghis Khan*, trans. by John A. Boyle, New York: Columbia University Press, 1971.
Rashīd/Jahn I	Rashīd al-Dīn, *Ta'rīkh-i mubārak-i Ghāzānī*, ed. by Karl Jahn, 's-Gravenhage: Mouton, 1957.
Rashīd/Jahn II	Rashīd al-Dīn, *Ta'rīkh-i mubārak-i Ghāzānī*, ed. by Karl Jahn, London: Luzac, 1940.
Rashīd/Karīmī	Rashīd al-Dīn, *Jāmiʿ al-tavārīkh*, ed. by B. Karīmī, Tehran: Eqbal, 1959, 2 vols.

Rashīd/Quatremère	Raschid-eldin [Rashīd al-Dīn], *Histoire des Mongols de la Perse*, trans. and ed. by E. Quatremère, repr., Amsterdam: Oriental Press, 1968.
Rubruck/Jackson	Jackson, Peter, trans., and David O. Morgan, ed., *The Mission of Friar William of Rubruck*, London: Hakluyt Society, 1990.
Seifeddini	Seifeddini, M. A., *Monetnoe delo i denezhnoe obrashchenie v Azerbaidzhane XII–XV vv.*, Baku: Elm, 1978–81, 2 vols.
SH/Cleaves	*The Secret History of the Mongols*, trans. by Francis W. Cleaves, Cambridge, Mass.: Harvard University Press, 1982.
SH/de Rachewiltz	de Rachewiltz, Igor, *Index to the Secret History of the Mongols*, Indiana University Publications, Uralic and Altaic Series, vol. CXXI, Bloomington, 1972.
TP	*T'oung Pao.*
ʿUmarī/Lech	Al-ʿUmarī, Ibn Faḍl Allāh, *Das mongolische Weltreich: al-ʿUmarīs Darstellung der mongolischen Reiche in seinem Werk Masālik al-abṣār fī mamālik al-amṣar*, trans. by Klaus Lech, Wiesbaden: Otto Harrassowitz, 1968.
Vaṣṣāf	Vaṣṣāf al-Ḥaẓrat, *Taʾrīkh-i Vaṣṣāf*, Tehran: Ibn-i Sina, 1959.
YS	*Yuan shih*, Peking: Chung-hua shu-chü, 1978.
YTC	*Ta-Yuan sheng-cheng kuo-ch'ao tien-chang*, repr. of the Yuan edn, Taipei: Kuo-li ku-kung po-wu yuan, 1976.
Yule, *Cathay*	Yule, Sir Henry, *Cathay and the Way Thither, being a Collection of Medieval Notices of China*, repr., Taipei: Ch'eng-wen Publishing Company, 1966, 4 vols.
YWL	Su T'ien-chüeh, *Yuan wen-lei*, Taipei: Shih-chiai shu-chü ying-hsing, 1967.

PART I

Background

ONE

Introduction

The goals and themes of this work have undergone substantial change in the course of the basic research. As originally conceived, this monograph was to explore the political and diplomatic relationship between the Mongolian courts of China, the Yuan, and Iran, the Il-qans/Il-khāns. I was particularly interested in their joint efforts to stave off the military challenge of their rivals and cousins in central Asia, the lines of Chaghadai and Ögödei, and the western steppe, the line of Jochi, in the last half of the thirteenth century and the early decades of the fourteenth century. To sustain one another against their mutual enemies, the regimes in China and Iran shared economic resources, troops, and war matériel. As time passed, I became increasingly aware that this exchange was far more wide-ranging and diverse, embracing as it did an extensive traffic in specialist personnel, scholarly works, material culture, and technology. My interest in these issues grew and I soon came to the conclusion that these cultural exchanges were perhaps the most consequential facet of their relationship.

This, however, was only the first phase of the work's transformation. Having settled on the issue of cultural exchange as the central theme, I naively assumed that I would proceed by identifying specific exchanges and then assess their "influence": for example, the impact of Chinese physicians in Iran on Islamic medicine. This, I quickly discovered, posed formidable problems of method, interpretation, and evidence. The most obvious difficulty is that any attempt to establish such influence requires a detailed knowledge of Chinese and Islamic medicine before, during, and after the Mongolian conquests. The same stricture, of course, applies to all other areas of contact, such as agronomy, astronomy, etc. And, beyond the intimidating range of topics, I came to realize that I simply lacked the formal training and experience to make meaningful evaluations of these complex issues, most of which are highly technical.

This realization led to one further modification of the goals and themes of the work: in this monograph I will speak primarily to the question of the nature and conditions of the transmission of cultural wares between China and Iran, not the vexed issues of receptivity or rejection of new elements on the part of subject peoples. In other words, I am mainly concerned with how these two courts utilized the cultural resources of their respective domains, Iran and China, in their efforts to succor and support one another.

This reorientation means that early sections on the diplomatic, ideological, and economic relations between the Chinese and Iranian courts, while interesting in themselves, are presented here to provide the political and institutional context in which the Mongolian-inspired cultural exchange took place. A full-scale diplomatic history of Yuan China and Il-qan Iran, sensitive to the changing power relations between the Mongolian, Christian, and Muslim polities of medieval Eurasia, is certainly desirable but not the objective of this study. In fact, it is the overall range, frequency, and intensity of the contacts that are of primary interest here, not the diplomatic goals of specific embassies – a kind of information that in any event is rarely supplied in the sources.

The core of the work, then, is devoted to the movement of specific cultural wares between China and Iran. In each case, I will seek to provide full information on given exchanges, some of which, like astronomy, have been previously studied, while others, such as agronomy, have yet to be investigated. These sections will be for the most part descriptive, with an occasional suggestion, opinion, or hypothesis on the more problematical issue of long- and short-term influences. This, it is hoped, will profitably serve as a guide to specialists interested in tracing contacts and influences between East and West.

The final sections will be devoted to questions of agency and motivation, and here the Mongols, their cultural priorities, political interests, and social norms take center stage. Indeed, the overarching thesis of this work is the centrality of the nomads to East–West exchange.

The nomads of Inner Asia made some notable contributions to world culture, horse riding and felting to name just two, and this, to be sure, has been duly acknowledged.[1] More commonly, however, studies of the cultural traffic across Eurasia have focused on the extremities: the desire and receptivity of the great sedentary societies for one another's products and ideas.[2] When the nomads are brought into the picture their influence on the course of events is usually addressed under the twin rubrics of "communication" and "destruction."[3] In the former, the nomads create a *pax* which secures and facilitates long-distance travel and commerce, encouraging representatives of sedentary civilizations, the Polos for example, to move across the various cultural zones of Eurasia and thereby take on the role of the primary agents of diffusion. In

[1] William Montgomery McGovern, *The Early Empires of Central Asia* (Chapel Hill: University of North Carolina Press, 1939), pp. 1–6.

[2] S. A. Huzayyin, *Arabia and the Far East: Their Commercial and Cultural Relations in Graeco-Roman and Irano-Arabian Times* (Cairo: Publications de la société royale de géographie d'Egypte, 1942), pp. 18–19 and 39.

[3] John A. Boyle, "The Last Barbarian Invaders: The Impact of the Mongolian Conquests upon East and West," *Memoirs and Proceedings of the Manchester Literary and Philosophical Society* 112 (1970), 1–15. Reprinted in his *The Mongolian World Empire, 1206–1370* (London: Variorum Reprints, 1977), art. no. I.

the latter, the nomads, conversely, and perversely, impede contact and destroy culture by their ferocity and military might. For some nationalist historians, nomadic conquest, especially that of the Mongols, was a regressive force in human history accounting for their country's "backwardness" in modern times.[4]

These two visions of nomadic history, as Bernard Lewis points out, are not mutually exclusive alternatives; the nomads destroyed some cultural resources and at the same time created conditions in which long-distance cultural exchange flourished.[5] There was, in fact, both a Pax Mongolica and a Tartar Yoke, inhering and coexisting in the very same polity. But such a formulation, while true so far as it goes, leaves out too much and has limited explanatory power. For a fuller understanding of the place of the nomads in transcontinental exchanges we must look more deeply at the nomads' political culture and social norms which functioned as initial filters in the complex process of sorting and selecting the goods and ideas that passed between East and West.

Indeed, such possibilities of cultural transmission were embedded in the very structure of Mongolian rule and in the basic ecological requirements of nomadism. Because of the need to distribute large numbers of herd animals and small numbers of people over sizable expanses of territory, the Mongols' demographic base was quite limited compared to their sedentary neighbors. In Chinggis Qan's day the population of the eastern steppe, modern Mongolia, was somewhere between 700,000 and 1,000,000.[6] Moreover, as pastoralists, they could hardly provide specialists from their own ranks to administer and exploit the sedentary population that fell under their military control. This critical issue was soon recognized and squarely faced: immediately after the conquest of West Turkestan, ca. 1221, Chinggis Qan sought the advice of Muslim subjects with commercial and/or administrative backgrounds who, in the words of the *Secret History*, were "skillful in the laws and customs of cities [*balaqasun-u törö yasun*]."[7]

As a decided minority in their own state, the Mongols made extensive use of foreigners, without local political ties, to help them rule their vast domains. This technique received its most elaborate development in China, where the Mongols, for purposes of official recruitment and promotion, divided the Yuan population into four categories: Mongols, Central and Western Asians

4 For the conflicting Russian and Chinese views, see Paul Hyer, "The Re-evaluation of Chinggis Khan: Its Role in the Sino-Soviet Dispute," *Asian Survey* 6 (1966), 696–705. For the Mongols' views, see Igor de Rachewiltz, "The Mongols Rethink Their Early History," in *The East and the Meaning of History* (Rome: Bardi Editore, 1994), pp. 357–80.

5 Bernard Lewis, "The Mongols, the Turks and the Muslim Polity," in his *Islam in History: Ideas, Men and Events in the Middle East* (New York: Library Press, 1973), pp. 179–98.

6 On population densities, see N. Ts. Munkuev, "Zametki o drevnikh mongolakh," in S. L. Tikhvinskii, ed., *Tataro-Mongoly v Azii i Evrope*, 2nd edn (Moscow: Nauka, 1977), p. 394; Bat-Ochir Bold, "The Quantity of Livestock Owned by the Mongols in the Thirteenth Century," *JRAS* 8 (1998), 237–46; and A. M. Khazanov, "The Origins of the [sic] Genghiz Khan's State: An Anthropological Approach," *Ethnografia Polska* 24 (1980), 31–33.

7 *SH*/Cleaves, sect 263, p. 203, and *SH*/de Rachewiltz, sect. 263, p. 157.

Table 1 *Personnel exchanges*

"Westerners" in the East		"Easterners" in the West
Italians		**Ongguts**
merchants	physicians	clerics
envoys	musicians	**Khitans**
clerics	administrators	soldiers
French and Flemings		administrators
clerics	envoys	**Uighurs**
goldsmiths	servants	soldiers
Greeks		administrators
soldiers		court merchants
Germans		physicians
miners	artillerymen	scribes
Scandinavians		translators
merchants	soldiers	**Tibetans and Tanguts**
Russians		soldiers
princes	goldsmiths	clerics
envoys	clerics	physicians
soldiers	carpenters	**Mongols**
Hungarians		soldiers
household servants		envoys
Alans		administrators
soldiers	envoys	scribes
armorers	princes	translators
Armenians		wrestlers
clerics	princes	**Chinese**
merchants	envoys	soldiers
Georgians		envoys
envoys	princes	physicians
Nestorians of Iraq and Syria		astronomers
merchants	translators	administrators
physicians	textile workers	"scholars"
astronomers	lemonade makers	cooks
administrators		wetnurses
Arabs and Persians		wives
wrestlers	administrators	carpenters
musicians	translators	stonemasons
singers	scribes	"fire makers" (gunpowder makers?)
merchants	textile workers	artillerymen
envoys	accountants	accountants
astronomers	architects	engineers
physicians	sugar makers	agriculturalists
soldiers	"leopard" keepers	
clerics	geographers	
artillerymen	historians	
valets	carpet makers	

(*se-mu-jen*), North Chinese, and South Chinese.[8] Moreover, quotas were established so that the Mongols and West Asians were assured "equal" representation with those selected from the two Chinese personnel pools. Those so appointed were in turn served by a large number of assistants and secretaries of equally diverse social and cultural origins.[9] Further, there was a decided tendency in the Yuan to promote these low-level officials – clerks, gatekeepers, scribes, and, most particularly, translators and interpreters – to high positions in the government and court.[10] Thus, the Mongolian rulers of China systematically placed peoples of different ethnic, communal, and linguistic backgrounds side by side in the Yuan bureaucracy. There were, in other words, quite literally thousands of agents of cultural transmission and change dispersed throughout the Yuan realm.

Some idea of the extent to which these specialists were transported from one cultural zone of the empire to another can be conveyed graphically. In table 1 "Easterners" are defined for our purposes as subject peoples of the Yuan serving or traveling in the Islamic and Christian lands, the "West," while "Westerners" are Christians and Muslims who took up residence anywhere within the Yuan regime, the "East."

Even a cursory examination of the raw data reveals the extraordinary geographical mobility and ethnic-occupational diversity of the servitors of the Empire of the Great Mongols. How the Mongols, in the furtherance of their imperial enterprise, went about the business of selecting and appropriating the vast cultural resources of their sedentary subjects and why they initiated the transference of cultural wares and cultural specialists across Eurasia forms the subject of this work.

[8] Meng Ssu-ming, *Yuan-tai she-hui chieh-chi chih-tu* (Hong Kong: Lung-men shu-tien, 1967), pp. 25–36. This system was operational by 1278.

[9] This diversity was first noted by Erich Haenisch, "Kulturbilder aus Chinas Mongolenzeit," *Historische Zeitschrift* 164 (1941), 46.

[10] This, at least, was the complaint of Confucian scholars. See *YS*, ch. 142, p. 3405. On the elevated position of language specialists at the Mongol court, see Thomas T. Allsen, "The *Rasūlid Hexaglot* in its Eurasian Cultural Context," in Golden, *Hexaglot*, pp. 30–40.

TWO

Before the Mongols

By the time of the Mongolian Empire, China and Iran had been in political, cultural, and commercial contact for more than a millennium. In fact, to a large extent China and Iran anchored the exchange of spiritual and material culture between East and West in the premodern era, arguably the longest sustained example of intercultural communication in world history.[1] So extensive were these relations in the past that they have been invoked in recent times as a solid basis for closer diplomatic and cultural cooperation between their modern governments.[2]

To the ancient Iranians, the Middle Kingdom was Chēnastān and its inhabitants, Chēnīk. In Chinese, Iran was initially known as An-hsi, after the Arsacid dynasty of Parthia (ca. 247 BC to AD 227), and later, with the rise of the Sasanians (ca. 222–651), as Po-ssu, Persia.[3] The Chinese, it seems clear, had no direct knowledge of the Far West before the second century BC, the period of the Former Han (202 BC to AD 9). In the reign of Wu-ti (140–87 BC), the Chinese official Chang Ch'ien was sent west to seek an alliance with the Yueh-chih (Tokharians) against the Hsiung-nu, the dominant power in the eastern steppe. When he returned to court in 126 BC he brought the first concrete information on Bactria (Ta-hsia) and Parthia. Following the consolidation of their position in central Asia, the Han in 106 BC sent an embassy to the East Roman Empire (Ta-ch'in) and Parthia which reached the Persian Gulf. The Later Han (AD 25–220), however, progressively lost its influence in the Tarim Basin and official contacts with the West were terminated.[4]

[1] For an overview of cultural and political contacts between East and West, see Needham, *SCC*, vol. I, pp. 150–248. For a succinct account of some of the controversies generated by the scholarly study of the exchange, see Lionel Casson, *Ancient Trade and Society* (Detroit: Wayne State University Press, 1984), pp. 247–72.

[2] See the article by Shen Chin-ting, the Taiwan ambassador to Iran in the 1960s, "Introduction to Ancient Cultural Exchange between Iran and China," *Chinese Culture* 8 (1967), 49–61.

[3] H. W. Bailey, "Iranian Studies," *BSOAS* 6 (1932), 945 and 948, and Paul Wheatley, "Geographical Notes on Some Commodities Involved in Sung Maritime Trade," *Journal of the Malayan Branch of the Royal Asiatic Society* 32/2 (1961), 14–15.

[4] William Watson, "Iran and China," in Ehsan Yarshater, ed., *The Cambridge History of Iran* (Cambridge University Press, 1983), vol. III/1, pp. 537–58.

In the following two centuries there is no evidence of any diplomatic exchanges between China and Iran. Only in the course of the fifth century, when first the Kidarites and then the Hephthalites pressured the Sasanians' northeastern frontiers, was the relationship renewed. Prompted by these threats, the Persian court sought allies in the East and made contact with the Northern Wei (386–535) in 455. Thereafter, regular embassies were sent east, nine more to the Wei, one to its successor state, the Western Wei (535–57), and two to the Liang (502–57) in the south. Indirect evidence suggests that for the most part the envoys traveled overland.[5] These ties continued into the early T'ang (618–906), which played an active role in the affairs of the Western Regions (Hsi-yü). It is well known that Pēroz, the son of Yazdagird III (632–51), the last Sasanian emperor, driven from his homeland by the advancing Arab–Muslim armies, took refuge at the Chinese court. In 662 he was recognized as "King of Persia" but given no effective support in his efforts to regain his throne and kingdom. Remnants of the deposed dynasty consequently stayed on at the T'ang court as political exiles and are noted in the Chinese records down to 737.[6]

The T'ang position in central Asia was eroded in the early decades of the eighth century, first by Tibetan expansion into the Tarim Basin and later by the Arabs' defeat of a Chinese army along the Talas River in 751. But despite these setbacks the T'ang court still received envoys from the local Persian dynasty of Ṭabaristān in the 740s and 750s.[7] In subsequent decades the T'ang, weakened by internal revolts and pressured by the Uighur qaghanate, the successors of the Türk, became less a factor in central Asian affairs. When it finally disintegrated, it was replaced in the extreme north by the Liao dynasty (907–1125), whose rulers, the Qitans, took an interest in the Western Regions. In 923 the Liao received "tribute" from Po-ssu, most certainly the Sāmānids (875–999) who ruled Khurāsān and Transoxania, and a year later there arrived an embassy from "Ta-shih," that is, the ʿAbbāsid Caliphate of Baghdad. In 1027 the Qitans sent an envoy to the court of Maḥmūd (r. 998–1030), the ruler of the Ghaznavids of Khurāsān and Afghanistan.[8]

The Qitans' near neighbor, the Chinese dynasty of the Northern Sung (960–1126), also had quite regular intercourse with the governments of the

[5] I. Ecsedy, "Early Persian Envoys in the Chinese Courts (5th–6th Centuries AD)," in J. Harmatta, ed., *Studies in the Sources on the History of Pre-Islamic Central Asia* (Budapest: Akadémiai Kaidó, 1979), pp. 153–62.

[6] J. Harmatta, "Sino-Iranica," *Acta Antiqua Academiae Scientiarum Hungaricae* 19 (1971), 135–43.

[7] Edouard Chavannes, *Documents sur les Tou-kiue (Turks) occidentaux*, repr. (Taipei: Ch'eng wen, 1969), pp. 70, 71, 91–92, and 173.

[8] Karl A. Wittfogel and Feng Chia-sheng, *History of Chinese Society, Liao (907–1125)* (Transactions of the American Philosophical Society, n.s., vol. XXXVI; Philadelphia, 1949), p. 347, and Marvazī, *Sharaf al-Zamān Ṭāhir Marvazī on China, the Turks and India*, trans. by V. Minorsky (London: Royal Asiatic Society, 1942), pp. 19–21 and 76–80.

West. In 1081 and 1091 they received envoys from Fu-lin, the Seljuqs of Rūm. More frequent were their contacts with Ta-shih, the ʿAbbāsid Caliphate, which sent fifty or so missions to the Sung between 966 and 1116.[9] In some cases the "embassies" might have been merchants falsely assuming diplomatic status but none the less exchanges with the eastern Islamic world were intense and fairly regular. Following their defeat at the hands of the Jürchens in 1126, the Sung court moved to the south and thereafter its contacts with the West decreased dramatically: the ʿAbbāsids sent missions in 1086 and 1094 and then no more until 1205–8. The Southern Sung, which survived until the Mongolian conquest of 1279, was simply more isolated, cut off from the routes through central Asia, a fact well recognized by traditional Chinese historiography.[10]

While official diplomatic relations between Iran and China were intermittent, cultural and commercial contacts were far more constant; there were, to be sure, peaks and valleys but few complete or extended interruptions once regular communication was established. Exactly when such relations began is, however, open to interpretation. Millennia before the movement of Chinese silk to the West, there was certainly a long-distance trade in prestige goods, principally semi-precious stones such as lapis lazuli, nephrite, and turquoise.[11] Whether this constituted a Bronze Age "world system," an extended network of interactive economic exchange, is now being debated.[12] More conventionally, scholars have argued that regular exchange came much later, with Alexander the Great's campaigns or with Chang Ch'ien's mission to the Yueh-chih. Most would agree, however, that the so-called "Silk Route" was in operation by the century before Christ and that it reached an early peak during the period from 50–150, when the Roman, Parthian, Kushan, and Han empires dominated the political landscape of Eurasia.[13]

In addition to the commercial goods, mainly silk, coming west, many cultural wares, from folklore motifs to alphabets and religions, moved eastward.[14]

[9] Robert M. Hartwell, *Tribute Missions to China, 960–1126* (Philadelphia: n.p., 1983), pp. 71, 72, and 195–202.

[10] Chau Ju-kua, *His Work on Chinese and Arab Trade in the Twelfth and Thirteenth Centuries, entitled Chu-fan-chi*, trans. by Friedrich Hirth and W. W. Rockhill, repr. (Taipei: Literature House, 1965), pp. 117–19, and Mary Ferenczy, "Chinese Historiographers' Views on Barbarian–Chinese Relations," *AOASH* 21 (1968), 354 and 357.

[11] V. I. Sarianidi, "The Lapis Lazuli Route in the Ancient East," *Archaeology* 24/1 (1971), 12–15.

[12] André Gunder Frank, "Bronze Age World System Cycles," *Current Anthropology* 34 (1993), 383–429 with invited commentary.

[13] Osamu Sudzuki, "The Silk Road and Alexander's Eastern Campaign," *Orient: Report of the Society for Near Eastern Studies in Japan* 11 (1975), 67–92, and J. Thorley, "The Silk Trade between China and the Roman Empire at its Height, circa AD 90–130," *Greece and Rome*, 2nd series, 18 (1971), 71–80. On the historical geography of these routes, see Huzayyin, *Arabia and the Far East*, pp. 87–110.

[14] Paul Pelliot, "Les influences iraniennes en Asie centrale et en Extrême Orient," *Revue Indochinois* 18 (1912), 1–15, and Donald Daniel Leslie, "Moses, the Bamboo King," *East Asian History* 6 (1993), 75–90.

Almost all of the major religious movements originating in the Middle East – Zoroastrianism, Judaism, Christianity, Manichaeanism, and Islam – reached China, while Chinese ideological systems made no inroads in the West. This intriguing and persistent pattern, which has never been explained, was apparently established quite early. It has been argued recently that by the eighth century BC there were itinerant ritual specialists, the Iranian Magi, dispensing their services in Chou China.[15]

Naturally, the movements of religions and commercial goods across Eurasia brought a growing awareness and appreciation of distant, and initially quite alien, artistic traditions. For many in the medieval Middle East, any foreign object expertly made was automatically called "Chinese" whatever its real origin.[16] The extensive exchanges in ceramics, metal work, architectural decoration, and textiles between China and Iran resulted in the acceptance and adaptation of new materials, styles, and manufacturing techniques. In the T'ang, for instance, "Sasanian" silks were imported from the West, and imitated by the Chinese. In some cases, textiles of this period reveal extensive syncretism in which Chinese and Iranian motifs were fully integrated.[17]

Among the Chinese and Persians there was a general expansion in the knowledge of each other's history and geography. While early Persian sources are fragmentary and vague, the Armenians, very much in Iran's cultural orbit, make some explicit and informative references to China (Chenats'n) and the Chinese (Siwnik) in the seventh and eighth centuries.[18] Clearly, the Armenian knowledge of China was one shared by their Sasanian overlords. The Chinese, on the other hand, were much more systematic, acquiring and preserving considerable data on the places, peoples, and products of West Asia, those of Iran in particular.[19]

This growing familiarity can also be seen in the cultural sphere. By the T'ang, the Iranian world had contributed much to Chinese entertainments, especially music and dance. And in this same period Chinese customs,

15 Victor H. Mair, "Old Sinitic *Myag, Old Persian Maguš and English Magician," *Early China* 15 (1990), 27–47.

16 Tha'ālibī, *The Book of Curious and Entertaining Information: The Latā'if al-Ma'ārif of Tha'ālibī*, trans. by C. E. Bosworth (Edinburgh University Press, 1968), p. 141.

17 Jane Gaston Mahler, "Art of the Silk Route," in Theodore Bowie, ed., *East–West in Art* (Bloomington: Indiana University Press, 1966), pp. 70–83; Dorothy G. Shepherd, "Iran between East and West," in *ibid.*, pp. 84–105; Jessica Rawson, *Chinese Ornament: The Lotus and the Dragon* (London: British Museum Publications, 1984), pp. 33–62; and Aurel Stein, *Innermost Asia: Detailed Report of Explorations in Central Asia, Kan-su and Eastern Iran* (Oxford: Clarendon Press, 1928), pp. 675–78.

18 Moses Khorenats'i, *History of the Armenians*, trans. by Robert W. Thomson (Cambridge, Mass.: Harvard University Press, 1970), pp. 229–31, and Ananias of Širak, *The Geography of Ananias of Širak*, trans. by Robert H. Hewsen (Wiesbaden: Ludwig Reichert, 1992), p. 76A.

19 See Donald Daniel Leslie and K. H. J. Gardiner, "Chinese Knowledge of Western Asia during the Han," *TP* 68 (1982), 254–308, and Chavannes, *Documents*, pp. 170–74 which translates the chapter on Persia (Po-ssu) in the *Hsin T'ang-shu* (Peking: Chung-hua shu-chü, 1986), ch. 221B, pp. 6258–60.

including the nature of their writing system, were described by the noted Muslim bibliographer, al-Nadīm, who had seen at first hand Chinese books.[20] Fauna, flora, and their many by-products were likewise part of this transcontinental traffic. Many Persian plants and aromatics entered China. For a long time there was a tendency to ascribe all such transfers to Chang Ch'ien, when in fact they arrived over a period of several centuries: alfalfa and grapes in the Han, pomegranates and coriander during the Northern and Southern Dynasties, and date palm and spinach in the T'ang.[21] Persian medicinal plants and drugs became in time so prevalent in China that several specialized pharmacopeias were devoted to them.[22]

Additionally, the Western Regions and Iran sent to China horses, gold and silver vessels, boxes, and plates as well as glass and quartz bowls and precious gems.[23] In return, China exported a wide variety of commodities, mainly processed goods, to the Western Regions. According to an Arabic commercial handbook dating to the late ninth century, the Middle Kingdom sent to the Muslim world silks, sables, felts, aromatics, porcelains, paper, ink, exotica such as peacocks, saddles, cinnamon, and "unmixed" (unadulterated) rhubarb famed for its healing properties.[24]

Obviously, this commercial, cultural, and religious communication was closely entwined and it is difficult and perhaps misleading to isolate the various strands from one another. For example, the spread of world religions provided both a medium and a motive for commercial exchange, and the trade goods themselves, textiles, metal, and glassware, functioned, as Huzayyin correctly noted decades ago, "as the best media for the introduction of artistic motifs from one region to another."[25] Given these linkages, merchants, who often doubled as missionaries, were among the most important agents of cultural transmission. In large part they were Western and Central Asians rather than Chinese. Typically, they operated through networks of merchant communities of the same ethnic and religious background that were situated at key points along the great trade routes. In different times and places, different communal groups came to dominate and organize the long-distance trade: Jews, Khwārazmians, Varangians, Armenians, Soghdians, Indians, Uighurs, Persians, and Bukharans. In many cases, one ethnic group served as the

[20] Mikinosuke Ishida, "Etudes sino-iraniennes, I: A propos du *Huo-siun-wou*," *Memoirs of the Research Department of the Toyo Bunko* 6 (1932), 61–76, and Al-Nadīm, *The Fihrist of al-Nadīm*, 2 vols., trans. by Bayard Dodge (New York: Columbia University Press, 1970), vol. I, p. 31 and vol. II, pp. 836–40.

[21] The classic work on this subject is Laufer, *Sino-Iranica*. See especially pp. 190–92, 208–45, 276–87, 297–99, and 395–98. See also the major contribution of Edward H. Schafer, *The Golden Peaches of Samarkand: A Study of T'ang Exotics* (Berkeley: University of California Press, 1963).

[22] Needham, *SCC*, vol. I, pp. 187–88.

[23] Yang Hsüan-chih, *A Record of Buddhist Monasteries in Lo-yang*, trans. by Yi-t'ung Wang (Princeton University Press, 1984), pp. 192–93.

[24] Ch. Pellat, "Ǧāhiẓiana, I," *Arabica* 2 (1955), 157, 158, and 159.

[25] Huzayyin, *Arabia and the Far East*, pp. 217–18. Cf. the comments of S. A. M. Adshead, *China in World History* (London: Macmillan, 1988), pp. 22–27, especially p. 24.

commercial agents of another. One of the Persian rulers of Ṭabaristān, for example, had ties with a Jewish merchant operating in the Tarim Basin on the fringes of the T'ang Empire around 718.[26]

By the mid-eighth century there were also substantial Persian merchant communities in Ch'ang-an, the terminus of the overland trade routes, and in Canton, Yang-chou, and Ch'üan-chou, the major entrepôts of the seaborne trade. These included both long-distance traders in transit and shop owners who had settled permanently in China. So visible and numerous were they that the locals developed well-defined stereotypes of these strangers in their midst: as seen through the prism of popular literature, the Persian merchants were wealthy and generous, usually specialists in the rare gem trade, and often possessed of supernatural powers.[27]

Commercial concerns were not the only reasons individuals or groups took up residence in foreign lands. Ta Huan, captured at the Battle of Talas in 751 and thereafter a temporary prisoner in the ʿAbbāsid Caliphate, saw in Kūfah, its early capital, Chinese weavers, gold- and silversmiths and painters.[28] This, however, is one of the few reports we have on Chinese in the West before the Mongolian era. Much more common, or perhaps better documented, are the Iranians resident in China. One of the earliest was An Shih-kao, a Parthian prince who arrived in the Han capital Loyang in AD 148 as a hostage and spent the rest of his life in China. This is very likely the same An Shih-kao famed for his translations of Buddhist works into Chinese.[29] More members of the Iranian ruling elite found refuge in China following the collapse of the Sasanian regime. Among them was a female member of the Sūrēn clan, one of the major aristocratic lineages of the Parthian and Sasanian eras, whose death in 874 was commemorated in a bilingual Chinese–Middle Persian inscription found near Ch'ang-an.[30]

Taken together, the Iranian exiles and merchants constituted a sizable and permanent foreign presence in medieval China, one that could support, for several centuries, numerous shrines and temples devoted to various "Persian" religions – Zoroastrianism, Manichaeanism, and Nestorian Christianity.[31] In addition to the capital and the southern ports, they were found in the lower Yangtze where, the Japanese pilgrim Ennin notes, the local Persian community contributed 1,000 strings of cash toward the repair of a damaged

[26] Aurel Stein, *Ancient Khotan* (Oxford University Press, 1907), pp. 306–9 and 570–74.

[27] Edward Schafer, "Iranian Merchants in T'ang Dynasty Tales," in *Semitic and Oriental Studies: A Volume Presented to William Popper* (University of California Publications in Semitic Philology, vol. XI; Berkeley, 1951), pp. 403–22, and David Whitehouse and Andrew Williamson, "Sasanian Maritime Trade," *Iran* 11 (1973), 45–49.

[28] Paul Pelliot, "Des artisans chinois à la capitale Abbaside en 751–762," *TP* 26 (1928), 110–12.

[29] Antonio Forte, *The Hostage An Shigao and his Offspring* (Italian School of East Asian Studies, Occasional Papers 6; Kyoto, 1995), pp. 88–90.

[30] Harmatta, "Sino-Iranica," 113–34, and I. Ecsedy, "A Middle Persian–Chinese Epitaph from the Region of Ch'ang-an (Hsian) from 874," *Acta Antiqua Academiae Scientiarum Hungaricae* 19 (1971), 149–58.

[31] Donald Daniel Leslie, "Persian Temples in T'ang China," *MS* 35 (1981–83), 275–303.

Buddhist monastery.[32] So significant were these Iranian populations and their religious establishments that the Chinese government created a special institution to administer them. Interestingly, the name of this office, transcribed as *sa-po* and later as *sa-pao*, derives from the Sanskrit term *sārthavāha*, meaning "caravan leader." In the T'ang this office was specifically charged with regulating Zoroastrian shrines, but it is clear that its brief also encompassed commercial and diplomatic responsibilities, yet another telling reminder of the intimate linkages between cultural, religious, and economic exchange in Eurasian history.[33]

With the advent of the Chinggisids and the creation of their vast and unprecedented transcontinental empire, a new chapter in the history of East–West exchange was suddenly and unexpectedly opened. And between China and Iran, the Mongols, for their own ends, initiated a dramatic and ofttimes traumatic intensification of this centuries-old relationship.

[32] Edwin O. Reischauer, *Ennin's Diary: The Record of a Pilgrimage to China in Search of the Law* (New York: Ronald Press, 1955), pp. 69–70.

[33] On this office and its antecedents, see Albert E. Dien, "The *Sa-pao* Problem Reexamined," *JAOS* 82 (1962), 335–46.

PART II

Political–economic relations

THREE

Formation of the Il-qans, 1251–1265

In 1206, after decades of struggle with rival tribes of the eastern steppe, Chinggis Qan proclaimed the formation of the Great Mongolian State (*Yeke Mongghol Ulus*), a polity which in the course of three generations became the largest land empire in world history.[1] The empire began its expansion southward, launching a series of campaigns against the Tanguts and the Jürchen Chin dynasty which culminated in the capture of Chung-tu (Peking) in 1215. The commercial overtures of the Khwārazmshāh Muḥammad in 1218 turned Mongolian attention westward. The incident at Utrār, where a Mongolian caravan was despoiled by Khwārazmian officials, led to an invasion of Transoxania in 1219. Between 1220 and 1221 the armies of the Khwārazmshāh were overwhelmed and West Turkestan and Khurāsān ravaged and subdued.

Chinggis Qan returned to Mongolia in 1224 to organize further campaigns against the Tanguts and died three years later in the midst of these operations. This necessitated a temporary halt in military expansion while the Chinggisid princes and their advisers assembled in Mongolia to confirm Ögödei, Chinggis Qan's third son and designated heir, as the new qaghan (r. 1229–41). Operations were restarted in 1229 to complete the conquest of West Asia. Progress was substantial: Mongolian armies forced the capitulation of the Armenians and Georgians in 1236 and the Seljuqs of Rūm in 1243. Under Güyüg (r. 1246–48), Ögödei's son and successor, expansion was, however, slowed in the face of increased tension among the imperial princes.

At Güyüg's death these divisions became quite visible and, in a much disputed succession, Möngke (r. 1251–59), the son of Tolui, Chinggis Qan's youngest son, became qaghan. In part to stifle the opposition and to direct Mongolian energies outward, Möngke initiated a series of large-scale campaigns against Korea, the Southern Sung and the ʿAbbāsid Caliphate. The latter operation was entrusted to Hülegü, Möngke's younger brother who

[1] In Chinese the Chinggisid state was called *ta Meng-ku kuo*, "Great Mongolian State," in internal documents. The name *Yuan ch'ao*, adopted in 1271, also meant "Great Dynasty." See the detailed discussion of Hsiao Ch'i-ch'ing, "Shuo Ta-ch'ao: Yuan-ch'ao chien-hao ch'ien Meng-ku te Han-wen kuo-hao," *Han-hsüeh yen-chiu* 3/1 (1985), 23–40.

began his march west in 1253. By early 1258 Baghdad and Mesopotamia were occupied and the Mongols continued their drive into Syria until defeated by the Egyptian Mamlūks at ʿAin Jālūt in 1260.

While the basic stages of the Mongols' military conquest of the Middle East are readily discernible, the political status of the territories so acquired has a very tangled history, one in which there is much obscurity and uncertainty. What is certain, however, is that disputes over princely rights in Khurāsān and the consequent emergence of the Il-qan state under Hülegü contributed to the breakup of the Mongolian Empire and, at the same time, opened a new chapter in the relationship between Iran and China.

The contention over rival claims in Iran has its roots in Chinggis Qan's initial, and somewhat nebulous, dispensation of lands to his four eldest sons. At an unknown date, but presumably after the conquest of Transoxania, Chinggis apportioned in typical nomadic fashion his vast holdings among his various kinsmen. According to Juvaynī, our earliest source, he granted to his brother and grandchildren specific territories in China; to his eldest son Jochi he gave Khwārazm and the as yet unconquered Qipchaq steppe; Chaghadai, his second son, received most of Transoxania; Ögödei, his third son and heir, obtained areas in Jungaria; and Tolui, his youngest son, was given unnamed territories in the Mongolian homeland.[2] Iran is simply not mentioned in this connection. It is, of course, possible that Iran was included, assigned to a particular Chinggisid line, but that this information was suppressed by later partisan historians for political reasons. On balance, however, I think that Juvaynī's report of this division should be taken at face value. The most striking feature of this account is that neither of the great sedentary societies, China and Iran, then falling under Mongolian control, were apportioned to a specific son. These regions, the richest in the empire, were to be administered by the qaghan for the benefit of the Chinggisid lines at large. Further, each line enjoyed territorial holdings in Iran and China and each had some say in the administration of these territories.

Certainly, from the evidence at hand, the qaghan in Mongolia always claimed sovereignty over West Asia and exercised a decisive influence on matters of policy and administration. From the very inception of Mongolian rule in the region the emperor's name appears exclusively on the coinage. The earliest of these issues, undated silver and copper coins minted in Kirmān, contain the inscription, in Arabic, "The Just/the Great/Chīngīz Khān."[3] Under Ögödei various coins struck in Iran and Georgia bear the inscription "Qaghan/the Just."[4] Even more telling are the coins issued in 1244/45 in Transcaucasia during the regency of Töregene Qatun which contain the inscription "*Ulugh Manqul ūlūs bik.*"[5] Various interpretations have been

[2] Juvaynī/Qazvīnī, vol. I, pp. 31–32, and Juvaynī/Boyle, vol. I, pp. 42–43. See also M. Brosset, trans., *Histoire de la Géorgie*, pt. 1: *Histoire ancienne jusqu'en 1469 de JC* (St. Petersburg: Académie des sciences, 1850), pp. 508–9. [3] Seifeddini, vol. I, pp. 154–55.

[4] *Ibid.*, pp. 155–58. [5] *Ibid.*, pp. 159–63.

made, but this is clearly a Turkic rendering of the Mongolian *Yeke Mongghol Ulus*, "Great Mongolian State," with the addition of the Turkic *beg* which answers to the Mongolian *noyan*, "commander." Thus, in the absence of a sitting monarch, West Asian coins were issued in the name of the empire at large by the local commander, probably Chormaqan noyan, an appointee of the deceased Ögödei.

With the accession of Güyüg, the inscriptions on coins became rather pointed. A dirham of 1247 from Tbilisi bears the legend "By the Power of God/Dominion of Kūyuk/Qā'ān-Slave Dā'ūd" (i.e., David Narin).[6] Moreover, Baiju noyan, Güyüg's military governor in West Asia, corresponded with Pope Innocent IV "by the divine disposition of the qaghan [*chaam*] himself."[7] Güyüg, whose rise was opposed by the line of Jochi, was pointedly advertising his authority in a region in which the Jochids were aggressively asserting their princely rights.

The nature of these rights is brought out in the career of Arghun Aqa, an Oyirad Mongolian official in West Asia. First appointed governor of Khurāsān by Töregene, he then served Güyüg and was reappointed to the same position by Möngke, despite the fact that he was closely associated with the rival Ögödeid line.[8] What explains this decision is that Arghun, although an appointee of the qaghan, had on his staff representatives, Mongolian *nökör*, from each princely line, who looked after the interests of their respective masters in Iran and adjoining regions.[9] As was the case in China, incomes from various agricultural lands in Khurāsān had been assigned to specific princes – their "shares" in the profits of empire – and therefore they had the right to monitor, through their agents, major administrative initiatives such as census taking and tax collecting.[10]

How this system of joint administration was effectively ended, and how Iran became the "share" of a particular prince is, of course, intimately tied to the arrival of Hülegü in West Asia. Möngke's decision to send his younger brother west to complete Mongolian conquests in that direction was taken shortly after his enthronement in 1251. Hülegü received military command over Iran, Mesopotamia, Syria, Egypt, Asia Minor, and Transcaucasia. A short while later he was given very precise instructions on the empire's military objectives in the region. In the summer of 1253 he set out from Mongolia to fulfill his sovereign's commission in the West.[11] Following a successful assault on the

[6] David M. Lang, *Studies in the Numismatic History of Georgia in Transcaucasia* (New York: American Numismatic Society, 1955), p. 37.

[7] Karl-Ernst Lupprian, *Die Beziehungen der Päpste zu islamischen und mongolischen Herrschern im 13. Jahrhundert, anhand ihres Briefwechsels* (Vatican: Biblioteca Apostolica Vaticana, 1981), p. 191.

[8] His reappointment is noted in both Chinese and Persian sources. See *YS*, ch. 3, p. 45; Rashīd/Karīmī, vol. I, p. 596; and Rashīd/Boyle, p. 218.

[9] On the *nökör*, see Juvaynī/Qazvīnī, vol. II, p. 255, and Juvaynī/Boyle, vol. II, pp. 515–18.

[10] The evidence for such assignments of land and income in Iran and China will be taken up in chapter 7, "Economic ties."

[11] Rashīd/Karīmī, vol. II, pp. 685–87, and *YS*, ch. 3, p. 47.

strongholds of the Ismāʾīlīs, Hülegü's armies converged on Baghdad, which fell in early 1258. Hülegü dutifully sent a complete report of his operations and "victory presents" to Möngke in the East.[12]

Even though Möngke, his main supporter, died in the following year and his own armies met with a major military defeat in Syria in 1260, Hülegü managed to solidify his hold on West Asia. His main rivals were the Jochids, who had been instrumental in bringing about the enthronement of Möngke. With territories in North Caucausia and Khwārazm, the rulers of the Golden Horde pressed their rights in Khurāsān and Georgia, hoping, perhaps, to use these assignments as stepping stones to extend their influence throughout the Middle East. Certainly once Hülegü reached Khurāsān there was growing tension between him and the Jochid princes sent to support his military operations against the ʿAbbāsid as well as confrontations between Hülegü's officials and representatives of Batu (r. 1237–ca. 1256), the qan of the Golden Horde.[13] Indeed, these became so acrimonious that Hülegü drove the Jochid princes and agents from the lands under his military control.

This termination of Jochid rights in Iran and Transcaucasia has been viewed as a usurpation, and to some extent this is an accurate characterization. Rashīd al-Dīn, a partisan of the Toluids, admits as much when he states, after enumerating Möngke's many instructions to Hülegü, that:

> Although [the idea] was formed and fixed in the mind of Möngke qaghan that Hülegü qan, with the armies he had given him, would always be sovereign [*pādshāh*] and reside in the domains of Iran and that these domains would belong, in a firm and secure manner, to him and his august line, [Möngke] nevertheless said for appearance sake [*zāhiran*] that "when the matter is concluded return to the homeland [i.e., Mongolia]."[14]

Möngke, as Jean Aubin has argued, presented the dispatch of Hülegü to Iran as a temporary military measure, when in fact he always intended that Iran should come under exclusive Toluid control.[15] Thus, Iran was no longer to be administered on behalf of the Chinggisids as a whole but transformed into a qanate on an equal footing with that of the Chaghadaids and Jochi. In this way Toluid power could be projected along the southern flank of the Golden Horde and the vast economic and cultural riches of the Middle East monopolized rather than shared.

This interpretation is sustained by the numismatic evidence. Before Hülegü's arrival, Möngke's name appears alone on coinage. A dirham issued in Georgia in 1252 reads: "by the power of God/by the good fortune of the

[12] Rashīd/Karīmī, vol. II, p. 717; *YS*, ch. 3, p. 51; Jūzjānī/Lees, p. 431; Jūzjānī/Raverty, vol. II, pp. 1255–57; and Grigor of Akancʿ, "History of the Nation of Archers," trans. by Robert P. Blake and Richard N. Frye, *HJAS* 12/3–4 (1949), 305 and 307.

[13] On these disputes, see the pioneering study of Peter Jackson, "The Dissolution of the Mongol Empire," *CAJ* 22 (1978), 186–243, and especially 208–35.

[14] Rashīd/Karīmī, vol. II, p. 687.

[15] See Jean Aubin, *Emirs mongols et vizirs persans dans les remous de l'acculturation* (Studia Iranica, vol. XV; Paris, 1995), p. 17.

emperor/of the world, Munkū Qā'ān."[16] This inscription, written in Persian, incorporates all the basic elements of Mongolian ideology – charisma, a heavenly mandate, and universal rule – and replicates very accurately Chinese formulations in stelae dating to Möngke's reign.[17] When, however, Hülegü reached the Middle East his name was added. Coins issued in 1254/55 and 1255/56 read: "Qā'ān the Supreme, Mūnkkā Qā'ān/Hūlāgū Khān."[18] This attempt to promote Hülegü to the rank of qan was not, however, successful, for he soon abandoned the title qan for the less exalted il-qan/īl-khān.

The timing of this adoption is somewhat uncertain. As late as 1262 Hülegü, in a Latin letter addressed to King Louis, styles himself *cham*, "qan," and *dux milicie Mungalorum*, "commander of Mongolian military forces."[19] On the other hand, the Armenian historian Vardan (d. 1271), a contemporary, regularly calls Hülegü an il-qan (*ēl-łan*) from the time of his arrival in Iran in 1255 to his death in 1265.[20] Similarly, Juvaynī, also a contemporary, uses the term īl-khān with reference to events of 1256.[21] The latter, however, are very likely anachronistic. Recent research strongly suggests that this title is first applied to Hülegü in literary sources in AH 657/AD 1258–59 and on coinage in AH 658/AD 1259–60.[22]

Before the Mongolian era the term appears as a name, Elkhane, among the Seljuqs of the late eleventh century and as a title, il-qan, in an eleventh-century Uighur translation of the seventh-century Chinese biography of the noted Buddhist pilgrim Hsüan Tsang.[23] Originally, *il* or *el*, a Turkic word, meant "country" or "polity," but by the time of the Chinggisids it had acquired a secondary meaning of "submissive," "peaceable," "obedient," or "subservient."[24] It is also possible that il-qan should be connected with the Chinese term *kuo-wang*, both of which mean literally "polity prince." This title was borrowed

[16] E. A. Pakhomov, *Monety Gruzii* (Tbilisi: Izdatel'stvo "Metsniereba," 1970), p. 133.

[17] A stela dated 1257 begins: "By the strength of Eternal Heaven and the protective good fortune of the emperor Meng-ko [Möngke]." See Ts'ai Mei-piao, *Yuan-tai pai-hua pei chi-lu* (Peking: K'o-hsüeh ch'u-pan-she, 1955), p. 20.

[18] Seifeddini, vol. I, pp. 171–72, and Michael Weiers, "Münzaufschriften auf Münzen mongolischer Il-khane aus dem Iran," *The Canada–Mongolia Review* 4/1 (1978), 46.

[19] Paul Meyvaert, "An Unknown Letter of Hulagu, Il-khan of Persia, to King Louis of France," *Viator* 11 (1980), 253.

[20] Vardan Arewelcʻi, "The Historical Compilation of Vardan Arewelcʻi," trans. by Robert W. Thomson, *Dumbarton Oaks Papers* 43 (1989), 217, 218, 220, and 221.

[21] Juvaynī/Qazvīnī, vol. III, p. 130, and Juvaynī/Boyle, vol. II, p. 632.

[22] Nitzan Amitai-Preiss and Reuven Amitai-Preiss, "Two Notes on the Protocol on Hülegü's Coinage," *Israel Numismatic Journal* 10 (1988–89), 117–21; and Reuven Amitai-Preiss, "Evidence for the Early Use of the Title *īlkhān* among the Mongols," *JRAS* 1 (1991), 353–61.

[23] Anna Comnena, *The Alexiad*, trans. by E. R. A. Sewter (New York: Penguin Books, 1985), pp. 210, 211, 299, and 312, and L. Iu. Tugusheva, trans., *Fragmenty uigurskoi versii biografii Siuan-tszana* (Moscow: Nauka, 1980), p. 23, Uighur text and p. 44, Russian translation.

[24] See, for example, Naṣīr al-Dīn Ṭūsī, a contemporary of Hülegü who uses *il* for "obedient," "subservient," a term which he pointedly contrasts with *yaghi*, the Turkic word for those who are "rebellious," or "disobedient." John A. Boyle, "The Death of the Last ʿAbbāsid Caliph: A Contemporary Muslim Account," *Journal of Semitic Studies* 6 (1961), 151–52. Further, the fourteenth-century Yemeni lexicon equates the Mongolian and Turkic *il* with the Arabic *muṭīʿ*, "obedient" or "compliant." See Golden, *Hexaglot*, 187C2, p. 79 and 190C7, p. 112.

into Mongolian in the form of *güi-ong* and first bestowed upon Chinggis Qan's chief commander in North China, Muqali, in 1217.[25] Perhaps the adoption of the term il-qan by Hülegü was designed to accentuate his military responsibilities in West Asia, to focus attention on his function as a guardian of a far corner of the empire, and thus to disguise or underplay his political intentions and ambitions in the region.[26]

But however one understands the title il-qan at the time of its adoption, there is little doubt that it conferred upon Hülegü and his immediate successors a subordinate position in the hierarchy of Chinggisid rulers. In my opinion this was done quite consciously because their overlordship of Iran was not part of Chinggis Qan's original dispensation and therefore they simply could not claim equal status with the rulers of the Golden Horde and Chaghadai Qanate. Such a posture, however contrived, did permit them effective control over the Middle East while at the same time avoiding the charge that they had violated the will of the founding father.

This reconstruction of events is substantiated by the testimony of the early fourteenth-century Arab encyclopedist, al-ʿUmarī, whose view clearly reflects those of the rival Jochid line. At one point he states that "Hülegü b. Tūlī was the representative [*mandub*] of his brother Munkū Qān," and at another he says more specifically that "Hülegü did not rule as an independent monarch but was the deputy [*nāʾib*] of his brother Munkū Qān." Because of this, he continues, the other "Chinggisid princes disparaged the house of Hülegü, saying that they did not inherit royal authority [*mulk*] from Chingiz Khān or from the successors of Chingiz Khān but [obtained it] by means of usurpation and through the passage of time."[27]

With the death of Möngke in 1259 and the outbreak of open hostilities with the Golden Horde in 1262, Hülegü's position in Iran was jeopardized militarily and politically. To make matters worse, two of his brothers, Qubilai and Ariq Böke, contested the succession to the throne, which resulted in a Toluid civil war in 1260–64. Whatever his initial feelings, Hülegü came out in favor of Qubilai, the eventual winner, and secured his political support. In 1262 envoys from China arrived in Iran conveying a decree (*jarliq*) that Hülegü was the

[25] *SH*/Cleaves, sect. 202, p. 141, sect. 206, p. 147, and sect. 220, p. 161; *SH*/de Rachewiltz, sect. 202, p. 114, sect. 206, p. 118, and sect. 220, p. 127; and Paul Pelliot and Louis Hambis, *Histoire des campagnes de Gengis Khan* (Leiden: E. J. Brill, 1951), pp. 363–64.

[26] In this regard it is interesting to note that Ch'ang Te, Möngke's ambassador to Hülegü in 1259, equates the Muslim title *sulṭān* (*suan-t'an*) with the Chinese *kuo-wang*. See Emil Bretschneider, *Medieval Researches from Eastern Asiatic Sources*, 2 vols. (London: Routledge and Kegan Paul, 1967), vol. I, p. 134.

[27] ʿUmarī/Lech, pp. 2, 19, and 20, Arabic text, and pp. 91–103, and 104, German translation. On the term *nāʾib*, given to a sulṭān's lieutenant, not to royal princes, see H. A. R. Gibb, "*Nāʾib*," *EI*, 2nd edn, vol. VII, pp. 915–16. The lowly status of a *nāʾib* is further underscored by the fact that when this term passed into Mongolian, in the form *nayib*, it did so as the title of a garrison commander. See Didier Gazagnadou, "La lettre du gouverneur de Karak: A propos des relations entre Mamlouks et Mongols au XIIIe siècle," *Etudes Mongoles et Sibériennes* 18 (1987), 129–30.

rightful ruler of the Mongol holdings in the Middle East.[28] In return, in 1264 Hülegü sent a message to Qubilai counseling him to take a hard line against the "pretender" Ariq Böke, advice which the new qaghan followed.[29]

In the last years of his life, Hülegü kept in close contact with his sovereign, Qubilai. He sent Bayan, later the conqueror of the Southern Sung, to the emperor "to memorialize on [certain] matters," and in 1265 the elder Polos, after a three-year stay in Bukhara, encountered another envoy of Hülegü and accompanied him to China.[30] Hülegü and Qubilai had become firm allies against their cousins and rivals elsewhere in the fragmented empire and in consequence China and Iran were drawn into a new and intimate relationship.

[28] Rashīd/Karīmī, vol. I, p. 623, vol. II, p. 732, and Rashīd/Boyle, pp. 255–56.

[29] Rashīd/Karīmī, vol. I, p. 628, and Rashīd/Boyle, pp. 261–62.

[30] *YS*, ch. 127, p. 3099; Francis W. Cleaves, "Biography of Bayan of the Barīn in the *Yuan-shih*," *HJAS* 19 (1956), 205; Marco Polo, p. 76; Rashīd/Alizade, vol. I, pt. I, p. 194; and Rashīd/Karīmī, vol. I, p. 247.

FOUR

Grand Qans and Il-qans, 1265–1295

Hülegü's campaigns against the Ismāʾīlīs and ʿAbbāsids were the last joint military ventures of the unified Mongolian Empire. Thereafter, the Chinggisid princes increasingly turned their military energies inward in a confrontation that lasted, with fits and starts, into the fourteenth century. The accumulating tensions between rival lines which had temporarily surfaced at the accessions of Güyüg and Möngke became permanent divisions during the Toluid civil war. By the time Qubilai successfully claimed the qaghanate in 1264, the empire had fragmented into four regional and independent qanates.

To summarize, the new alignment saw the formation of one Jochid, one Chaghadaid, and two Toluid polities. In the East, Qubilai, who vanquished Ariq Böke by relying on the resources of China, moved the Mongolian capital from Qara Qorum to Peking. While his administrative authority was restricted to his own domains, he continued to assert his sovereignty as Grand Qan over the whole of the empire.[1] His territories, formally called the Yuan in 1271, ultimately embraced China, Manchuria, Mongolia, East Turkestan, Tibet, Korea, and parts of Southeast Asia. In central Asia, most of the Chaghadaids first supported Qubilai but in 1269 joined forces with the deposed Ögödeid line, under the leadership of Qaidu (d. 1301), in an attempt to drive the qaghan from his throne. The major battlegrounds between these rivals were the Uighur lands and western Mongolia. The Jochids, centered on the lower Volga, controlled western Siberia, Khwārazm, North Caucasia, the Qipchaq steppe, and the majority of the Rus principalities. Initially, they supported Ariq Böke, but following his submission they joined the coalition of princes fighting Qubilai. Finally, the Hülegüid realm, which included Iran, Afghanistan, Transcaucasia, Asia Minor, and Mesopotamia, was the only Chinggisid state that initially and consistently supported Qubilai. They faced and fought the Chaghadai princes in Khurāsān and their Jochid rivals in Transcaucasia. In pursuing interests in West Asia, the Jochid ruler Berke (1257–66), a convert to Islam, forged an alliance with the Mamlūks who had defeated Hülegü's armies at ʿAin Jālūt. This marked the first time a Chinggisid

[1] See, for example, Marco Polo, p. 167.

prince had involved a sovereign, outside power in the Mongols' internal disputes.

The Il-qans, nearly surrounded by hostile states, made every effort to maintain close ties with the court in China: their political legitimacy and their physical survival depended to a large extent on the support of the Grand Qan in China. As self-proclaimed subordinate rulers, Hülegü and his heirs all sought patents to rule in the name of their acknowledged sovereign.

Before his death, Hülegü named his eldest son Abaqa (r. 1265–82) as his successor. While there is no unequivocal evidence that Abaqa was Qubilai's nominee in the first instance, there is every reason to conclude that the qaghan fully approved and endorsed his selection.[2] For his part, Abaqa, as was expected of a ruler-elect, made a great show of reticence. According to Rashīd al-Dīn, Abaqa, when notified of his father's demise, replied: "My elder brother [senior kinsman] is Qubilai Qaghan; without his patent [*farmān*] how can one sit [upon the throne]?" His supporters, of course, persuaded him to accept and on June 19, 1265 he ascended the throne in Azerbaijan. He then exercised a kind of provisional authority while, Rashīd al-Dīn continues, waiting for "the arrival of envoys from the court of Qubilai Qaghan and the dispatch of a decree [*jarligh*] in his name."[3]

For his formal investiture Abaqa had to wait five years. Finally in October of 1270 envoys arrived from Qubilai bringing a patent, crown, and robe of honor. In the following month he was enthroned yet again.[4] The delay was caused by communications problems – the great distances involved and the flareup of warfare in central Asia.[5] Yet, despite these difficulties, there was a steady stream of envoys between the two courts, some with intelligence on their mutual enemies, the Chaghadai Qans, some in connection with commercial ventures and yet others to receive imperial largesse, as when Qubilai granted the servitors of Abaqa (A-pa-ha) silk and paper money in 1280.[6] Unfortunately, we are given little guidance as to the specific diplomatic purposes of these and many other exchanges.[7]

Abaqa was quite content to advertise his dependency on the Grand Qan and did so in many ways. In his exchange of letters with Clement IV in 1267–68 the Pope calls him "elchani Apacha" and he addresses the pontiff "by the power of the qaghan [chaam]."[8] Similarly, in his correspondence with the Mamlūk Sūlṭan Baybars in 1269, the opening formula invokes his sovereign, the qaghan, while in the text he refers to himself and his father, Hülegü, as

[2] There are, however, hints that Qubilai "pre-approved" Abaqa. See Rashīd/Karīmī, vol. I, p. 632; Rashīd/Boyle, p. 265; and Hayton [Het'um], *La flor des estoires de la terre d'Orient*, in *Recueil des historiens des croisades, Documents arméniens*, vol. II (Paris: Imprimerie nationale, 1906), p. 175. [3] Rashīd/Jahn I, p. 7. [4] *Ibid.*, p. 28.

[5] Because of such disturbances it took the elder Polos three and a half years to travel from Lesser Armenia to North China in the mid-1260s. Marco Polo, pp. 80 and 84.

[6] Rashīd/Jahn I, p. 19; Bar Hebraeus, p. 456; and *YS*, ch. 11, pp. 222–23.

[7] Rashīd/Alizade, vol. I, pt. 1, pp. 220 and 443–44.

[8] Lupprian, *Beziehungen*, pp. 221 and 224.

īl-khāns.[9] Abaqa also sent an envoy east to procure a seal, and in fact on a safe conduct the il-qan issued in 1267 or 1279 there is an imprint in Chinese reading "Seal of the Supporter of the State and Pacifier of the People (*Fu-kuo an-min chih pao*)."[10] Domestically, his coinage, as remarked in the literary sources, was minted in the name of his sovereign in China.[11] On some of his coins there is the Arabic formula "Qā'ān/the Supreme, Abāgā/īl-khān, the Supreme, King/of the Necks [*al-riqāb*, i.e., subordinate peoples]," and on others a Mongolian legend in Uighur script "struck/by Abaqa/in the Qaghan's/Name [*Qaghan-u*/*nereber*/Abaqa-*yin*/*deletkegülüksen*]."[12]

When Abaqa died in 1282 there was a certain amount of contention over the succession between Tegüder, Hülegü's oldest surviving son, and Arghun, Abaqa's eldest son. In the end Arghun stepped aside, thereby averting a military confrontation and possibly a civil war. The first of his line to convert to Islam, Tegüder took the name Aḥmad and the title sulṭān: moves that clearly alarmed his Christian subjects but presumably pleased the Muslim majority.[13] It is even possible that his succession was not recognized by the Yuan court since the table of Chinggisid rulers of Iran found in the Yuan dynastic history lists Hülegü (Hsü-lieh-wu), Abaqa (A-pa-ha) and then skips over Aḥmad/Tegüder to Arghun (A-lu-[hun]).[14] Perhaps his reign was too short for an exchange of envoys or perhaps the list is simply faulty or perhaps he was recognized and his name deleted after the fact. In any event, there is no record in either the Chinese or Persian sources that he requested or received a patent of investiture from Qubilai.

This is not to say, however, that Aḥmad broke with the qaghan. When, for instance, certain Nestorian bishops, disgruntled over the election of Mar Yahbh-Allāhā to the patriarchate, approached him with claims that the new patriarch had "sent calumnies about him to the king of kings, Kūblāi Khān," he became alarmed and ordered a thorough investigation of the matter.[15] It is therefore more accurate to conclude that Aḥmad was trying to broaden or diversify the bases of his legitimation by appealing to the religious sensibilities of the majority of his subjects. This is revealed in the ideological formulas and titulature inscribed on his coins. On some types he used the Mongolian formula of his predecessors: "Struck by/Aḥmad/in the name/of the Qaghan."

9 Reuven Amitai-Preiss, "An Exchange of Letters in Arabic between Abaγa Ilkhān and Sultan Baybars," *CAJ* 38 (1994) 16–17, 21–23, and 26–27.

10 Rashīd/Alizade, vol. I, pt. 1, p. 143; and Antoine Mostaert and Francis W. Cleaves, "Trois documents mongols des Archives Secrètes Vaticanes," *HJAS* 15 (1952), 483.

11 ʿUmarī/Lech, p. 19, Arabic text and p. 103, German translation.

12 Seifeddini, vol. I, pp. 188–89; Lang, *Numismatic History*, pp. 43–44; and Weiers, "Münzaufschriften," 49.

13 Christian sources all emphasize his use of the title Sulṭān. See, for example, A. G. Galstian, *Armianskie istochniki o Mongolakh* (Moscow: Izdatel'stvo vostochnoi literatury, 1962), p. 38, from the Chronicle of Bishop Step'anos; and Marco Polo, pp. 457–66.

14 *YS*, ch. 107, p. 2720.

15 Ernest A. Wallis Budge, trans., *The Monks of Kūblāi Khān* (London: Religious Tract Society, 1928), pp. 158–60.

There is also a variant in which his name, Amad in the Mongolian script, is replaced by the Arabic "al-sulṭān Aḥmad." Lastly, there is a third type, entirely in Arabic, which contains on the obverse "Qā'ān/the Supreme/Aḥmad, īl-khān," and on the reverse the standard Islamic formula "There is no God but Allah/Muḥammad is the prophet of God/Sulṭān Aḥmad."[16]

These ideological shifts clearly angered many Mongols. Various contemporary sources all testify to the fact that his political opponents accused him of betraying Mongolian tradition, the legacy of Chinggis Qan, and that they laid these charges before Qubilai.[17] Aḥmad's relationship with his Mongolian followers may also have suffered because of his peace overtures to the Il-qans' traditional enemies, the Golden Horde and their allies, the Egyptian Mamlūks.[18] In any event, the growing discontent afforded Arghun another opportunity to claim the throne, one which Qubilai seems to have backed at an early date.

Aḥmad, aware that the opposition was coalescing around Arghun, had his nephew arrested and imprisoned. One of Aḥmad's chief officials, Buqa, was sent to dispatch Arghun, but instead freed him and provided him with counsel and intelligence that enabled him to defeat his rival, who in 1284 was himself executed together with numerous supporters.[19]

Qubilai's interest in these matters is revealed in the embassies he hastened to Iran. The first was headed by a very senior court official, Bolad noyan, the Po-lo of the Chinese texts. He was accompanied by ʿIsā *kelemechi*, "Jesus the Interpretor," a native of Syria with long service in China, where he was known as Ai-hsieh *ch'ieh-li-ma-ch'ih*. Nominations for this assignment were made in the spring of 1283 and at some later date, not specified in the sources, the embassy left China escorted by an Alan military officer.[20] They arrived at the very end of 1285 while Arghun was in Arrān and a short while later, in January of 1286, another envoy, Ūrdūqiyā, whom Arghun himself had sent east for assistance, arrived back in Iran with the desired patent of investiture from the Grand Qan.[21]

Several features of this embassy call for further comment. First, the time lapse between Aḥmad's execution on August 10, 1284 and the arrival of the patent in Arghun's name on January 23, 1286 is only seventeen months, a remarkably rapid response to the crisis in Iran. This, in my opinion, argues that Qubilai knew in advance of the efforts to depose Aḥmad and that he fully

16 Seifeddini, vol. I, pp. 195–96; Lang, *Numismatic History*, p. 46; and Weiers, "Münzaufschriften," p. 53.

17 Hayton, *La flor des estoires*, p. 186; Marco Polo, p. 460; and Bar Hebraeus, p. 474.

18 Peter M. Holt, "The Īlkhān Aḥmad's Embassies to Qalāwūn: Two Contemporary Accounts," *BSOAS* 49 (1986), 128–32.

19 This famous incident is recounted in many sources. See Galstian, *Armianskie istochniki*, p. 41; Brosset, *Histoire de la Géorgie*, p. 601; Bar Hebraeus, pp. 460–72 and 477–79; and Marco Polo, pp. 464–65.

20 *YS*, ch. 123, p. 3038 and ch. 134, p. 3249; and *MSC*, ch. 1, p. 14a (p. 47), ch. 3, p. 5b (p. 82) and ch. 4, p. 3b (p. 114).

21 Rashīd/Jahn I, p. 66. On Ūrdūqiyā and his name, see Pelliot, *Notes*, vol. I, p. 581.

approved them. To put it another way, Qubilai backed Arghun before the outcome of the struggle was known at the Yuan court. Second, his support for Arghun is further underscored by the fact that Qubilai granted Buqa, the architect of victory, the prestigious title of *ch'eng-hsiang*, "chancellor." Significantly, this bestowal was widely reported in West Asian sources and was viewed by contemporaries and later chroniclers as one of the major events of the day.[22] Indeed, this was a singular event since *ch'eng-hsiang* (Persian *chīnksānk*) was the title reserved for the very highest-ranking officials in the Yuan government; at the time Buqa was so honored, 1286, there was only one other *ch'eng-hsiang* on the books in China.[23] In short, Buqa's title was a most dramatic and effective means of conveying Qubilai's support for Arghun's coup to the Mongolian elite in Iran and elsewhere in the empire. Third and last, Qubilai's choice of representatives at the Il-qan court, Bolad and ʿIsā, also betrays the importance the Grand Qan attached to the maintenance of loyal allies in Iran. Although described initially as an ambassador (*rasālat*), Bolad, too, was a *ch'eng-hsiang* and a long-time confidant of Qubilai who had held many important positions in China.[24] More importantly, as matters turned out, Bolad remained in West Asia for nearly thirty years, where he functioned as the major conduit of cultural exchange between Iran and China. His second in command, ʿIsā, returned to China and there performed similar offices, albeit on a more modest scale. Both figures will loom large in later sections of this study.

Arghun (r. 1284–91), the beneficiary of so much aid and encouragement, responded in kind. In the first place, he, like his father Abaqa, made a great show of awaiting Qubilai's patent before assuming full powers.[25] Naturally, Buqa, the kingmaker, became his chief minister and adviser. Initially he was allowed to exercise wide powers but his pride in office and title soon led to excess and in 1289 Arghun had his erstwhile savior executed.[26]

Not surprisingly, Arghun took care to broadcast his subordination to his sovereign and benefactor. The coinage of his reign carries combinations of the formulas "Struck by/Arghun/in the name of the Qaghan" or "Qā'ān/the Supreme/Ārghūn, īl-khān."[27] In his diplomatic correspondence with the papacy and Philip the Fair of France he addresses these princes in the "good

[22] Besides Rashīd al-Dīn, the grant is noted by Abū Bakr al-Ahrī, *Ta'rīkh-i Shaikh Uwais, an Important Source for the History of Adharbaijān*, trans. by J. B. Van Loon ('s-Gravenhage: Mouton, 1954), p. 139, Persian text and pp. 41–42, English translation; Galstian, *Armianskie istochniki*, p. 40; Brosset, *Histoire de la Géorgie*, pt. 1, pp. 602 and 606; and Stephannos Orbelian, *Histoire de la Siounie*, trans. by M. Brosset (St. Petersburg: Académie imperiale des sciences, 1864), p. 204.

[23] On this title, see *YS*, ch. 85, pp. 2120–21, ch. 112, pp. 2794–2800; and Paul Ratchnevsky, *Un code des Yuan*, 4 vols. (Paris: Collège de France, 1937–85), vol. I, pp. 17–19.

[24] Rashīd/Alizade, vol. I, pt. 1, p. 518.

[25] Hayton, *La flor des estoires*, p. 188.

[26] Bar Hebraeus, pp. 477–79.

[27] Seifeddini, vol. I, pp. 206–14; Lane, *Numismatic History*, p. 47; and Weiers, "Münzaufschriften," 53–54.

fortune of the qaghan" and refers to himself as an il-qan.[28] Finally, he sent missions to China and received envoys from the Yuan court. On the objectives of these exchanges we are, again, poorly informed. Qubilai's dispatch of envoys to Iran in 1286 may have been prompted by concern over the growing military pressure on Uighuristan mounted by Qaidu, the leader of the Ögödeids, and his ally Du'a, the ruler of the Chaghadai Qanate (r. 1282–1307).[29]

With the demise of Arghun in March of 1291, there was yet another contested election. The principal contenders were Arghun's son Ghazan, his paternal uncle Geikhatu, and a more distant relative, Baidu. Geikhatu (r. 1291–95), who received the Tibetan name Irinjin Dorje from Buddhist monks (*bakhshiyān*) resident at the court, emerged the eventual winner and was enthroned in July and again a month later.[30] As was the case with Tegüder/Aḥmad, there is no direct evidence that Geikhatu received or asked for a patent from the Grand Qan. On the other hand, unlike Aḥmad, Geikhatu is included in the list of Hülegüid rulers in the Yuan dynastic history; he appears there as I-lien-chen To-erh-chih, the Chinese transcription of his Tibetan name.[31]

In a general way, Geikhatu continued to recognize the qaghan's authority but he was not as careful or consistent as his predecessors in his outward expressions of subordination to the Yuan court. While the majority of his coins contain the Mongolian formula stating they were struck in the qaghan's name, there are a few issues from Baghdad and Tabrīz that were minted in his name alone and contain no reference to the Grand Qan. Equally revealing, the term il-qan no longer appears; on all known coin types of his reign, his name stands alone without titulature.[32]

Despite these significant changes in ideological formulas, there was, however, continuing contact with the Yuan court. Toward the end of his reign Arghun had sent three of his retainers east to obtain a wife in China. In response, Qubilai sent a Mongolian noblewoman, Kökejin, to Arghun, and the three Polos accompanied this embassy back to Iran. They traveled by sea because communications overland were again disrupted by war among the Chinggisid princes. When they arrived in Iran they found Arghun dead and his brother Geikhatu on the throne.[33] The returning envoys were warmly

[28] Lupprian, *Beziehungen*, p. 245; Mostaert and Cleaves, "Trois documents," 450, Mongolian text and 451, French translation; and Antoine Mostaert and Francis W. Cleaves, *Les Lettres de 1289 et 1305 des ilkhan Aryun et Öljeitü à Philippe le Bel* (Cambridge, Mass.: Harvard University Press, 1962), p. 17, Mongolian text, p. 18, French translation.

[29] *YS*, ch. 11, p. 293. Arghun's mission to China will be discussed below in another context.

[30] Rashīd/Jahn I, pp. 81–82 and 85. The Persian *bakhshī* is derived from the Turkic *baqshi* which in turn goes back to the Chinese *po-shih*, "learned man" or "teacher." See *DTS*, p. 82.

[31] *YS*, ch. 107, p. 2721.

[32] Seifeddini, vol. I, pp. 222–23; Lang, *Numismatic History*, p. 49; and Weiers, "Münzaufschriften," 58–60.

[33] Marco Polo, pp. 88–91.

received and Kūkājīn (Kökejin), in conformity with Mongolian custom, was now betrothed to Ghazan, the son of the deceased. According to Rashīd al-Dīn, a contemporary, Ghazan also received various "Cathayan [Khitāʿī] wonders and Chinese [Chīnī] rarities."[34] From other sources we know that Kūkājī[n] was given the lands, properties, and camps (*ordos*) of Doquz Qatun (d. 1265), the principal wife of Hülegü, a very high honor.[35]

The Polos, it should also be noted, were well treated at the court of Geikhatu, who sent them on their way home with four tablets of authority in "the name of the great kaan."[36] From the data available it therefore appears that while Geikhatu distanced himself from the Yuan court, asserting a measure of independence, he still recognized, in a vague way, the Grand Qan as his sovereign, and he evinced no desire to precipitate a complete break. His reign, however, represents an important period of transition in the relationship between the Mongolian courts of China and Iran, a transformation that was accelerated and solidified under Ghazan and his successors.

[34] Rashīd/Jahn II, pp. 13 and 39. For further details on this embassy and the Polos' traveling companions, see Yang Chih-chiu and Ho Yung-chi, "Marco Polo Quits China," *HJAS* 9 (1945–47), 51, and Francis W. Cleaves, "A Chinese Source Bearing on Marco Polo's Departure from China and a Persian Source on his Arrival in Persia," *HJAS* 36 (1976), 181–203.

[35] Qāshānī/Hambly, p. 8. [36] Marco Polo, pp. 91–92.

FIVE

Continuity and change under Ghazan, 1295–1304

In late 1294, Baidu, one of the unsuccessful claimants of the throne in 1291, launched a rebellion against Geikhatu which ended in the latter's death early the next year.[1] During Baidu's six months on the throne chaos reigned in Iran; the incessant plots and counterplots led to fragmentation and the near collapse of the Hülegüid state into civil war.[2] Like his deceased rival, Baidu struck his limited coin stock in the name of the Grand Qan but deleted the title il-qan.[3] Because of the extreme brevity of his reign, he hardly had time, whatever his inclination, to solicit, much less secure, a patent from the newly enthroned Grand Qan, Temür (r. 1294–1307), Qubilai's son and successor. Not surprisingly, the Yuan dynastic history does not mention Baidu among the Mongolian rulers of Iran.

Ghazan (r. 1295–1304) led the opposition to Baidu's faltering regime. Although the governor of Khurāsān and the designated heir apparent of his father, Arghun, Ghazan had stepped aside for Geikhatu in 1291.[4] Now he moved energetically to claim his delayed but rightful inheritance. In the course of the struggle against Baidu, Ghazan converted to Islam in mid-June 1295. He did so, according to a recent study, because a sizable and influential group among the Mongolian army and elite in Iran had already become Muslims.[5] Whatever his reason, once he had defeated his rival and ascended the throne in November 1295, he moved quickly to establish his credentials as a Muslim ruler.

This is clearly apparent in his coinage. The essential change, as the Arab encyclopedist al-ʿUmarī correctly recognized, was that Ghazan "inscribed his own name alone upon his coins and omitted the name of the Grand Qan [*al-qān ṣāhib al-takht*]."[6] The coins, for the most part, confirm this testimony. On

[1] Abū'l-Fidā, *The Memoirs of a Syrian Prince*, trans. by P. M. Holt (Wiesbaden: Franz Steiner, 1983), pp. 24–25. [2] See the description in Budge, *Monks of Kūblāi Khān*, p. 209.

[3] Seifeddini, vol. I, pp. 223–24, and Weiers, "Münzaufschriften," 60–62.

[4] Rashīd/Jahn II, p. 15; Rashīd/Karīmī, vol. I, p. 850; Seifeddini, vol. I, p. 209; and Weiers, "Munzaufschriften," 56.

[5] Charles Melville, "Pādshāh-i Islām: The Conversion of Sulṭān Maḥmūd Ghāzān Khān," *Pembroke Papers* 1 (1990), 159–77.

[6] ʿUmarī/Lech, p. 19, Arabic text and p. 103, German translation.

some of his earliest issues, which carry Arabic inscriptions, he styles himself "Ruler [*Pādshāh*] of the World/Sulṭān Supreme/Ghāzān Maḥmūd/May God Prolong his Reign." Others bear a wide variety of Perso-Islamic titles: "Ruler of Islam/Emperor [*Shāhanshāh*], the Supreme, Ghāzān Maḥmūd"; "Sulṭān of Islam/Ghāzān Maḥmūd"; and "Sulṭān, the Supreme, Ghāzān Sulṭān Maḥmūd." There are also coins from Transcaucasia inscribed with a modified Mongolian formula: "In the might of Heaven [*Tngri*]/Struck by Ghazan."[7] This shift in ideology is also apparent in Ghazan's diplomatic correspondence. In his Mongolian letter to Pope Boniface VIII in 1302 he drops all reference to the Grand Qan and to the title il-qan.[8]

It would be a mistake, however, to view this change as immediate or absolute; rather, the transformation was incremental and incomplete. For example, an Armenian scribe refers to Ghazan as a *p'ašah łan*, "*pādshāh khān*," which combines Persian and nomadic tradition.[9] More bombastic, but equally syncretic, is Rashīd al-Dīn's reference to Ghazan, in an invocation to God to protect his sulṭānate, as the

> Pādshāh of the World, Shāhānshāh of Earth and Time, Sovereign Lord of the Kings of Iran and Turan, Manifestation of the Copious Grace of God, the Visible Sign of Islam and the Faith, a Jamshid, Dispenser of Justice, Animator of the Custom of World Domination, the Elevated Banner of Sovereignty, Bestower of the Carpet of Justice, an overflowing Sea of Compassion, King of the Domains of Monarchs, Heir to the Chinggisid Throne, Shadow of God, Defender of the Faith of Allah to the Ends of the Earth and Time.[10]

Here are invoked the various bases of legitimacy, mainly Muslim to be sure, but with passing reference at least to both ancient Iranian and Mongolian sources of political authority. Many such passages can be found in Rashīd al-Dīn's *Collected Chronicles*, a compilation which Ghazan initiated and patronized.

The piecemeal character of the ideological shift is clearly evident in his letter to Boniface; while the title of the qaghan is no longer invoked, the Grand Qan's Chinese seal is still used, a seal that declares Ghazan to be a prince (*wang*).[11] And on a few coin types Ghazan is styled an il-qan and issues from the Georgian mints continued to carry the traditional Mongolian formula "Struck by/Ghazan/in the Name/of the Qaghan," down to the last years of his reign.[12] In the latter case two explanations can be advanced for public use of the qaghan's authority. First, since Georgia was Christian, the Islamization of Ghazan's legitimacy was inappropriate or at least not a pressing issue there.

[7] Seifeddini, vol. I, pp. 227–28, and Lang, *Numismatic History*, p. 52.
[8] Mostaert and Cleaves, "Trois documents," 470, Mongolian text and 471, French translation.
[9] Avedis K. Sanjian, *Colophons of Armenian Manuscripts: A Source for Middle Eastern History* (Cambridge, Mass.: Harvard University Press, 1969), p. 49.
[10] Rashīd/Karīmī, vol. I, p. 386. For another example, see p. 214.
[11] Mostaert and Cleaves, "Trois documents," 483.
[12] Seifeddini, vol. I, pp. 226–27 and 231, and Lang, *Numismatic History*, p. 51.

Second, the Golden Horde had long made claims on Georgia and perhaps Ghazan found it politically expedient to advertise the Grand Qan's nominal sovereignty of this region.

But however we understand and interpret these changes in titles and formulas, this did not presage a break with the Grand Qan in China. Ghazan's famed banishment of the Buddhist clerics (*bakhshiyān*) from Iran in no way terminated East Asian influence at the court nor, moreover, is there any evidence that it was intended to do so. Indeed, in many respects, Ghazan's reign represents one of the high points in the cultural exchange between China and Iran. This is not too surprising since Ghazan, in his formative years, was raised by East Asians. His wetnurse, a certain Mughāljīn, was the wife of a Chinese named Ishang (I Shang).[13] At age five, according to Rashīd al-Dīn, his grandfather Abaqa "entrusted him to Bāraq, a Chinese *bakhshī*, in order that he educate and teach him Mongolian and Uighur writing and their [i.e., *bakhshī*] sciences and manners [*ādāb*]."[14] He showed, reportedly, great aptitude and enthusiasm for these subjects. Nor should it be forgotten that one of his wives, the Mongol Kökejin, had spent considerable time at the Yuan court and that she came "together with wonders of Cathay and rarities of China."[15] As an adult, years after his conversion, he participated fully in purely Mongolian traditions such as the White Festival, the Mongolian New Year celebration.[16] In short, his conversion, however sincere, in no way precluded a continuing interest in Chinese science, history, and cuisine or in Mongolian customs.

The same strictures also apply in matters of state. Conversion did not automatically make Ghazan a friend of Muslim polities and an enemy of infidel states. Three years after his adoption of Islam, Ghazan executed Nawruz, the Oyirad Mongol instrumental in his own conversion, for unauthorized communication with Muslim states.[17] And in his negotiations with the Mamlūks in 1301, Ghazan, while he invoked his Islamic faith, still consulted with "old Mongolian" advisers in his native tongue.[18] More basically, the Mongolian court in Iran, regardless of its ideological reorientation, was inextricably enmeshed in Chinggisid princely politics and rivalries. Troubles with the Golden Horde had temporarily eased but the coalition of Ögödeids and Chaghadaids in central Asia still posed a serious threat to the security of the Yuan dynasty and its long-time ally in Iran. Basic self-interest therefore dictated a continuing relationship between the two.

There were, in fact, many ties that now bound the two courts together. This is well illustrated in two exchanges between Ghazan and Qubilai's successor. The first, known exclusively in the Chinese sources, was mounted by Temür

[13] Rashīd/Jahn II, pp. 3–4. [14] *Ibid.*, II, p. 8. [15] *Ibid.*, II, pp. 13 and 39.

[16] Budge, *Monks of Kūblāi Khān*, pp. 250–51. For further discussion see Reuven Amitai-Preiss, "Ghazan, Islam and Mongol Tradition: A View from the Mamlūk Sultanate," *BSOAS* 54 (1996), 1–10. [17] Abū'l-Fidā, *Memoirs*, p. 30.

[18] Heribert Horst, "Eine Gesandtenschaft des Mamlūken al-Malik an-Naṣīr am Il-khān Hof in Persien," in Wilhelm Hoernerbach, ed., *Der Orient in der Forschung: Festschrift für Otto Spies zum 5. April 1966* (Wiesbaden: Otto Harrassowitz, 1967), pp. 357 and 358.

Qaghan (Ch'eng-tsung, r. 1294–1307). In 1296 he dispatched Baiju (Pai-chu), a promising military officer, to the Western Region (Hsi-yü). Ghazan (Ha-tsan) was so impressed with Baiju's abilities that he made him a valet (*shang-i*) in his household and an adjutant in his campaign army (*hsing-chün*). He gave excellent service and was rewarded by the appreciative prince. At some unspecified time thereafter he returned to the Yuan court where Temür, most pleased with his performance, bestowed further awards and "imperial favor" upon him.[19] Obviously, this "loan" of military talent indicates that the two courts were on friendly, indeed intimate, terms.

The second was initiated in Iran. According to Vaṣṣāf, Ghazan selected two of his retainers, Malik Fakhr al-Dīn Aḥmad and Noghai Elchi (the "envoy"), to head the mission to the Grand Qan. They traveled by sea since the overland routes were disrupted by war with Qaidu and Du'a. Their travels, however, were not without misadventure; in 1301 Yang Shu, an official in Kiangsu province, encountered Noghai (Na-huai) and his colleagues drifting off the China coast. Subsequently, in 1304, they presented tribute to the Yuan court, and inspected properties granted to Hülegü in North China. They returned by sea and Fakhr al-Dīn died near Maʿbar in India in 1305; Noghai and Yang Shu, Temür's envoy, pressed on and reached Hurmuz (Hu-lu-mu-ssu) in 1307, nearly nine years from the date of departure. By this time, of course, Öljeitü (r. 1304–16), Ghazan's brother, was on the throne.[20]

Besides the time involved, this embassy is instructive on several accounts. First, it is obvious that these envoys had a number of functions. We are not told of their political goals, but their economic activities are clearly stated: they took capital to trade and brought back proceeds from Hülegü's properties in China (a subject discussed at greater length in chapter 7). Second, they were also involved in cultural exchange. They took West Asian exotica such as "hunting leopards" (cheetahs) to the East and brought back similar gifts with them. Thus, at the end of Ghazan's reign the full range of relationships – political, economic, and cultural – that had developed between the Mongolian courts of China and Iran since Hülegü's time were very much intact and still quite active.

[19] Yuan Chüeh, *Ch'ing-jung chü-shih chi* (Ssu-pu ts'ung-k'an ed.), ch. 34, p. 22b. The author, 1267–1327, wrote Baiju's biography.

[20] Vaṣṣāf, pp. 505–6; H. M. Elliot and John Dowson, trans., *The History of India as Told by its Own Historians*, repr. (New York: AMS Press, 1966), vol. III, pp. 45–47; Huang Chin, *Chin-hua Huang hsien-sheng wen-chi* (Ssu-pu ts'ung-k'an ed.), ch. 35, p. 16a; and *YS*, ch. 21, p. 460. For further comment and analysis, see V. V. Bartol'd, "Evropeets XIIIv. v Kitaiskikh uchenykh uchrezhdeniiakh (K voprosu pizantse Izole)," in his *Sochineniia* (Moscow: Nauka, 1968), vol. V, pp. 385–87; and Paul Pelliot, "Les grands voyages maritimes chinois au début du XVe siècle," *TP* 30 (1933), 431.

SIX

Sulṭāns and Grand Qans, 1304–1335

The enthronement of Öljeitü as Ghazan's successor coincided with the establishment of a general peace among the Chinggisid princes. Öljeitü's relationship with the Grand Qan must therefore be placed, first of all, within the context of these important developments.

As noted previously, the conflict between Ariq Böke and Qubilai provided dissident lines an opportunity to seek independence and pursue individual interests. The result was frequent warfare between the four regional qanates. The Golden Horde and the Hülegüids clashed over territories in Caucasia in 1262–63, 1265, 1288, and 1290. Meanwhile, in the East the Ögödeid/Chaghadaid coalition led by Qaidu launched attacks on Qubilai's forces in Mongolia and Uighuristan in 1268, 1275, 1286, and 1290. Initially, the Jochids, whose territories extended into central Siberia, supported or were at least on friendly terms with Qaidu and in general sympathy with his efforts to topple Qubilai. This, however, began to change in the 1280s when the eastern wing of the Golden Horde, increasingly fearful of their powerful and aggressive neighbors, Qaidu and Du'a, made a number of overtures to their cousins in China and Iran.[1] In consequence, enmity between the Jochids and Hülegüids ended so that they could concentrate their attention on the more immediate threat posed by the coalition in central Asia. Gradually Qaidu and Du'a were isolated, and between 1298 and 1301 the Yuan forces, in concert with those of the Jochids, decisively defeated them in a series of battles fought along the Irtysh River in southern Siberia.[2] After some further desultory fighting, Chabar, the son of the deceased Qaidu, and the war-weary Du'a decided to end hostilities. They sent envoys to the Yuan court in August of 1301 and began negotiations; in October of 1304 they formally offered their "submission."[3]

Although the Hülegüids were not participants in the climactic battles nor

[1] Rashīd/Karīmī, vol. I, pp. 352–53, and Rashīd/Boyle, p. 160.

[2] For details and documentation, see Thomas T. Allsen, "The Princes of the Left Hand: An Introduction to the History of the *Ulus* of Orda in the Thirteenth and Early Fourteenth Centuries," *AEMA* 5 (1985–87), 18–25.

[3] Qāshānī/Hambly, pp. 32–41, and *YS*, ch. 21, pp. 454 and 460.

direct participants in the peace negotiations, they were well informed of events and rejoiced at the Grand Qan's triumph over their common enemies.[4] Moreover, the newly crowned Öljeitü lost little time in informing his neighbors that the empire was reunited. In his missive to Philip the Fair of France in 1305, he dwells at some length on the fact that all the descendants of Chinggis Qan are at peace after forty-five years of civil war and that the postal relay stations (*jamud*) have been reconnected.[5]

While celebrating this nominal reunification of the empire and his friendship with his fellow Mongolian princes, Öljeitü, a Christian who first converted to Sunni Islam and then became a Shīʿite, took care to appeal to his Muslim subjects. The main chronicler of his reign, Qāshānī, portrays Öljeitü as deeply devoted to the Faith, especially in comparison with other Muslim rulers, and notes his respect for the descendants of the Prophet and the favors he bestowed on Muslim divines.[6] Originally named Nicolas and then Muḥammad Khudābandah, he took the title of Ūljāītū Sulṭān at his coronation in 1304.[7] His succession and adopted title was a purely local decision and there is no indication that a patent from the Grand Qan was ever requested or received.

To his own subjects, including the Christian component, he was certainly a sulṭān, a defender of the Islamic faith.[8] Inscriptions on public buildings erected or remodeled during his reign convey the same message. On these he is styled sulṭān, shāhānshāh, "shadow of God on Earth, etc."[9] Strangely enough, the title il-qan reappears in Öljeitü's certificate commissioning the Mosul Qurʾān of 1311–12 which states in part that this copy was ordered by

> Our Lord the Sulṭān, the supreme Īl-khān, the Exalted, King of Subject Peoples, Sulṭān of the Arab and non-Arab [*al-ʾajam*], Sulṭān, King of Kings of the World, Shadow of God on Earth, and His Caliph over His Slaves and Dominions.[10]

Here the import of the title il-qan, with its implication of subordination, is much diminished, embedded as it is in such a lengthy catalog of Perso-Islamic formulas. The certificate, in other words, accurately reflects the relative weight accorded the two ideological systems under Öljeitü.

An ideological admixture of roughly similar proportions can be found in a diplomatic document. In the text of a letter to Philip the Fair, Öljeitü titles himself a sulṭān and while he gives Temür, the reigning Yuan emperor, his

[4] Qāshānī/Hambly, p. 235.

[5] Mostaert and Cleaves, *Lettres de 1289 et 1305*, p. 53, Mongolian text, and p. 54, French translation. [6] Qāshānī/Hambly, p. 228. [7] Qāshānī/Hambly, pp. 17–18 and 42.

[8] Sanjian, *Colophons*, pp. 51 and 53.

[9] Sheila S. Blair, "The Inscription from the Tomb Tower at Bastām: An Analysis of Ilkhanid Epigraphy," in C. Adle, ed., *Art et société dans le monde iranien* (Paris: ADPF, 1982), p. 267, Arabic text and p. 265, English translation, and André Godard, "Historique du Masdjid-é Djumʿa d'Iṣfahān," *Athar-é Irān* 1 (1936), 234–36.

[10] David James, *Qurʾāns of the Mamluks* (New York: Thames and Hudson, 1988), p. 257, Arabic text and p. 100, English translation. Certificates of other Qurʾāns commissioned by Öljeitü contain similar attributions. See pp. 92, 112–13, 236, and 238.

proper title, qaghan, he in no way implies his subordination to him.[11] On the other hand, the Chinese seal on this document conveys a message of dependency on the Yuan emperor. This inscription which reads "Seal [*pao*] of the Truly Mandated August Emperor for Whom Heaven Indulges the Ten Thousand Things" has, however, been interpreted quite differently. Mostaert and Cleaves, in their study of the seal, have argued that the "Truly Mandated Emperor" (*Chen-ming huang-ti*) is Öljeitü and that the seal was produced in Iran because it is most unlikely that the Yuan emperor would have conceded the title *huang-ti*, with its claim of absolute, unabridged sovereignty, to another.[12] Their authority in such matters is deservedly high but in this instance I think their interpretation is mistaken. The seal in question bears the character *pao*, which always indicates that it was made for the emperor.[13] It is far more likely, therefore, that the "Truly Mandated Emperor" refers to Temür Qaghan in China. In short, I believe that the Yuan court sent this *pao* to Iran for Öljeitü's use around the time of his enthronement. In any case, a Chinese-language seal on such a document, while usefully invoking the backing and authority of a powerful, if nominal, sovereign in diplomatic exchanges, would in no way undermine Öljeitü's efforts to gain the acceptance of his Muslim subjects.

On the coins issued in Öljeitü's time, however, the message is uniformly Muslim. He is called "Sulṭān most Mighty/Defender of the World and the Faith" or "Lord/Sulṭān most Mighty/Ruler over Subject Peoples [*riqāb al-umam*]."[14] For purposes of internal politics there was then a consistent effort to domesticate the sources of legitimacy, to place a Muslim face on Mongolian rule. This, however, did not preclude, as Het'um, a contemporary, asserts "Carbanda's deference to and reverence" for the emperor in the east, "Tamor Can."[15] And beyond the long habit of respect for the office of qaghan, Öljeitü still had much important business to conduct with its holder.

Their relationship, so far as it can be reconstructed, was amiable and fairly intense. It began at the very outset of Öljeitü's reign when in October of 1304 envoys of Temür Qaghan arrived together with those of Chabar to announce peace among the princes. After a stay of six weeks the envoys of Temür, who included a Muslim whose family was long resident in China, departed on the return trip.[16] The next embassy arrived in early 1306 "bringing favorable news and good reports" from the court of Temür. They were feted several times before their departure sometime in the spring.[17] Two years later, according to the Chinese sources, another mission was dispatched westward to prince

[11] Mostaert and Cleaves, *Lettres de 1289 et 1305*, p. 55, Mongolian text, and p. 56, French translation. [12] Mostaert and Cleaves, "Trois documents," 484–85.

[13] David M. Farquhar, "The Official Seals and Ciphers of the Yuan Period," *MS* 25 (1966), 393.

[14] Seifeddini, vol. I, pp. 235–40, and Lang, *Numismatic History*, pp. 57–59.

[15] Hayton, *La flor des estoires*, p. 214.

[16] Qāshānī/Hambly, pp. 31–32 and 41. One of the envoys, Muṣṭafā Khwājah, was a descendant of Ja'far Khwājah, the Chu-pa-erh Huo-che of the *YS*, ch. 120, p. 2960, Chinggis Qan's first imperial agent (*darughachi*) in Peking in 1215. [17] Qāshānī/Hambly, p. 49.

Khudābandah (Ha-erh-pan-da), this time, presumably, to announce the death of Temür and the accession of Qaishan (r. 1307–11) as the new qaghan.[18] In 1314 a further mission arrived from Qaishan's successor Buyantu (r. 1311–20), again "bringing good reports."[19] Around 1316 an envoy from Khudābandah (Ha-erh-pan-ta) arrived in China where he bestowed much cash and gifts on Temüder (T'ieh-mu-tieh-erh), the chief political and financial officer of the Yuan realm (d. 1322).[20]

In addition to the diplomatic missions, there were exchanges of personnel. Shortly after Öljeitü's enthronement in 1304 new amirs were appointed, among them a certain Saraqān Bashqird who had previously served the Yuan prince, Ananda, a grandson of Qubilai and a convert to Islam, whose territory was in the Tangut land, the area of the Kansu Corridor.[21] We know, too, from the *Yuan shih* that in 1307 "people subordinate to Imperial Prince Ha-erh-pan-ta" were dispersed after some unspecified disturbance and that the emperor "gave orders to punish those who went into hiding."[22] While cryptic, the passage clearly indicates that Khudābandah had some kind of staff in China. It is this ongoing contact and communication between the two courts that best accounts for the fact that the chronicler Qāshānī possesses extremely detailed information on the commanders and deployment of Yuan military units in Uighuristan and Tibet, and that the historian Vaṣṣāf knows so much about the accession of Khaishān (Qaishan) and Būyāntūq (Buyantu).[23]

On his death in 1316, Öljeitü was succeeded by his ten-year-old son Abū Saʿīd. Again, this was a local arrangement and there is no suggestion in either the Persian or Chinese sources that the Grand Qan had a hand in the affair or issued a patent. The kingmaker in this instance was Chuban, a senior Mongolian official who had long served Öljeitü and now became the regent for his young son. His power and prestige were in fact so great throughout most of Abū Saʿīd's reign that contemporary observers considered him co-ruler, a sovereign prince who sent his own ambassadors to foreign courts.[24]

On Muslim inscriptions Abū Saʿīd is called "Sulṭān of the World, Elevated of the Earth and the Faith" and following the suppression of an uprising in Georgia he took the additional title of Bahādur Khān, "Brave Qan," which is also attested in Mongolian documents in the form Busayid Baghatur qan.[25] In the Armenian sources, his various titles, Łan, Bahatur Łan and sultan are used quite interchangeably.[26]

The ideological formulas on his coins are consistently Muslim and his title

[18] *YS*, ch. 21, p. 501.

[19] Qāshānī/Hambly, pp. 166–67. This source says these envoys came from Tīmūr Qān, clearly a mistake, since he died in 1307.

[20] *YS*, ch. 205, p. 4579. Since Temüder was viewed by Confucians as an "evil minister," perhaps these gifts were actually bribes for some unknown ends.

[21] Qāshānī/Hambly, pp. 9 and 29.

[22] *YS*, ch. 21, p. 472.

[23] Qāshānī/Hambly, pp. 202–3, and Vaṣṣāf, pp. 498–505.

[24] Abū'l-Fidā, *Memoirs*, pp. 72, 73, 83, 85, 86, and 87, and Sanjian, *Colophons*, pp. 63 and 64.

[25] V. V. Bartol'd, "Persidskaia nadpis na stene anniskoi mechete Manuche," in his *Sochineniia*, vol. IV, pp. 317–18, and Francis W. Cleaves, "The Mongolian Documents in the Musée de Téhéran, *HJAS* 16 (1953), 27.

[26] Sanjian, *Colophons*, pp. 65, 67, 68, 70, 72, and 73.

is most usually "Sulṭān."[27] There is, however, an interesting exception. Coins struck in Anatolia and Azerbaijan in 1316–18 use the title "Il-khān" as well as "Sulṭān."[28] This limited revival of the term il-qan is not explained in the available sources but it may be connected with the renewal of hostilities with the Chaghadai Qanate which launched major attacks in Uighuristan and Khurāsān at this time. In such circumstances perhaps the court in Iran felt it a propitious moment to advertise its ties with the Yuan.

In any event, the renewal of hostilities certainly encouraged regular communication with the Yuan. From the Chinese sources it is known that around twenty embassies passed between the two courts in the years 1324–32. Most were initiated by Abū Saʿīd and most are described conventionally as "tribute" missions. Occasionally, however, we are told of other business conducted by these embassies: congratulations for newly enthroned qaghans, problems with the behavior of diplomatic personnel, and the bestowal of titles and honorifics.[29] In the latter category there was the grant of an honorary office to Chuban, an episode which indicates the continuing relevance of the Grand Qan in the politics of Iran.

Chuban's dominance at the court began to wear thin in the early 1320s. First his son, Temür Tash, the governor of Anatolia (Rūm), rebelled in 1321–22. While Chuban was still sufficiently powerful to secure his son's pardon and reappointment to the same office, his prestige suffered and his political vulnerability was exposed for the first time. As a means of shoring up his position in Iran, he somehow induced Abū Saʿīd to solicit honors from the Grand Qan. According to the account in the *Yuan shih* dated November 28, 1324:

> Imperial Prince Abū Saʿīd [Pu Sai-yin] sent word that his minister [*ch'en*] Chuban (Ch'u-pan) was meritorious and requested that he be given an office. [The Emperor] made Chuban a Commander Unequalled in Honor [*K'ai-fu i-t'ung san-ssu*] and Duke who Assists the State [*I-kuo kung*] and granted him a silver seal and golden tablet.[30]

The Grand Qan's representative arrived in Iran, by way of the Chaghadai Qanate and the Golden Horde, in mid-1327 and bestowed these honors upon Chuban. In the Persian sources his new Chinese title, "Commander Unequalled in Honor," which ranked just below that of Prince (*wang*) in the Yuan system, is translated quite appropriately as "Commander of Commanders [*Amīr al-umarā*]" or as "Commander of the Four Qanates [*ulūs-hā*]."[31]

[27] Seifeddini, vol. II, pp. 23–37; Lang, *Numismatic History*, pp. 61–65; and M. N. Fedorov, "Klad serebrianykh khulaguidskikh monet iz Iuzhnogo Turkmenistana," in *Kul'tura Turkmenii v srednie veka* (Trudy Iu. TAKE, vol. XVII; Ashabad: Ylym, 1980), pp. 97–98.

[28] Sheila S. Blair, "The Coins of the Later Ilkhanids: A Typological Analysis," *Journal of the Economic and Social History of the Orient* 26 (1983), 299–301.

[29] *YS*, ch. 29, pp. 643, 645, 646, 651, 661, 662; ch. 30, pp. 667, 671, 672, 673, 674, 675, 677, 678; ch. 34, pp. 754, 760; ch. 35, pp. 789, 792; ch. 36, pp. 801, 803, 805; and ch. 37, p. 812. These missions will be examined in more detail in chapter 7, "Economic ties."

[30] *YS*, ch. 29, p. 651.

[31] Abū Bakr al-Ahrī, *Tarīkh-i Shaikh Uwais*, p. 153, Persian text, and pp. 54–55, English translation; and Ḥāfiẓ-i Abrū, *Ẓayl jāmiʿ al-tavārīkh-i Rashīdī*, ed. Khānbābā Bayānī (Salsalat-i intishārāt-i anjuman-i aṣar millī, no. 88; Tehran, 1971), p. 167.

By this time, however, the relations between Abū Saʿīd and his chief minister had reached breaking point. Just a few months after the bestowal Abū Saʿīd, smarting over new affronts, executed one of Chuban's sons and a military confrontation ensued. Chuban's support soon evaporated and for a while he contemplated a plea for support from the Grand Qan. In the end, he sought refuge in Herat, where he was seized by the local ruler and executed on Abū Saʿīd's order.[32]

Although his titles did not save Chuban's career or life, it is significant that the original request was made at all; clearly, there were important figures in Iran who felt the "China card" was still worth playing in their domestic politics. And it is equally revealing that the Yuan court pointedly announced Chuban's honors to the Jochids and Chaghadaids, thereby reminding these rival lines that the Grand Qan's special relationship with Iran was still intact, a political fact best not forgotten or ignored.

On Abū Saʿīd's death in 1335 succession disputes led to civil war and chaos, and Mongolian rule in Iran rapidly disintegrated. Abū Saʿīd is the last Hülegüid ruler mentioned in the Chinese annals and soon thereafter the Yuan regime itself was facing dire domestic crises. A political partnership of eighty years, characterized by regular contact and consultation, had come to an end.

[32] For more details on this episode, see Thomas T. Allsen, "Notes on Chinese Titles in Mongol Iran," *Mongolian Studies* 14 (1991), 32–34.

SEVEN

Economic ties

To obtain a full and balanced picture of the nature and intensity of the relationship between the two courts, we need to explore briefly their economic ties. Again, this does not pretend to be exhaustive (or economic history); rather, the intention in this chapter is to supply additional context for their cultural exchanges.

During the reign of Abaqa, a certain Yaʿqub, described by Bar Hebraeus as "a great merchant and a Christian," died in Khurāsān while returning from the court of Qubilai. He was accompanied on his travels, we are further informed, by Abaqa's ambassador, an Uighur named Yashmut.[1] Such overland trading ventures, conducted in association with official diplomatic missions, must have been a common occurrence whenever land travel was safe. As the thirteenth century wore on, however, it seems likely that disturbances and military confrontation in central Asia increasingly forced merchants and envoys onto alternative routes.[2] Consequently, the Indian Ocean assumed an important, if not central, place in the economic relations between China and Iran. In any event, we have much fuller information on this seaborne commercial traffic.

The Indian Ocean trade, of course, long predated the Mongols and was in no sense created or controlled by them.[3] This network of exchange reached from the ports of South China, such as Zaiton (Ch'üan-chou), to Alexandria on the shores of the Mediterranean. The principal transit point was Maʿbar on the eastern coast of India. This kingdom was well known to the Yuan court and from the Chinese sources it appears likely that the Mongols first began to exploit the sea route from Ch'üan-chou to Maʿbar (Ma-pa-erh) to Iran during the reign of Abaqa (A-pu-ha) when civil war made the overland routes

[1] Bar Hebraeus, p. 456.

[2] On the question of the alternative routes, their changing advantages and disadvantages, see the comments of John of Monte Corvino, a Franciscan in China in the early fourteenth century, in *Mongol Mission*, p. 226.

[3] For an overview of the trade between China and the Persian Gulf, its periodization, ports, products, routes, and commercial institutions, see Moira Tampoe, *Maritime Trade between China and the West: An Archaeological Study of the Ceramics from Siraf (Persian Gulf), 8th to 15th Centuries AD* (Oxford: BAR Publications, 1989), pp. 77–81 and 97–153.

unsafe.[4] In any event, as Marco Polo and Rashīd al-Dīn testify, to Maʿbar came the wares of China, Hind, and Sind, which were then reexported to Iraq, Rūm, and Europe.[5] The exchange of goods between the Mongolian courts of China and Iran was therefore part of a much larger commercial traffic in which private merchants, such as the Egyptian-based Karīmī family, played a prominent role.[6]

The Mongols' active participation in this trade is frequently noted in the contemporary sources. Marco Polo, for instance, relates that the Persian port of Curmos (Hurmuz) was a major entrepôt for the goods arriving from China and India, testimony that is confirmed by Ibn Baṭṭuṭah, who several decades later (ca. 1327) speaks of the many ships from China that plied the waters of the Persian Gulf.[7] Qāshānī, the chronicler of Öljeitü's reign, is also well informed on this trade, noting that the rarities of Chīn and Machīn were first delivered to Maʿbar and then transshipped to Iran "on great vessels, that is the *jung*."[8] This, of course, is the famous junk. Marco Polo, who spent some time on one, describes in detail these ocean-going vessels of the Chinese – their large size, carrying capacity, watertight compartments, axial rudders, rigging, and anchors.[9] The actual capacity of Sung–Yuan ships is a matter of uncertainty and dispute. In recent scholarship the estimates have ranged from 1,200 tons to a more modest 375 tons.[10] But whatever the correct figures, medieval Chinese vessels were large, comfortable, and always impressed Westerners, Christians, and Muslims, who encountered them.

We even know something of the individual merchants who made use of these impressive ships to bring East Asian wares to Iran. In the late thirteenth and early fourteenth centuries, the Shaikh al-Islam, Jamāl al-Dīn Ibrāhīm ibn Muḥammad al-Tībī, the Mongols' superintendent of taxes in southern Iran and Iraq, ran an extensive transcontinental trading operation from his base on the island of Qais in the Persian Gulf. This successful enterprise, in the words of Vaṣṣāf, "was so managed that the produce [*biżāʿat*] of remotest China was consumed in the farthest West."[11] From other literary sources we know that the produce so conveyed to Iran included spices, copper, sandalwood, pearls, and jewels.[12] Textiles, of course, were also a major item of

4 *YS*, ch. 210, p. 4669.

5 Marco Polo, pp. 351, 417, and 418–19, and Rashīd al-Dīn, *Die Indiengeschichte des Rashīd al-Dīn*, trans. by Karl Jahn (Vienna: Verlag der österreichischen Akademie der Wissenschaft, 1980), folio 335r–v, *tafeln* 14–15, Persian text, and pp. 37–38, German translation.

6 Arthur Lane and R. B. Serjeant, "Pottery and Glass Fragments from the Aden Littoral, with Historical Notes," *JRAS* nos. 1–2 (1948), 108–33, especially 113–16.

7 Marco Polo, p. 123, and Ibn Baṭṭuṭah/Gibb, vol. II, p. 320.

8 Qāshānī/Hambly, p. 182.

9 Marco Polo, pp. 354–57.

10 Zhou Shide, "Shipbuilding," in *Ancient China's Technology and Science* (Peking: Foreign Language Press, 1983), p. 479, and H. C. Lee, "A Report on a Recently Excavated Sung Ship at Quanzhou and a Consideration of its True Capacity," *Sung Studies* 11–12 (1975–76), 4–9.

11 Elliot and Dowson, *History of India*, p. 35; Vaṣṣāf, p. 303; and Jean Aubin, "Les princes d'Ormuz du XIIIe au XVe siècle," *Journal Asiatique* 241 (1953), 89–99.

12 Marco Polo, p. 415.

import. The amounts of the goods conveyed, while unrecorded, were certainly substantial. Qāshānī, a contemporary, gives us some notion of the volume when he reports that in 1311 a fire in Baghdad destroyed Egyptian and Chinese cloth and wares valued at 100 *tūmān*.[13] From the archeological evidence, it is clear that Chinese ceramics reached Iran in large quantities.[14] A more thorough search of the archeological literature would likely shed additional light on the nature and extent of Chinese wares in Iran.

Besides the private- and government-sponsored trade, there were formalized exchanges between the courts of China and Iran. These are usually presented in the sources as "tribute" but from the perspective of Mongolian social norms and usages they are better understood as examples of reciprocity, of gift exchange. While such presentations began in the thirteenth century (e.g., Ghazan's receipt of Chinese rarities), we are best informed on what passed between the two courts during the reign of Abū Saʿīd (1316–35).

According to "The Book of the Estate of the Great Caan," written ca. 1330 by the archbishop of Sulṭāniyyah, Boussay (Abū Saʿīd) and other Chinggisid princes "send year by year live libbards [leopards], camels, gyrfalcons, and great store of precious jewels besides, to the said Caan [Qaghan], their Lord."[15] Although this is a curious and problematic source, its data in this respect accord well with the accounts in the *Yuan shih*. The frequent exchanges of presents found there can best be presented in a table (see table 2).

Several comments are called for. First, the purpose of the dispatch of lions, tigers, and leopards to China is not stated in the sources but it is fairly certain that these animals were destined for the various hunting parks maintained by the Yuan, the most famous of which was Shang-tu, Coleridge's Xanadu. Second, the Yuan court frequently responded to Abū Saʿīd's gifts with huge sums of "cash" which took the form of paper money or *ch'ao*. This, too, is noticed in "The Book of the Estate of the Great Caan" which says of the Yuan that "all their royal grants are also made on paper [money]."[16] Obviously, paper money could not be taken back to West Asia, with its system of metallic currency. The solution, of course, was to use paper money in China to purchase silk and other valuables. Such practice was well known to both Christian and Muslim authors of the age.[17]

The "allotted territories" that individual princes were assigned throughout the vast Chinggisid domains constitute another, and important, economic bond between the courts of China and Iran. Much has been written on these bestowals of lands and peoples in debates over the supposed "feudal"

[13] Qāshānī/Hambly, p. 109.

[14] B. A. Shelkovnikov, "Kitaiskaia keramika iz raskopok srednevekovykh gorodov i poseleni Zakavkaz'ia," *Sovetskaia arkheologiia* 21 (1954), 368–78.

[15] Yule, *Cathay*, vol. III, p. 89.

[16] *Ibid.*, p. 98.

[17] Marco Polo, p. 239; Francesco Balducci Pegolotti, "La Practica della Mercatura," in Yule, *Cathay*, vol. III, pp. 154–55; and Ḥāfiẓ-i Abrū, *A Persian Embassy to China*, trans. by K. M. Maitra, repr. (New York: Paragon Book Corp., 1970), pp. 97–98 and 111–12.

Table 2 *Table of gift exchanges*

Date of presentation	Presentations to Yuan emperor	Presentations to Abū Saʿīd (Pu Sai-Yin)	*Yuan shih* Reference ch.	p.
Apr 22, 1324	"tribute"		29	645
May 9, 1324	"tribute"		29	651
Jan 1, 1326		"20,000 ingots of cash and 100 rolls of silk"	29	661
Jan 12, 1326	"pearls"	"20,000 ingots of cash"	29	662
Feb 10, 1326	"western horses"		30	667
Aug 15, 1326	"camels and horses"		30	671
Sept 23, 1326	"precious stones and single-humped camels"		30	672
Nov 25, 1326	"tigers"		30	674
Dec 6, 1326	"horses"		30	675
Apr 5, 1327	"tigers, western horses, daggers, pearls and other valuables"	"gold and cash reckoned at 10,000"	30	677
Apr 21, 1327	"lions and tigers"	"8,000 ingots of cash"	30	678
July 24, 1330	"congratulation presents"		34	760
Nov 18, 1331	"tribute"	"materia medica"	35	795
Mar 28, 1332		"240 rolls of embroidered, multicolored silk"	36	801
May 13, 1332	"local products"		36	803
Aug 17, 1332	"seven pieces of precious quartz"		36	805
Nov 7, 1332	"88 catties of t'a-li-ya [theriaca] and daggers"	"3,300 ingots"	37	812

tendencies exhibited by the Mongolian Empire.[18] Relatively little attention, however, has been paid to these allotted territories as a form of transcontinental economic exchange.

Nomadic society and political culture require leaders to redistribute part of their wealth and possessions among their retainers and followers. This could be accomplished in various ways: the organization of large-scale feasts and drinking parties, or the bestowal of clothing. The chase also offered an oppor-

[18] See, for example, Meng Ssu-ming, *Yuan-tai she-hui chieh-chi chih-tu* (Hong Kong: Lung-men shu-t'ien, 1967), pp. 115–26; G. V. Melikhov, "Ustanovlenie vlasti mongol'skikh feodalov v Severo-Vostochnom Kitae," in Tikhvinskii, *Tataro-Mongoly*, pp. 72 ff.; and I. P. Petrushevskii, *Zemledelie i agrarnye otnosheniia v Iran, XIII–XIV vekov* (Moscow and Leningrad: Izdatel'stvo akademii nauk SSSR, 1960), pp. 233 ff.

tunity to display royal munificence. Describing the massive and carefully organized hunts of Ögödei's time, Rashīd al-Dīn records that at the end of the day "the commissaries [*büke'üls*] distributed with justice, the accumulated game among all the various princes, commanders and troops so that no one went without a share [*naṣīb*]."[19]

Booty of all kinds, including cattle and humans, was similarly apportioned. According to the *Secret History*, Chinggis Qan regularly shared out defeated peoples and prisoners of war among his family.[20] Initially, of course, these were nomadic, tribal peoples, but when Mongolian rule was established over sedentary societies this practice was extended to agricultural populations, some of which were now allotted to imperial princes and meritorious officials. The scale of this undertaking is nicely captured in Juvaynī's statement that at the *quriltai* of 1252 Möngke "apportioned [*taḥsīs farmud*] the whole of the realm and gave a share [*bakhsh*] to all his kin, sons and daughters, brothers and sisters."[21]

The generic term in Mongolian for such "shares" was *qubi*, but there developed over time a complex, and at times confusing, Chinese and Mongolian vocabulary related to territories and peoples granted to notables; among the more common were *t'ou-hsia*, "appanage," *ai-ma* (Mongolian *ayimagh*), "tribe," and most important for our purposes, *fen-ti*, "allotted territory."[22] On a large scale at least, *fen-ti* were first bestowed under Ögödei. The decision to do so generated much controversy and political debate and was vigorously resisted by the Mongols' most influential Chinese advisers, notably Yeh-lü Ch'u-ts'ai.[23] None the less, the plan to share out large areas of North China (Chung Yuan) was implemented, with modifications, in 1236. The consequence was that a sizable part of the population was "apportioned"[24] among the imperial family. In this dispensation Ögödei generously assigned senior Chinggisid princes entire prefectures: for instance, Orda and Batu, the eldest sons of Jochi, received P'ing-yang; Chaghadai the prefecture of T'ai-yuan, etc. It was, however, stipulated by the emperor, on the insistence of Yeh-lü Ch'u-ts'ai, that while each recipient might place his own agent (*ta-lu-hua-ch'ih* > Mongolian *darughachi*) in his allotted territory, court-appointed officials would collect the taxes and then turn the proceeds over to the grantee or his agent.[25]

19 Rashīd/Alizade, vol. II, pt. 1, pp. 248–49, and Rashīd/Boyle, p. 65.

20 *SH*/Cleaves, sect. 186, 187, pp. 114–15, sect. 203, pp. 143–44, and sect. 242, p. 175; and *SH*/de Rachewiltz, sect. 186, 187, pp. 95–96, sect. 203, pp. 115–16, and sect. 242, pp. 138–39.

21 Juvaynī/Qazvīnī, vol. I, p. 31, and Juvaynī/Boyle, vol. I, p. 42.

22 For further discussions of terminology, see Paul Ratchnevsky, "Zum Ausdruck 't'ou-hsia' in der Mongolenzeit," in Walther Heissig, ed., *Collectanea Mongolica: Festschrift für Professor Dr. Rintchen zum 60. Geburtstag* (Wiesbaden: Otto Harrassowitz, 1966), pp. 173–91; and Chou Liang-hsiao, "Yuan-tai t'ou-hsia fen-feng chih-tu ch'u-t'an," *Yuan shih lun-ts'ang* 2 (1983), 53–59.

23 See Hsiao Ch'i-ch'ing, "Yen Shih (1182–1240)," *Papers on Far Eastern History* 33 (1986), 121–22.

24 The Chinese term is *fen-tz'u*, literally "divide and bestow."

25 This event is reported most fully in the *YS*, ch. 2, p. 35. See also *YWL*, ch. 40, pp. 23a–b.

The tax imposed on this category of the populace was called **aqa-tamur* in Mongolian and *wu-hu-ssu*, literally, "five households silk," in Chinese. Such households, accordingly termed *wu-hu-ssu-hu*, "five households silk households," paid their tax in silk floss at an annual rate of one *chin* (596.82 grams) to the central government and six *liang*, four *ch'ien* (238.72 grams) to the grantee. The central government therefore received 2.5 times as much as the holder of the allotted territory.[26]

We are fairly well informed on Hülegü's allotted territories and other economic interests in China. The *Yuan shih* records that in 1257 Möngke, as part of a much larger dispensation, fixed Hülegü's (Hsü-lieh) annual grant at 100 ingots of silver and 300 rolls of cloth. At the same time the emperor "apportioned" 25,056 households in Chang-te in Honan as five households silk households. By 1319, the text continues, there were only 2,929 households producing 2,201 *chin* of silk.[27] The sharp reduction in the number of households is not explained in this passage but it is almost certainly connected with the Yuan court's efforts to assert control over the allotted territories. This task, it is interesting to note, was placed in the hands of Temüder, the Minister of the Right, on whom Öljeitü lavished so many gifts in 1316. By about 1319 he had succeeded in reducing the overall number of silk households by 75 percent, thereby increasing central government revenues at the expense of imperial princes and meritorious officials.[28] It appears, then, that the Hülegüids' loss of assets in China was a by-product of general policy trends, not a consequence of deteriorating relations between the two courts.

As regards the administration of Chang-te, we know little beyond the fact that Hülegü exercised his right to place an agent in this territory. Some time toward the end of his reign the il-qan appointed a Chinese scholar, Kao Ming, to be the "general administer of Chang-te." The selection process, involving as it did protracted negotiations, occasioned three separate missions from Iran to China before the nominee accepted.[29]

There is information, too, on another of Hülegü's officials in China. This was a certain Po-te-na, a native of Balkh (Pan-le-ho) in Afghanistan, whose entire family submitted to the Mongols in 1220. According to his biography in the *Yuan shih*, Po-te-na later served (Hsü-lieh) and was "given [the post] of assistant revenue officer for the people of Ho-tung; in consequence [of this assignment] he lived in Ho-chung and I-shih counties [*hsien*] and later moved to Chieh-chou." From other biographical sources, it appears that Po-te-na's brief extended to Ch'ang-an as well.[30] Since all these locales are in Shansi or

[26] *YS*, ch. 93, pp. 2361–62. For a complete translation, see Herbert F. Schurmann, *The Economic Structure of the Yuan Dynasty* (Cambridge, Mass.: Harvard University Press, 1956), p. 99. On the Mongolian term, see Farquhar, *Government*, p. 338 and p. 363 note 244.

[27] *YS*, ch. 95, pp. 2417–18.

[28] See Elizabeth Endicott-West, *Mongolian Rule in China: Local Administration in the Yuan Dynasty* (Cambridge, Mass.: Harvard University Press, 1989), pp. 97 ff.

[29] *YS*, ch. 160, p. 3758.

[30] *YS*, ch. 137, p. 3309, and Ch'eng Chü-fu, *Ch'eng hsüeh-lou wen-chi* (Taipei, 1970), ch. 18, p. 1b.

Shensi Province, Po-te-na was clearly not associated with the administration of Chang-te in Honan. It is likely, therefore, that he was managing or monitoring other economic assets Hülegü possessed in the neighboring provinces of Shansi and Shensi.

More certainly, Hülegü also had rights to families in China assigned to him by his grandfather. This is detailed in a long and sometimes opaque passage:

> Originally Chinggis Qan transferred more than 7,000 families of hunters and falconers from various circuits and placed them under the authority of Imperial Prince Hülegü [Hsü-lieh]. In 1261 arrangements were instituted [to administer them]. In 1275 the Imperial Prince Abaqa [A-pa-ha] sent an envoy with a memorial [requesting] they be returned to the courts [authority]. They were attached to the Ministry of War. [For purposes] of control they were basically subordinated to the General Administration of Hunters, Falconers and Various Classes of Artisans in Ta-tu [Peking] and Other Circuits. [The officers of which] held the rank of 3a and they managed the affairs relating to Imperial Prince Ghazan [Ha-tsan]. In 1304 [new] arrangements were instituted and officials for all princes were selected for employment. In 1311 all [these] offices were suppressed. Because Imperial Prince Kharbandah [Ha-erh-pan-ta, i.e., Öljeitü] guarded a far distant corner and further [because] there were no officials attached [to this office], the existing arrangement was not wasteful.[31]

While the early sections of this text are clear enough, the events of 1311 and afterward call for clarification. As I understand the latter passages, the "new arrangements" of 1304 were abolished in 1311 and administrative responsibility for these households devolved upon the General Administration of Hunters, Falconers, etc., that is, matters reverted back to the arrangement of 1275. This interpretation is borne out by another passage in the *Yuan shih* which speaks directly to the administrative status of those "subordinate to Imperial Prince Abū Saʿīd [P'u Sai-yin]," Öljeitü's successor, and states that "control [over these households] was basically turned over to the *Darughachi* of the General Administration of Hunters, Falconers, and Various Classes of Artisans in Ta-tu and Other Circuits." By Abü Saʿīd's time, our source adds, the number of households had dwindled from 7,000 to 780.[32]

We know, too, that Hülegü had properties in Tibet. Möngke allotted territories there to all his family and Hülegü's share was the Yar-lung Valley in southern Tibet. A resident commissioner (*yul bsrungs*) was assigned to these lands down to ca. 1300, when the Il-qans' rights seem to have lapsed, quite possibly because of the great difficulties of communications.[33]

To round out the picture of the Hülegüids' holdings in the East, there are some relevant but elusive data in the Persian sources that deserve brief examination. Hülegü, according to Rashīd al-Dīn, had inherited rights over the *ordo* or camp of Linkqūn (Lingqum) Qatun, one of Tolui's secondary wives.

[31] *YS*, ch. 85, pp. 2141–42, and Pelliot, *Notes*, vol. I, pp. 5 and 120. [32] *YS*, ch. 101, p. 2600.

[33] Luciano Petech, *Central Tibet and the Mongols: The Yuan-Sa-skya Period in Tibetan History* (Rome: Istituto Italiano per il Medio ed Estremo Oriente, 1990), pp. 11, 16, 38, 56–57, and 88–90, and Elliot Sperling, "Hülegü and Tibet," *AOASH* 45 (1990), 147–53.

The location of this *ordo* is not indicated but apparently it was in Mongolia. Sometime in the 1270s or 1280s, Melik Temür, a son of Ariq Böke, who had aligned himself with Qaidu against Qubilai, seized control of this *ordo*.[34] While certainly not as valuable as his allotted territories in China, the seizure of this *ordo* with its attached servitors, herds, tents, and equipment was surely reckoned as a substantial loss by the grandchildren of Chinggis Qan.

Because of the tradition of bureaucratic record keeping that underlies Chinese historiography, the data on allotted lands in North China are quite full and have often been discussed in the scholarly literature. It is far less appreciated, however, that the Mongolian leadership also "apportioned" agricultural lands in Iran in a similar fashion. These data are quite scattered and less explicit but the evidence as a whole points to the unmistakable conclusion that there were allotted territories in the Hülegüid realm set aside for princes and officials, some of whom were non-residents.

Such assignments of land are first noted in the reign of Ögödei. Speaking of members of the Onggirad tribe in Iran, Rashīd al-Dīn relates that "Amīr Tesü [Tasū] had originally come from the Qa'an [Ögödei] as a companion [*nökör*] of Arghun Aqa in order to manage a district [*vilāyat*] which belongs to the person of the Qa'an."[35] Jūzjānī, writing of the life and times of Batu (d. 1256), qan of the Golden Horde, says that "from each district [*vilāyat*] that had come under the control of the Mongols in Iran, he [Batu] had an assigned share [*naṣīb*], and his agents [*gumāshtagān*] were installed in those portions allotted to him."[36] Finally, Juvaynī, like Jūzjānī a contemporary to the events he describes, also alludes to the establishment of allotted territories in Iran:

> And since at this time [1257] the census [*shumār*] of the districts [*vilāyat*] had been completed, the Emperor of the World [Möngke Qaghan] apportioned [*takhsīs farmūd*] the districts among all his kinsmen and brothers and this shall be mentioned in its proper place.[37]

Most unfortunately, Juvaynī never returns to this subject but the Chinese sources fully confirm his testimony. According to an entry in the *Yuan shih* dating to the winter of 1256–57, Möngke "apportioned [*fen-tz'u*] the subject Muslim [Hui-hui] population of the Amu Darya [A-mu River] among the imperial princes and high officials."[38] That northern Iran is meant here is verified by an earlier passage in the same source which has Möngke assigning Arghun Aqa [A-erh-hun] to the A-mu River, an assignment, we know from Persian sources, that sent him to Ṭūs in Khurāsān.[39]

Piecing the data together, it is evident that allotted lands were established in Iran and China at approximately the same time: in both places the system was

[34] Rashīd/Karīmī, vol. I, p. 668, and Rashīd/Boyle, p. 312.
[35] Rashīd/Alizade, vol. I, pt. 1, p. 413.
[36] Jūzjānī/Lees, p. 406, and Jūzjānī/Raverty, vol. II, p. 1172.
[37] Juvaynī/Qazvīnī, vol. II, p. 260, and Juvaynī/Boyle, vol. II, p. 523.
[38] *YS*, ch. 3, p. 49.
[39] *YS*, ch. 3, p. 45.

inaugurated under Ögödei and further expanded under Möngke. In the latter instance the timing (1257) and the terminology ("apportioning," *fen-tz'u*) are exactly the same. Moreover, in Iran as in China, the grantee's own agents, variously called *nökör*, *darughachi*, or *gumāshtagān*, played a prominent role in the administration of these "shares" (*fen-ti*, *qubi*, *bakhsh*, or *naṣīb*). Lastly, the territories in Iran, like those in China, were assigned to many notables, resident and non-resident. In 1265, for example, Masʿūd Beg, a long-time civil official in the Chaghadai Qanate, arrived in Iran as an envoy of Qaidu and his Chaghadaid ally Baraq and "asked to go over the accounts of their hereditary assignments [*injū-hā*]."[40] And more to the point, so, too, did the representatives of Qubilai. Around 1265, Rashīd al-Dīn relates, the Grand Qan sent two envoys, Sartaq and ʿAbd al-Raḥmān, to Hülegü to inquire after Bayan, temporarily assigned to Iran. Shortly thereafter Sartaq and Bayan returned to China but ʿAbd al-Raḥmān "remained here [in Iran] for the purpose of clearing accounts [*āfragh-i muhāsabāt*]."[41] There is no indication of what accounts were gone over but it is easy to believe that the object of the inquiry was the proceeds of Qubilai's allotted lands in the Hülegüid realm.

Besides land, the qaghan had movable property in the West. Down to Ghazan's time the Yuan emperor had herds in Iran, cattle, sheep, and camels that were tended by *qānchī*, "the qaghan's men," or perhaps the Mongolian *qonichi*, "shepherds." It is interesting that Ghazan carefully investigated the management of these animals and ordered that all losses through disease, theft, or straying be replaced. Apparently, he wished to encourage the qaghan to take a similar attitude toward his holdings in China.[42]

For ease of presentation, I have isolated various modes of economic exchange between China and Iran. In point of fact, however, the varied strands of their economic relations were usually intertwined, and often under the management of the same individual. This can be illustrated by taking a closer look at the range of economic activities of the aforementioned embassy Ghazan dispatched to China in AH 697/AD 1297–98. This, it will be recalled, was headed by Malik Fakhr al-Dīn and Noghai, who were sent east, according to Vaṣṣāf, with costly presents and "ten *tūmān* [100,000] of gold dinars from the great treasury [*khizanat-buzurg*]" as capital for trade. At the same time Fakhr al-Dīn filled the assigned ships with his own merchandise and that of his relatives and business associates such as Shaikh al-Islām Jamāl al-Dīn. Once they arrived in South China, they were conducted, free of costs or duties, to Ta-tu (Peking) where they presented Ghazan's gifts to Temür Qaghan and displayed their wares. When they were ready to depart, after a stay of four years, presents for Ghazan were turned over to them, together with silk stuffs from Hülegü's holdings in China that had not been collected since the days of

40 Rashīd/Jahn I, p. 9.

41 Rashīd/Alizade, vol. I, pt. 1, p. 523. See also p. 455, and Rashīd/Karīmī, vol. I, p. 637, and Rashīd/Boyle, pp. 270–71.

42 Rashīd/Jahn II pp. 339–40.

Möngke Qaghan. An ambassador (i.e., Yang shu) took charge of these proceeds on a separate junk and accompanied Fakhr al-Dīn on the return trip.[43]

In the course of this single expedition all the modes of exchange are clearly evident: the formal presentation of tribute and exotica; government trade capitalized by the royal treasury; "private" commerce, involving semi-official merchant capitalists like Jamāl al-Dīn, whose transportation costs were underwritten by the imperial court; and, finally, the transfer of proceeds from long-established allotted territories, those princely shares in the profits of empire. While exact numbers are lacking, the account of this embassy provides arresting anecdotal evidence that the volume of exchange between the two courts could reach impressive levels, thus providing yet another reason for these two Chinggisid lines to remain in contact and maintain their partnership and alliance.

[43] Elliot and Dowson, *History of India*, pp. 45–47, and Vaṣṣāf, pp. 505–6.

EIGHT

Overview of the relationship

The purpose of this chapter is to identify some of the basic characteristics of the relationship between the courts of China and Iran and at the same time to try to cast additional light on the underlying structures and political dynamics of the Mongolian Empire as a whole. The place to begin this exploration is with Chinggis Qan's original dispensation of territories among his sons and kin.

This consequential event, crucial to understanding the subsequent evolution of the Mongolian polity, is not extensively reported in the sources. As already noted, the earliest and most complete account is provided by Juvaynī, who wrote in the 1260s. Because of its extreme importance, this passage is quoted at length:

> And when in the age of the dominion of Chinggis Qan, the area of the kingdom became vast, he assigned every one their own place of abode called a *yurt*. To Otchigin [Ūtakīn], who was his brother, and some other of his grandchildren he designated [territory] in the region of China [Khitāi]. To his eldest son Jochi [Tūshī] he gave [the territory] from the regions of Qayaliq and Khwārazm to the far reaches of Saqsin and Bulghār [on the Volga] and from those parts to whatever places the hooves of the Tatar horses had reached. To Chaghadai [he gave the territory extending] from the country of the Uighur to Samarqand and Bukhara and his place of residence was Quyas in the vicinity of Almaliq. The royal residence of the heir apparent, Ögödei, during his father's reign was his *yurt* in the region of the Emil and Qobaq [Rivers in Jungharia]. When he sat upon the royal throne, he transferred [his royal residence] to the [Mongols'] original homeland which is between China and the country of the Uighur, and gave that [other] place of residence to his own son Güyüg . . . [The territory of] Tolui [his fourth son] likewise was contiguous with and adjacent to his [Ögödei's], and indeed this place [of Tolui's] is in the middle of their kingdom just like the center of a circle.[1]

While short on specifics, Juvaynī's account gives us an accurate depiction of the division of the territorial spoils made, apparently, in the last years of Chinggis Qan's lifetime. The Jochids in fact received and subsequently occupied what is

[1] Juvaynī/Qazvīnī, vol. I, pp. 31–32, and Juvaynī/Boyle, vol. I, pp. 42–43.

now the Kazakh steppe, southern Siberia, the lower Volga, the Qipchaq steppe, North Caucasia, and the Rus principalities. Chaghadai, his second son, obtained West Turkestan; Ögödei, his third son and political heir, had his personal territory in Jungharia and later moved to central Mongolia, the site of the imperial capital, Qara Qorum; and, finally, Tolui, the youngest, received eastern Mongolia, the *urheimat* of the Mongolian tribes.

China, it is critical to recognize, was given out piecemeal as shares to kinsmen such as Otchigin who held 62,156 silk households in I-tu circuit in Shantung.[2] It was a kind of joint property in which all Chinggisids came to have an interest, a share. And later, when Mongolian rule was extended into Iran and an administrative apparatus was fashioned there, it, too, was shared out among the imperial princes. Consequently, as Paul Buell pointed out some time ago, this territory was governed by a "joint satellite administration," a branch of the imperial secretariat in Mongolia. The staff of such branch secretariats was composed of joint appointees of the qaghan and the imperial princes.[3] And the latter, it will be recalled, also had the right to assign their personal agents in their allotted territories. Thus, the administrative personnel, at least in theory, represented the interests of all the Chinggisid lines with the qaghan enjoying the status of the first among equals. This meant, it must be reemphasized, that there was no direct princely control over China and Iran, as there was in central Asia and the steppe. In other words, as Peter Jackson has argued, the four qanates that emerged in the mid-thirteenth century did not arise from Chinggis Qan's primary territorial dispensation; rather the fourfold division of the empire was the unintended consequence of intense struggle among his immediate descendants who reinterpreted and redistributed his legacy.[4]

The main source of this princely tension was not, therefore, confrontation over "borders," but conflict over allotted territories. Naturally, the qaghan and the officials of the central secretariat tried to limit the authority of the princely shareholders and their access to the resources of the realm. This competition was particularly acute in Iran, which was so distant from Qara Qorum. There is little doubt that Batu, the son of Jochi, tried to use his allotted territories as a base from which to assert his control over, or at least extend his influence in, Iran and Transcaucasia.

To eliminate such possibilities, Möngke, soon after he came to the throne, made a new dispensation, one that forever changed the political alignment among the princely lines. At about the same time that he granted new allotted

[2] This, at least, was the number in 1236. See *YS*, ch. 95, p. 2413 under Wo-chen na-yen, Otchigin noyan.

[3] Paul Buell, "Sino-Khitan Administration in Mongol Bukhara," *Journal of Asian History* 13 (1979), 147. For further comment, see Thomas T. Allsen, *Mongol Imperialism: The Policies of the Grand Qan Möngke in China, Russia and the Islamic Lands, 1251–1259* (Berkeley: University of California Press, 1987), pp. 100–13.

[4] Peter Jackson, "From *Ulus* to Khanate: The Making of the Mongol States," in Amitai-Preiss and Morgan, *Mongol Empire*, pp. 12–37, particularly 35–36.

territories to family and officials in China and Iran, he asserted and established direct Toluid princely control over both countries. In the words of Rashīd al-Dīn, the new emperor

put one of his brothers, Qubilai Qaghan, in charge of the countries of Khitāi [North China], Māchīn [South China], Qarājāng [Yünnan], Tangut, Tibet, Jurche, Solanga [North Korea], Kūlī [Kao-li, or Korea], and that part of Hindustan which is contiguous to Khitāi and Māchīn, and to Hülegü he assigned the countries of the West, Iran, Syria, Egypt, Rūm, and Armenia, so that each of them, with the armies they would have, would be his right and left wings.[5]

More simply, the *Yuan shih* states that in 1251 Möngke "ordered his younger brother Qubilai [Hu-pi-lai] to take charge of the population of the Chinese territory [held by] the Mongols" and a year later he ordered his other brother "Hülegü [Hsü-lieh] to subdue the states of the Western Region and of the Sulṭān [Su-tan]."[6]

This assertion of immediate control over the richest and most populous parts of the empire made the Toluids the most powerful of the princely lines, not only in name but in fact. The result, of course, was new tension and new enmity. The Ögödeids already viewed Möngke as a usurper and now the Jochids, his erstwhile allies, saw him as an unwanted and unexpected meddler in what had long been considered their special preserve; it was no doubt particularly frustrating that the new qaghan with one hand affirmed and extended their allotted territories in West Asia and with the other introduced measures that had the effect of restricting their rights and undermining their influence in the region.

The growing hostility can be seen in the confrontation over access to the Jochids' allotted territories in Khurāsān. Sometime in the late 1250s two nephews of Batu, Balaghai and Tutar, made repeated demands for supplies and monies on Herat. The local ruler, Shams al-Dīn Kart, rebuffed them and this decision, after a long period of bickering, was sustained by Hülegü.[7]

Even more consequential and long-lasting was the rivalry over Transcaucasia. From the time of their establishment in the Lower Volga, the Jochids had been extending their influence in Georgia. No doubt as a counterbalance to the qaghan's officials in the area, the Georgian monarchy seems to have welcomed these attentions. Queen Rusudan (r. 1223–45), for instance, dispatched Georgian nobles to serve at Batu's court.[8] This special relationship was even recognized by Möngke. After consolidating his hold on the throne, the qaghan in 1252 rewarded his princely supporters in a new dispensation. According to the *Yuan shih* account, Möngke

[5] Rashīd/Karīmī, vol. II, p. 685. [6] *YS*, ch. 3, pp. 44 and 46.

[7] Sayf ibn Muḥammad ibn Yaʿqub al-Havarī, *Tarīkh nāmah-i Harāt*, ed. by Muḥammad Zubayr al-Ṣiddīqī (Calcutta: Baptist Mission Press, 1944), pp. 228–33; and Jackson, "Dissolution of the Mongol Empire," 222–23.

[8] S. S. Kakabadze, trans., *Gruzinskie dokumenty IX–XV vv.* (Moscow: Nauka, 1982), p. 71.

allotted [*fen-ch'ien*] each prince of the blood [*chu-wang*] his own place: Qadan [Ho-tan] with the territory [*ti*] of Besh Baliq [Pieh-shih Pa-li]; Melik [Mieh-li] with [territory] on the Irtysh [Yeh-erh-te-shih] River; Qaidu [Hai-tu] with Qayaliq [Hai-ya-li]; Berke [Pieh-erh-ko] with the territory of Georgia [Ch'ü-erh-chih > Persian Gurj]; Totoq [T'o-t'o] with the territory of Emil [Yeh-mi-li]; and Mönggetü [Meng-ko-tu] and Ögödei's empress Ch'i-li-chi-hu-t'ien-ni with [territory] to the west of that inhabited by Köden [K'uo-tuan]. Further, [the emperor] allotted [*fen-tz'u*] Ögödei's wives, concubines and family property to the imperial princes [*ch'in-wang*].[9]

Juvaynī, a contemporary, also reports on this same dispensation. He states, in conformity with the *Yuan shih* account, the division of Ögödei's camps (*urdū*) and women (*khavātīn*) among the princes, but most revealingly, while he mentions Qadaghan (i.e., Qadan), Melik, and Batu's brother Berke by name, he suppresses all reference to the territories allotted them, since, obviously, the rights of Berke in Georgia were a politically sensitive issue for his patrons, the Hülegüids.[10]

During Möngke's reign the contest for influence in Georgia was limited to a series of political and bureaucratic struggles over census taking, taxation, etc., struggles which Hülegü, with the qaghan's backing, always won. However, once Berke (r. 1257–66) became qan of the Golden Horde and Möngke passed from the scene, open warfare broke out in the Caucasus. In 1262 Berke launched a major assault which devastated northern Azerbaijan and in the next year Hülegü countered with a campaign that reached the Terek in southern Daghestan.[11] In consequence of this contention, the Toluids now lost their last firm ally among the Chinggisids: henceforth they would be faced with three rival lines who not only contested their legitimacy but who joined forces to secure their destruction.

Möngke's new dispensation of allotted territories and his imposition of Toluid princely control over China and Iran laid, therefore, the geographical foundations for the subsequent emergence of the Il-qan state and the Yuan dynasty, and, at the same time, intensified preexisting princely rivalries that resulted in a Chinggisid civil war that lasted intermittently into the early fourteenth century. In this internecine struggle, the Mongolian courts in China and Iran, by virtue of their very origins, became fast allies against the remaining princely lines who saw them as usurpers – usurpers of the imperial throne and, subsequently, usurpers of territories that were supposed to be held and managed by the Chinggisid family collectively.

Under these circumstances it is hardly surprising that the two courts became so interdependent, militarily and ideologically. As we have seen, from Hülegü to Baidu the Il-qans' legitimacy was derivative in character. Their right to rule was dependent on a formal grant of authority from the qaghan in the East. This is understandable because Hülegü, the founder of the state, received his

9 *YS*, ch. 3, p. 45.

10 Juvaynī/Qazvīnī, vol. III, pp. 69–70, and Juvaynī/Boyle, vol. II, pp. 594–95.

11 Rashīd/Karīmī, vol. II, pp. 732–33, and Kirakos, *Istoriia*, p. 237.

territory and administrative authority in a secondary dispensation from Möngke and not, as the Il-qans were painfully aware, in consequence of the primary dispensation of Chinggis Qan.

Under Ghazan and his successors, however, there was a decided shift in ideological emphasis; now the legitimacy of the Mongolian rulers of Iran arose directly from their function as propagators and defenders of the faith. This is well reflected in the changing titulature on the coinage of the realm and in the emerging historiographic tradition. For Rashīd al-Dīn, his sovereign and patron Ghazan was no longer an Il-qan subordinate to a Grand Qan but a sulṭān of Islam, a *pādishāh*, a Persian emperor, and his domain was not, in the Mongolian fashion, the *ulus* of Hülegü[12] but the kingdom of Iran (*mamālik-i* Irān).[13] All the available evidence seems to indicate that the change in the basis of legitimacy was initiated in Iran to meet local conditions; certainly, there was no visible external event to explain this shift, no known breakdown in the relations between the Yuan court and their ally in Iran. On the contrary, Ghazan's reign was a crucial period in the relationship between the Chinggisid princes, coinciding with the defeat of Qaidu and Du'a and the negotiations leading to the peace of 1304. As for the Yuan attitude, it seems likely that they were either oblivious to the change in ideology or simply accepted it as a necessary means of securing the stability of the regime in Iran. After all, the continued existence of the Hülegüids as an effective military partner was more important than formal ideological dependence. In any event, the Yuan court, as many passages in the *Yuan shih* make clear, continued to view Ghazan, Öljeitü, and Abū Saʿīd as subordinate rulers, imperial princes (*chu-wang*), who properly sent envoys east to present "tribute."

While the Hülegüids' adoption of a new ideological framework was an important event, a means of domesticating the bases of legitimacy, it should also be borne in mind that the Mongolian element in their political culture did not disappear completely. Even after adopting Islamic precepts, Ghazan and his successors still felt bound to defend their predecessors' right to rule on the bases of conventional Mongolian formulations. No attempt was made – as was done in the Yuan dynasty, where early qaghans were turned into *cakravartinrajas* for the benefit of their Buddhist constituencies – to transform, retroactively, the Il-qans into Muslim rulers.[14] They remained exactly what they claimed to be: subservient rulers who derived their legitimacy from the qaghan.

Indeed, the new sulṭāns made every effort to strengthen these claims on behalf of their forerunners. This is brought out clearly in Rashīd al-Dīn's treatment of Qubilai's rise to power. The great Persian historian, who wrote his chronicles at Ghazan's behest, makes every effort to demonstrate that Qubilai's

[12] Rashīd al-Dīn repeatedly refers to the territory of the Golden Horde as the *ulus* of Jochi.
[13] I. P. Petrushevskii, "Rashīd al-Dīn's Conception of the State," *CAJ* 14 (1970), 153–54.
[14] Herbert Franke, *From Tribal Chieftain to Universal Emperor and God: The Legitimation of the Yuan Dynasty* (Munich: Bayerische Akademie der Wissenschaften, 1978, heft 2), pp. 52–76.

disputed succession received the sanction of the senior Chinggisid lines and was therefore completely legitimate. To achieve this end Rashīd al-Dīn maintains that Berke, the qan of the Golden Horde, was at first neutral in the struggle between Qubilai and Ariq Böke and that after the defeat of the latter he freely acceded to Qubilai's enthronement.[15] His recounting of this episode, however, is contradicted by other sources, literary and numismatic, which prove conclusively that Berke supported Ariq Böke from the very beginning.[16]

Why did Rashīd al-Dīn engage in such studied and conscious deception? Peter Jackson, the first scholar to point out these discrepancies, argues that this was done because Berke's support for Ariq Böke, if openly admitted, would have undermined "the legitimacy of the status quo in China, with which Rashīd's patrons were so closely connected."[17] In other words, if Qubilai's right to the throne was seriously called into question, then the legitimacy of his dependants, the Il-qans, also evaporated. Thus, while Ghazan converted himself into a Muslim ruler for domestic reasons, he was still quite sensitive about his dynasty's anomalous status within the fragmented empire, and sought to reaffirm, against the counterclaims of his Chinggisid rivals, the rights of his infidel precursors to West Asia in purely Mongolian terms. Different constituencies ofttimes require different ideologies.

To sum up this enduring partnership, from the arrival of Hülegü in Khurāsān in 1256 to the death of his great-great-grandson Abū Saʿīd in 1335, there was constant communication between the Mongolian courts of China and Iran. They supported one another diplomatically, ideologically, and militarily; they exchanged intelligence, commodities, tribute, personnel, and envoys. And, most importantly for our purposes, they also appropriated, apportioned, and exchanged the varied cultural resources of their subject peoples. It is to this transcontinental cultural traffic that we now turn.

[15] Rashīd/Karīmī, vol. I, pp. 623 and 631, and Rashīd/Boyle, pp. 256 and 265.

[16] The major proofs are two: the Armenian chronicler Kirakos, a contemporary and neutral observer, states plainly that while Hülegü helped Qubilai, Berke "assisted Ariq Böke." See Kirakos, *Istoriia*, p. 236. Equally persuasive is the fact that Berke minted coins in Ariq Böke's name. See A. G. Mukhamadiev, *Bulgaro-Tatarskaia monetnaia sistema* (Moscow: Nauka, 1983), pp. 49–50.

[17] Peter Jackson, "The Accession of Qubilai Qa'an: A Re-Examination," *Journal of the Anglo-Mongolian Society* 2/1 (1975), 3.

PART III

Intermediaries

NINE

Marco Polo and Po-lo

The study of cultural contact and exchange is intimately connected to the question of agency. Culture, of course, can be transmitted by a number of mechanisms – commodities, ideologies, literary works – as well as people. Material culture, transported as trade, tribute, or booty, can diffuse artistic motifs and technology over great distances. Texts, particularly religious texts, also convey culture over time and space and most particularly between large-scale, urban-based civilizations. The extensive corpus of Chinese translations of the Indian Buddhist canon well illustrates this phenomenon.[1] In the Mongolian era, the fourth mechanism, direct human agency, assumed, as already argued, a very special importance in East–West cultural communication. Given the Mongols' penchant for moving imperial personnel, subject peoples, and specialists from one cultural zone of the empire to another, there were innumerable face-to-face encounters between individuals and communities of the most diverse ethnic, linguistic, and religious backgrounds. In this part of the study, we will investigate the major "brokers" in medieval Eurasian cultural history.

By far the most famous of these intermediaries is Marco Polo. As is well known, from his own day to the present, his travels have been the center of controversy; indeed, many deny that the Venetian ever set foot in China.[2] His defenders, naturally, have tried to confirm his accounts by detailed geographical–historical commentaries and most particularly by seeking references to his name in the Chinese sources of the Yuan era, which are studded with foreign names, Turkic, Iranian, Muslim, and Tibetan, as well as Christian.

Efforts to find Marco Polo in the Asian sources were inaugurated in 1865 by the French scholar Pauthier who was the first to identify the Venetian with

[1] Walter Fuchs, "Zur technischen Organisation der Übersetzungen buddhischer Schriften ins Chinesische," *Asia Major* 6 (1930), 84–103.

[2] My own view is that Marco Polo was in China and that his travels are a valuable source on medieval Eurasia. For recent and persuasive defenses of this position, see Igor de Rachewiltz, "Marco Polo Went to China," *Zentralasiatische Studien* 27 (1997), 34–92; Jørgen Jensen, "The World's Most Diligent Observer," *Asiatische Studien* 51 (1997), 719–28; and Jean-Pierre Voiret, "China 'Objektiv' Gesehen: Marco Polo als Berichterstatter," *Asiatische Studien* 51 (1997), 805–21.

a certain Po-lo mentioned in the *Yuan shih*. Well into the twentieth century some scholars, e.g., Charignon in his biography of Marco Polo, clung to this identification. Chinese savants also made this connection. T'u Chi, a noted historian of the late Ch'ing to the early Republican era, thought this Po-lo was Marco Polo (Ma-k'o Pao-lo) and prepared a biography of the "Venetian" on that assumption.[3]

This identification of the two names, made repeatedly, poses many serious, and indeed insurmountable problems, historical and philological. In the first place, as Olschki points out, it is probably mistaken to search for Marco Polo under his family name since the regular practice of the contemporary Chinese sources is to use first names or biblical names – Luke (Lu-ho), Nicholas (Nieh-ku-la), etc. – for the Mongols' many Christian servitors of the Latin, Greek, and Nestorian rite.[4] His belief is very likely correct: if any of the Polos come to light in the Yuan accounts, it will be under their Christian names, not their surnames.

Second, and irrespective of the problems of nomenclature, the Po-lo of the *Yuan shih* is most certainly another historical personage, a Mongol who, as we shall see, has his own legitimate claims as a cultural broker of great importance. This identification was first made by the great French orientalist Paul Pelliot. As early as 1914, and thereafter on many subsequent occasions, Pelliot demonstrated that the Po-lo of the Chinese texts was to be equated with the Mongolian name Bolad, not Marco Polo, and that this same person appears in the Persian histories under the name Pūlād/Fūlād, that is, the envoy of Qubilai, who arrived in Iran in 1285 in the company of ʿIsā *kelemechi*.[5] At about the same time, Japanese scholars, working quite independently, came to this same and quite correct conclusion.[6]

Since his name has been a source of so much misunderstanding, it will be helpful to establish its various forms from the outset of our examination of his life and times. Po-lo is the Chinese transcription of the Mongolian *bolad* and the Uighur *bolod*.[7] Indeed, our Bolad bore a most appropriate name for a cultural intermediary between China and Iran. His personal name is the Mongolian form of the Persian *pūlād/fūlād*, "steel." His title, *chīnksānk* in the Persian sources, as already noted, is the Chinese *ch'eng-hsiang*, "chancellor," a very high-ranking position in the Yuan government.[8] Lastly, his honorific, *aqa*, Mongolian for "elder brother" or "uncle," is often used as a term of great respect for non-kinsmen.[9] In his case, its use certainly declares his membership

[3] T'u Chi, *Meng-wu-erh shih-chi* (Taipei: Shih-chieh shu-chü, 1962), ch. 117, p. 1b.

[4] Leonardo Olschki, "Poh-lo: Une question d'onomatologie chinoise," *Oriens* 3 (1950), 183–89.

[5] Paul Pelliot, "Chrétiens d'Asie centrale et d'Extrême-Orient," *TP* 15 (1914), 638–40, and Paul Pelliot, "Review of Charignon, *Le livre de Marco Polo*," *TP* 25 (1928), 157–64.

[6] K. Enoki, "Marco Polo and Japan," in *Oriente Poliano* (Rome: Istituto Italiano per il Medio ed Estremo Oriente, 1957), p. 38.

[7] Cleaves, "Mongolian Documents," 46–47, note 9.

[8] *Chingsang* is the Mongolian form. See *SH*/Cleaves, sect. 132, p. 62 and note 9, and *SH*/de Rachewiltz, sect. 132, p. 56.

[9] Francis W. Cleaves, "*Aqa minu*," *HJAS* 24 (1962–63), 64–81.

in a prince's extended political family, his imperial household establishment, and perhaps even indicates his elevated status as an honorary member of the Chinggisid line.

Besides the superficial similarity of their names in Chinese transcription, there was another reason Marco Polo and Bolad were often confused by earlier commentators: their respective careers were in many ways parallel. The two were of course near contemporaries; Bolad's dates are ca. 1240 to 1313 and Marco Polo's 1254 to 1324. Both served the emperor Qubilai, and since their tours of duty in China overlapped between 1275 and 1283, it is conceivable, but not demonstrable, that they may have encountered one another. Both traveled extensively in China, central and West Asia, and both were sent on official embassies from the Yuan court to Iran, Bolad in 1283 and Polo in 1291.

In light of this intriguing parallelism, we should not be too harsh on pioneers such as Pauthier who in their enthusiasm for the search found what they wanted and rushed into a mistaken identification. But, at the same time, it is now long past time to give Bolad his due, his proper place in the historical sun.

To date, Bolad's chief claim to fame in the scholarly literature is that many have mistaken him for Marco Polo; and naturally any quick comparison between this obscure Mongolian and the heralded Venetian puts Bolad at an immediate disadvantage. After all, in the context of global history, Marco Polo, whether he was ever in China or not, excited the interest of later generations of Europeans in the peoples, products, and fabled riches of the Orient and encouraged the belief that the "Great Caam" in Cathay would warmly welcome Christians. Moreover, some of his most avid readers, Christopher Columbus, for example, were principal agents in the maritime expansion of Europe and Marco Polo's account of Asia greatly affected the way in which Europeans understood Amerindian culture in the early years of contact.[10]

However, if one judges the two in the context of their own historic time, a somewhat different assessment emerges. Bolad, as we shall see, was a major political player in both China and Iran, a shaper of events, while Polo, at best, was an observer, a low-level official on the periphery of events. As a cultural middleman, Bolad's role was also the more substantial. In fact, as subsequent chapters will demonstrate, he was a pivotal figure in the flow of science, technology, and culture between China and the Islamic world. It in no way detracts from Marco Polo's long-term historical legacy to say that in his own lifetime he cannot be credited with similar accomplishments. Even his supposed introduction of Chinese noodles into Italy can no longer be accepted.[11] The growing importance of pasta (macaroni) in Italian cuisine has nothing to do

[10] On these themes, see Abbas Hamdani, "Columbus and the Recovery of Jerusalem," *JAOS* 99 (1979), 39–48; Bertold Laufer, "Columbus and Cathay, and the Meaning of America to the Orientalist," *JAOS* 51 (1931), 87–103; and Zhang Zhishan, "Columbus and China," *MS* 41 (1993), 177–87.

[11] On this mythology, see Maguelonne Toussaint-Samat, *A History of Food* (Oxford: Blackwell, 1992), pp. 187–89.

with the Venetian and everything to do with the diffusion of glutinous, hard-grained wheat from the Islamic lands to southern Europe in the early thirteenth century.[12]

To substantiate the claims so far made on Bolad's behalf, we must begin this exploration of cultural exchange with a detailed examination of his career in China and later on in Iran. Most unfortunately, he has no biography in the Yuan sources, presumably because he died in the West long after leaving China. Consequently, his career must be pieced together from passing references in the dynastic history, Yuan documentary collections, and literary collections (*wen-chi*), and from various Persian works, especially but not exclusively those of Rashīd al-Dīn. Such an undertaking is well worth the investment because his appointments and personal experiences, and the contacts he made in the course of his varied official duties, have a direct bearing on the cultural transfers between these two civilizations in the Mongolian era.

[12] Andrew M. Watson, *Agricultural Innovation in the Early Islamic World: The Diffusion of Crops and Farming Techniques, 700–1100* (Cambridge University Press, 1983), pp. 20–24, and Louis Dupree, "From Whence Cometh Pasta," in Peter Snoy, ed., *Ethnologie und Geschichte: Festschrift für Karl Jettmar* (Wiesbaden: Franz Steiner, 1983), pp. 128–34.

TEN

Qubilai and Bolad Aqa

Bolad was a member of the Mongolian-speaking Dörben tribe. In the latter half of the twelfth century, when Temüjin, the future Chinggis Qan, began his rise to power, they were numbered among the many nomadic tribes of eastern Mongolia. According to Mongolian tradition, the Dörben were descended from the four sons of Duua Soqor, a semi-legendary figure in the *Secret History*. While a Dörben was present in 1187 (or 1189) when Temüjin first announced his political intentions, most of this tribal grouping was in the opposition camp. In fact, the Dörben with great consistency allied themselves with all of Chinggis Qan's principal rivals: the Tayichi'ud in 1200; Jamugha, the erstwhile *anda* (sworn brother) of Temüjin, in 1201; the Tatar in 1202; and the Naiman, the most powerful tribal confederation in western Mongolia, in 1204. Only after the defeat of the latter, which broke nomadic resistance in the eastern steppe, did the Dörben as a whole finally submit to Chinggis Qan.[1]

Bolad's father, according to Rashīd al-Dīn's account, was Yurkī (Mongolian Jürki), who was a *ba'urchi*, cook or steward, attached to the camp (*orda*) of Chinggis Qan's senior wife, Börte Üjin. Concurrently, he was a commander of a unit of one hundred in the Personal Thousand (*Hazārah-i khaṣṣ*) of Chinggis Qan.[2] To modern ears the title of cook, one which Bolad himself later held, sounds quite menial. But to the Mongols, with their patrimonial notions of society and government, this was a title of great prestige and announced to all that the bearer was an individual with access to the qan and explicitly trusted by him. Moreover, as a member of the Personal Thousand of Chinggis Qan, Jürki was an officer in the most elite unit of the Mongolian military establishment, the imperial guard. Thus, while his tribe had long opposed the Mongolian leader, Bolad's own family had the most intimate ties to the imperial house. And these connections, in combination with his many talents, led

[1] *SH*/Cleaves, sect. 11, p. 3, sect. 120, p. 52, sect. 141, p. 68, and sect. 196, p. 129; Rashīd/Alizade, vol. I, pt. 1, pp. 160, 174, 297, and 517–18; and Rashīd/Karīmī, vol. I, p. 305. On their role in the formation of the Western Mongols in later centuries, see Hidehiro Okada, "Origins of the Dörben Oyirad," *Ural-Altaische Jahrbücher*, 7 (1987), 197–203.

[2] Rashīd/Alizade, vol. I, pt. 1, p. 518; Rashīd/Karīmī, vol. I, p. 400; and Rashīd al-Dīn, "Shuʿab-i panjgānah" (ms., Topkapi Sarayi Museum, cat. no. 2932), folio 105v.

to a long and distinguished career, in fact two careers, one at either end of Eurasia.

We first hear of Bolad in 1248 when Qubilai, still a prince, ordered Chang Te-hui (1197–1274), a noted scholar, "to tutor his eldest son [Dorji] and Po-lo and others."[3] At this juncture Bolad was probably a child of seven or eight serving as a cadet in Qubilai's guard/household establishment. In any event, it appears that young Bolad was an attentive pupil with a talent for languages. This is borne out by documents preserved in the *Yuan-tien chang*, a collection of administrative and legal precedents compiled in 1320–22. We learn from this source that in 1269 the General Secretariat (*Chung-shu sheng*) heard "Bolad's [Po-lo's] hurried and rough oral translation [*ch'uan*]" of an imperial rescript regulating burials in the vicinity of the capital. Two years later, another document in the same collection reports that Bolad prepared for the General Secretariat "a written translation [*wen-tzu i*]" of an imperial rescript prohibiting construction in cemetery grounds.[4] As a Mongol who knew Chinese well, Bolad's services would always be in demand.

While there is no information on Bolad's activities in the 1250s, it is clear he rose steadily in Qubilai's entourage, which, it should be remembered, was a most cosmopolitan body, recruited as it was from among Mongols, Muslims, Uighurs, Chinese, and many other ethnic and communal groups. Once Qubilai assumed the throne in 1260 he naturally formed his own imperial guard (*wei*) and Bolad was one of its rising young officers. On one occasion the emperor charged Bolad with the task of preparing Tieh-ko, a member of a distinguished Kashmiri Buddhist family, for service in the guard.[5] At this time, too, Bolad received his first active military command when in 1264 he led a contingent against "rebels" in the city of T'ung-shih in Shantung. He successfully suppressed the uprising and then on the emperor's orders took charge of pacifying and rehabilitating the region.[6]

Obviously, he carried out these and other duties to his sovereign's satisfaction, for his next assignment propelled him into the realm of high politics. In 1264, following Ariq Böke's submission to Qubilai, the qaghan, in the words of Rashīd al-Dīn,

> ordered the amīrs to seize and bind Ariq Böke [Arīq Būkā] and further ordered that, of the princes Shiregi [Shīrikī], Taqai [Taqaī], Charaqu [Charāqū] and Bai Temür [Bā Tīmūr] and, of the amīrs, Hantum Noyan Dörbetai [Dūrbātaī] and Bolad *Ch'eng-hsiang* [Pūlād *Chīnksāng*] . . . to convene [together] to interrogate Ariq Böke and his amīrs and then issue a report.[7]

The result of their deliberations was that his amīrs were punished and Ariq Böke temporarily spared. What is important here is that Qubilai, confronted with the most sensitive of political issues, one upon which his legitimacy

[3] *YS*, ch. 163, p. 3824. [4] *YTC*, ch. 30, p. 11a. [5] *YS*, ch. 125, p. 3075.
[6] *YS*, ch. 166, p. 3910. [7] Rashīd/Karīmī, vol. I, p. 629; and Rashīd/Boyle, p. 262.

turned, selected senior Chinggisid princes and several of his most trusted advisers to investigate and resolve this matter. Clearly Bolad was now included in a most select company, Qubilai's inner circle, and he would soon be charged with other important tasks and appointments.

In one of the first such assignments he assisted in the establishment of the Office of State Ceremonial (*Shih-i ssu*) which oversaw audiences, enthronements, receptions of foreign envoys, and grants of honorary titles. This is a most revealing episode, for we now see Bolad collaborating, closely and successfully, with Qubilai's Chinese advisers, a pattern of association that persists throughout the Yuan phase of his career. In this particular instance he was paired with Liu Ping-chung, who had first met Qubilai in 1242 and who became one of his intimates after 1251 when the prince took over the administration of the Chinese territories. Once Qubilai assumed the throne, Liu regularly urged upon his sovereign the adoption of Chinese models and methods of governance. In 1269 he memorialized the throne on the need for appropriate rites and ceremonies.[8] Qubilai responded favorably and ordered Liu and Bolad (Po-lo) to select scholars to investigate the court ceremonies of former dynasties. Chao Ping-wen and Shih Kung, students of Liu, were nominated and began their inquiries. In the fall of 1269 the throne gave further encouragement to the project when it ordered Hantum (An-t'ung), a grandson of Muqali, and Bolad "to select 200 or so capable learners [of pleasant] demeanor from among the Mongolian imperial guardsmen and train them within a month [to conduct court ceremonies]."[9] The *Yuan shih* reports that in February of the following year the emperor, while on an imperial progress "beheld Liu Ping-chung, Bolad, Hsü Heng and the Director of the Court of Imperial Sacrifices [*T'ai-ch'ang ch'ing*], Hsü Shih-lung, who were setting up ceremonies for the court. He was greatly pleased, offered them wine and favored them."[10] The harmonious working relationship between Bolad and his Chinese colleagues produced the desired results and in October of 1271 the Office of State Ceremonial was officially founded.

This office, however, was only part of a larger effort to fashion an effective ritual and ideological framework for Yuan court life. Regularized ancestor worship had begun in the reign of Möngke and under Qubilai it was expanded and formalized, acquiring in the course of time a pronounced syncretic character through an eclectic blending of Mongolian, Chinese, shamanistic, and Buddhist elements.[11] One result of this elaboration of ritual life was the aforementioned Court of Imperial Sacrifices, founded in 1260 to conduct ceremonies at the imperial ancestral temples and at the temples for Heaven, Earth, and Grain. These ceremonies, in true nomadic fashion, often involved animal

[8] Hok-lam Chan, "Liu Ping-chung (1216–74): A Buddhist–Taoist Statesman at the Court of Khubilai Khan," *TP* 53 (1967), 98–146, and especially 132–33 for his interest in rites and ceremonies. [9] *YS*, ch. 67, p. 1665. [10] *YS*, ch. 7, p. 128.

[11] Paul Ratchnevsky, "Über den mongolischen Kult am Hofe der Grosskhane in China," in Louis Ligeti, ed., *Mongolian Studies* (Amsterdam: B. R. Grüner, 1970), pp. 417–43.

sacrifices. Bolad, one of the Court's two directors (*ch'ing*), in the mid-1270s was ordered to inquire into the "feathers and blood sacrifice," a query that the Chinese scholar Shen-t'u Chih-yuan was able to answer.[12] Bolad, it is evident, was extremely well suited for such a position; he knew something of Chinese ritual, and as a cook, or *ba'urchi*, he knew the proper (that is, the Mongolian) way to dispatch an animal. As the *Yuan shih* makes clear in its depiction of the four animal sacrifices conducted by the imperial family, "a Mongolian *ba'urchi* [*po-erh-ch'ih*] kneels down and kills the sacrificial animal."[13] Bolad was comfortable in two cultural worlds and in the not-too-distant future would be operating with equal effectiveness in a third.

His next posting was to the Censorate (*Yü-shih t'ai*). This traditional Chinese institution was reinstituted by Qubilai in 1268 to monitor the activities of both civil and military officials to ensure honesty and efficiency. Because the Censorate had the right of direct communication with the emperor and the powers of impeachment and punishment, it exercised substantial political influence.[14] This body was headed by two Censors-in-Chief (*Yü-shih ta-fu*) and two Vice Censors-in-Chief (*Yü-shih chung-ch'eng*). The date of Bolad's initial appointment is not indicated but by early 1271 he was serving as a Vice Censor-in-Chief and continued to do so until promoted to Censor-in-Chief in the spring of 1275. Later that year Qubilai named Yü-su (or Yü-hsi) T'ieh-mu-erh as his opposite number.[15] This individual, an Arulad Mongol descended from one of Chinggis Qan's "companions" (*nököd*), appears in Rashīd al-Dīn's history as Ūz Tīmūr (Mongolian, Öz Temür).[16] Apparently, the two did not function well together because Yao T'ien-fu, a Chinese censor, memorialized the throne that this dual leadership was cumbersome and ineffective, and that the situation could only be improved by dismissing one of the Censors-in-Chief. Qubilai approved the suggestion, sent it on to the parties in question, and Bolad, the younger man, resigned sometime after 1277.[17] This forced resignation was obviously without prejudice since Bolad continued to hold other important posts and indeed acquired new ones.

While just beginning his service in the Censorate, Bolad received an additional appointment to the Office of the Grand Supervisors of Agriculture (*Ta-ssu nung-ssu*), another quintessentially Chinese institution, one that went back to the Former Han. The Mongols first acknowledged the need for such an institution in 1261 when an Office for the Encouragement of Agriculture (*Ch'üan-nung ssu*) was created, at least on paper.[18] Then sometime in the late

12 *YS*, ch. 170, p. 3989. 13 *YS*, ch. 77, p. 1923.

14 Charles O. Hucker, *The Censorial System of Ming China* (Stanford University Press, 1966), pp. 25–28; and Charles O. Hucker, "The Yuan Contribution to Censorial History," *Bulletin of the Institute of History and Philology, Academia Sinica*, extra vol., no. 4 (1960), 219–27.

15 *YS*, ch. 7, p. 132, ch. 8, pp. 166 and 170.

16 *YS*, ch. 119, p. 2947; and Rashīd/Alizade, vol. I, pt. 1, p. 430.

17 Po-chu-lu Ch'ung, *Chü-t'an chi* (Ou-hsing ling-shih ed.), ch. 2, p. 31b; and *YS*, ch. 168, p. 3960. The exact date of his resignation is uncertain but he was still called Censor-in-Chief as late as April 1277. See *YS*, ch. 9, pp. 188–89.

18 On this office, its antecedents and later transformation, see Farquhar, *Government*, pp. 214–17.

1260s a campaign was launched to upgrade and extend its activities. The manner in which this campaign was orchestrated tells us much about Yuan court politics and Bolad's role as a cultural broker. The effort to gain higher status for this office was initiated by Kao T'ien-hsi, a *pi-she-ch'ih* (Mongolian, *bichēchi*), "secretary," in Qubilai's guard, whose family had long served in the household of the Toluids. According to his biography in the *Yuan shih*, Kao

> spoke to *Ch'eng-hsiang* Bolad [Po-lo] and the Minister of the Left [*Tso-ch'eng*] Chang Wen-ch'ien saying: "Agriculture and sericulture is the source [*pen*] of clothing and food; if one does not devote attention to the source, the people will not have sufficient clothing and food, culture cannot flourish, and kingly government, for this reason, will not come to the fore here. You should be willing to consider this." [Bolad] *Ch'eng-hsiang* made [this proposal] known to [the throne]. The Emperor was pleased and ordered the establishment of the Office of Supervisors of Agriculture [*Ssu-nung ssu*].[19]

Here Bolad is certainly used as a stalking horse, a front man, by his Chinese associates, indicating that the Chinese cause at court was at times best served by a Mongolian advocate.

The new office was officially founded in March 1270 and its first director was Chang Wen-ch'ien, who separately memorialized the throne "requesting that the Emperor begin plowing the imperial estates [*chi-t'ien*] and that the former sacrifices to agriculture, sericulture and other ceremonies be introduced."[20] This demonstrates that there were actually close ties between the seemingly separate campaigns to revive agriculture and ceremonial life and that Bolad was linked to both.

Bolad's involvement in agricultural affairs, so far in the role of an advocate, by no means ends here. In 1271 the office, by imperial order, was again upgraded to the Office of the Grand Supervisors of Agriculture (*Ta-ssu-nung ssu*). Qubilai further ordered that Vice Censor-in-Chief Bolad become its first director (*Ta-ssu-nung ch'ing*). Hantum (An-t'ung), another of the pro-Chinese Mongols at court, found this unacceptable and remonstrated, saying that "Bolad is combining the duties of a censor with [that of] directing; formerly there was no such practice." In short, according to Chinese precedent and norms, this constituted a flagrant case of conflict of interest. Qubilai, however, was unmoved and returned a rescript stating "The Office of Agriculture [*Ssu-nung*] is no trifling matter; I have thought deeply and proclaim Bolad to be its Director."[21] In this way, a man of nomadic background, over the objections of another nomad, came to preside over one of the oldest and most productive agricultural systems in the world.

In his capacity as Director, Bolad had varied responsibilities and experiences. He oversaw the Directorate of Waterways (*Tu-shui chien*), which was charged with the maintenance of bridge, canals, dikes, and embankments along the Yellow River and its tributary system. He was also in charge of

[19] *YS*, ch. 153, p. 3614. This passage is dated to 1264 (*Chung-t'ung*, 4th year); more likely it should be dated to 1268 (*Chih-yuan*, 4th year).

[20] *YS*, ch. 157, p. 3697. See also ch. 7, p. 128, and *YWL*, ch. 40, p. 17a.

[21] *YS*, ch. 7, p. 132.

Mobile Offices for the Stimulation of Agriculture (*Hsün-hsing ch'üan-nung ssu*), whose task was to disseminate new agronomic information and technology among the rural populace.[22] Naturally, too, the Director had a hand in rewarding and punishing officials and underlings for their performance in the encouragement of agriculture.[23]

That Bolad still retained a measure of his nomadic heritage and a certain sensibility to pastoral production emerges from an exchange between his office and the throne in 1275. This interesting episode is reported in the *Yuan shih* as follows:

> The Office of the Grand Supervisors of Agriculture said: "The General Secretariat [*Chung-shu*] sent a directive to begin gathering in the autumn crops within the imperial domain; we request that you prohibit the peasants from plowing again [as] we fear that it will interfere with the grazing [*ch'u-mu*]." Because [,however,] agriculture has [such] benefit, [the emperor] rejected the prohibition [against plowing].[24]

What Bolad is advocating here is an arrangement, well known in West Asia, in which nomads and agriculturalists arrive at reciprocal agreements that allow herders to pasture their animals on recently harvested fields to graze the stubble and return manure.[25] For Qubilai, apparently, no interference with the regular annual agricultural rounds, at least on his estates, was to be tolerated.

Although obviously preoccupied with multiple official duties, Bolad was drawn into yet another project, the creation of an imperial archive. Following a by now familiar pattern, the task was entrusted to Bolad and a Chinese associate, Liu Ping-chung, who received an imperial decree in late 1273 to establish the Imperial Library directorate (*Mi-shu chien*). As originally constituted, the directorate had, besides administrative personnel, historians and archivists.[26] Its function was the collection and preservation of books, maps, pictures, and prohibited works on sorcery and geomancy.[27]

Bolad, while not an officer of the directorate, took an active part in its development. Various records and personnel were transferred there on his initiative, and Bolad and Liu jointly memorialized the throne for additional funding.[28] He was concerned, too, with the control of prohibited books and in 1277 was ordered by the throne to investigate, in conjunction with Chinese colleagues, the damage and theft of "drafts, dispatches, books and pictures" in the directorate's keeping.[29]

In 1277 Bolad received a new and important assignment. Because of its importance in elucidating his Chinese career, the *Yuan shih* account will be quoted in full:

22 *YS*, ch. 7, p. 138 and ch. 8, pp. 148 and 166. 23 *YS*, ch. 7, p. 138 and ch. 8, p. 152.

24 *YS*, ch. 8, p. 152.

25 Anatoly M. Khazanov, *Nomads and the Outside World* (Cambridge University Press, 1984), pp. 33–37. 26 *MSC*, ch. 1, pp. 1a–b (pp. 21–22). 27 Farquhar, *Government*, p. 137.

28 *MSC*, ch. 1, pp. 2a–b (pp. 23–24) and ch. 2, pp. 1a–b (pp. 51–52).

29 *T'ung-chih t'iao-ko* (Hangchou: Che-chiang ku-chi ch'u-pan-she, 1986), ch. 28, p. 316, and *MSC*, ch. 6, p. 1a (p. 169).

[The Emperor] selected Bolad [Po-lo], the Grand Supervisor of Agriculture [*Ta ssu-nung*], who combined [the duties] of Censor-in-Chief [*Yü-shih ta-fu*], Director of Imperial Household Provisions [*Hsüan-hui shih*], and Administrator of the Office of State Ceremonial [*Ling shih-i ssu shih*], to be Assistant Director of the Bureau of Military Affairs [*Shu-mi fu-shih*] and concurrently Director of Imperial Household Provisions and Administrator of the Office of State Ceremonial.[30]

From this most informative passage we learn the following:

1. As Director of Imperial Household Provisions, Bolad was a commissary, in charge of food and drink at the court.[31] In other words, following the family tradition, Bolad was a *ba'urchi*.
2. Bolad held high rank in the Office of State Ceremonial, an appointment not mentioned elsewhere.
3. Bolad was promoted to the Bureau of Military Affairs (*Shu-mi yuan*), a very powerful institution.
4. Lastly, and perhaps most importantly, this passage establishes unequivocally that the various "Bolads" mentioned in the *Yuan shih* as servitors of Qubilai are one historical personage, our Bolad.

The Bureau of Military Affairs, to which Bolad was now seconded, was established in 1263. As an assistant director, Bolad was now among a small number of officials who formulated and debated military policy. After Chiang-nan, on the lower course of the Ch'ang-ch'iang, fell, Bolad helped to set up a system of garrisons in the south to consolidate Mongolian rule in Sung territory. These decisions were made through consultations between field commanders such as Bayan, who actually conquered the area, and officials of the Bureau of Military Affairs such as Bolad.[32] He was also immediately drawn into discussions of military recruitment, replacement, and advancement. In early 1278 Qubilai involved Bolad in a debate on the guidelines to be followed when military households without an able-bodied male hired substitutes for service in the army.[33] A short time later, Bolad memorialized the throne, recommending that the Mongolian practice of permitting meritorious officers to bequeath their vacated posts to sons or nephews be modified. Qubilai approved and henceforth replacements would be selected on the basis of merit unless an officer was killed in combat or died of illness while on active duty. In such cases, sons or nephews might succeed to the office or to one reduced a degree in rank.[34]

In the spring of the same year Bolad went on campaign. He accompanied the Jalayir commander Toghan (T'o-huan) and the imperial prince Urughtai

[30] *YS*, ch. 9, pp. 188–89.

[31] On the Bureau for Imperial Household Provisions (*Hsüan-hui yuan*) and its innumerable subordinate agencies, see Farquhar, *Government*, pp. 73–82.

[32] *YS*, ch. 99, p. 2545, and Hsiao, *Military*, p. 118 for translation.

[33] *YTC*, ch. 34, p. 30a, and Gunter Mangold, *Das Militärwesen in China unter der Mongolenherrschaft* (Bamberg: aku Fotodruck, 1971), p. 126.

[34] *YTC*, ch. 8, p. 16a; *YS*, ch. 98, p. 2516; and Hsiao, *Military*, p. 84.

(Wo-lu-hu-t'ai), who formed part of the forces Qubilai sent against Qaidu in Jungaria and the Irtysh. Under the overall command of Nomoghan, Qubilai's son, the operations soon faltered, owing to princely dissension and defection, and by late 1279 Bolad was back at court.[35]

Here he resumed his administrative duties. These included appointing military commanders, in this instance for a punitive campaign against the Man in Fukien, and recommending a person for the position of *darughachi*, imperial agent, a ubiquitous office found in all levels of the Yuan governmental and military system.[36] As an assistant director, Bolad also performed intelligence functions: he interrogated Wen T'ien-hsiang, a scholar and famous Sung loyalist who played an active role in the defense of his doomed dynasty to its final collapse. Wen arrived in Ta-tu (Peking) in November 1279 as a prisoner of war and a month later underwent a "hostile interrogation" at the hand of Bolad and Aḥmad (A-ho-ma), Marco Polo's Acmat the Bailo. Throughout, the prisoner engaged Bolad in a vigorous debate on the nature of public duty and political loyalty. Steadfast in his defense of the fallen regime, he was returned to prison and executed three years later.[37]

By far the most momentous event during Bolad's tour as an assistant director in the Bureau of Military Affairs was the investigation of Aḥmad's assassination. Indeed, this is one of the most widely heralded events of the century since it was reported at length by Rashīd al-Dīn and by Marco Polo.[38]

Aḥmad, the infamous financial minister, entered Qubilai's service around 1262.[39] A skilled bureaucratic politician and financial officer who produced a steady flow of revenue for the Yuan coffers, Aḥmad soon acquired high position and the emperor's trust. However, his arrogance, corrupt practices, and foreign origin soon led to conflict with Chinese officials in the central government. In 1278 Ts'ui Pin memorialized the throne, denouncing Aḥmad. The next year Qubilai ordered Bolad and Hsiang Wei, an official of the Censorate, to investigate Aḥmad's activities, particularly his appointment of supernumerary officials. The two traveled by post horse from K'ai-p'ing (Shang-tu) to Ta-tu, where Aḥmad successfully evaded interrogation by pleading illness.[40] Qubilai none the less retained his confidence in Aḥmad and even when his own son and heir apparent, Jimjim, attacked the minister as cruel and corrupt in 1280, he steadfastly refused to believe the charges against him.

The failure of officialdom to curb Aḥmad's great power led to action by

[35] *YS*, ch. 133, p. 3233; Rashīd/Karīmī, vol. I, pp. 632–33; and Rashīd/Boyle, p. 266.

[36] *YS*, ch. 131, p. 3193 and ch. 134, p. 3261.

[37] Liu Yüeh-shen, *Shen-chai Liu hsien-sheng wen-chi* (Yuan-tai chen-pen wen-chi hui-k'an ed.), ch. 13, pp 12a ff.; H. W. Huber, "Wen T'ien-hsiang," in Herbert Franke, ed., *Sung Biographies* (Wiesbaden: Franz Steiner, 1976), vol. III, pp. 1187–1201, especially 1198–99; and Richard L. Davis, *Wind against the Mountain: The Crises of Politics and Culture in Thirteenth Century China* (Cambridge, Mass.: Harvard University Press, 1996), pp. 177–79.

[38] Marco Polo, pp. 214–16.

[39] A. C. Moule, *Quinsai with Other Notes on Marco Polo* (Cambridge University Press, 1957), pp. 79–88, and Herbert Franke, "Aḥmad (?–1282)," in Igor de Rachewiltz *et al.*, eds., *In the Service of the Khan: Eminent Personalities of the Early Mongol–Yuan Period (1200–1300)* (Wiesbaden: Harrassowitz, 1993), pp. 539–57.

[40] *YS*, ch. 128, p. 3130 and ch. 173, p. 4038.

private individuals who now plotted to assassinate the hated minister. This popular movement, led by Chinese "monks" and "magicians," successfully killed Aḥmad in early 1282. In the tumult that followed the assassination, Qubilai, still trusting in Aḥmad's integrity, sent Bolad and other officials to investigate the matter and punish the guilty. They reached the capital on May 1 and on the next day executed the ringleaders. The deceased minister was buried with great honor and his family, by imperial orders, was exempted from further inquiries. Only when Qubilai later discussed the matter with Bolad did the emperor come to realize the full extent of Aḥmad's "villainy." Greatly angered, he ordered an immediate investigation of the whole affair, which resulted in the execution and punishment of many of Aḥmad's associates and family members.[41]

This was Bolad's last major service to his sovereign while still in China. But before following him to his new posting in Iran, we need to assess, however briefly, his career and experiences in the Yuan domain.

First, to evaluate his political status, the basic organizational character of the regime must be made clear. Under Qubilai there were three major agencies of governance: the General Secretariat (*Chung-shu sheng*), with overall responsibility for civil administration; the Bureau of Military Affairs (*Shu-mi yüan*), charged with formulating military policy and controlling guards units in the north; and, lastly, the Censorate (*Yü-shih t'ai*), the surveillance arm that monitored other units of government. All three communicated directly with the emperor and Bolad was a member of two of them. Further, as a *ba'urchi*, the Director of Imperial Household Provisions (*Hsüan-hui shih*), Bolad was a true insider, a member of the emperor's household establishment; thus, he not only had direct administrative communication with his sovereign, but ongoing personal contact as well. This is why his Chinese colleagues found his support and mediation so important to their policy initiatives. He was a very important personage in the government, the military, and the imperial household. In modern political parlance, he was "connected." Not surprisingly, therefore, when a certain Chang Yang-lu of An-chou tried to counterfeit the official seal of Bolad *Ch'eng-hsiang* in 1282 he was immediately put to death.[42]

Second, and of particular importance for our purposes, Bolad's varied postings afforded him an opportunity to observe Chinese society and culture at close range. He knew the language, the institutions, and many representatives of the Chinese elite with whom he frequently collaborated on joint projects. His support for their initiatives indicates that he found much to admire in Chinese civilization. The knowledge gained and attitudes formed during this first phase of his career shaped in substantial ways his subsequent activities in Iran, where he served for the last twenty-eight years of his life as an ambassador, political adviser, and principal conduit of cultural interchange between China and the eastern Islamic world.

[41] *YS*, ch. 205, pp. 4563–64; Rashīd/Karīmī, vol. I, p. 603; and Rashīd/Boyle, p. 292.
[42] *YS*, ch. 12, p. 240.

ELEVEN

Rashīd al-Dīn and Pūlād *chīnksānk*

The decision to send Bolad on an embassy to Arghun (A-lu-hun) is most fully reported in the Chinese biographies of his traveling companion, ʿIsā (Ai-hsieh). According to these sources, ʿIsā was selected to accompany *Ch'eng-hsiang* Po-lo as an aide (*chiai*) because of his previous experience as an "envoy to distant parts."[1] Though left unsaid, it is obvious that as a native of the West he could function there as an interpreter.

As we have already seen, Bolad and ʿIsā arrived in Iran in late 1285 after a perilous overland journey and there conferred Qubilai's blessings on Arghun's second elevation. In early 1286 the two envoys then began their long journey home. Their respective fates are noted by Ch'eng Chü-fu, ʿIsā's biographer:

> Because they encountered the rebellion [of Qaidu and Du'a] on their return trip the envoy [Bolad] and the aide [ʿIsā] were separated from one another. [ʿIsā], braving slings and arrows, emerged from this land of death and two years [later] finally reached the capital [Ta-tu]. He presented the precious garment and belt offered by Prince Arghun [A-lu-hun] and was ordered to make a full report of his observations on the outward and return journeys. The emperor [Qubilai], greatly pleased, turned to his court officials and said with a sigh: "Bolad was born in our land, enjoyed our emoluments and yet is content to stay there; ʿIsā, was born there, has his [original] home there and yet is faithful to me. How different they are!"[2]

From this we can conclude that Bolad's mission was temporary and that when he was unable to return he was persuaded to take up service at the Il-qan court. It is also the case that Qubilai's disappointment in Bolad was somewhat exaggerated by ʿIsāʿs biographer to dramatize the loyalty and courage of the latter. There is, for example, no hint that Qubilai ever ordered Bolad home; on the contrary, there is every evidence that by staying in Iran he well served the Toluid cause, a fact the Yuan court later recognized in public and dramatic fashion.

Before proceeding to the details of Bolad's second career, it is well worth

[1] Ch'eng Chü-fu, *Ch'eng hsüeh-lou wen-chi*, ch. 5, p. 3b. See also *YS*, ch. 134, p. 3249, and A. C. Moule, *Christians in China before the Year 1500* (London: Society for Promoting Christian Knowledge, 1930), p. 229, who provides a translation of ʿIsā's *YS* biography.

[2] Ch'eng Chü-fu, *Ch'eng hsüeh-lou wen-chi*, ch. 5, pp. 3b–4a.

while, given the history of confusion over his identity and the centrality of this identification to the arguments of this book, to assert and reaffirm the obvious: the Po-lo of the Chinese texts and the Pūlād of the Persian sources are one and the same person. The Chinese texts, for instance, tell us that Po-lo was a *ch'eng-hsiang* and the Director of Imperial Household Provisions (*Hsüan-hui shih*), while Rashīd al-Dīn notes in one place that Pūlād was "a commissary [*ba'urchī*] as well as a *chīnksānk*," and in another that Būlād Āqā "was in the service of Qūbīlāi Qā'ān as a *chīnksānk* and as a *bā'urchī*."[3] In short, there is absolutely no doubt that Qubilai's Po-lo is Rashīd's Pūlād and our Bolad.

Whatever Qubilai's attitude toward his missing minister, it is evident that Bolad was warmly received in Iran. He had arrived as the "ambassador of the Grand Qan [*īlchī-i* Qā'ān]" but stayed on as an adviser to the Il-qans.[4] His new status and duties are noted obliquely by al-ʿUmarī, who reports that "the Holder of the Throne [*sāhib al-takht*, i.e., the qaghan] assigned to the Kingdom of Iran, to the court of Hülegü and his sons a permanent official [*amīr*] who is held in great esteem."[5] Though not mentioned by name, this must be Bolad, a conclusion that finds support in contemporary court records. On the back of a badly damaged Mongolian document of the il-qan Arghun, dating to 1287, there is the "attestation" (Mongolian *barvan-a* > Persian *parvānah*) of Bolad and several other officials.[6] Given the date and the fact that Bolad is first on the list of signatories, it is fair to conclude that he assumed an important place at the Il-qan court from the very first.

Further evidence of the esteem in which he was held can be seen in his new domestic arrangements: he took as his wife (*qatun*) a certain Shirin, a former concubine (*egechi*) of the deceased il-qan Abaqa (d. 1281).[7] Such a privilege may not have been entirely unprecedented, but it was certainly rare, a real mark of distinction and a reaffirmation of Bolad's membership in the Chinggisids' extended political family. This union, interestingly, indicates that he started in Iran a second family as well as a second career, since Rashīd al-Dīn records that amīr Būlād had "sons in the service of the Qā'ān [Qubilai]."[8] Regrettably, there is no further information on those Bolad left behind.

As adviser and representative of the qaghan, Bolad naturally took an active role in court politics. His access to the il-qan and his great prestige gave him considerable influence, which, the sources tell us, he was willing to use. On one occasion he secured the accession of a dependent ruler. When Yūsuf Shāh, the atabeg of Lur-i Buzurg, died, his son Āfrāsiyāb, who served at the imperial camp, and who, Naṭanzī relates, was a great favorite of Pūlād *jinksānk*, was named to replace his father. In typical Mongolian fashion, his other brother

[3] Rashīd al-Dīn, "Shuʿab-i panjgānah," folio 131v, and Rashīd/Alizade, vol. I, pt. 1, p. 518.
[4] Vaṣṣāf, p. 272. The *īlchī* of this text is the Mongolian *elchi*, "envoy."
[5] ʿUmarī/Lech, p. 19, Arabic text, and p. 103, German translation.
[6] Gerhard Doerfer, "Mongolica aus Ardabīl," *Zentralasiatische Studien* 9 (1975), 206–7.
[7] Rashīd/Jahn I, p. 5. [8] Rashīd/Alizade, vol. I, pt. 1, p. 518.

Aḥmad then replaced Āfrāsiyāb as a hostage at court.[9] As he had done in China, Bolad evidently introduced and trained newcomers to his prince's guard/household establishment, one of the principal recruiting grounds for high-level officials in the Mongolian system of governance.

Bolad also had a hand in purging officials in disrepute, most notably Malik Jalāl al-Dīn, who had been dismissed from office for his part in the intrigues of Buqa, but who had escaped further punishment through the intercession of unnamed friends at court. In the summer of 1289 the malik, on his way to the imperial camp, encountered Pūlād Āqā, who made "inquiries about the circumstances of his dismissal and its causes." The malik in response proclaimed his innocence and blamed his travails on his sovereign's poor judgment. These words soon reached the ears of Arghun and once he verified their accuracy with Pūlād, the malik was seized by a member of the guard and executed.[10] Bolad obviously was in a position to make and break careers and lives.

During the reign of Geikhatu, Bolad was still consulted on important issues of the day, the ill-fated introduction of paper money, for example, but he seems somewhat less prominent and powerful. Upon the death of Geikhatu two claimants, Baidu and Ghazan, vied for the throne. Throughout this tense period, when it appeared that the Il-qan regime might disintegrate in civil war, Bolad served as an intermediary between the rival camps. In May 1295, while the two rivals were negotiating in southern Azerbaijan, Baidu sent Bolad to Ghazan to insure that his challenger return from the meeting site by the same road he had arrived. He did so, Rashīd al-Dīn informs us, because Baidu feared that if Ghazan took his intended, alternative route through the Siyah Kuh mountains near Ardabīl, some of his supporters stationed there might defect to the opposition.[11]

On the surface it appears that Bolad was Baidu's man, but this impression is probably misleading. It seems more likely that Bolad, given his status and background, served in these circumstances in a more neutral capacity, perhaps as an honest broker, to prevent a costly civil war. In any event, while we do not know his precise role in the transition, he emerges, following Ghazan's victory, as a respected member of the new regime, and this makes it extremely unlikely that he was ever strongly associated with Baidu's cause.

This is not to say that Ghazan's enthronement did not affect Bolad's position at court. Al-ʿUmarī asserts that the new ruler "paid no heed to the authority of his [i.e., the qaghan's] amīr [Bolad] who in consequence lost his standing and repute."[12] Clearly Bolad's political influence was diminished, but this was

[9] Muʿīn al-Dīn Naṭanzī, *Muntakhab al-tavārīkh-i muʿīnī*, ed. by Jean Aubin (Tehran: Librairie Khayyam, 1957), pp. 45–46. [10] Rashīd/Jahn I, p. 84.

[11] Rashīd/Jahn II, pp. 65 and 71. The continuer of Bar Hebraeus' chronicle mentions a number of ambassadors Baidu sent Ghazan, but not by name. See Bar Hebraeus, pp. 500–4.

[12] ʿUmarī/Lech, p. 19, Arabic text, and p. 103, German translation.

less a matter of partisanship in the struggle for the throne than a result of Ghazan's efforts to present a more recognizable face to his numerous Muslim subjects.

To some extent the reduction in Bolad's standing may well have been orchestrated for public consumption, part of the effort to highlight Ghazan's new status as an independent Islamic ruler. Most certainly Bolad remained on good terms with Ghazan and apparently wielded some power behind the scenes. In any event, it is during this period that Bolad became associated with one of the most visible and influential political figures of the realm, Rashīd al-Dīn. And since from this point on Bolad's activities and projects were usually a product of his partnership with Rashīd al-Dīn, we need to look briefly at the life and times of this famed statesman and scholar.

Rashīd al-Dīn was born ca. 1247 in Hamadān, the son of a Jewish apothecary.[13] Trained as a physician, he converted to Islam at age thirty and apparently entered the service of the Il-qans during the reign of Geikhatu (1291–95). He rose to prominence under Ghazan as an advocate and architect of reform. The major thrust of these measures was the revival of the economy and court revenues. To this end Ghazan, under Rashīd al-Dīn's guidance, sought to regularize and reduce taxes and rents, end corruption in the fiscal administration, repopulate abandoned agricultural lands through tax immunities, restore damaged irrigation systems, compile a new land register, protect peasants from nomadic depredations, and encourage new agricultural methods and techniques.[14]

Henceforth, Rashīd al-Dīn was at the center of power, but always paired with other ministers who were his rivals. His final protagonist, Taj al-Dīn ʿAlī Shāh, brought about Rashīd al-Dīn's destruction in 1318. Accused of poisoning Öljeitü, he was cruelly executed on orders of Abū Saʿīd.[15] In the aftermath, his extensive properties were destroyed or confiscated. This accounts for the fact that some of Rashīd al-Dīn's rich literary legacy, including, as we shall see, works from and about China, has been unhappily lost.[16]

Rashīd al-Dīn and Bolad were of course very busy men. We know, however, that they met on a variety of occasions. In 1305 when the new Sulṭān Öljeitü

[13] Amazingly enough, despite his uncontested importance as a political and cultural figure, there is no full-scale biography of Rashīd al-Dīn. For brief sketches of his life and activities, see David O. Morgan, "Rashīd al-Dīn," *EI*, 2nd edn, vol. VIII, pp. 443–44; Josef Van Ess, *Der Wesir und seine Gelehrten* (Wiesbaden: Franz Steiner, 1981), pp. 1–13; Reuven Amitai-Preiss, "New Material from the Mamlūk Sources for the Biography of Rashīd al-Dīn," *Oxford Studies in Islamic Art* 12 (1996), 23–37; and Edward G. Browne, *A Literary History of Persia*, vol. III: *The Tartar Domination (1265–1502)* (Cambridge University Press, 1969), pp. 68–87.

[14] Petrushevskii, *Zemledelie*, pp. 55–62, and Bertold Spuler, *Die Mongolen in Iran*, 4th edn (Leiden: E. J. Brill, 1985), pp. 263–69.

[15] On the court factionalism that led to Rashīd al-Dīn's fall and execution, see Charles Melville, "Abū Saʿīd and the Revolt of the Amirs in 1319," in Denise Aigle, ed., *L'Iran face à la domination Mongol* (Tehran: Institut français de recherche en Iran, 1997), pp. 92–94.

[16] Karl Jahn, "The Still Missing Works of Rashīd al-Dīn," *CAJ* 9 (1964), 113–22.

married, Pūlād *chīnsāng* stood up for the groom while Rashīd al-Dīn gave the bride away.[17] Obviously, too, they encountered one another in the conduct of state business. Since Bolad traveled with, and at times was in charge of, Öljeitü's "base camp" (*a'urugh*), this must have been a frequent occurrence.[18]

By the time of Öljeitü's reign, Bolad had made a political comeback of sorts: he was again acknowledged as one of the senior ministers of state. In the list of officials which opens Qāshānī's history of Öljeitü's reign, third place is held by "the great amīr Pūlād *chīnsānk*," who ranked behind Qutlugh Shāh and Chuban.[19] The three often worked in tandem: Öljeitü consulted the three soon after his enthronement to discuss general government policy and specific projects, and they jointly petitioned Öljeitü on such matters as the honesty and efficiency of the officials of the realm.[20] This is not to say that the three were nearly equal. One gets the strong impression from the sources that Qutlugh Shāh and later on Chuban were the dominant figures; certainly foreign observers identified them as such.[21]

Besides tendering advice as a senior statesman, Bolad still received active commands. In May 1307 when Öljeitü was campaigning in the mountainous and inaccessible Gīlān, a region the Mongols had yet to subdue, Bolad was placed in charge of logistics and supply.[22] And he was still in the saddle in 1312, by which time he must have been in his seventies. On this occasion his sovereign entrusted him with the security of Darband and Arrān, the main invasion route of the Golden Horde into Azerbaijan.[23]

This, however, was to be his last assignment in a career of numerous important postings; as befits a man of nomadic origin, Bolad died on April 26, 1313 "in the meadow of Arrān at the winter camp."[24]

In life and in death, Bolad was a much honored figure. Rashīd al-Dīn frequently sang his praises and the Mongolian court in Iran mourned his passing. Nor was he forgotten in China. Several years before his demise, the Yuan court bestowed upon him high honors. According to the *Yuan shih*, on July 6, 1311 "The Bureau of Military Affairs Official [*Shu-mi ch'en*] Bolad [Po-lo] was enfeoffed as the Duke of State of Tse [Tse *kung-kuo*]."[25] This passage, though laconic, is quite informative. In the first place, despite the fact that he had left China twenty-eight years previously, he was still carried on the books as an official of the Bureau of Military Affairs and therefore still considered a servitor of the Yuan court. Second, and more obviously, his original employers continued to hold Bolad in high esteem. This is brought out by a closer exam-

17 Qāshānī/Hambly, p. 42. 18 Qāshānī/Hambly, p. 236.

19 Qāshānī/Hambly, p. 8. Here Bolad is called a Qarākitāi. He was, of course, a Dörben. Perhaps this slip is to be explained as an error for "from Khitāi."

20 Ḥafiẓ-i Ābrū, *Ẓayl*, p. 67, and Qāshānī/Hambly, p. 239.

21 Abū'l-Fidā, *Memoirs*, pp. 41 and 42.

22 Ḥafiẓ-i Ābrū, *Ẓayl*, p. 73, and Charles Melville, "The Ilkhān Oljeitü's Conquest of Gīlān (1307): Rumor and Reality," in Reuven Amitai-Preiss and David O. Morgan, eds., *The Mongol Empire and its Legacy* (Leiden: Brill, 1999), p. 105. 23 Qāshānī/Hambly, p. 142.

24 *Ibid.*, p. 147. 25 *YS*, ch. 24, p. 543.

ination of the title he received, Duke of State. This was the third highest of the nine titles of nobility in the Yuan, following that of Prince (*wang*) and Commandery Prince (*chün-wang*), two ranks normally reserved for princes of the blood. To such elevated ranks were usually added a territorial appellation, in this case Tse, a prefecture (*fu*) of Chung-shu, the metropolitan province of the Yuan, now part of the modern-day Shansi.[26] It was in Chung-shu that many princes and high officials were granted their shares (*qubi*/*fen-ti*).

Whether this honor reached Bolad before his death is not known. Most certainly his next honor did not. In 1313, the year of his death, the Yuan court again sent Baiju west to consult with Ha-erh-pan-ta (Kharbandah/Öljeitu) and "to bestow a gold seal [*chin-yin*] on *Ch'eng-hsiang* Po-lo."[27] Thus, it is obvious that Qubilai's "disappointment" aside, the Yuan court was kept informed and approved of Bolad's long tour of "detached duty" in Iran. He had, in their judgment, continued to render good service and was rewarded accordingly.

It is apparent as well that Bolad, in the course of this service, had acquired rewards of a more tangible nature. In the spring of 1314, a marriage contract was signed between Shāhmalikī and Pīr Ḥāmid "the son of Būlād *chīnsānk*," which stipulated "a bride price of 6,000 *man* of silk carpets."[28] Since this is something in the neighborhood of 4,000 pounds, the bride price represents considerable family wealth.

As a starting point for our discussion of Rashīd al-Dīn's and Bolad's many joint cultural enterprises, we can begin with an exploration of their political collaboration, which led, I believe, quite naturally to Chinese matters and Chinese models. To a degree, this must have begun unconsciously, with two ministers discussing mutual interests and common problems. That enquiries about how things were done at the Yuan court actually came up in these exchanges is quite apparent from Rashīd al-Dīn's writings. In his account of Qubilai's reign the Persian historian discusses a range of Chinese governmental procedures, offices, titles, and terms.[29] He mentions, for instance, that in depositions "fingerprints [*khaṭṭ-i angusht*]" are sometimes taken to identify individuals, a venerable practice in China that goes back to T'ang times.[30] Titles and offices he discusses are typically provided with their Chinese names, and for the most part quite accurately. Rashīd al-Dīn's *vangshaī* answers to the Chinese *Yuan-shuai*, "Regional Military Commander," and his *finjān* equates to *P'ing-chang* (*ch'eng-shih*), "Privy Councillor." Not surprisingly, the organizations with which Bolad was affiliated are prominently featured: the

[26] See T'an Ch'i-hsiang, ed., *Chung-kuo li-shih ti-t'u chi*, vol. VII: *Yuan Ming-te ch'i* (Shanghai: Ti-t'u ch'u-pan she, 1982), map 7–8, lat. 35° 30′, long. 112° 50′.

[27] Yuan Chüeh, *Ch'ing-jung chü-shih chi*, ch. 34, p. 22b.

[28] Qāshānī/Hambly, p. 154.

[29] Rashīd/Karīmī, vol. II, pp. 642–44, and Rashīd/Boyle, pp. 278–81, where all terms are explicated.

[30] On the practice in China, see Bertold Laufer, "History of the Finger Print System," *Annual Report of the Board of Regents of the Smithsonian Institution, 1912* (Washington, D.C.: Government Printing Office, 1913), pp. 631–52, especially pp. 641 ff.

chubīvan, from the Mongolian pronunciation, *chümui ön*, of the Chinese *Shu-mi yuan*, "Bureau of Military Affairs," and the *zhūshitāi* or *Yü-shih t'ai*, "Censorate," the Mongolian form of which is *üshi-tai*.

Rashīd al-Dīn also notes that in Khān Bālīgh (Peking) there are "the archives of the court [*dafātir-i dīvān*]," in which "they well preserve [everything]." In this instance the Chinese name is not provided, but it is reasonable to connect this institution with the *Mi-shu chien*, "Imperial Library Directorate." In any event, Rashīd al-Dīn informs us that these archives "contain fine precepts [*dasātīr*]," precepts in which he had more than just a passing interest. This emerges from the general catalog of Rashīd al-Dīn's works which is extant in both a Persian and an Arabic version. This source records four volumes translated "from Chinese into the Persian language," including one "about the organization and administration of the Chinese state and about the conduct of affairs according to their customs."[31]

What Chinese works underlie this very general description is not indicated, but another work of Rashīd al-Dīn, the *Tanksūq-nāmah*, "The Book of Rarities," provides, I think, the answer. In its table of contents there is listed a similarly titled work on politics, translated from the Chinese, consisting of two parts: the first records the amīrs of the right and left hand according to rank, while the second, a work on the "laws, organization and measures of government," bore the title "*Tāi khū lū lun*."[32] As Herbert Franke correctly surmised decades ago, this is the *T'ai-ho lü*.[33] This work, "The Statutes of the T'ai-ho Reign," was a legal code promulgated in 1201 under the Jürchen–Chin dynasty (1126–1234), one based on T'ang models. The Mongols utilized this code in North China from the fall of the Chin until 1271. Interestingly, the code is no longer extant in Chinese; all that remains are fragments in later Chinese codes and the partial Persian translation in the *Tanksūq-nāmah*.[34]

This interest in and familiarity with Chinese governmental practice and terminology is also expressed in the form of calques or loan translations found in the writings of Rashīd al-Dīn. For example, his repeated use of the Persian *buzurg*, "great" or "grand," to modify the offices, titles, and institutions of the empire parallels the Chinese use of *ta*, "great," in official nomenclature.[35] During the Yuan *ta* was regularly and widely employed to signify imperial status, most notably in the name of the dynasty itself, Ta Yuan. And, of

[31] A. M. Muginov, "Persidskaia unikal'naia rukopis Rashīd al-Dīna," *Uchenye zapiski instituta vostokovedeniia* 16 (1958), 374. The Arabic catalog lists a similar work on politics translated "from the native tongue of China into the Persian and Arabic languages." See Rashīd/Quatremère, pp. CXXXIX and CLX–CLXI.

[32] Rashīd al-Dīn, *Tanksūq nāmah yā ṭibb ahl-i Khitā*, ed. by Mujtabā Mīnuvī (Tehran: University of Tehran, 1972), p. 81.

[33] See Karl Jahn, "Some Ideas of Rashīd al-Dīn on Chinese Culture," *CAJ* 14 (1970), 137 note 8.

[34] Paul Heng-chao Ch'en, *Chinese Legal Traditions under the Mongols: The Code of 1291 as Reconstructed* (Princeton University Press, 1979), pp. 10–14.

[35] For examples, see Shimo Hirotoshi, "Two Important Persian Sources of the Mongol Empire," *Etudes Mongoles et Sibériennes* 27 (1996), 222–23.

course, Rashīd al-Dīn's chief informant on such matters, Bolad Aqa, once held the title *Ta ssu-nung*, "Grand [or Imperial] Supervisor of Agriculture."

On a more practical and personal level, Bolad's experiences in China were drawn upon in the search for solutions to pressing problems in Iran. For example, when Ghazan became exercised over the number of Mongols sold into slavery or reduced to beggary, he instituted a program to redeem those so debased and then to advance them "ready money" so that they could resume their proper station and function in life, service in the imperial army. After several years 10,000 unfortunates were collected and formed into a guards unit (*kabtūvāl* > Mongolian *kebte'ül*) and placed under the command of Bolad.[36] As we have already seen, Bolad began his career in China training new recruits for the imperial guard, but – of equal relevance – he was also involved in the social welfare measures of the Yuan court. In early 1281, the emperor transferred ready cash in the form of paper money (*ch'ao*), gold, and silver to Bolad (Po-lo) which he was to "hand over to needy people."[37]

His experience in China therefore provided the court in Iran with both praxis and precedent. For Ghazan and Rashīd al-Dīn, Bolad must have been a most useful and frequently consulted adviser. Here was a respected and high-ranking Mongolian official who favored accommodation and innovation, and who had facilitated reform in China as well as Iran. After all, no one could easily accuse Bolad, an old campaigner steeped in his own people's traditions and the agent of the Grand Qan in China, of betraying the Chinggisid legacy or of trying to subvert the empire through "un-Mongolian activities."

In court debates with nomadic traditionalists Bolad was certainly a major asset, long experienced in such struggles. Throughout his extended and varied career he demonstrated his capacity to work with local scholar–officials such as Liu Ping-chung and Rashīd al-Dīn, and to operate effectively as a middleman between the nomadic conquerors and the native elites in the sedentary sectors of the empire.

When acknowledged at all, our Bolad is usually described, quite accurately, as a literate Mongolian and as the informant of Rashīd al-Dīn.[38] But he was much more than that. He may be justly characterized as a Mongolian intellectual – literate, cosmopolitan, and a man of affairs. Although continuously exposed to foreign cultures and to their leading representatives, he never abandons his ties to Mongolian traditions. Many former nomads won their intellectual spurs in Chinese eyes by acculturating and writing passable Chinese poetry. These people, however, were Chinese, not Mongolian intellectuals. Bolad, of course, knew much about Chinese and later Persian culture,

36 Rashīd/Jahn II, pp. 311–12. For a full translation, see A. P. Martinez, "The Third Portion of the History of Ǧāzān Xan in Rašīdu'd-Dīn's *Ta'rīx-e mobārak-e Ǧāzānī*," *AEMA* 6 (1986–88), 111–13. 37 *YS*, ch. 11, p. 229.

38 D. [György] Kara, *Knigi mongol'skikh kochevnikov* (Moscow: Glavnaia redaktsiia vostochnoi literatury, 1972), p. 21.

but he remained to his dying day "the expert" on Mongolian customs and genealogy.

In Rashīd al-Dīn Bolad had the perfect collaborator. Today Rashīd al-Dīn is chiefly famous because he made the most of the opportunities afforded by the rise and expansion of the Mongolian empire. He, like his friend Bolad, acquired high office, wielded great influence, and amassed a substantial personal fortune.[39] In this they were like many others; but what makes them so unique, and to me such attractive figures, is that they were among the very few who recognized and personally realized the cultural possibilities presented by the Mongols' trans-Eurasian state. As we shall now see, Rashīd al-Dīn and Bolad regularly created and exploited such opportunities. The most famous of their joint enterprises was, appropriately enough, the first large-scale, systematic history of the principal sedentary and nomadic cultures of their world, Eurasia.

[39] See the discussions of I. P. Petrushevskii, "Feodal'noe khoziaistvo Rashīd al-Dīna," *Voprosy istorii* no. 4 (1951), 87–104, and Birgitt Hoffman, "The Gates of Piety and Charity: Rashīd al-Dīn Faḍl Allāh as Founder of Pious Endowments," in Aigle, *Iran*, pp. 189–202.

PART IV

Cultural exchange

TWELVE

Historiography

Rashīd al-Dīn was the first scholar to try to treat in a systematic and comprehensive fashion the history of the known world.[1] The resulting corpus, called the *Jāmiʿ al-tavārīkh* or "Collected Chronicles," is unprecedented in its scope and unique in its research methods, as the author himself is at pains to point out in the introduction to the work:

> Until now [he writes], no work has been produced in any epoch which contains a general account of the history of the inhabitants of the regions of the world and different human species. In this land [Iran] no book is available concerning the histories of other countries and cities and among the sovereigns of old none investigated or examined this [possibility]. Today, thanks to God and in consequence of him, the extremities of the inhabited earth are under the dominion of the house of Chinggis Qan and philosophers, astronomers, scholars and historians from North and South China, India, Kashmir, Tibet, [the lands] of the Uighurs, other Turkic tribes, the Arabs and Franks, [all] belonging to [different] religions and sects, are united in large numbers in the service of majestic heaven. And each one has manuscripts on the chronology, history and articles of faith of his own people and [each] has knowledge of some aspect of this. Wisdom, [which] decorates the world, demands that there should be prepared from the details of these chronicles and narratives an abridgement, but essentially complete [work] which will bear our august name . . . This book [he concludes], in its totality, will be unprecedented – an assemblage of all the branches of history.[2]

In its final form, completed around 1308, the *Collected Chronicles* included a history of the biblical prophets, Muḥammad, and the emergence of Islam, the Caliphates and major sulṭānates, a history of the Mongolian and Turkic peoples, the rise of the Chinggisid dynasty, and separate accounts of the Chinese, Indians, Jews, and Franks, as well as an extensive genealogical supplement and a geographical compendium.

There were, of course, efforts in Iran to write a history of the Mongols and the nations they subdued before Rashīd al-Dīn. The most famous of these is

[1] The best introductions are Karl Jahn, "Rashīd al-Dīn as World Historian," in *Yadname-ye Jan Rypka* (Prague: Academia; The Hague: Mouton, 1967), pp. 79–87, and John A. Boyle, "Rashīd al-Dīn: The First World Historian," *Iran* 9 (1971), 19–26.

[2] Rashīd/Alizade, vol. I, pt. 1, pp. 16–17.

the *History of the World Conqueror* by Juvaynī, written in the 1260s and much appreciated and utilized by the Syriac chronicler Bar Hebraeus writing in the 1280s.[3] Both these works are extremely valuable, but stand in sharp contrast to Rashīd al-Dīn's history not only in terms of organization and coverage but in the manner of compilation, a fact well understood by later generations of Persian historians.[4]

To take up the latter issue first, Rashīd al-Dīn recognized the limits of Muslim historiography in preparing a world history. While the Muslim tradition is for him the "most authentic of all," he readily concedes that "one cannot rely upon it for the history of others."[5] The solution, of course, was the utilization of an amazing array of foreign sources and informants – Chinese, Kashmiri, Uighur, Mongolian, Hebrew, Arabic, Tibetan, and Frankish. In his own words Rashīd al-Dīn says that "I queried and interrogated the scholars and notables of the aforementioned peoples and made extracts from the contents of [their] ancient books."[6]

In some instances we know the identity of his collaborators. His history of India and his account of Buddhist doctrine was prepared with the assistance of Kamālashri, a Kashmiri monk who supplied Rashīd al-Dīn with Sanskrit sources on the life and teachings of Buddha.[7] Such a collaborator was available because Kashmir became a Mongolian dependency during the reigns of Ögödei and Möngke and thereafter had close political ties to the Il-qan court.[8] It is relevant in this regard that one of Bolad's first commissions in China was to train T'ieh-ko, a member of a prominent Kashmiri Buddhist family, for service in Qubilai's guard.[9] Thus, Rashīd al-Dīn's close associate may have had knowledge and connections that proved useful in the recruitment of Kamālashri.

The best-known and most important of Rashīd al-Dīn's collaborators and informants was, of course, Bolad himself. In thanking his numerous assistants in the preparation of his history, Rashīd al-Dīn records his special indebtedness and gratitude to:

> the great amīr, the commander of the armies of Iran and Turan, the governor of the kingdoms of the world, Pūlād chīnksāng – long may his greatness endure – who in the inhabited quarters of the earth has no equal in the various branches of learning and in knowledge of the genealogies of the Turkish tribes and the events of their history, especially that of the Mongols.[10]

3 Bar Hebraeus, p. 473.

4 For example, Faḍlallāh ibn Rūzbihān (d. 1521) says that Rashīd al-Dīn stands apart from other classes of Muslim historians "by his method [*uslūb*]." See Vladimir Minorsky, *Persia in AD 1478–1490* (London: Royal Asiatic Society, 1957), p. 10.

5 Rashīd/Alizade, vol. I, pt. 1, p. 23.

6 *Ibid.*, p. 17.

7 Karl Jahn, "Kamālashri – Rashīd al-Dīn's Life and Teaching of Buddha," *CAJ* 2 (1956), 86 note 12, 99, 105, 120, and 121 ff. In keeping with his ecumenical proclivities, the Persian historian also drew on central Asian–Uighur materials for his portrayal of Buddhism. See Klaus Röhrborn, "Die islamische Weltgeschichte des Rašīduddīn als Quelle für den zentralasiatischen Buddhismus?," *Journal of Turkish Studies* 13 (1989), 129–33.

8 Karl Jahn, "A Note on Kashmir and the Mongols," *CAJ* 2 (1956), 176–80.

9 *YS*, ch. 125, p. 3075.

10 Rashīd/Alizade, vol. I, pt. 1, pp. 66–67.

This assessment, though certainly effusive, was very probably the opinion held by most contemporaries, including Ghazan, the sitting monarch, who prided himself on his extensive knowledge of tribal history and genealogy. He, too, praised Bolad, who instructed his sovereign on the finer points of early Mongolian history.[11]

This reliance on native sources and informants meant, of course, that the *Collected Chronicles* are best seen as a composite work, the by-product of a large and diverse research team coordinated by Rashīd al-Dīn. Moreover, since he was a very busy minister of state, and because he did not command all the foreign languages involved, the basic compilation of raw data was frequently delegated to others. Bolad, naturally, made the preliminary reconnaissance in the Mongolian sources and then provided Rashīd with Persian renderings or summaries. And if we are to believe a later tradition, preserved in Abū'l Ghāzī, a seventeenth-century historian, Bolad's own busy schedule was such that he, too, needed assistants: "five or six persons who knew the Old Mongolian language" to help run down data for the project.[12]

Thus, this vast historiographical enterprise was undertaken and executed by Rashīd al-Dīn with the aid of a hierarchy of research assistants and committees who provided access to the literary traditions of the principal cultures and civilizations of Eurasia, from China to Latin Europe. This method of compilation also explains why in the years after Rashīd al-Dīn's death, one former committee member, Qāshānī, advanced a very unconvincing claim that he was the real author of the *Collected Chronicles* and that the deceased minister falsely took credit and reaped the financial rewards for another's work.[13]

According to Rashīd al-Dīn's testimony, it was Ghazan who initiated and patronized this remarkable enterprise; fearful that the Mongols in Iran were forgetting their glorious past, he commissioned Rashīd to provide a detailed summary of the rise and expansion of the Mongolian Empire. This, the core of the *Collected Chronicles*, is organized into four long sections: the first treats the Mongolian and Turkic tribes; the second, the life and times of Chinggis Qan; the third, his successors from Ögödei to Temür Qaghan; and the last, the Hülegüids in Iran. These volumes, particularly the first three, together with the separately produced *History of China*, contain a vast amount of data on East Asia and constitute a quantum leap in Muslim knowledge of the region. They also reveal very clearly the character and extent of Rashīd al-Dīn's intellectual partnership with, and indebtedness to, Bolad.

In many ways the section on the tribes is the most remarkable in the *Collected Chronicles*. It covers all of the nomadic peoples of Inner Asia from the Oyirad in southern Siberia to the Qipchaqs in the western steppe. For most

[11] Rashīd/Jahn II, pp. 142 and 172.

[12] Aboul Ghāzī Bēhādour Khān, *Histoire des Mongols et des Tatares*, trans. by Petr I. Desmaisons, repr. (Amsterdam: Philo Press, 1970), p. 35. There is no contemporary confirmation of Bolad's research assistants, but Abū'l Ghāzī's data are quite plausible.

[13] Qāshānī/Hambly, pp. 54 and 240. For further comments see David O. Morgan, "Rashīd al-Dīn and Ghazan Khan," in Aigle, *Iran*, pp. 182–84.

entries, Rashīd al-Dīn begins with their geographical location, tribal origins and divisions, and their history to the time of Chinggis Qan. Usually he then provides some account of the circumstances leading to their incorporation into the Chinggisid state. In some cases this is quite brief and in others very detailed, especially in the treatment of major tribal groupings such as the Önggüd, Kereyid, and Naiman. To this basic data are sometimes added comments on the peculiarities of individual tribes' lifestyles and beliefs.

Following the general characterization of each tribe there is a history of its most famous personages. Often these lists are long and provide considerable detail on these individuals, their families, offices, and major events in their lives. Those covered include major figures such as Muqali and Sübedei, as well as lesser persons serving Chinggisid princes. The majority of those discussed served in China or Iran, but occasionally persons serving in the Golden Horde and Chaghadai Qanate are also included.

Some of Rashīd's data on the tribes come, by his own testimony, from written sources in Mongolian and kept "in the treasury of the Qans."[14] Much of his information, however, derives from the oral tradition, as one would expect in a tribal society with restricted literacy. The collection of oral traditions focused on tribesmen serving in Iran, particularly those who were famous or celebrated.[15] When local sources were inadequate, he or his assistant queried travelers and envoys, and the "learned men" of tribes such as the Qipchaqs. In this latter case the informant was probably a certain Qūmūrbīsh, "from the ruling line of the Qipchaqs," who was sent on an embassy to Ghazan.[16] In similar fashion, Rashīd knew of certain Jalayir officials serving in China because one of their relatives came on a mission to Iran.[17]

Much of the information on the cultural life of the tribes came, however, from Bolad, the acknowledged expert on Mongolian tradition. The range and nature of this data is as valuable as it is unexpected: discussions of dialectical differences between the Mongolian languages, comparisons of customs between different tribal groupings, the peculiarities of the climatic conditions and religious observances in the territory of the Uriyangqadai, a forest tribe, and the special titulature of household officials among the Naiman.[18]

Bolad is surely responsible, too, for the detailed information on Qubilai's wetnurse, wives, and concubines, their names, offspring, families, tribal affiliations, and titles. In speaking of Chabui, Qubilai's favorite wife, Rashīd al-Dīn says that her title "in the Chinese language was *qūnqū*, meaning senior wife [*khatun-i buzurg*]," an accurate transcription and rendering of *huang-hou*, "empress."[19]

In most cases, of course, Rashīd does not indicate his precise source of

[14] Rashīd/Alizade, vol. I, pt. 1, p. 480, and Rashīd/Karīmī, vol. I, pp. 173 and 178. See further, Shimo Satoko, "Three Manuscripts of the Mongol History of *Jāmiʿ al-tavārīkh*, with Special Reference to the History of the Tribes," *Etudes Mongoles et Sibériennes* 27 (1996), 225–28.

[15] Rashīd/Alizade, vol. I, pt. 1, pp. 192–93. [16] *Ibid.*, pp. 66 and 351–52.

[17] *Ibid.*, p. 145. [18] *Ibid.*, pp. 222, 293, 374–75, and 461–62. [19] *Ibid.*, pp. 300, 400, and 519.

information, but with the help of other sources we can often pinpoint Bolad's contribution. For example, in his discussion of the Arulad tribe, Rashīd notes that many of the sons of Boraldai, a high-ranking military commander, were serving Qubilai, and then adds that "of this number, one, Ūz Tīmūr [Öz Temür] the *ba'urchi*, was a great amīr and was specially favored and is famous and celebrated."[20] This Ūz Tīmūr is the same person as the Yü-hsi T'ieh-mu-erh with whom Bolad served in China. Both were *ba'urchis* and at one point during the 1270s both were chief censors. Rashīd's brief characterization of Öz Temür's career is quite accurate. Particularly interesting is the reference to the favor (*inaq*) bestowed upon him. This, clearly, is an allusion to an incident recorded in his much fuller biography in the *Yuan shih*:

> In Shih Tsu's [Qubilai's] time, Yü-hsi T'ieh-mu-erh, because he had been [unjustly] dishonored, experienced favor receiving the style *Yü-lü-lu na-yen*, which is similar to the Chinese expression "able official."[21]

Obviously, Rashīd's information on Öz Temür's position at the Yuan court derived from Bolad's personal experience and firsthand knowledge.

The result of their collaboration is truly a unique work systematically treating the history, geographical distribution, ethnogenesis, and folklore of all the principal nomadic peoples of Inner Asia. No study of similar scope and content precedes it, except for Herodotus' account of the Scythians of the western steppe, and nothing similar follows it until the nineteenth century when Russian geographers and ethnographers began to compile accounts of the nomadic subjects of the empire. As a source of information on medieval steppe history this work is unparalleled, a veritable gold mine that is still largely untapped. To take but one example, the native legends and mythology about tribal origins recorded here provide important ideological information and in some cases contain, like many oral traditions, a core of historical data as well. Rashīd al-Dīn's account of the Jalayir is a case in point. As Zuev has shown, their tribal history, migrations, and divisions, though typically conflated and distorted in the indigenous oral tradition, can in fact be connected to real historical events reported in Chinese and other sources.[22] The ethnogenetic myth of the Onggirad, the consort clan of the Chinggisids, also contains valuable information on the cosmological beliefs, political culture, and mythology of the steppe peoples, some of which can be traced back to the Scythian era.[23]

If the section on the tribes relied, in the main, on oral tradition, the account

[20] *Ibid.*, p. 430.

[21] *YS*, ch. 119, p. 2947. The transcription *Yü-lü-lu* is Turkic *ürlüg*, "constant," "everlasting," and *na-yen*, the Mongolian *noyan*, "commander."

[22] Iu. A. Zuev, "*Dzhāmiʿ al-tavārīkh* Rashīd al-Dīna kak istochnik po rannei istorii Dzhalairov," *Pis'mennye pamiatniki vostoka, 1969* (Moscow: Nauka, 1972), pp. 178–85.

[23] Rashīd/Alizade, vol. I, pt. 1, pp. 389–90, and Thomas T. Allsen, *Commodity and Exchange in the Mongol Empire: A Cultural History of Islamic Textiles* (Cambridge University Press, 1997), pp. 69–70.

of Chinggis Qan's life that follows is largely dependent on literary sources in Mongolian, both documents and narratives, now unfortunately lost. Here again, there can be no doubt that Bolad was the major, if not the exclusive, contributor of data.

The Mongolian materials made available to Rashīd al-Dīn are described by him on several occasions, and most fully in the following passage:

> In earlier days several notables of the age and learned men of the time produced fragments on the circumstances of the world-conquest, fortress-taking and dominion of Chinggis Qan and his descendants [but] they were contrary to the facts and to the beliefs of the Mongolian princes and commanders. In consequence, [there is] incomplete knowledge concerning the facts and circumstances of this polity [*dawlat*] and little information on the great and worthy deeds [associated with] these events. Nevertheless, reign by reign [they wrote] an authentic chronicle about them in the Mongolian idiom and letters; it was neither unified nor ordered and they kept [all] the separate fragments in the treasury. It was hidden and concealed from outsiders and worthies and no one who might have understood and penetrated them was given the opportunity or authority [to do so].[24]

Collectively, these materials were called, at least at the western end of the empire, the *Altan Debter* or "Golden Register," which, Rashīd al-Dīn adds, was always "in the keeping of the Great Amīrs."[25] This work, or, more accurately, archive, bore this title because gold was the imperial color and everything associated with the Chinggisid line was characterized as "golden."[26] There is, for example, another, and completely unrelated, work that circulated somewhat later in China and Mongolia also called the *Altan Debter*, which was a compendium of ritual texts for the Chinggis Qan cult.[27]

It is quite evident that the Mongolian elite considered these materials, at least in the Mongolian versions, sacrosanct, possessing great spiritual force since they were associated with the founding father. Rashīd al-Dīn relates that there is "much that is secret and there are narratives of the Mongols which [Ghazan] alone knows and they have not been recorded in this history."[28] Naturally, access to them was strictly controlled; they were secured in the treasury and entrusted only to the "intimates" of his Majesty Ghazan.[29] Clearly, as a great amīr and recognized authority, Bolad was one of those with such access and it was he (and his research team) who provided Rashīd al-Dīn with Persian translations and extracts from the Mongolian originals. It is also possible that Bolad and his associates passed on such data to others such as Het'um, a prince of Lesser Armenia and an intimate of Ghazan, who wrote an account of the Mongols in the early fourteenth century which he claims recounts "everything just as the histories of the Tartars say."[30]

[24] Rashīd/Alizade, vol. I, pt. 1, pp. 63–64. [25] *Ibid.*, p. 479.

[26] *Ibid.*, p. 390, and Henry Serruys, "Mongol *Altan* 'Gold' = Imperial," *MS* 21 (1962), 357–78, especially 375.

[27] Klaus Sagaster, trans., *Die Weisse Geschichte* (Wiesbaden: Otto Harrassowitz, 1976), pp. 192, 200, 222, and 365. [28] Rashīd/Jahn II, p. 171. [29] Rashīd/Alizade, vol. I, pt. 1, p. 65.

[30] Hayton, *La flor des estoires*, p. 213.

As regards their physical appearance, Rashīd al-Dīn speaks in one passage of what was written in "the books [*kutub*] and scrolls [*tavāmīr*] of the Mongolian histories."[31] From this we can conclude that we are dealing with a large array of materials of different origins, some of which, the scrolls, were in all likelihood produced in China or under Chinese influence. The diversity of the format is well reflected in the contents. As Rashīd al-Dīn makes abundantly clear, the *Altan Debter* should not be thought of as a connected or finished narrative. Rather these were different chronicles (*tavārīkh*) and registers (*dafātir*), usually incomplete, prepared by different hands. Moreover, even the character of individual narratives changes over time: chronology absent in the beginning is added for later years.[32] Thus, Rashīd al-Dīn had to deduce the "dates" of Alan Gho'a and Dobun Bayan (Mergen), the mythical ancestors of the Mongols, "from the tenor of the section of their chronicle . . . and [from] the statements of experienced and worldly elders."[33]

In addition to these diverse, contradictory, and fragmentary narratives, there were also original documents preserved in whole or in summary. At one point, Rashīd al-Dīn, trying to establish the names and the number of the sons of Jochi Qasar, Chinggis Qan's brother, compares data found "in the narratives and chronicles" with an imperial decree (*jarligh*).[34]

Diplomatic correspondence is also in evidence. One such document is the Uighurs' request for submission in 1209, versions of which have been preserved in Rashīd al-Dīn, the Chinese chronicle entitled *The Record of the Personal Campaigns of the Holy Warrior*, and in the *Secret History*. A comparison of these texts tells us something of the contents of the *Altan Debter* and the international character of historiography in the Mongolian Empire.

To set the scene, by 1209 the Uighurs had become restive under Qara Qitai authority and, realizing the power of the Mongols was growing, their ruler dispatched a message to Chinggis Qan. In Rashīd al-Dīn, the missive reads:

> I was intending to send envoys and make a full and detailed report [to you] about the circumstances of the Gür Qan and all else I know, and with a pure heart serve you. In the midst of these reflections, [just] before the envoys of Chinggis Qan arrived, I felt as if
>
> > "the heavens had become clear of clouds, and bright sun appeared from behind them, and the ice which congeals upon the river was broken, and the clear, pure water was revealed."
>
> In heart and bowels I greatly rejoiced. Hereafter I place before [you] the whole Uighur land and become the servant and son of Chinggis Qan.[35]

Next, the Chinese version:

> [I] was just about to send an envoy communicating [my] sincere intention to personally offer [my] submission. How is it, considering the distance, [you] condescended to cause [your] heavenly envoys to descend on [our] dependent state? It was as if

[31] Rashīd/Karīmī, vol. I, p. 416. [32] *Ibid.*, p. 229. [33] *Ibid.*, p. 166. [34] *Ibid.*, p. 204.
[35] *Ibid.*, pp. 309–10.

the clouds opened
to reveal the sun, and
the ice melted
to produce water

[My] joy was unequalled. Henceforth [I] will endeavor to lead [my] people as [your] servant and son.[36]

Lastly, the slightly fuller Mongolian version in Cleaves' translation:

The *idu'ud* [ruler] of the Ui'ud sent ambassadors unto Chinggis Qan. When he came, petitioning by the two ambassadors, Adkiragh and Darbai, he came, saying,

[Even] as having seen Mother sun
When the clouds became clear;
[Even] as having found the water of the river,
When the ice becometh clear,

I greatly rejoiced, when I heard the name and fame of Chinggis Qan. If [thou], Chinggis Qan favor [me], If I get [were it but one]

From the rings of [thy] golden girdle; [were it but one]
From the shreds of [thy] crimson garment

I will become thy fifth son and give [my] might [unto thee].[37]

These and other parallel passages in the three sources have led to the erroneous conclusion that Rashīd al-Dīn had direct access to a version of the *Secret History*.[38] The *Secret History*, however, is quite a distinct work, whose textual history and dating is still much debated.[39] While a problematical text, it is certainly not to be equated with the *Altan Debter*; rather the *Altan Debter* contained raw materials that were common to three historiographical traditions. In the case of the Uighurs' submission, the underlying document obviously goes back to an Uighur or Mongolian original carefully preserved by the Chinggisid court. Thus, the *Altan Debter*, with its diverse contents, is perhaps best described as a collection of materials toward a history of the early Mongols, the generation of which, as we will see later, was initiated in China by Chinese scholars for their own cultural purposes.

The third volume on Chinggisid history, detailing the founder's successors, contains discussions of Chinese themes and for the most part this is based on contemporary eyewitness accounts of individuals serving at Qubilai's court. Not surprisingly, Bolad is a major source of information, a fact that Rashīd

[36] *Sheng-wu ch'in-cheng lu*, in Wang Kuo-wei, *Meng-ku shih-liao ssu-chung* (Taipei: Cheng-chung shu-chü, 1975), p. 152. [37] *SH*/Cleaves, sect. 238, p. 172.

[38] Chirine Bayani, "L'histoire secrète des Mongols – une des sources de *Jāme-al-tawārīkh* de Rachīd ad-Dīn," *Acta Orientalia* (Copenhagen) 37 (1976), 201–12.

[39] Igor de Rachewiltz, "The Dating of the *Secret History of the Mongols*," *MS* 24 (1965), 185–206, and Hidehiro Okada, "The Chinggis Khan Shrine and the *Secret History of the Mongols*," in Klaus Sagaster, ed., *Religious and Lay Symbolism in the Altaic World and Other Papers* (Wiesbaden: Otto Harrassowitz, 1989), pp. 284–92.

al-Dīn readily acknowledges in general terms.[40] Bolad's interrogation of high Sung officials and participation in court debates on military policy explain why Rashīd al-Dīn is so well informed on the details of the fall of the Sung dynasty. For example, the Kiyāī Dāū[41] he mentions as the Sung general who directed the relief of Ūchū, Chinese O-chou, the modern Wu-ch'ang on the Yangtze, is certainly the infamous Chia Ssu-tao, "the bad last minister," traditionally blamed for the fall of the southern Sung.[42]

This is not to say that everything related by Bolad is accurate or trustworthy. Clearly this text must be read critically for bias, faulty memory, and confusion in transmission. Bolad, it will be recalled, was a major investigator of Aḥmad, and Rashīd al-Dīn has him conducting these inquiries in conjunction with Hantum (An-t'ung) noyan; this, however, is clearly impossible since in 1282, the date of these events, Hantum was being held captive in the Golden Horde.[43] Despite such lapses, Rashīd al-Dīn's depiction of Qubilai's China provides us with a much needed Mongolian perspective on events, and even the obvious biases and the suppression of inconvenient facts tell us something useful about the ideology and politics of the early Yuan court. In any event, together Rashīd al-Dīn and Bolad provided readers in Iran with an unprecedented picture of contemporary Chinese life and government, and in another work provided their readers with an extended account of Chinese culture and history.

The history of China, commissioned when Öljeitü extended Rashīd al-Dīn's original brief to include the known world, is also a composite work to which a number of people contributed. The introduction was prepared with the help of Bolad, who provided his friend with general information on the population, cities, and communications of China, as well as specifics on certain aspects of Chinese culture such as printing, a topic which will be taken up in a separate chapter.[44]

The second part of this work is of a completely different character and was produced with the help of a different set of assistants. This comprises, in Rashīd al-Dīn's own words:

> The history and stories of the emperors of North and South China, starting with early times, in the manner it appears in their [own] books – divided year by year and ruler by ruler – this we have made a supplement to the *Fortunate History of Ghazan* [i.e., the *Collected Chronicles*].[45]

[40] Rashīd/Karīmī, vol. I, p. 638, and Rashīd/Boyle, p. 273.

[41] Probably Kiyāī should be read Kiyās.

[42] Rashīd/Karīmī, vol. I, p. 604; Rashīd/Boyle, p. 229 and note 135; and Herbert Franke, "Chia Ssu-tao (1213–75): A 'Bad Last Minister'?" in Arthur F. Wright and Denis Twitchett, eds., *Confucian Personalities* (Stanford University Press, 1962), pp. 224–27.

[43] Igor de Rachewiltz, "An-t'ung," in de Rachewiltz *et al.*, *In the Service of the Khan*, p. 10.

[44] Rashīd al-Dīn, *Die Chinageschichte des Rašīd al-Dīn*, trans. and ed. by Karl Jahn (Vienna: Herman Böhlaus, 1971), folio 391v, *tafel* 1, Persian text, and pp. 19–20, German translation.

[45] Rashīd/Karīmī, vol. I, p. 235.

There is no useful information on Chinese history here, since it is a bare-bones outline of dynasties and rulers interspersed with fanciful tales, but it is an invaluable cultural document because for the first time Muslims acquired a direct knowledge of Chinese historiography.[46]

In carrying out this project Rashīd al-Dīn records that he enjoyed the assistance of two Chinese collaborators, named Lītājī (Li Ta-chih?) and K.msūn (Ch'in/Ch'ien Sun/Sung?), who provided him with data from a Chinese chronicle compiled by three authors. Their given names, Fūhīn (Fu Hsin/Hsien?), Fīkhū (Fei Ho?), and Shīkhūn (Shih Huan?), can only be tentatively restored, but all three have the title *Hūshāng*, which Rashīd al-Dīn says is *bakhshi*, a good rendering of the Chinese *ho-shang*, "Buddhist monk."[47] From this information, Herbert Franke rightly concludes the Chinese original underlying Rashīd's *History of China* must be sought in the Buddhist tradition. And, indeed, his account has much in common with the *Fo-tsu li-tai t'ung-tsai* of the Buddhist scholar Nien-ch'ang. Since, however, Nien-ch'ang's work was only completed in the 1340s, Rashīd's history cannot rest directly on this particular chronicle but, as Franke points out, upon its sources, which have yet to be traced.[48] In any event, the Chinese section of Rashīd al-Dīn's world history is anchored, like the rest, in native sources.

Another supplement to the *Collected Chronicles*, and the last in which Bolad had a direct hand, was the "Shuʿab-i panjgānah," or "The Five Genealogies," which covers the Franks, Jews, Arabs/Muslims, Chinese, and Mongols. The latter section contains extensive genealogical tables of all the descendants of Chinggis Qan down to the fourteenth century. In most cases their names are given in both the Arabic and Mongolian/Uighur script. Additionally, for the more important Chinggisid princes such as Qubilai, there are long lists of their wives and ministers which include data on their titles, family, and ethnic background. This work, known in a single unpublished manuscript, forms the basis of the more famous Temürid genealogy, the *Muʿizz al-ansāb*, which updates the Mongolian section but drops those on the Franks, Jews, etc.[49]

Although little used, the "Shuʿab-i panjgānah" is in fact quite valuable, containing information not found elsewhere. The discrepancies between the genealogies produced during the Mongolian era and those of the Temürid period reveal much about the importance of these "political charters" in tribal soci-

[46] For another appreciation of this text, historical and philological, see Karl H. Menges, "Rašidu'd-Dīn on China," *JAOS* 95 (1975), 95–98.

[47] Rashīd al-Dīn, *Chinageschichte*, folio 393r, *tafel* 4, Persian text, and pp. 23–24, German translation.

[48] Herbert Franke, "Some Sinological Remarks on Rašīd al-Dīn's History of China," *Oriens* 4 (1951), 21–24.

[49] Zeki Velidi Togan, "The Composition of the History of the Mongols by Rashīd al-Dīn," *CAJ* 7 (1962), 68–71. The original of the "Shuʿab-i panjgānah" is in the Topkapi Sarayi Museum, cat. no. 2932.

eties.[50] In the introduction to this work, Rashīd al-Dīn says that the genealogical material on the Chinggisids conforms to the Mongolian book (*Kitab-i mugūl*).[51] This he surely checked with the living descendants of the earlier generation and with his expert on such matters, Bolad.

Taken together, the extensive information on East Asia in the *Collected Chronicles* is accurate, and its coverage, while certainly focused on China, extends to many neighboring lands as well: Tibet, Uighuristan, Southeast Asia, Japan, Korea, Siberia, and Manchuria. All in all, this was the most complete and engaging picture Muslims had of the eastern end of Eurasia in medieval times. And through the work of Banākatī, a fourteenth-century historian who epitomized Rashīd al-Dīn's histories, this account of China was reproduced in various forms down to the seventeenth century.[52]

While much historical information flowed west in the Mongolian era, to what extent was the reverse also true? Did the Chinese gain an equivalent body of literature on Islam and West Asia? In answering this question it must be remembered that while the *Collected Chronicles* were written for a sitting monarch, Ghazan, the *Yuan shih* was not. In the tradition of Chinese historiography it was based on records kept during the Yuan but was compiled and ideologically edited by scholars of the Chinese Ming dynasty (1368–1644). This is why the Persian history shows such great interest in all parts of the empire while the Yuan dynastic history has a very parochial outlook. For example, the *Yuan shih* contains a lengthy section on the Liu-ch'iu Islands and virtually ignores the Golden Horde. Certainly in the minds of the Yuan rulers the Jochids were more important than the Liu-ch'ius but to the Ming authors of the *Yuan shih* this was not the case. Consequently, there was no Chinese Rashīd al-Dīn nor anything similar to the *Collected Chronicles* produced at the eastern end of the empire. There was, however, new information that circulated in Yuan China and at least one new work devoted to the Western Regions.

Before the Yuan, Chinese knowledge of Iran, Mesopotamia, and the eastern Mediterranean was scattered through the dynastic histories, travel accounts, and literary collections. There were no systematic regional histories of these areas before the Mongols.[53] The first to write one was the Yuan scholar Shan-ssu, Shams [al-Dīn], 1278–1351, whose ancestors came from Arabia (Ta-shih). Following the Mongolian invasion of West Asia his grandfather Lu-k'un,

[50] See the study of Sholeh A. Quinn, "The *Muʿizz al-ansāb* and the 'Shuʿab-i panjgānah' as Sources for the Chaghatayid Period of History: A Comparative Analysis," *CAJ* 33 (1989), 229–53. [51] "Shuʿab-i panjgānah," folio 4r.

[52] Banākatī, *Tārīkh-i Banākatī*, ed. by Jaʿfar Shiʿār (Tehran: Chāpkhānah-i Bahram, 1969), pp. 337–59, and Karl Jahn, "China in der islamischen Geschichtsschreibung," *Anzeiger der phil.-hist. Klasse der österreichischen Akademie der Wissenschaften* 108 (1971), 63–73.

[53] For a summary of Chinese knowledge of the Western Regions from the Han through the T'ang, see Wolfram Eberhard, "Die Kultur der alten Zentral- und West-asiatischen Völker nach chinesischen Quellen," *Zeitschrift für Ethnologie* 73 (1941), 231–32, 240–42, and 261–63.

Rukn [al-Dīn], moved to China. In the reign of Ögödei he was placed in charge of tax collection in several circuits (*lu*) of North China and settled in Chen-ting in Hopei. His father, Wo-chih, pursued Confucian learning and Shan-ssu followed suit at the age of nine; he made rapid progress and his scholarly fame soon reached the court. In 1330 he received his first official appointment. Thereafter he held a variety of posts, the duties of which he discharged with diligence. According to his biography in the *Yuan shih*, his learning embraced the Chinese classics as well as "astronomy, geography, music, mathematics, water control, and even some foreign literature." But, in addition to these pursuits, his biography indicates a profound interest in history. His works in this field, now unfortunately all lost, included *Chin Ai-tsung chi*, "Records of the Reign of Ai-tsung of the Chin" and the *Cheng-ta Chu ch'en lieh-chuan*, "Biographies of Eminent Officials of the Cheng-ta Era" (1224–31). And most important from our perspective is his *Hsi-yü i-jen chuan*, "Biographies of Extraordinary People of the Western Regions."[54]

Shan-ssu's *Biographies*, so far as I know, is the only Chinese work of the Yuan devoted to the history of West Asia. In the absence of the work, last mentioned in a seventeenth-century catalog, one can only note that this genre of historical literature has deep roots in the Chinese, Arabic, and Greco-Roman traditions. In China it can be traced back to the second century BC, and in Islamic and most particularly Arab society to the ninth century AD. In both cases, once the genre was established, tens of thousands of biographies were produced and collected. There are, to be sure, differences of method, selection, and presentation, but the motives were quite similar: to provide examples, and counterexamples, upon which later generations might mold their behavior.[55] Shan-ssu, as a sinicized Arab, could have drawn on either tradition as his model or synthesized elements of both without undue difficulty. Obviously, which individuals he selected for inclusion, the sources of his information, and the historical data his works may contain are questions that cannot at present be answered, but there can be little doubt that his *Biographies of Extraordinary People of the Western Regions* will constitute, if ever found, an extraordinary cultural document in its own right.

On the whole, then, historical data generally flowed west. It remains to investigate the reasons for this, some of which are obvious and some of which are linked to less visible cultural currents.

We can begin by examining a particular episode that Rashīd al-Dīn recorded in detail: the death of the last Chin emperor in 1234. In discussing this event, he quotes several versions and notes their discrepancies. In one, the

[54] *YS*, ch. 195, pp. 4351–53, and Ch'en Yuan, *Western and Central Asians in China under the Yuan*, trans. by Ch'ien Hsing-hai and L. Carrington Goodrich (Los Angeles: Monumenta Serica and the University of California, 1966), pp. 60–62 and 174–76.

[55] For a general orientation to these two traditions, see Denis Twitchett, "Chinese Biographical Writing," in W. G. Beasley and E. G. Pulleyblank, eds., *Historians of China and Japan* (London: Oxford University Press, 1961), pp. 95–114, and R. Stephen Humphreys, *Islamic History: A Framework for Inquiry* (Minneapolis: Bibliotheca Islamica, 1988), pp. 173–75.

Āltān Khān (Ai-tsung) disguises himself and escapes into hiding. In another, taken, Rashīd al-Dīn says, from the *Ta'rīkh-i Khitāi*, the emperor is burnt to death in a great conflagration attending the Mongolian assault on Ts'ai-chou, the last Chin capital. These accounts, in his view, are wrong; in actuality, Rashīd al-Dīn asserts, the Āltān Khān abdicated, placed his *qorchi* (quiver-bearer) on the throne, and then hanged himself on the eve of the Mongolian seizure of the city. Because of the ensuing chaos and the conflicting rumors of his fate, his burned body could not be found.[56] And, indeed, Rashīd al-Dīn's conclusions accord in all essentials with the known facts: Ai-tsung made his chief military adviser, Wang-yen ch'eng-lin, his successor and then committed suicide by hanging.[57] Further, it is quite true that his body was never found.

How is it that Rashīd al-Dīn selected the correct version of events? The answer, not too surprisingly, is Bolad, with his manifold experiences and extensive personal connections in China. In the first place, Bolad and Wang O (1190–1273), the principal recorder of the last days of the Chin dynasty, were both intimate servitors of Qubilai. Wang's personal memoir on the fall of the Chin, the *Ju-nan i-shih*, in fact served as the major source of the basic annals (*pen-chi*) of the Chin dynastic history prepared during the Yuan. Coincidentally, it was the Arab historiographer Shan-ssu who recast and expanded this memoir in the preparation of the Chin dynastic history.[58]

And even if Bolad and Wang O never met, which seems unlikely since they served at the same court for over a decade, the expert on Mongolian history had other sources of such information. Here it will be recalled that Bolad was instrumental in the founding and development of the *Mi-shu chien*, the Imperial Library Directorate which was in charge, among other things, of the "records of successive generations," that is, it was a historical archive of great importance.[59] Bolad, who of course had access to this depository (which Rashīd al-Dīn knew under the name *Dafātīr-i dīvān*, "Archives of Court"), was therefore already involved in the production and preservation of Chinese and Mongolian historical materials long before his arrival in Iran. Thus, it should occasion no surprise when Rashīd al-Dīn and Chinese records reflect the same data.

Bolad's ties to Chinese historiography do not end here, however. There can be little doubt that he was aware of the efforts to prepare a new set of dynastic histories initiated in the mid-thirteenth century by Qubilai's Chinese advisers. The major figure behind this initiative was the aforementioned Wang O, who had been reared and educated under the Chin. With great tenacity he continually encouraged Qubilai to authorize and sponsor an official history of "his" dynasty. In 1266, with imperial approval, Wang organized a court

[56] Rashīd/Karīmī, vol. I, p. 461, and Rashīd/Boyle, pp. 40–41.

[57] *Chin shih* (Peking: Chung-hua shu-chü, 1975), ch. 18, pp. 402–3.

[58] Hok-lam Chan, "Prolegomena to the *Ju-nan i-shih*: A Memoir on the Last Chin Court under the Mongol Siege of 1234," *Sung Studies Newsletter* 10, supplement 1 (1974), 2–19, especially 13.

[59] *YS*, ch. 90, p. 2296.

discussion on historiographic matters.[60] In pressing his case for a Chin history he adroitly and wisely always connected this enterprise with the preservation and compilation of sources relevant to early Mongolian history. He rightly argued that the historical sources needed for the Chin and Liao would cast additional light on the rise of the Mongols and the glorious deeds of Chinggis Qan. At the same time he urged that the earliest records in Mongolian be sought out and preserved as raw material for the Mongols' own dynastic history.[61]

Eventually, the Mongolian court accepted these recommendations and in the fourteenth century produced official dynastic histories for all of their immediate predecessors, the Liao (907–1125), Chin (1115–1234), and Sung (960–1279).[62] As a start on the immense enterprise, individuals were selected for the preliminary collection of data in Chinese and Mongolian.

While there is no direct evidence that Bolad participated in this project, he knew several of the principals. He was, for example, a close associate of Liu Ping-chung, who regularly supported Wang O's recommendation for a Chin history. Further, Hsu Shih-lung, an academician in the Han-lin Academy who helped collect Chinese data on the Chin, was also an acquaintance with whom Bolad worked in 1270 on court ceremony. Given Bolad's relationship to these individuals and his own interest in history, it is not hard to imagine that he knew of their activities.

Of equal importance, there is evidence that he knew the individual charged with collecting old Mongolian records, a certain Sa-li-man. To properly assess this possibility, we must first sketch in his career (he has no official biography) from scattered references in the Chinese sources. Judging from his name, also transcribed as Sa-erh-man (Sarman or Sarban), he was a Mongol.[63] He is first mentioned in 1270 at an informal court discussion on "sharing thoughts and influencing people," in which he contributed an appropriate maxim of Chinggis Qan on the subject.[64] When he next appears in 1281 he is a Han-lin academician and Recipient of Edicts, and a joint director of the Hostel for Foreign Envoys (*Hui-t'ung kuan*). Later on, in 1284 and 1291 he was assigned posts in the Court of Imperial Sacrifice.[65]

Most importantly from our perspective, Sa-li-man was assigned the task of assembling and editing the surviving Mongolian records on the qaghans before Qubilai. Starting in 1287 he received imperial approval "to compile the successive court records of T'ai-tzu [Chinggis Qan] . . . in the Uighur [Wei-wu] script."[66] His labors, carried out in conjunction with another Mongol named

60 *YS*, ch. 5, p. 86.

61 Chan, "Wang O's Contribution to the History of the Chin Dynasty," in Chan Ping-leung, ed., *Essays in Commemoration of the Golden Jubilee of the Fung Ping Shan Library, 1932–1982* (Hong Kong University Press, 1982), pp. 355–56 note 34, and 366–67.

62 Chan, "Chinese Official Historiography at the Yuan Court: The Composition of the Liao, Chin, and Sung Histories," in John D. Langlois, ed., *China under Mongol Rule* (Princeton University Press, 1981), pp. 56–106.

63 *MSC*, ch. 1, p. 11b (p. 44).

64 *YS*, ch. 115, p. 2888.

65 *YS*, ch. 11, p. 235, ch. 13, p. 264, and ch. 16, p. 353.

66 *YS*, ch. 14, p. 294.

Wu-lu-tai (Urughdai), resulted in a Mongolian-language veritable record which at first circulated in manuscript. By 1290 the records of the reigns of Güyüg and Ögödei were ready and in 1303 the Han-lin and National History Academy (*Han-lin kuo-shih yuan*) translated and revised this material and presented it to Temür Qaghan under its Chinese title *Wu-ch'ao shih-lu*, "Veritable Records of the Five Reigns," a work which covers the era of Chinggis Qan, his nominal successor and regent, Tolui, and the reigns of Ögödei, Güyüg, and Möngke.[67]

Here, clearly, was the principal investigator for early Mongolian history at the Yuan court, the individual who not only collected and selected the raw material but drafted the veritable records as well. This effort initiated by Chinese scholars most certainly generated that diverse body of historical sources used later by Rashīd al-Dīn and known to him generically as the *Altan Debter*. Obviously, too, Bolad is again the most likely conduit.

The evidence that Bolad had contact with Sa-li-man is circumstantial but none the less persuasive. First, they shared common interests and traveled in the same circles. For example, in 1284 when Sa-li-man presided over sacrifices on the imperial estates, he did so under the auspices of the Court of Imperial Sacrifices. Bolad, to be sure, was on his way to Iran at this time, but he had helped to found this organization, headed it in the 1270s, and was made responsible for training its Mongolian personnel. Certainly it is not stretching the evidence to suggest that if Sa-li-man presided over a major sacrifice in 1284 he was not then a neophyte, and that his preparation for this task had been acquired while Bolad was still in China and actively involved in the Court of Imperial Sacrifices. Further, Sa-li-man had dealings with another of those organizations Bolad helped to establish, the Imperial Library Directorate, that depository of historical materials. In this case there is positive evidence that these contacts occurred both before and after Bolad went west.[68] Finally, there are data that connect Sa-li-man with ʿIsā *kelemechi*, Bolad's traveling companion. In March of 1283, just before his departure on the embassy, ʿIsā (Ai-hsieh) with Sa-li-man jointly participated in a court discussion on commercial policy. Characteristically, Sa-li-man's role in this debate was to supply appropriate precedent from Chinggis Qan's reign.[69] And Sa-li-man's association with trade makes it all the more likely that he is to be identified with Rashīd al-Dīn's Sārbān, whom the Persian historian says was involved, together with ʿIsā *kelemechi* and other amīrs, in some questionable dealings with foreign merchants.[70]

Granted that Bolad and therefore Rashīd al-Dīn had knowledge of these historiographical enterprises in China, what were the consequences? First, and most apparently, there is the matter of common sources. This, surely, was unprecedented; as already noted, the same Mongolian materials fed into the *Collected Chronicles*, the *Secret History*, and the Chinese chronicle, *The*

[67] *YS*, ch. 15, pp. 308–9, ch. 16, pp. 338 and 341–42, and ch. 21, p. 455.
[68] *MSC*, ch. 1, p. 11a (p. 41) and ch. 7, p. 13a (p. 207). [69] *YTC*, ch. 27, p. 1a.
[70] Rashīd/Karīmī, vol. I, p. 679, and Rashīd/Boyle, p. 330.

Record of the Personal Campaigns of the Holy Warrior. The latter, it is relevant to emphasize, supplied some of the data for the basic annals of the *Yuan shih*, a work hurriedly compiled and edited by a committee of eighteen Chinese scholars in the second year of the Ming dynasty.[71]

There is also the question of the organizational affinities of the various historiographical projects carried out in Iran and China at this time. In China the tradition of dynastic histories was initiated by individual scholars such as Ssu-ma Ch'ien and Pan Ku, but from T'ang times onward this task of compiling and writing such works was turned over to committees. This practice, as we have seen, continued into the Yuan, where "research and editorial boards" were formed to collect material on the early Mongols and to produce the three dynastic histories. Certain individuals always took the lead in this, Wang O and Sa-li-man, but it is also true that they never worked alone. Typically they had their research assistants, translators, etc. Indeed, the committees that finally produced the three dynastic histories in the fourteenth century had a very cosmopolitan flavor: they included Chinese, Mongols, Turks, Jürchens, and a few Muslims.[72] The same, of course, can be said of the preparation of the *Collected Chronicles*. It, too, was an "international" project prepared by a committee or series of sub-committees: a pair of Chinese, a team of Mongols, and a host of individual informants of the most diverse background, including the Persian contingent headed by the editor-in-chief and principal author, Rashīd al-Dīn.

The search for sources on the early Mongols simply required teamwork and a very wide net, with repeated plunges into what we would now call trans-national or cross-cultural historiography, and it did so at both ends of the empire: in 1307, and again a few years later, the Yuan court solicited and obtained older Korean records on the era of Chinggis Qan, while at about the same time Rashīd al-Dīn sought data in older Arabic sources, such as Ibn al-Athīr's famous chronicle, on the first appearance of the Mongols in the Far West.[73]

Such a collective, multiethnic approach to historiography, generated in part by the scale and formidable nature of the task at hand, was in all likelihood reinforced by the Mongols' own administrative style, which always favored shared/divided responsibility and a collegial system of decision making. This can be seen in the Yuan dynasty's studied duplication of offices, usually pairing native-born and foreign officials, and in the requirement that officials

[71] Pelliot and Hambis, *Histoire des campagnes de Gengis Khan*, pp. xiii–xv. On the preparation of the *YS*, see Francis W. Cleaves, "The Memorial for Presenting the *Yuan shih*," *Asia Major* 1 (1988), 59–69 and especially 66–67.

[72] Chan, "Wang O's Contribution," pp. 347 and 367–71, and Herbert Franke, "Chinese Historiography under Mongol Rule: The Role of History in Acculturation," *Mongolian Studies* 1 (1974), 17.

[73] Walter Fuchs, "Analecta zur mongolischen Uebersetzungsliteratur der Yuan-Zeit," *MS* 11 (1946), 57–58; Rashīd/Karīmī, vol. I, pp. 229 and 381–82; and Ibn al-Athīr, *Al-Kamīl fī al-ta'rīkh*, ed. by C. J. Thornberg, repr. (Beirut: Dar Sader, 1966), vol. XII, p. 385.

consult and then take action (and responsibility) in a collective manner.[74] While various influences are probably at work here, the Chinese precedent for collective historical research and writing is clear, and once again we can suspect Bolad, Rashīd's principal collaborator, as the channel of this subtle cultural current from East Asia.

Finally, the methods of historical compilation used in China seem to have had some influence in the eastern Islamic world during and after the Mongolian era.

In China, the production of official historical knowledge followed a set pattern. The "basic annals" (*pen-chi*) of the dynastic histories, which comprised a straight chronological account of court activities, were dependent upon "veritable records" (*shih-lu*) that were compiled at the end of each reign by the deceased emperor's successor. In their turn, the veritable records were derived from the "Diaries of Activity and Repose" (*Ch'i chü-chu*). These were kept by court diarists who took down the words and actions of the emperor and then turned these raw records over to the office of historiography for preservation and later editing.[75]

This system is in evidence in the early empire if only on an informal basis. We know, for example, that on two of the occasions when Chinggis Qan met the Taoist master Ch'ang Ch'un in 1222, at the end of the campaign in Turkestan, the emperor ordered, according to the eyewitness Li Chih-ch'ang, that their conversation be recorded (*chi, lu*).[76] By the time of the Yuan, these procedures had been regularized and formalized. According to Odoric of Pordenone, who visited the Mongolian court in China in the 1320s, "there be four scribes also, to take down all the words that the king may utter."[77] Unlike in Chinese courts, these diaries were of course composed in Mongolian and then turned into veritable records in the native tongue. The Chinese sources called these narratives *to-pi-ch'ih-yen*, Mongolian *tobchiyan*, "summary," "abridgement," and unmistakably equate them with their *shih-lu*.[78] These were then translated into Chinese in anticipation of their later use in the Yuan dynasty's history. One such translation, carried out around 1315, was undertaken by Chaghan, an official whose family home was Balkh in Afghanistan.[79] But even when rendered into Chinese, these records, considered the Mongols' "national history (*kuo shih*)," were secret, restricted in circulation, especially

[74] For an informative and well-documented discussion of this point, see Endicott-West, *Mongolian Rule in China*, pp. 44 ff.

[75] Charles S. Gardner, *Chinese Traditional Historiography* (Cambridge, Mass.: Harvard University Press, 1961), pp. 88–94.

[76] Li Chih-ch'ang, *Hsi-yü chi*, in Wang, *Meng-ku shih-liao*, pp. 342 and 356, and Li Chih-ch'ang, *The Travels of an Alchemist*, trans. by Arthur Waley (London: Routledge and Kegan Paul, 1963), pp. 102 and 113.

[77] Odoric of Pordenone, "The Eastern Parts of the World Described," in Yule, *Cathay*, vol. II, p. 224.

[78] Francis W. Cleaves, "The Sino-Mongolian Inscription of 1362 in Memory of Prince Hindu," *HJAS* 12 (1949), 67, Mongolian text, and 91, English translation; and *YS*, ch. 36, p. 803.

[79] *YS*, ch. 137, p. 3311.

those parts relating to Chinggis Qan, and sometimes denied to high-ranking Chinese officials as being "outsiders."[80] This, of course, fits nicely with Rashīd al-Dīn's statement, quoted above (p. 88), that the *Altan Debter* "was hidden and concealed from outsiders."

The preparation of these narratives from the raw court diaries must have been an ongoing process and a matter of some importance to the court because we know from the *Yuan shih* that both the Mongolian and Chinese versions of the *shih-lu* for Qubilai's reign were presented to Temür Qaghan in 1304, just ten years after the death of the Yuan founder. The presenter and, presumably, the compiler/editor was the Han-lin Academician and Recipient of Edicts, Sa-li-man.[81]

There are various indications that these methods of compilation were known in Iran and were even followed there to some extent. Rashīd al-Dīn, in his account of Qubilai's ministers, says that one of their number, Yighmish, an Uighur, "records the words of the qaghan as is their practice."[82] But not only did Rashīd know of the practice, he very likely had access to some of the Mongolian *tobchiyan* which Sa-li-man and associates produced for the Yuan court.[83] In one passage discussing his Mongolian sources, Rashīd makes reference to an *ʿahd ba-ʿahd taʾrīkh-i ṣaḥiḥ*, literally a "reign-by-reign authentic chronicle."[84] This terminology neatly and accurately describes and defines the *shih-lu* of the Chinese historiographic tradition. This conclusion is reinforced by the fact that the Chinese *shih* and the Arabo-Persian *ṣaḥiḥ* have a very similar range of meanings: "genuine," "real," "authentic," and "veritable." Thus, *taʾrīkh-i ṣaḥiḥ* is best understood as a calque translation of the Chinese original.

Although indirect, there is evidence that this technique was actually employed in Iran. Rashīd al-Dīn himself seems to have based his account of the Il-qans, particularly of the later reigns, on some kind of court diary. This procedure is even more apparent in another of the histories produced under the Hülegüids, Qāshānī's *History of Öljeitu*, which certainly has the flavor of Chinese official historiography. As in the basic annals and the veritable records, he presents events in a straight chronological order, year by year, month by month, and sometimes day by day, all of which points, as others have noticed, to the existence of a diary. In consequence, Öljeitü's movements throughout his reign can be reconstructed in detail, on a weekly if not a daily basis.[85]

80 Hsü Yu-jen, *Kuei-t'ang hsiao-kao* (Ying-yin wen-yuan ko-ssu k'u-ch'uan ed.), ch. 10, p. 9a; and *YS*, ch. 35, p. 789 and ch. 181, p. 4179. 81 *YS*, ch. 21, p. 457.

82 Rashīd/Karīmī, vol. I, pp. 643 and 657; Rashīd/Boyle, pp. 279 and 298; and "Shuʿab-i panjgānah," folio 131r.

83 In sinological scholarship there is an opinion that the *tobchiyan* might have come west with the embassy of 1304, and that once in Iran it became known as the *Altan Debter*. See William Hung, "The Transmission of the Book Known as the *Secret History of the Mongols*," *HJAS* 14 (1951) 469–81 and especially 470 and 474. 84 Rashīd/Alizade, vol. I, pt. 1, p. 64.

85 Qāshānī/Hambly, editor's "Introduction," p. vi; and Charles Melville, "The Itineraries of Sultan Öljeitü," *Iran* 28 (1990), 56–57 and appendix, 64–66.

There is evidence, too, that the method was adopted in the Chaghadai Qanate. Speaking of the 1230s, Rashīd al-Dīn relates that "it was the custom to write down daily every word the ruler spoke" and that "every one [of the princes] appointed one of their courtiers to write down their words." Chaghadai's scribe was a certain Vazīr/Hujīr, a Turk who came from China (Khitāi).[86] The practice, moreover, was continued and became a permanent feature at the Temürid court. According to Yazdī, Temür had "Uighur scholars [*bakhshiyān*] and Persian secretaries [*dabīrān*]" record his words and actions. These rough notes were first verified by Temür himself and then turned into more finished works, the very procedure Shāh Rukh's envoys later encountered at the Ming court in 1420.[87] The mediators in this instance seem to have been the ubiquitous Uighur scribes who played such an active role in Yuan and Temürid historiography.[88] This precedent was followed by the Temürids' political heirs, the Mughals of India. At the court of Akbar (r. 1556–1605) there was a *vāqiʿ-navīs*, "event-" or "news-writer." From a pool of fourteen, two were on duty at any given time, responsible for recording the words and deeds of the emperor. This resulted in a diary which the emperor himself corrected and from which a "summary" (*taʿliqah*) was made, that is, a *tobchiyan* or *shih-lu*. Although Abū'l-Faẓl concedes that "a trace of this office may have existed in ancient times," he none the less claims that "its higher objects were but recognized in the present reign."[89] Clearly, however, this was patterned after Temürid practice, which goes back, ultimately, to Chinese models.

To conclude, the linkages between the historiographical projects sponsored by the Yuan and Il-qan courts can be summarized as follows:

- They shared common sources and methods of compilation, both developed in China.
- They shared organizational peculiarities – the committee approach to official history so characteristic of the Chinese tradition.
- Rashīd al-Dīn's principal historical adviser, Bolad, was familiar with such traditions, had contacts with Yuan historiographers, e.g., Hsu Shih-lung and Sa-li-man, and was long associated with one of the major historical depositories of the Yuan, the Imperial Library Directorate, before coming west.

86 Rashīd/Karīmī, vol. I, p. 549, and Rashīd/Boyle, p. 155; and Juvaynī/Qazvīnī, vol. I, p. 227, and Juvaynī/Boyle, vol. I, p. 272.

87 Sharaf al-Dīn ʿAlī Yazdī, *Ẓafar-nāmah*, vol. I, ed. by M. ʿAbbāsī (Tehran: Chap-i rangin, 1957), pp. 18–19, and John E. Woods, "The Rise of Tīmūrid Historiography," *Journal of Near Eastern Studies* 46/2 (1987), 82. On the Ming practice, see Ḥafiẓ-i Abrū, *Persian Embassy*, pp. 56–57.

88 See also V. V. Bartol'd, "Otchet o komandirovke v Turkestan," in his *Sochineniia*, vol. VIII, p. 131 and note 25 for more on Uighur influence in Temürid historiography.

89 Abū'l Faẓl, *The ʿĀīn-i Akbarī*, trans. by H. Blochmann and H. S. Jarret, repr. (Delhi: Atlantic Publishers, 1979), vol. I, pp. 268–69. Cf. the comments of Pierre du Jarric, *Akbar and the Jesuits: An Account of Jesuit Missions to the Court of Akbar*, trans. by C. H. Payne (London: Routledge, 1926), p. 11, whose data come from contemporary Jesuit letters.

This is not to argue that their respective historiographical efforts were actively or consciously coordinated, but rather that they were convergent and connected, and arose out of similar cultural and political concerns. And, taken together, the production of the *Collected Chronicles* and the three Chinese dynastic histories under Mongolian patronage must be accounted as one of the great historiographical enterprises and achievements of the premodern age.

THIRTEEN

Geography and cartography

As indicated in the preceding chapter, there was a considerable body of geographical data incorporated into the *Collected Chronicles*. According to Rashīd al-Dīn, the historical narrative was to be "accompanied by maps [*ṣuvar*] of the climes, routes and countries." This work, he continues, "composed in two parts, will form an appendix to the aforementioned *Chronicle*."[1] Further on, he expands upon this, stating that his geographical treatise presents:

> maps of the climes, countries, routes and distances, researched and authenticated to the extent possible [on the bases] of that which previously had been known in this country [Iran] and described in books and [from] that which, in this fortunate age, the philosophers and learned men of India, South China, France, North China, etc., found in their books and subsequently verified. All of this, in substance and detail, has been affirmed in this, the Third Volume [devoted to geography].[2]

In the Arabic and Persian digests of Rashīd al-Dīn's literary output, his geographical compendium, entitled the *Ṣuvar al-āqālīm*, or "Configuration of Climes," is further described. According to these texts, this work constitutes volume four, not three, of the *Collected Chronicles*. Its contents include a discussion of the borders of the seven climes, that is, the world, the extent and position of the major countries and states, their principal cities, rivers, lakes, seas, valleys, and mountains, their longitude and latitude, the mileposts placed along the great roads, and an enumeration of the postal relay stations (*yām-hā*) established throughout Eurasia by order of the Mongolian rulers. All this, we are told, was derived from literary sources and eyewitness testimony. Finally, all these data were depicted on maps according to a system devised by the author.[3]

Most unfortunately, this geographical section has not come down to us. Indeed, some scholars, starting with Bartol'd, doubt that it was ever completed.

[1] Rashīd/Alizade, vol. I, pt. 1, pp. 16–17. [2] *Ibid.*, p. 39.

[3] Muginov, "Persidskaia unikal'naia rukopis," pp. 373–74, and Rashīd/Quatremère, pp. LXXIII–LXXIV, French translation, and p. CLX, Arabic text.

Krawulsky, for example, argues that the *Ṣuvar al-āqālīm* was planned but not executed.[4] Others, Togan and Jahn, have, on the contrary, asserted that it was completed and subsequently lost.[5] The evidence, in my opinion, strongly favors the latter proposition. Most compelling is the fact that Rashīd al-Dīn's *Vaqf-nāmah* of 1310 mentions that among his "collected works [*jāmiʿ al-taṣānīf*]" are two volumes, the *Ṣuvar al-āqālīm* and the *Ṣuvar al-buldān*, the "Configuration of Countries," which require large-format paper for reproduction because they were "illustrated [*muṣauvar*]."[6] Clearly, some copies of this existed during his lifetime; many were perhaps lost in the disturbances that destroyed Rashīd al-Dīn's quarter in Tabrīz following his execution in 1318, but some seem to have survived until the Ṣafavid era. At least the noted historian Iskandar Munshī (ca. 1561–1634) makes mention of a *Ṣuvar-i āqālīm* as one of the "standard geographical works" of his day.[7]

Whatever the fate of the compendium, it is obvious that its disappearance is a major loss for modern scholarship. This is fully borne out by an examination of Rashīd al-Dīn's geographical knowledge of East Asia contained in his surviving works, information which is extensive, detailed, and surprisingly accurate.

We can begin with Rashīd al-Dīn's familiarity with the topography of the Mongolian homeland. He provides in his histories of Chinggis Qan and of the Turkic–Mongolian tribes a wealth of information on the mountains, rivers, and other natural features of the eastern steppe. Native toponyms are abundantly provided and, although sometimes deformed by copyists' errors, they are readily reconstructible and generally accurate. Indeed, a work written in northwest Iran can frequently clarify the historical geography of Mongolia as recorded in native sources, principally the *Secret History*.[8] This is the case, most certainly, because Rashīd al-Dīn effectively used both native literary sources and native informants for his data.

Though he offers fewer details, Rashīd al-Dīn had a fair understanding of the basic geography of the farthest East, Korea and Japan. Earlier generations of Muslim geographers called Korea al-Shīlah, from the native dynasty Silla,

[4] Dorthea Krawulsky, *Iran – Das Reich der Īlhāne: Eine topographische-historische Studie* (Wiesbaden: Ludwig Reichert, 1978), pp. 26 ff.

[5] Ahmet Zeki Validi [Togan], "Islam and the Science of Geography," *Islamic Culture* 8 (1934), pp. 514–15, 517, 522 note 17, and 525 note 29; Jahn, "The Still Missing Works of Rashīd al-Dīn," 119–20; and Karl Jahn, "Study of the Supplementary Persian Sources for the Mongol History of Iran," in Denis Sinor, ed., *Aspects of Altaic Civilization* (Bloomington: Indiana University, 1963), p. 197.

[6] Rashīd al-Dīn, *Vaqfnāmah-i Rabʿ-i Rashīdī*, ed. by M. Minuvī and I. Afshār (Tehran: Offset Press, 1972), p. 212.

[7] Iskandar Munshī, *History of Shah ʿAbbas the Great*, trans. by Roger M. Savory (Boulder, Colo.: Westview Press, 1978), vol. II, p. 1170.

[8] See Nicholas Poppe, "On Some Geographical Names in the *Jāmiʿal-Tawārīx*," *HJAS* 19 (1956), 33–41; John A. Boyle, "Sites and Localities Connected with the History of the Mongol Empire," *The Second International Congress of Mongolists* (Ulan Bator: n.p., 1973), vol. I, pp. 75–80; and Kh. Perlee, "On Some Place Names in the *Secret History*," *Mongolian Studies* 9 (1985–86), 83–102.

668–935; their knowledge was sketchy and stereotyped, and they tended to view it as an island.[9] Rashīd al-Dīn, who calls the north Sūlāngah (from the Mongolian Solangghas), and the central and southern portions Kūlī (from the Chinese Kao-li), understands that Korea is a peninsula, separated from China by a moderate-sized gulf, the Po-hai, which he does not name. The only city he mentions, Jūnjū, is either Chōngja in the north or Ch'ungju in the south. Japan, which the Persian historian calls Jaminkū (from the Chinese Jih-pen-kuo), he describes as an island in the Pacific, called by him the Ocean Sea (Daryā-i muḥīṭ). It is large, populous, mountainous, and has many mines, a possible reference to Japan's rich copper deposits.[10]

Far more extensive and explicit is his treatment of China. Muslims, of course, had long known of the Middle Kingdom which is frequently mentioned in travel accounts and in the systematic geographical literature. In the Mongolian era, however, their information greatly increases in volume and detail, a dramatic infusion of new knowledge much of which was derived from foreign sources. Rashīd al-Dīn, for instance, mentions twenty-five or so Chinese towns never before named by earlier Muslim authors.[11] To take yet another example, he was extremely well informed on the postal relay system which he says the *Ṣuvar al-āqālīm* describes at length. This is confirmed in his discussion of Qubilai's conflict with Qaidu and Du'a in central Asia, in which he relates that the Yuan court had recently established a network of postal relay stations (*yām*) "running from the *sübe* [strategic point] of Ajiqi in the extreme west to the *sübe* of Muqali in the far east and that patrols have been attached to each of them."[12] His testimony in this instance is fully corroborated by the Chinese sources which report in 1281 that A-chih-chi (Ajiqi), a descendant of Chaghadai in Yuan service, laid out a new network of thirty stations (*chan*) from T'ai-ho ling in northern Shansi to Pieh-shih Pa-li (Besh Baliq) in Uighuristan.[13] Clearly, Rashīd al-Dīn's maps of the Mongols' postal system and mile markers on the "great roads," if ever recovered, would constitute a major addition to our knowledge of the historical geography of Eurasia and to medieval cartography.

Equally impressive, Rashīd al-Dīn's extended account of the administrative geography of the Yuan provinces, *shīng* (Chinese *sheng*), is detailed and on the whole accurate. Certainly no previous Muslim author had as deep or as comprehensive a knowledge of the territorial organization of a Chinese

[9] Kei Won Chung and George F. Hourani, "Arab Geographers on Korea," *JAOS* 58 (1938), 658–61. Persian didactic literature also mentions Sīlā, a dependency of China. See Julie Scott Meisami, trans., *The Sea of Precious Virtues (Baḥr al-Favā'id): A Medieval Islamic Mirror for Princes* (Salt Lake City: University of Utah Press, 1991), pp. 279 and 376 note 38.

[10] Rashīd/Karīmī, vol. I, pp. 461, 639, 644–45, and 646–47, and Rashīd/Boyle, pp. 41, 274, 281, and 284.

[11] Donald Daniel Leslie, "The Identification of Chinese Cities in Arabic and Persian Sources," *Papers on Far Eastern History*, 26 (1982), 4–17.

[12] Rashīd/Karīmī, vol. I, p. 675, and Rashīd/Boyle, p. 326.

[13] *YS*, ch. 11, p. 231 and ch. 63, p. 1569.

state. Moreover, both the administrative terminology and the place names are given in their Chinese forms, most of which are readily recognizable or reconstructible.[14]

His treatment again raises the issue of his sources and again we must first look to Bolad. There are places in Rashīd al-Dīn's text where Bolad's imprint is unmistakable. Rashīd, for example, describes Shang-tu, the summer capital and hunting park, in detail – its grounds and facilities, and the routes, distances, and communities between it and Peking. He also knows the current Chinese name of Shang-tu, Kāi Mink Fū, which answers to K'ai-p'ing fu, as well as the Chinese name of one of the palaces in the summer capital, Lank Tan or Liang T'ien. That this came from Bolad is evident from the fact, noted in the Chinese sources, that his Mongolian informant was often at Shang-tu and that in the course of his investigations of Aḥmad he rode the postal relays from K'ai-p'ing to Ta-tu (Peking) several times.[15]

This, however, is only part of the story. In compiling information on the geography of foreign climes, Rashīd al-Dīn on more than one occasion notes he relied on foreign books, including those of China. While specific works cannot be identified, the source and means of transmission can be sketched with a measure of confidence.

The Mongols, although they did not produce an indigenous tradition of cartography until the eighteenth century, evinced early on a deep and abiding interest in maps, which in East Asia, at least, were closely associated with notions of legitimacy and sovereignty.[16] In 1255 the ruler of the Ta-li kingdom in southwest China, by imperial order, submitted "geographical maps [*ti-t'u*]" of his realm to Möngke Qaghan and in 1292/93 the ruler of Java submitted such maps and population registers to the invading Mongolian armies. Further, in 1276 when Bayan entered the recently fallen Sung city of Lin-an, he immediately instituted an inventory of "maps [*t'u*] and books."[17] That the acquisition of foreign maps was systematically organized is underscored by the fact that the Hostel for Foreign Envoys (*Hui-t'ung-kuan*), established in 1277, undertook, among other tasks, the collection of data on foreign geography, postal stations, pasturage, products, and "maps [*t'u*] of difficult [*hsien*] and easy [*i*] mountain [passes] and river [crossings]."[18] Here it is pertinent that

[14] Rashīd/Karīmī, vol. I, pp. 644–46, and Rashīd/Boyle, pp. 281–84. On the accuracy of this account, see Romeyn Taylor, "Review of Rashīd al-Dīn, *Successors of Genghis Khan*," *Iranian Studies* 5 (1972), 189–92.

[15] Rashīd/Karīmī, vol. I, pp. 620 and 641–42; Rashīd/Boyle, pp. 252 and 276–77; and *YS*, ch. 128, p. 3130, and ch. 205, p. 4563.

[16] G. Henrik Herb, "Mongolian Cartography," in J. B. Harley and David Woodward, eds., *History of Cartography* (University of Chicago Press, 1992–94), vol. II, bk. 2, pp. 682–85. On "sacred maps" and political authority in the T'o-pa wei, see Yang, *Record of Buddhist Monasteries*, pp. 104 and 115.

[17] *YS*, ch. 166, p. 3910, ch. 162, p. 3802, and ch. 127, p. 3112; and Cleaves, "Biography of Bayan of the Bārin," p. 256.

[18] *YS*, ch. 85, p. 2140.

the character *hsien* in Chinese, "difficult," "narrow passage," "strategic locale," has the same semantic range as the Mongolian *sübe*, "narrow passage," "eye of a needle," as well as "strategic point."[19]

Maps of strategic points and postal relay systems certainly existed in Yuan China. The real question is how did Rashīd al-Dīn gain access to this material? The most plausible channel is, as usual, Bolad, who, it will be recalled, helped found and had close ties to the Imperial Library Directorate, the major depository of maps (*t'u*) for the Yuan court. Here is the obvious source of Chinese books on geography and cartography mentioned by Rashīd al-Dīn and the reason why some of the illustrations in his *Collected Chronicles* are executed in a way reminiscent of Chinese maps and topographies.[20]

The flow of geographical knowledge was, however, a two-way street: the Imperial Library Directorate, staffed in part by Muslim scholars, undertook their own original compilations for the Yuan court which drew extensively on West Asian traditions in geography and cartography. Indeed, it is evident that the Directorate was actively engaged in exchanging scientific and scholarly information between East and West. As we shall see here and in later chapters, the interests of its staff were wide and their intellectual resources extensive; on the scholarly plane the directorate faithfully mirrored the cosmopolitanism of the empire and court it served. This is nicely exemplified by the fact that the directorate, long the center of traditional learning and monitor of cultural norms in China, was headed for a time by ʿIsā *kelemechi*, who received his appointment shortly after he returned from his extended stay in the West.[21]

The key figure in the eastward transmission of geographical knowledge was Jamāl al-Dīn, who arrived in China during the reign of Möngke. Primarily an astronomer and mathematician, he, like his illustrious predecessors al-Bīrūnī and al-Khwārazmī, also made a substantial contribution in the field of geography.[22] The first such occurred in 1267 when, according to the *Yuan shih*, Jamāl al-Dīn (Cha-ma-lu-ting) presented to the throne a series of astronomical instruments, one of which was a *k'u-lai-i a-erh-tzu*, which transcribes very accurately the Persian *kurah-i arẓ*, or "terrestrial globe." This instrument, the text continues,

19 Ferdinand D. Lessing, *Mongolian–English Dictionary* (Bloomington, Ind.: Mongolia Society, 1973), p. 74.

20 *YS*, ch. 90, p. 2296, and Priscilla Soucek, "The Role of Landscape in Iranian Painting to the 15th Century," in *Landscape and Style in Asia* (Percival David Foundation Colloquies in Art and Archaeology in Asia 9; London, 1980), pp. 91–92.

21 The *mi-shu ch'ien*, also called the *mi-shu sheng*, had its origins in the third century AD and survived through the Ch'ing. On its historical development and activities, see P. A. Herbert, "From *Shuku* to *Tushuguan*: An Historical Overview of the Organization and Function of Libraries in China," *Papers on Far Eastern History* 2 (1980), 93–121. On ʿIsā's appointment, dated July 25, 1287 see *MSC*, ch. 9, p. 5a (p. 253), and *YS*, ch. 134, p. 3249.

22 His background and career will be detailed in chapter 17, "Astronomy."

> is in the Chinese language a geographical record [*ti-li chih*]. Its [method of] manufacture was to take wood and fashion it into a sphere, seven parts [of which] are water, its color being green, and three parts [of which] are land, its color being white. They drew the streams, rivers, lakes, and seas [like] interconnected veins and arteries over the whole [of the sphere]. They also marked off small squares in order to calculate the breadth and length of countries and distance [lit., farness and nearness] in miles [*lī*] of the roads.[23]

Most certainly, this and the other instruments were made in China but their inspiration closely followed West Asian models and traditions. In the terrestrial globe the Yuan court possessed a representation of the known world that must have given considerable attention to the geography of the Islamic world and western Eurasia.

Jamāl al-Dīn's next geographical project was the preparation of a massive geographical compendium which the court ordered the Imperial Library Directorate to prepare in 1285. The *Yuan-shih* calls this, as it did Jamāl al-Dīn's terrestrial sphere, a *ti-li chih*, "geographical record," whereas documents from the directorate itself call it the *Ta-*[*Yuan*] *i-t'ung chih*, or "Comprehensive Gazetteer of the Great [Yuan]." More specifically, the latter source says that the court ordered the directorate to prepare "a great compilation of the topographies [*t'u-chih*] of all regions" and further "to unify them making them known."[24] From this description it certainly sounds as if the scope of the project embraced the whole of the Mongolian Empire, if not the known world.

The project leader was Jamāl al-Dīn. Another document from the directorate, dating to 1288, relates that "because the directorate official compiling and editing the geographical gazetteer [*ti-li t'u-chih*] was Cha-ma-lu-ting, a man of the Western Region [who] did not speak and was unable to understand [Chinese], he was assigned an interpreter."[25] The final product, undertaken with the assistance of Yü Ying-lung, a Chinese scholar attached to the directorate, was a massive descriptive geography with maps. According to the Yuan literatus Hsü Yu-jen, "In 1291 the work was completely finished in 755 chapters and called the *Ta* [*Yuan*] *i-t'ung chih*; it was secured in the Imperial Library [Mi-fu]."[26]

Some twelve years later a second *Ta* [*Yuan*] *i-t'ung chih* was submitted to the court, this one in 1,000 chapters. Its compilers, Po-lan-hsi (Boralqi), a Mongol, judging from his name, and the Chinese scholar Yüeh Hsüan, were

[23] *YS*, ch. 48, p. 999, and Walter Fuchs, *The Mongol Atlas of China by Chu Ssu-pen and the Kuang-yü-t'u* (Peking: Fu Jen University, 1946), p. 5. On the construction of such globes from wood, papier-mâché, and later from various metals, see Emilie Savage-Smith, "Celestial Mapping," in Harley and Woodward, *History of Cartography*, vol. II, bk. 1, pp. 48–49.

[24] *YS*, ch. 13, p. 277; *MSC*, ch. 4, p. 1a (p. 109); and Kōdō Tasaka, pp. 78–79.

[25] *MSC*, ch. 1, p. 10a (p. 39).

[26] Hsü Yu-jen, *Chih-cheng chi* (Ying-yin wen-yuan ko-ssu k'u-ch'üan shu ed.), ch. 35, pp. 4a–b.

both employees of the directorate and their work should be understood as a second, expanded edition of Jamāl al-Dīn's gazetteer.[27]

Sadly, all of the first edition appears to be lost and only fragments of the second have survived. These number about thirty or so chapters scattered in various collections and libraries. These remnants for the most part cover North China and are quite detailed – they record even small villages, their distances to larger towns, rivers, etc.[28]

What the *Ta* [*Yuan*] *i-t'ung chih* had to say on the "Western Regions" is impossible to tell, but that it included much information on the Muslim West becomes quite evident when we investigate the cartographical legacy of the Muslim geographers working in Yuan China. The most visible and dramatic testimony of Muslim influence in East Asian geographical knowledge is found in a number of Chinese and Korean maps of the fourteenth to sixteenth centuries.

The preeminent Chinese cartographer of the Yuan era, Chu Ssu-pen (1273–?), was a man of many parts – traveler, geographer, poet, and noted Taoist figure.[29] Around 1320 he produced the *Yü-t'u*, "Terrestrial Map," which covered China, Mongolia, and central Asia. His maps, utilizing the Chinese grid system, are detailed and accurate, showing major cities, rivers, and landforms. Separate maps were provided for each Chinese province. At about the same time, Li Tse-min, an associate of Chu's, compiled *Sheng-chiao kuang-pei t'u*, "Map of the Vast Diffusion of Resounding Teaching," which included much material on the Far West. Both originals are now lost, but fortunately their important cartographic work is preserved in a number of later maps. The earliest of these is the Korean map of Kwōn Kun, *Hun-i chiang-li li-tai kuo-tu chih t'u*, "Map of Integrated Lands and Regions of Historical Countries and Capitals," which dates to 1402. Next, there is the work of Lo Hung-hsien, *Kuang Yü-t'u*, the "Extended Terrestrial Map," of 1541 in which he states explicitly that his work is based upon that of Chu and Li. Lastly, there is the anonymous *Ta-ming hun-i t'u*, "Integrated Map of the Great Ming," which can be dated to ca. 1600.[30]

27 *YS*, ch. 21, p. 450. This text names as the presenters "Hsiao-lan-hsi, Yüeh Hsüan and others." In this passage *hsiao*, "little," is clearly a mistake for the graphically similar *pu*, "to divine," the character used by *MSC*, ch. 9, pp. 1a (p. 245) and 10b (p. 264) to transcribe Pu-lan-hsi. See also Ch'ien Ta-hsin, *Pu-Yuan shih i-wen chih* (Shih-hsüeh ts'ung-shu ed.; Taipei, 1964), ch. 2, p. 9b.

28 On the *Ta* [*Yuan*] *i-t'ung chih* as it has come down to us, see L. Carrington Goodrich, "Geographical Additions of the XIV and XV Centuries," *MS* 15 (1956), 203–6, and Endymion Wilkinson, *The History of Imperial China: A Research Guide* (Cambridge, Mass.: Harvard University Press, 1973), p. 113.

29 For a brief sketch, see K'o-k'uan Sun, "Yü Chi and Southern Taoism during the Yuan," in John D. Langlois, ed., *China under Mongol Rule* (Princeton University Press, 1981), pp. 251–52.

30 Fuchs, *The "Mongol Atlas" of China*, pp. 7–14; Needham *SCC*, vol. III, pp. 551–56, and map 44; Gari Ledyard, "Cartography in Korea," in Harley and Woodward, *History of Cartography*, vol. II, bk. 2, pp. 235–45, and map, p. 246; and Walter Fuchs, "Drei neue Versionen der chinesischen Weltkarte von 1402," in Herbert Franke, ed., *Studia Sino-Altaica: Festschrift für Erich Haenisch* (Wiesbaden: Franz Steiner, 1961), pp. 75–77.

What is so arresting about these maps is their treatment of the West: most surprisingly, Africa is depicted as a triangle and the general shape of the Mediterranean is immediately recognizable. Moreover, for Africa there are over 30 place names registered and for western Europe over 100, many of them recognizable. For Germany, we have A-lu-man-ni-a.

While the most spectacular, this by no means exhausts Yuan cartographic depiction of the West. Between 1329 and 1332 the Yuan court officially issued the *Hsi-pei pi ti-li t'u*, "Map of the Countries of the Northwest." Preserved in the *Yung-li ta-tien*, a vast collection of historical materials from the early Ming, this map covers the Mongolian realm beyond the Yuan. Laid out in a grid, with each square representing about 100 Chinese *li*, the map registers about thirty cities in the lands of Pu Sai-yin (Abū Saʿīd), e.g., I-ssu-fa-hang (Iṣfahān) and Sun-tan-ni-ya (Sulṭāniyyah). There are also several localities west of the Il-qan state noted, such as Damascus and Egypt. A majority of these place names are also mentioned in the *Yuan shih* chapter on geography without context or comment.[31]

Finally, there is the "atlas" of the sinicized Arab Shan-ssu (Shams [al-Dīn]) who authored in the fourteenth century a work entitled *Hsi-kuo t'u-ching*, "Map Book of the Western Countries." The Chinese character *t'u* denotes, of course, both "illustration" and "map," so that this title might be translated as "An Illustrated Work on Western Lands," as do Ch'en and Goodrich. Since, however, Shan-ssu is credited with a profound knowledge of "astronomy, geography [*ti-li*] and mathematics" but no artistic skills, the title probably indicates a map book or atlas. No longer extant, nothing further is known of its contents and coverage.[32] Like Rashīd al-Dīn's *Ṣuvar al Āqālīm*, the loss of this atlas is to be deeply regretted.

Clearly, these cartographic works, all produced in fourteenth-century China, particularly that of Li Tse-min, are indebted to Muslim intermediaries. While we cannot identify with confidence the Muslim sources utilized in specific cases, the basic contours and channels of transmission are evident. First, of course, is Jamāl al-Dīn's terrestrial sphere which provided much information on the world known to the Muslims of the thirteenth century. Further, Jamāl al-Dīn also accumulated many maps from the West. A document concerning the progress of the Imperial Library Directorate in preparing the *Ta* [*Yuan*] *i-t'ung chih* dating to 1286 relates that following discussion among the principals, which included Cha-ma-lu-ting, a report was made to

[31] For a reproduction of the Chinese original, see Sven Hedin, *Southern Tibet* (Stockholm: Lithographic Institute of the General Staff of the Swedish Army, 1922), vol. VIII, plate 8, facing p. 278. For a schematic representation, with extensive commentary on the names, consult Bretschneider, *Medieval Researches*, vol. II, map facing title page and pp. 96–138. See also, Paul Pelliot, "Note sur la carte des pays du Nord-Ouest dans le *King-che ta-tien*," *TP* 25 (1928), 98–100; and *YS*, ch. 63, pp. 1571–74.

[32] *YS*, ch. 195, p. 4353, and Ch'en Yuan, *Western and Central Asians in China*, p. 62. It appears that the *Hsi-kuo t'u-ching* was still extant in the eighteenth century. See Ch'ien Ta-hsien, *Pu-Yuan shih*, ch. 2, p. 9b.

the throne on the "geographical materials [*ti-li te wen-tzu*]" available to the compilers. For example, on the "former Han [i.e., Sung] territories," they had "some forty or fifty registers [*ts'e*]" and most importantly for our purposes, the memorial then adds: "As for Muslim maps [Hui-hui *t'u-tzu*] we, as a foundation [for our work], have an abundance [of them] and we have summarized them, making a single [i.e., composite] map."[33] From this passage several important conclusions seem warranted: (1) the *Ta* [*Yuan*] *i-t'ung chih*, in its original recension, certainly included foreign countries and most particularly the Muslim world; (2) in preparing this section, the compilers relied upon a large number of Muslim cartographic sources; and (3) it is possible, therefore, either that these maps came with Jamāl al-Dīn or that he sent for them after his arrival in China.

Such resources, to be sure, were in the custody of the court and its agencies, but as all the cartographers in question, Chu, etc., were officials of the state they would have had access to Jamāl al-Dīn's globe and to the collections of the Imperial Library Directorate. While Muslim maps were available in some quantity, the issue of which cartographic traditions were represented remains elusive. What follows is of course simply a series of suggestions that seem plausible but are certainly not demonstrable with the evidence at hand.

The detailed treatment of western Europe in the Chinese–Korean maps has repeatedly evoked the name of al-Īdrīsī (1100–ca. 1165) as a possible source. As is well known, this great scholar worked at the court of the Norman king Roger of Sicily (1097–1154) where he produced geographical and cartographical works that contain extensive coverage of Europe. Moreover, in his youth Īdrīsī traveled in France and England, and in Sicily, of course, he had ready access to information on the Latin West.[34]

Īdrīsī's contribution to Chinese cartography is in fact potentially testable. A close comparison of the European and African place names on his maps and those dependent on Li Tse-min's in terms of the repertoire, arrangement, and linguistic form may well prove a connection. While this has often been talked about, to the best of my knowledge it has yet to be done.

Another plausible source is a cartographical work devoted to the West produced in the Il-qan realm in 1290, which provides ample time for it to reach China and influence the maps of 1320. This work, now lost, was presented to the court by Quṭb al-Dīn Shīrāzī when he entered the service of Arghun (r. 1284–91). It is described by Rashīd al-Dīn, a contemporary, as "a map [*ṣūrat*] of the Mediterranean Sea [Daryā-i Maghrib] and its gulfs and coastline which included within it many western and northern regions [*vilāyat*]."[35] Quṭb al-Dīn

[33] *MSC*, ch. 4, p. 3a (p. 114).

[34] S. Maqbul Ahmad, "Cartography of al-Sharīf al-Īdrīsī," in Harley and Woodward, *History of Cartography*, vol. II, bk. 1, pp. 156–74, especially 156–57, 163, and 167. For a photo of Īdrīsī's world map, see Howard R. Turner, *Science in Medieval Islam: An Illustrated Introduction* (Austin: University of Texas Press, 1995), p. 127, fig. 8.5.

[35] Rashīd/Karīmī, vol. II, p. 822.

(d. ca. 1309), a highly respected "learned man [*mard-i dānishman*]" in his own day, was an astronomer, a student of Ṭūsī, who worked for a time at the Marāghah observatory and later served the Il-qans as a judge in Rum and as Tegüder's envoy to Egypt in 1282.[36] That he was personally known to Rashīd al-Dīn, with his myriad connections, lends a measure of plausibility to the suggestion that his map may have reached China.

Lastly, we should not forget Rashīd al-Dīn himself. His geographical compendium with maps, which drew in part upon Frankish scholars and books, was in existence by 1310, again well in time to inform Chinese cartographical projects of the 1320s. Given the frequency of the contacts between the two courts in this period and the extended, transcontinental scholarly network in which Rashīd operated, this possibility cannot be excluded.

Geographical knowledge was obviously transmitted, but what of cartographical technique? Needham has argued that a true quantitative cartography began in China in the second century AD with the development of the grid system, thereby launching an uninterrupted mathematical approach to map making which climaxed in the Yuan and Ming. This grid system, he further implies, stimulated Muslim cartographic practice, particularly in the Mongolian era, and this in turn may have influenced European map makers.[37]

This line of argument, however, has been recently challenged by Cordell Yee on several grounds. First, the grid system in Chinese cartography is much later than claimed: the earliest unequivocal evidence is from 1136. Second, Yee argues that the grid was not a fixed coordinate system in any event; it was used to calculate distance, not to organize space or locate position as do true coordinates. In other words, the Chinese cartographic tradition was essentially textual, not quantitative as Needham thought.[38]

While I cannot offer an independent judgment on these technical matters, it is fairly obvious that in the Muslim cartographic tradition the use of graticule to indicate longitude and latitude begins with efforts to note the climes (āqālīm) on circular world maps.[39] The system of climes, of course, goes back to earlier Hellenistic tradition and is quite independent of the Chinese grid system, whatever its chronology or nature.

And, more to the point, any debate over priorities and the direction of influence must take into account "new" (that is, long overlooked) evidence that the use of longitude and latitude in Muslim cartography is much earlier than normally assumed. Most scholarship on the subject holds that the map prepared for Ḥamd-Allāh Mustawfī Qazvīnī's geography of 1340 was the first to employ

[36] Aydin Sayili, *The Observatory in Islam and its Place in the General History of the Observatory*, 2nd edn (Ankara: Türk Tarih Kurumu Basimevi, 1988), pp. 19, 206, and 214–18; Rashīd/Karīmī, vol. II, p. 788; and Bar Hebraeus, p. 467.

[37] Needham, *SCC*, vol. III, pp. 533–65.

[38] Cordell D. K. Yee, "Taking the World's Measure: Chinese Maps between Observation and Text," in Harley and Woodward, *History of Cartography*, vol. II, bk. 2, pp. 124–26.

[39] Gerald R. Tibbetts, "Later Cartographic Developments," in Harley and Woodward, *History of Cartography*, vol. II, bk. 1, pp. 148–52.

the grid system, and that the next was the map included in Ḥāfiẓ-i Abrū's treatise of 1420. The earliest grid, however, goes back to the beginning of the thirteenth century and is found on a map prepared by Muḥammad ibn Najīb Bakrān, a native of Ṭūs, in 1208. This map was composed on cloth and its data derived from old astronomical tables which Bakrān, by his own testimony, says he carefully collated to eliminate errors.[40] The map itself is lost but Bakrān describes its character and techniques in great detail in his *Jahān-nāmah* or "World Book." He begins by explaining the different colors and symbols used to indicate boundary markers, cities, rivers, seas, deserts, mountains, and climes (*āqālīm*). He then states that the "many red lines, some [running] from the east to the west and some from the north to the south, these are the lines [*khuṭūṭ*] of longitude [*ṭūl*] and latitude [*ʿarẓ*]," and adds that the "great advantage" of his map is that "by means of longitude and latitude the location of each city can be determined."[41] Thus, 130 years before Mustawfī, Muslims used the graticule and this of course fatally undermines the theory that this was a uniquely Chinese technique that flowed west to Iran under the Mongols. Or, to put it another way, the map Jamāl al-Dīn presented to the throne in 1267, with its color code and grid system, had a well-established precedent in the Muslim world.[42]

The issue of transfer of technique aside, exchange of geographical knowledge between China and Iran had a lasting legacy. Kwōn Kun's map of 1402 established a most interesting tradition in Korea; henceforth there was a widespread popularity of maps and atlases in Korean culture which from the inception always had a "global" dimension.[43] More consequentially, as Adshead has argued, one of the most important contributions of the Middle Ages to the creation of the modern world system was the diffusion and "integration of geographical information," a body of knowledge that once in existence became a "permanent" feature of the new world order.[44] And, undeniably, the Mongolian Empire played a critical role in the promotion, creation, and circulation of such knowledge. Sometimes this rapid extension of horizons is linked exclusively to the famous travelers, Marco Polo and Ibn Baṭṭuṭah, as well as to a legion of lesser figures who accompanied innumerable commercial, diplomatic, and religious missions across Eurasia under Pax Mongolica. Reichert, for example, has recently calculated that between 1242 and 1448, over 126 individuals or embassies, all from Eastern and Western Christendom,

[40] For biographical information and a discussion of the place of the map in Muslim cartography, see the editor's introduction to Mukhammad ibn Nadzhīb Bakrān, *Dzhakhān name* (*Kniga o mire*), ed. by Iu. E. Borshchevskii (Moscow: Izdatel'stvo vostochnoi literatury, 1960), pp. 10–11 and 16–19.

[41] Muḥammad ibn Najīb Bakrān, *Jahān nāmah* (Tehran: Ibn-i Sīnā, 1963), pp. 10–12, quote on p. 11.

[42] I would like to thank Dr. Charles Melville of Cambridge University, who first drew my attention to this passage and its significance.

[43] Shannon McClure, "Some Korean Maps," *Transactions of the Korean Branch of the Royal Asiatic Society* 50 (1975), 76–87.

[44] Adshead, *China in World History*, pp. 168 and 171–72.

undertook journeys to central or East Asia.[45] This, to be sure, was important but we must not forget the contribution of the cartographers and the exchanges of scholars, scholarly works, and data between Iran and China.

This exchange explains why the Chinese, from the Sung to the Ming, viewed the lands and seas to their west and southwest, as Wheatley says, "through Arabo-Persian spectacles."[46] Some of this information, particularly that accumulated by mariners in the Indian Ocean, circulated through unofficial channels,[47] but some, certainly, was introduced by Muslims in the employ of the Mongols, who consciously sought out such data for their own ends, political and cultural.

The consequence of these contacts and exchanges was that China, particularly in the Yuan, had a surprisingly detailed body of knowledge on the geography of Africa and Europe and the lands and seas between.[48] In contrast, European knowledge of Africa south of the Sahara and Asia before the voyages of exploration was less detailed and poorly represented cartographically. This can be explained in part by the fact that while Europeans eagerly tapped into Arabic philosophy, medicine, and science at an early date, their acquaintance with Muslim geographical literature came late, in the seventeenth century, whereas the Chinese introduction came, in direct consequence of Mongolian policies, in the thirteenth century.[49]

[45] Folker E. Reichert, *Begegnungen mit China: Die Entdeckung Ostasiens im Mittelalter* (Sigmaringen: Jan Thorbecke, 1992), pp. 288–93.

[46] Paul Wheatley, "Analecta Sino-Africana Recensa," in H. Neville Chittick and Robert I. Rotberg, eds., *East Africa and the Orient: Cultural Synthesis in Pre-Colonial Times* (New York: Africana Publishing Co., 1975), pp. 113–14.

[47] On mariner charts, see Marco Polo, pp. 235, 243, 319, and 434, and L. Carrington Goodrich, "The Connection between the Nautical Charts of the Arabs and those of the Chinese before the Days of the Portuguese Navigators," *Isis* 44 (1953), 99–100. For a discussion of an "unofficial" Yuan work on the Indian Ocean and Africa, see Shinji Maejima, "The Muslims in Ch'üan-chou at the End of the Yuan, Part I," *Memoirs of the Research Department of Toyo Bunko* 31 (1973), 47–51.

[48] Walter Fuchs, "Was South Africa Already Known in the 13th Century?" *Imago Mundi* 9 (1953), 50–51. On the superiority of Yuan geographical knowledge over that of the Ming, see Gang Deng, *Chinese Maritime Activities and Socioeconomic Development, c. 2100 BC–1900 AD* (Westport, Conn.: Greenwood Press, 1997), pp. 55–58.

[49] On the date of the European introduction to Muslim geographical literature, see Marina Tolmacheva, "The Medieval Arabic Geographers and the Beginnings of Modern Orientalism," *International Journal of Middle East Studies* 27 (1995), 141–56.

FOURTEEN

Agriculture

One of the most intriguing but least known facets of the cultural collaboration of Rashīd al-Dīn and Bolad is in the field of agronomy. Bolad, it will be remembered, helped to found and initially headed the Office of the Grand Supervisors of Agriculture (*Ta ssu-nung ssu*; Mongolian, *dai sinungsi*).[1] This was a very old institution in China going back to the Han; even dynasties of Inner Asian, nomadic origin commonly had such an office.[2]

Founded in 1270, the Office of the Grand Supervisor of Agriculture superseded the Office for the Encouragement of Agriculture (*Ch'üan-nung ssu*) created in 1261 when Qubilai came to power.[3] This office, whose name underwent frequent changes during the Yuan, was charged with the oversight of agriculture, sericulture, and water resources in North China, since, at the time of its inception, the Southern Sung was yet to be defeated.[4] During the period 1270–90 the office had regional organs at the level of the *tao* (region) called Mobile Offices for the Encouragement of Agriculture (*Hsün-hsing ch'üan-nung ssu*). On several occasions starting in 1275, the duties of these Mobile Offices were temporarily transferred to the regional censorial bureaus, an organization that Bolad also headed.[5] The basic responsibility of this organization was "to exhort [the people] to devote themselves to the completion of important agricultural tasks."[6] More specifically and concretely, the office worked with local communes (*she*), nominally fifty peasant families, to improve agricultural techniques, introduce new seeds, and raise productivity.

Consequently, when Bolad arrived in Iran he had a wealth of experience

[1] Cleaves, "The Sino-Mongolian Inscription of 1362," 66, Mongolian text and 90, English translation.

[2] Charles O. Hucker, *A Dictionary of Official Titles in Imperial China* (Stanford University Press, 1985), pp. 453 and 469; Gerhard Schreiber, "The History of the Former Yen Dynasty, part II," *MS* 15 (1956), 136; and Wittfogel and Feng, *History of Chinese Society, Liao*, pp. 135, 138, 139, and 149.

[3] For the founding date, organizational nomenclature, and tables of official ranks, see *YS*, ch. 87, p. 2188; *YTC*, ch. 2, p. 12a; and Ratchnevsky, *Un Code des Yuan*, vol. I, pp. 189–91 for French translations of the key passages.

[4] For a brief history of this office in the Yuan, see Farquhar, *Government*, pp. 214–17; *YS*, ch. 93, pp. 2354–56; and Schurmann, *Economic Structure*, pp. 43–48 and 50–56.

[5] *YS*, ch. 7, p. 128 and ch. 8, p. 166.

[6] *YS*, ch. 8, p. 148.

with Chinese agriculture, the most productive in the world at this time. And although the sources do not directly speak to the matter, Bolad assuredly communicated some of his knowledge to Rashīd al-Dīn and Ghazan, the chief architects of extensive reforms in the Il-qan realm which had as their principal objective the revival of agriculture. These measures, as already noted, included a rationalization of taxes, curtailment of the depredations of the Mongolian–Turkic elite, a crackdown on bureaucratic corruption, and measures to improve productivity.[7]

In pursuit of the latter goal, Ghazan sent off for new seeds and plants which were taken to Tabrīz where there were test gardens which acclimatized the new arrivals and in some cases grafted "their shoots and branches" to improve their yields.[8] Though not entirely unprecedented in the eastern Islamic world, this Iranian version of Offices for the Encouragement of Agriculture surely owes something to the Chinese model with which Bolad was so familiar.[9] This connection is most evident from a close examination of the means chosen to disseminate the results of efforts to improve the rural economy – the compilation of an agricultural manual.

Such manuals have a long tradition in the Islamic world, the earliest of which, written in Arabic, dates to the tenth century.[10] This and later productions regularly drew on earlier knowledge, particularly Mesopotamian and Greek, to which was added local experience and the innovations of the Muslim era.[11] Persian treatises, which came later, are clearly connected with the Arabic tradition and classical antiquity. Like their predecessors and models, the Persian manuals combined a textual tradition with practical experience.[12]

One of the most interesting of the Persian manuals was produced about the

7 For an overview, see Petrushevskii, *Zemledelie*, pp. 55–62.

8 Rashīd/Jahn II, p. 207. See also the comments of Aly Mazahéri, *La vie quotidienne des Musulmans au Moyen Age* (Paris: Librairie Hachette, 1951), pp. 242–43.

9 In Khwārazm there were water masters (*amīr-āb*) and agricultural officers (*miʿ-mār*) whose duty was the promotion of agriculture. See Heribert Horst, *Die Staatsverwaltung des Grosselǧūgen und Horazmšahs (1038–1231): Eine Untersuchung nach Urkundenformularen der Zeit* (Wiesbaden: Franz Steiner, 1964), pp. 59–60 and 137.

10 For a survey of this literature, see Mustafa al-Shihabi, "Filāha," *EI*, 2nd edn, vol. II, p. 900; Claude Cahen, "Notes pour une histoire de l'agriculture dans les pays musulmans médiévaux," *Journal of the Economic and Social History of the Orient* 14 (1971), 63–68; and Manfred Ullman, *Die Nature- und Geheimwissenschaften im Islam* (Handbuch der Orientalistik, Ergänzungband VI.2; Leiden: E. J. Brill, 1972), pp. 427–51.

11 On Muslim indebtedness to the Greeks, particularly the post-classical *Geponica*, see John L. Teall, "The Byzantine Agricultural Tradition," *Dumbarton Oaks Papers* 25 (1971), 40–44; J. Ruska, "Cassionus Bassus Scholasticus und die arabischen Versionen der griechischen Landwirtschaft," *Der Islam* 5 (1914), 174–79; and N. V. Pigulevskaia, *Kul'tura Siriitsev v srednie veka* (Moscow: Nauka, 1979), pp. 184–85. For an example of the local tradition in agricultural literature, see Daniel Martin Varisco, "Medieval Agricultural Texts from Rasulid Yemen," *Manuscripts of the Middle East* 4 (1989), 150–54.

12 Živa Vesel, "Les traités d'agriculture en Iran," *Studia Iranica* 15 (1986), 99–108; and Jürgen Jakobi, "Agriculture between Literary Tradition and Firsthand Experience: The *Irshād al-Zirāʿā* of Qāsim b. Yūsuf Abū Nasrī Havarī," in Lisa Golembek and Maria Subtelny, eds., *Timurid Art and Culture: Iran and Central Asia in the Fifteenth Century* (Leiden: E. J. Brill, 1992), 201–8.

time of Ghazan's reign and was connected with the agricultural work carried out at Tabrīz. For a long time the authorship and title of this treatise were unknown, but recently it has been demonstrated that this is the *Kitab-i Āthār va Aḥyā'*, "The Book of Monuments and Living Things" compiled by Rashīd al-Dīn. As he did with his other literary works, Rashīd al-Dīn endeavored to ensure their survival by establishing a regular program of copying. In the case of the *Āthār va Aḥyā'*, Rashīd in his *Vaqfnāmah* instructs its administrator (*mutawallī*) to hire scribes to produce each year a Persian and Arabic version of this work. Moreover, scholars in residence at his madrasa in Rabʿ-i Rashīdī in Tabrīz were expected to make a copy, in Persian or Arabic, of one of Rashīd al-Dīn's works, including the agricultural manual.[13] Despite these precautions the *Āthār va Aḥyā'* did not survive in many manuscript copies and its true identity was soon lost. In consequence, it became a bibliographical rarity. It was published in Tehran without indication of author or original title in a lithograph edition by Najm Daulah in 1905 as part of a collection of agricultural manuals entitled *Majmu'ah-i 'ilm-i Irānī dar zira'at va baghbānī va ghairah*.[14]

Because of its inaccessibility, little use was made of this valuable document by modern scholarship. The major exception was the Soviet historian I. P. Petrushevskii who cited the work extensively in his study of Persian agriculture under the Mongols and several times assessed its importance as a historical source. Although Petrushevskii did not realize that the manual was authored by Rashīd al-Dīn, his conclusions, based upon a careful reading of the lithograph edition, seem quite sound and bear repeating. First, the manual is practical in its approach and written in a simple, direct style. Second, and unlike other treatises, it is based in substantial part on firsthand experience rather than literary tradition. Third, the manual was started in Ghazan's reign and completed under his successor Öljeitü. Fourth, its basic organizational principles are specific crops, plants, and agricultural products, which it treats at length. Last, Petrushevskii rightly rates the manual a unique historical source because it describes in detail certain agricultural techniques, tree grafting for example, and because it provides unmatched data on the geography and diffusion of many important crops and plants.[15] To this we can add that Rashīd al-Dīn's perspective, as we might expect, is broad, embracing the whole of Eurasia from China to Egypt and all the lands in between. In its original form, as recorded in the digest of Rashīd al-Dīn's literary works, the *Āthār va Aḥyā'* contained the following chapter headings:[16]

[13] Rashīd al-Dīn, *Vaqfnāmah*, pp. 237 and 240.

[14] O. P. Shcheglova, *Katalog litografirovannykh knig na persidskom iazyke v sobranii LO IV AN SSSR* (Moscow: Nauka, 1975), vol. II, pp. 670–71.

[15] I. P. Petrushevskii, "Persidskii traktat po agrotekhnike vremeni Gazan-khan," in *Materialy pervoi vsesoiuznoi nauchnoi konferentsii vostokovedov v. g. Tashkente* (Tashkent: Akademii nauk Uzbekskoi SSR, 1958), pp. 586–98. Shorter but more accessible is Petrushevskii, *Zemledelie*, pp. 24–26.

[16] Muginov, "Persidskaia unikal'naia rukopis Rashīd al-Dīna," pp. 371–73, and Rashīd/Quatremère, pp. CLVI–CLVIII, Arabic text and pp. CXII–CXIV, French translation.

1. Years and seasons
2. Water, land, and weather
3. Types of cultivation, their timing and method
4. Canals and irrigation
5. Dams and their construction (missing in the Arabic text)
6. Seeds and roots
7. Seed plants and root crops
8. Trees, local and foreign
9. Tree grafting
10. Fertilizer
11. Melons, vegetables, and herbs
12. Wheat, barley, and cereals
13. Cash crops, cotton, etc.
14. Destruction of pests
15. Domesticated fowl
16. Domesticated and wild animals
17. Honeybees
18. Crop failures and their prevention
19. Storing of seed, cereal, wine, etc.
20. Construction of houses, forts, etc.
21. Construction of ships, bridges, etc.
22. Qualities of different animals
23. Methods of mining
24. Properties of metals and gems

As it has come down to us, however, the *Āthār va Aḥyā'* includes only the purely agricultural sections; those on construction, irrigation, mining, architecture, and animal husbandry are missing.[17]

From our perspective, of course, what is most interesting is that in the surviving portions of the text the data on Chinese agriculture is so extensive and so detailed that it invites the suspicion that Rashīd al-Dīn had access, albeit indirect, to the vast Chinese literature on agronomy.

The Yuan dynasty, founded by nomads, was, somewhat ironically, rich in agricultural manuals. Two of them, the *Nung-shu* of Wang Chen, issued in 1313, and the *Nung-sang i-shih ts'uo-yao* of Lu Ming-shen, issued in 1314, are obviously too late, since Rashīd al-Dīn's manual was begun in Ghazan's reign.[18] The most likely candidate for the agricultural information is the *Nung-sang chi-yao*, "Essentials of Agriculture and Sericulture," issued in 1273 by the Office of the Grand Supervisor of Agriculture. It was compiled by a committee of Chinese officials who drew heavily on earlier manuals, especially the *Ch'i-min yao-shu* of AD 535, to which they added a small amount of new data based on recent experience. For the most part the crops and techniques discussed were appropriate for agriculture in North China, not the as-yet-unconquered

[17] For a detailed, recent discussion of its contents, see A. K. S. Lambton, "The *Āthār wa aḥya'* of Rashīd al-Dīn and his Contribution as an Agronomist, Arboriculturist and Horticulturalist," in Amitai-Preiss and Morgan, *Mongol Empire*, pp. 126–54. Cf. also Jahn, "Still Missing Works of Rashīd al-Dīn," p. 118.

[18] On these works see the notices of A. Wylie, *Notes on Chinese Literature* (Shanghai: Presbyterian Mission Press, 1922), p. 94, and Francesca Bray, *Agriculture*, in Needham, *SSC*, vol. VI, pt. 2, pp. 53, 59–64, and 71–72. For a sense of the vastness of the traditional Chinese literature on agriculture, consult Liou Ho and Claudius Roux, *Aperçu bibliographique sur les anciens traités chinois de botanique, d'agriculture, de sericulture et de fungiculture* (Lyon: Bose Frères et Riou, 1927).

south.[19] Intended as an official manual for distribution to the peasant communes (*she*) to increase productivity, the *Nung-sang chi-yao* enjoyed considerable success, going through several Yuan and Ming editions.[20]

This work is organized in seven untitled chapters (*chuan*) and ten sections (*men*) with the following headings:[21]

Ch. I.	1. Words of wisdom
	2. Plowing and reclaiming
Ch. II	3. Scattering seed (cereal crops)
Ch. III	4. Mulberries
Ch. IV	5. Silkworms
Ch. V	6. Vegetables
	7. Fruit
Ch. VI	8. Bamboo and trees
	9. Medicinal herbs
Ch. VII	10. Domesticated animals (including fish)

This is the most attractive choice for several reasons. First, its contents overlap with Rashīd al-Dīn's coverage of Chinese agriculture, which includes discussions on fruit trees, cereal crops, vegetables, mulberries, and silkworms. Second, of course, the *Nung-sang chi-yao* was prepared and distributed while Rashīd al-Dīn's close collaborator, Bolad Aqa, was the Grand Supervisor of Agriculture. In short, at the time Rashīd al-Dīn undertook his collection of data on Chinese agriculture, the *Nung-sang chi-yao* was the most up-to-date and accessible manual available.

Now to the contents of the *Āthār va Aḥyā'*. Muslims, of course, long associated certain crops and agricultural products with the Chinese – rice, silk, cinnamon, etc. – but Rashīd al-Dīn's vast knowledge of Chinese agriculture truly represents a quantum leap. In a long section of the *Āthār va Aḥyā'* devoted to the crops of India and China (Chīn), Rashīd al-Dīn provides detailed information on the botanical characteristics, uses, and methods of propagation of many foreign, particularly Chinese, plants. He regularly indicates their names "in the language of Manzī [South China] and Khitāī [North China]," some quite accurately and some deformed but often reconstructible. The following lists a portion of the crops discussed as an indication of the range and nature of Rashīd al-Dīn's information on the subject.[22]

[19] Pelliot, *Notes*, vol. I, pp. 499–500; Amano Motonosuke, "On *Nung-sang chi-yao*," *Tōhōgaku* 30 (1965), English summary, 6–7; Amano Motonosuke, "Dry Farming and the *Ch'i-min yao-shu*," in *Silver Jubilee Volume of the Zinbun-Kagaku-Kenkyusyo Kyoto University* (Kyoto University, 1954), pp. 451–65; and Bray, in Needham, *SCC*, vol. VI, pt. 2, pp. 55–59.

[20] Wu Han, *Teng-hsia chi* (Peking: Hsin-chih san-lien shu-tien, 1961), pp. 11–13.

[21] *Nung-sang chi-yao* (Ssu-pu pei-yao ed.), table of contents, and Bray, in Needham, *SCC*, vol. VI, pt. 2, p. 71.

[22] Rashīd al-Dīn, *Āthār va Aḥyā'*, ed. by M. Sutūdah and I. Afshār (Tehran University Press, 1989), pp. 70, 77, 80, 83, 86–7, 89, and 95–6.

1. Coconuts, Persian *jawz-i hindī*, transcribed as *bādn*, a corruption of *yā-zū*, the Chinese *yeh-tzu*.
2. Cinnamon, Persian *dar-chīnī*, transcribed as *kūī-sī*, the first element of which is certainly the Chinese *kuei*.
3. Black pepper, Persian *filfil*, transcribed as *hursīū*, which answers to the Chinese *hu-chiao*.
4. Betelnut, Persian *fūlful*, transcribed as *fnām*, clearly *fin-lam*, the Chinese *pin-lang*.
5. Tea, Persian *chā*, transcribed as *chah*, the Chinese *ch'a*. Tea is described at some length, particularly its medicinal properties and Qubilai's efforts to encourage production in the north. This is not the first Muslim notice of Chinese tea but it is by far the longest until modern times.[23]
6. Sandalwood, Persian *sandal-i safīd*, transcribed as *tālī* (a corruption of *tān*) *h·ng*, the Chinese *t'an-hsiang*.
7. Litchi nut, transcribed as *līchīū*, the Chinese *li-chih*, an evergreen fruit tree. This tree (*dirakht*), Rashīd al-Dīn correctly notes, grows in Kwantung near the cities of Fr Jīūn (certainly Fu-chou) and Zaitun.[24]

Rashīd al-Dīn also discusses Chinese crops in more general contexts. For example, his treatment of oranges (*nāranj*) covers varieties in Kūfah, Baghdad, Iran, Egypt, and China, where, he notes quite accurately, there are numerous varieties.[25] Similarly, his discussion of jujubes (*'anāb*) ranges from Jurjān in northern Iran where jujubes "do well in some villages" to China and Uighuristan, a Yuan dependency, where they "are extremely large, lush and make a fine meal." These latter, he continues, "are so much better than the jujubes of other lands and in Uighuristan there is a city, Jūjūq, where they are the very best."[26]

Finally, Rashīd al-Dīn is also well informed on the diverse industrial uses of Chinese agricultural crops. In the subsection on mulberry trees (*dirakht-i tūt*) he notes that in addition to using the leaves as food for silkworms, the Chinese use the tree bark to make paper for everyday use, while the silk itself is used to prepare special paper for the imperial court. Further, he records that in South China (Chīn) they make a wine from the mulberries (*khar-tūt*).[27]

But to what extent was this increase in knowledge of Chinese agriculture

[23] Laufer, *Sino-Iranica*, pp. 533–54.

[24] On the litchi, see Frederick J. Simoons, *Food in China: A Cultural and Historical Inquiry* (Boca Raton, Ann Arbor, and Boston: CRC Press, 1991), pp. 206–10. There is a special work in Chinese devoted to the litchi, the *Li-chih p'u*, written in 1059 by Ts'ai Hsien. See Liou Ho and Roux, *Aperçu bibliographique*, pp. 20–21.

[25] Rashīd al-Dīn, *Āthār va Aḥyā'*, p. 51. On the "twenty-seven varieties," see Shiba Yoshinobu, *Commerce and Society in Sung China*, trans. by Mark Elvin (Ann Arbor: University of Michigan Center for Chinese Studies, 1970), p. 89.

[26] Rashīd al-Dīn, *Āthār va Aḥyā'*, p. 40, and Simoons, *Food in China*, pp. 223–25.

[27] Rashīd al-Dīn, *Āthār va Aḥyā'*, pp. 36–37 and 38. On paper making see Shiba, *Commerce and Society*, pp. 103–10.

and its products accompanied by the circulation of new crops and new preferences across Eurasia? Much evidence, I believe, points in this direction. First of all, there are several general indications of such movement in the writings of Rashīd al-Dīn himself. In one passage, he says that Ghazan

> issued a further order to bring from all countries seeds of various fruit-bearing trees, aromatic plants, and cereals which were not in Tabrīz and which no one there had ever seen before, and to graft these shoots and branches. They busied themselves with that project and now all are found in Tabrīz and every day the yield is more than can be adequately described . . . To all distant lands, such as the countries of India, China, and others, [Ghazan] sent envoys in order to obtain seeds of things which are unique in that land.[28]

In another place, Rashīd records that there was considerable traffic in the opposite direction as well: "Varieties of fruit trees," he relates, "have been brought from every country and planted in orchards and gardens there [Ta-tu, the new capital] and most are fruiting."[29] This is confirmed by Marco Polo, who notes also the fruit trees of many sorts growing in the palace complex at Ta-tu.[30]

To some extent, the preoccupation with trees is linked to Mongolian attitudes toward these plants as symbols of rebirth and longevity, and with the notion of the tree of life. Consequently, Mongolian qaghans, starting with Ögödei, encouraged and decreed the planting of trees throughout the realm to ensure a long life.[31] By the time of the Yuan there was even a special office (*chü*) in the Bureau for Imperial Household Provisions (*Hsüan-hui yuan*) that "managed the production of . . . fruit trees sent in as tribute."[32]

When it comes to the specific plants transferred, the sources are never as full or informative as one would like. There is, however, one such transfer that is unambiguously documented in *Āthār va Aḥyā'*. Speaking of millet (*gāvars*), Rashīd al-Dīn notes that "*tūkī* Khitāī is a variety of it" and then goes on to say:

> and in this kingdom [i.e., Iran] there is little *tūkī*. The Chinese [Khitāyān] from the region of North China [Khitāī] brought it to Marv and planted it there and when some of the Chinese were settled in Khūi [in Azerbaijan], they also planted it there and it multiplied. At this time, they [the Chinese] have carried it from there to Tabrīz and other districts and it has spread.[33]

This most informative passage calls for several comments. First, while no numbers are given, the fact that Mustawfī in his day (ca. 1340) says that the inhabitants of Khūi were "of Chinese [Khitāī] descent," indicates that the

[28] Rashīd/Jahn II, p. 207. [29] Rashīd/Karīmī, vol. I, p. 639, and Rashīd/Boyle, p. 274.
[30] Marco Polo, p. 210.
[31] *Mongol Mission*, p. 13; Marco Polo, p. 249; and Jean-Paul Roux, *La religion des Turcs et des Mongols* (Paris: Payot, 1984), pp. 171–74. [32] *YS*, ch. 87, p. 2204.
[33] Rashīd al-Dīn, *Āthār va Aḥyā'*, pp. 144–45.

community was substantial, the predominant element in a mid-sized town, and that it retained its ethnic identity over several generations.[34] Thus, it was an effective and long-term medium of Chinese cultural influence in Iran and may well have transmitted other crops and plants into the region. Second, the principal crop diffused, *tūkī*, can be identified with greater precision. Medieval lexicons of Turkic are most helpful in this regard; they consistently define the term, *tügü* and *tüki* in Turkic, as a kind of hulled or threshed millet.[35] Millets, of course, were long cultivated in North China and perhaps even domesticated there. They were a staple in the region and by Mongolian times numerous varieties had been developed. The most likely candidate for Rashīd al-Dīn's *tūkī* is what the Chinese call *shu*, a glutinous, hulled millet (*Panicum miliaceum L. Beauv.*).[36] This variety, in any event, would, as Rashīd al-Dīn implies, be an entirely new introduction into Iran, since there is good evidence that *shu* was not grown in the eastern Islamic world when the Mongols arrived.[37] It should be kept in mind, however, that the Chinese terminology for millet is by no means consistent or clear and that other possibilities cannot be excluded.

Plants moving eastward are also recorded, most prominently a variety of citrus that was introduced to South China in the thirteenth century. Here again we have information on the nature of the crop, its uses and the agency of its diffusion. The plant in question is called *līmū* in Persian and Arabic and was in all likelihood a variety of lemon. It was grown extensively in southwestern Iran, throughout Mesopotamia, long a center of citrus cultivation, and most particularly in the neighborhood of Baghdad.[38] From this fruit the locals made a lemonade (*ab-i līmū*) and a rub, that is, fruit juice made viscous by cooking in the sun, which was used as a medicine for cooling and for constipation.[39]

The question of the introduction of the *līmū* into China is complicated by the fact that citrus fruits of many varieties were extensively grown in the south by Mongolian times; for example, the *līmūn* of Khansā (Quinsai or

[34] Ḥamd-Allāh Mustawfī Qazvīnī, *The Geographical Part of the Nuzhat al-Qulūb*, ed. by Guy le Strange (London: Luzac, 1915), p. 85.

[35] Maḥmūd Kāšγarī, *Compendium of the Turkic Dialects* (*Dīwan Luγāt at-Turk*), trans. by Robert Dankoff (Sources of Oriental Languages and Literature, vol. VII; Cambridge, Mass.: Harvard University Printing Office, 1982), vol. II, p. 269; and Golden, *Hexaglot*, 202B19, p. 256.

[36] Bray, in Needham, *SCC*, vol. VI, pt. 2, pp. 434–48, and especially p. 440.

[37] This at least is the testimony of Yeh-lü Ch'u-ts'ai, who traveled through Samarqand in 1219–20. See Igor de Rachewiltz, trans., "The *Hsi-yü lu* by Yeh-lü Ch'u-ts'ai," *MS* 21 (1962), 21 and 57 note 99, where Yeh-lü Ch'u-ts'ai says that "all kinds of grain are found there [i.e., Samarqand] except glutinous millet [*shu*], glutinous rice and soya bean."

[38] L. P. Smirnova, trans. and ed., *'Ajā'ib al-dunyā* (Moscow: Nauka, 1993), pp. 493, Persian text, and 184, Russian translation; Muhammad Rashid al-Feel, *The Historical Geography of Iraq between the Mongolian and Ottoman Conquests, 1258–1534* (Nejef: al-Adab Press, 1965), vol. I, pp. 221–22; and 'Umarī/Lech, pp. 89, Arabic text, and 150, German translation.

[39] Al-Samarqandī, *The Medical Formulary of al-Samarqandī*, ed. and trans. by Martin Levy and Noury al-Khaledy, (Philadelphia: University of Pennsylvania Press, 1967), pp. 65 and 177 note 51.

Hangchow) reported by al-ʿUmarī.[40] Indeed, the history of lemons (*citrus-limon* L.) and limes (*citrus aurantifolia* Swing), like all members of the cultivated citrus family, is quite confused. While the current consensus holds that the lemon was first domesticated in India at a rather late date and then spread into the Islamic world by the tenth century and under the name *li-meng* into South China, particularly Hainan and Kwangtung, by the twelfth century, others hold that it was first cultivated in the eastern Himalayas and is therefore a "Chinese" domesticate.[41] Moreover, since all citrus species readily hybridize, there are endless special varieties and, consequently, a very confusing nomenclature which has tended, until very recently, to use the term "lemon" and its relatives, lime, *līmū*, *li-men*, *līmūnah* to cover all kinds of citrus – lemons, limes, and citrons.[42]

Despite the many sources of confusion, there is none the less good evidence that a particular variety of West Asian lemon was introduced into South China. As is often the case, Laufer was the first to suggest this possibility. According to passages assembled from local gazetteers and histories of the Ming and Ch'ing, there was at Li-chih Wan, near Canton, an imperial orchard, established during the Yuan, which specialized in the cultivation of *li-mu*. Eight hundred trees were planted and the responsible officials sent tribute to the court by special messenger in the form of *k'o-shui*, "thirst [allaying] water," which is explicitly equated with *she-li-pieh*, that is, *sharbat*, our sherbet, the Arabic and Persian drink made out of citrus, sugar, and rosewater. From this data, Laufer concluded, mainly on the close phonetic similarity between *li-mun* and *līmū*, that this particular variety of lemon was a recent West Asian import to Kwantung .[43]

To this linguistic evidence we can add supporting material from the Islamic end, again from the writings of Rashīd al-Dīn. The first comes from the correspondence traditionally ascribed to the Persian statesman. The authenticity of this source, to be sure, recently has been called into question and Morton's contention that the letters are a forgery of the Temürid era is persuasively argued.[44] None the less, this correpondence, whatever its origin, contains very specific and very accurate data bearing on the issue of West Asian citrus in China. In one of these missives there is a listing of various fruits being

40 ʿUmarī/Lech, pp. 30–31, Arabic text, and 111–12, German translation. On Khansā/Quinsai, see Moule, *Quinsai and Other Notes on Marco Polo*, p. 3.

41 Watson, *Agricultural Innovation*, pp. 46–48; Needham, *SCC*, vol. VI, pt. 1, pp. 363–77; Edward H. Schafer, *Shore of Pearls* (Berkeley: University of California Press, 1970), p. 47; and Shiu Iu-nin, "Lemons of Kwantung with a Discussion Concerning Origin," *Lingnan Science Journal* 12, supplement (1933), 271–94.

42 On nomenclature, see Helen M. Johnson, "The Lemon in India," *JAOS* 57 (1937), 381–96.

43 Bertold Laufer, "The Lemon in China and Elsewhere," *JAOS* 54 (1934), 148–51. Marco Polo, p. 245, notes that the runners who carry official correspondence also take fruit to the Great Khan in season.

44 A. H. Morton, "The Letters of Rashīd al-Dīn: Īlkhānid Fact or Timurid Fiction?," in Amitai-Preiss and Morgan, *Mongol Empire*, pp. 155–99.

prepared for winter storage, including "10,000 sweet lemons [*līmū-i shīrīn*] that are celebrated in Sīnī [South China]." Of this amount, he continues, "5,000 were due from Ba'qubā," just to the north of Baghdad and the remainder from Ḥillah, 15 km to the south of Baghdad.[45] Clearly, the writer was well informed on matters of Chinese agriculture and thought of the *līmū* as an introduction there. And whether in a forged letter or not, this aside on the *līmū* is fully consistent with the Chinese accounts cited above and with other remarks of Rashīd al-Dīn. In his discussion of the *līmū* in the *Āthār va Aḥyā'* he says that this variety of lemon was called *ya'qūbī* (a mistake for Ba'qubā) in Baghdad and that it had a delicate (*tanuk*) rind and unsurpassed fragrance. He also records that the *līmū* is found in Baghdad and its dependencies, and that the same variety is now found in Shabānkarah and Shustar.[46] These latter data give, in turn, a clue as to the agent of the introduction since one of the Mongols' governors in Canton (Chin-katān), according to Rashīd al-Dīn, was a certain Rukn al-Dīn of Tustar, an alternative name of Shustar, the town in Khūzistān where this fruit flourished.[47]

Taken together, the assembled data point to a West Asian introduction in Mongolian times to provide one of the essential ingredients for sherbet, a drink whose preparation at the Yuan court was in the hands of West Asian specialists. Because of foreign trade, contact, and settlement in Canton and Ch'üan-chou, the southeast coast of China had long been an important entrepôt of new crops and plants from the T'ang through the Ch'ing. Thus, the introduction of the *līmū* into the area of Canton was part of a well-established pattern of diffusion.[48]

Another likely introduction of the Yuan period is the carrot, Chinese Hu *lo-po*, "Iranian turnip"; at least there is no mention of this crop in China prior to the Mongolian era. Interestingly, Rashīd al-Dīn says that, in his day, carrots (*gazar*) were spreading rapidly throughout Iran wherever the soil was suitable.[49] This supports Laufer's contention that carrots were still in the process of establishing themselves in Iran and therefore did not reach China until a late date.[50]

But to obtain a balanced and complete picture of these crop exchanges we should not limit ourselves to first introductions. The history of several members of the bean family, which, like the citrus, has a very confused history, is most instructive in this regard.[51] The broad bean (*Vicia faba* L.), Chinese *ts'an-tou* or "silkworm bean," arrived during the Sung but never achieved pop-

[45] Rashīd al-Dīn, *Mukātabāt-i Rashīdī*, ed. by Muḥammad Shafī' (Lahore: Punjab Educational Press, 1947), p. 206.
[46] Rashīd al-Dīn, *Āthār va Aḥyā'*, p. 54.
[47] Rashīd/Karīmī, vol. I, p. 645, and Rashīd/Boyle, p. 283.
[48] See Hugh R. Clark, "Muslims and Hindus in the Culture and Morphology of Qanzhou from the Tenth to Thirteenth Century," *Journal of World History* 6 (1995), 69–70.
[49] Rashīd al-Dīn, *Āthār va Aḥyā'*, pp. 195–96.
[50] Laufer, *Sino-Iranica*, pp. 451–54.
[51] As Crosby notes, identifying beans and peas, even between Old and New World varieties, is difficult. Alfred W. Crosby, *The Columbian Exchange: Biological and Cultural Consequences of 1492* (Westport, Conn.: Greenwood Press, 1972), p. 172.

ularity until the Ming.[52] Thus, while not a Yuan import, this West Asian crop was clearly diffused *within* China during the Mongolian era. The same seems to be true of the common or garden pea (*Pisum sativum* L.), the Chinese *wan-tou*. In pre-Yuan times it was often styled the Hu *tou*, "Iranian bean," and then the Hui-ho *tou*, "Uighur bean," but by Ming times it was generally called the Hui-hui *tou*, "Muslim bean."[53] Here is another case of a Yuan popularization of a previously introduced crop, one that was quite familiar to the Muslim population of the Yuan and one whose planting we know was actively encouraged by the Mongolian court.[54]

This points up the fact that the initial introduction of a foreign cultural trait, the preoccupation of diffusion studies in the first half of the last century, is not always the most important date for the very obvious reason that acceptance, adaptation, and modification may come generations or even centuries later.[55] In short, chronologies focused on first contact say something about the length of the "demonstration period" but ofttimes very little about the actual process of cultural borrowing. This point is nicely illustrated by the history of the watermelon in China. Chinese of the Ming believed that the watermelon, *hsi-kua*, "western melon," was introduced under the Mongols. As Laufer has shown, the first introduction was in fact during the Five Dynasties period (907–60).[56] The Ming commentators were clearly wrong about the chronology but their mistaken opinion is itself an important cultural fact. Many new items, plants in particular, were demonstrated in the pre-Mongolian era and only popularized under the Yuan, which transformed social and cultural patterns in China, and this left Ming scholars with the mistaken impression that this constituted the initial introduction. It is possible as well that, as in the case of the *līmū*, a completely new variety of melon from the West was introduced at this time. Ibn Baṭṭuṭah speaks, suggestively, of the "wonderful melons" found in China that resemble "those of Khwārazm and Iṣfahān."[57] In any event, the fact that the Mongolian word for watermelon, *arbus*, derives from the Persian *kharbuzah* certainly indicates that there was a resurgence of interest in this crop under the Mongols.[58] So, too, does the existence of a Produce Superintendency (*Tsai-ching t'i-chü-ssu*) in North China that grew melons (*kua*) in several government gardens (*kuan-yuan*).[59]

Cotton is another, and very important, example of a foreign introduction that preceded the Yuan but only became widespread under the Mongols. Again, many people, including Chinese, attributed the original introduction

[52] Laufer, *Sino-Iranica*, pp. 307–8. For a detailed chronology of Chinese notices of the silkworm bean, see Li Ch'ang-nien, *Tou-lei* (Peking: Chung-hua shu-chü, 1958), pp. 351–54.

[53] Laufer, *Sino-Iranica*, pp. 305–6, and Li, *Tou-lei*, pp. 331–35.

[54] *YS*, ch. 183, p. 4214.

[55] As Deng, *Chinese Maritime Activities*, p. 156, has noted, the diffusion of crops typically takes place in "slow motion."

[56] Laufer, *Sino-Iranica*, pp. 438–45.

[57] Ibn Baṭṭuṭah/Gibb, vol. IV, p. 889.

[58] Antoine Mostaert, *Le matériel mongol du Houa I I Iu de Houng-ou (1389)*, ed. by Igor de Rachewiltz (Mélanges chinois et bouddhiques, vol. XVIII; Brussels: Institut belge des hautes études chinoises, 1977), vol. I, p. 37.

[59] *YS*, ch. 87, p. 2206.

to the Yuan era. In this case their conclusion seemed all the more plausible because the Yuan government actively encouraged the spread of cotton cultivation.[60]

The Mongols thus introduced new crops and new varieties from the Muslim world to China and, of equal importance, they helped to popularize many earlier introductions from the West. And as we shall see in the next chapter on cuisine, Mongolian rule had a similar effect on older Chinese introductions into Iran, such as rice.

[60] Pelliot, *Notes*, vol. I, pp. 484–506, especially 504–5, and Watson, *Agricultural Innovation*, pp. 31–41.

FIFTEEN

Cuisine

In the Mongolian Empire the office of *ba'urchi*, generally translated as "cook," or sometimes as "steward" or "commissary," had an unexpected importance.[1] As noted earlier, in the Mongols' patrimonial conception of government, which was rooted structurally and ideologically in the qaghan's household establishment, the title of *ba'urchi* clearly advertised the holder's closeness to the ruler and his right to act on his behalf. Cooks were officers in the imperial guard (*keshig*), one formation of which, the night guard (*kebte'ül*), oversaw the provision and preparation of drink and food (*undān ide'en*) during the reigns of Chinggis Qan and Ögödei; in addition to their titular duties these officers often held active military commands.[2] For example, Ked Buqa, who led the huge Mongolian field army against the Isma'īlīs and ʿAbbāsids in the 1250s, held the title of *ba'urchi*.[3]

Indeed, the kitchen was the starting point of many an illustrious career in the empire. Bolad and his father were both *ba'urchis* and Bolad's friend and ally, Rashīd al-Dīn, also served in the same capacity; his "entry level" appointment is reported in Bar Hebraeus:

> Now a certain Jew, whose name was Rashīd ad-Dāwlāh, had been appointed to prepare food which was suitable for Kaijātū [Gheikhatu], of every kind which might be demanded, and wheresoever it might be demanded.[4]

The Mamlūk sources fully confirm this, noting that by Ghazan's reign Rashīd al-Dīn had become the ruler's

> advisor, friend, table companion, comrade and cook. [Ghazan, the account continues] would not eat except from his hand and the hands of his son. They would cook for him in silver vessels and ladle it out on gold trays and cups, and carry it out to him themselves. Khwājah Rashīd would cut it up for him and serve him with his hand.[5]

[1] The standard Chinese translation is *ch'u-tzu*, "cook" or "chef." See Mostaert, *Le matériel mongol*, vol. I, p. 39. For a brief discussion of the word and its origin, see Gerhard Doerfer, *Türkishe und mongolische Elemente im Neupersischen* (Wiesbaden: Franz Steiner, 1963), vol. I, pp. 202–5.

[2] *SH*/Cleaves, sect. 213, pp. 153–54, sect, 232, p. 170, and sect. 278, p. 220; and *SH*/de Rachewiltz, sect. 213, p. 122, sect. 232, p. 134, and sect. 278, p. 168.

[3] Juvaynī/Qazvīnī, vol. III, pp. 72 and 94, and Juvaynī/Boyle, vol. II, pp. 596 and 611.

[4] Bar Hebraeus, p. 496.

[5] Amitai-Preiss, "New Material from the Mamlūk Sources," p. 25.

The trust placed in these cooks has rather obvious security implications. Ghazan came to power in a disputed succession and there was the ever present danger of poisoning, which could only be prevented by an absolutely loyal *ba'urchi*. And, in fact, poison (and rumors of poison) was an often used political weapon in the Mongolian Empire. Ghazan and other Chinggisid princes were well aware that Yisügei, Chinggis Qan's father, perished in this fashion, eating poisoned food proffered by his Tatar rivals.[6]

The food the Chinggisid *ba'urchis* were required to prepare changed over time. Initially, of course, it was traditional Mongolian fare which had much in common with that of the Turkic nomads of the steppe, for whom the basic sources of nutrition were meat, dairy products, and some vegetables. Such variations as did occur can be accounted for by differing ecological conditions and by specific historical–cultural factors.[7]

Horse flesh was the preferred meat but certainly not a staple. Mutton was more regularly eaten, some fresh, but most preserved by drying, freezing, jerking, and smoking. For the most part meat, of whatever type, was boiled and flavored with wild garlic or onions. There were distinct seasonal variations in the consumption of meat: in the winter meat of domesticated animals is more in evidence, while in the summer game became more important.

The by-products of milk, which was rarely drunk fresh, played a principal role in the nomads' diet. These include many nomadic innovations such as cheese, yoghurt, and the famous kumys, the lightly fermented mares' milk. These, too, were seasonal and their importance to the Mongols and other nomads is well reflected in their role in spiritual life. Dairy products, particularly libations of kumys, are a standard feature of Mongolian ceremonies from the time of empire to the present day.

The consumption of vegetables was generally limited to wild varieties and those extracted by trade or tribute from sedentaries. The grain obtained in this manner was made into porridge or dough fried in fat.

The initial conservatism of their food culture is revealed in the Mongols' attitude toward animal blood. Since blood, taken fresh or as an ingredient in broths and sausages, was seen as an important component of their diet, methods of animal slaughter were of major concern to the Mongols. When they kill an animal they do so by making an incision in the chest, squeezing the heart and thereby retaining the blood in the carcass for later use. This, of course, is just the opposite of the West Asian, Muslim, or Jewish notions of kosher, in which all the blood is drained off and discarded. These opposing methods often came into conflict within the empire which forbade the West

[6] *SH*/Cleaves, sect. 67, p. 18, and *SH*/de Rachewiltz, sect. 67, p. 26.

[7] The following discussion relies on Nurila Z. Shakanova, "The System of Nourishment among the Eurasian Nomads: The Kazakh Example," in Gary Seaman, ed., *Ecology and Empire: Nomads in the Cultural Evolution of the Old World* (Los Angeles: Ethnographics Press, 1989), pp. 111–17; N. L. Zhukovskaia, *Kategorii i simvolika traditsionnoi kul'tury Mongolov* (Moscow: Nauka, 1988), pp. 69–85; and John Masson Smith, "Mongol Campaign Rations: Milk, Marmots and Blood?," *Journal of Turkish Studies* 8 (1984), 223–28. For an eyewitness account, see Carpini, *Mongol Mission*, p. 17.

Asian techniques of killing an animal by cutting its throat. According to Rashīd al-Dīn, this proper, Mongolian method of slaughtering animals was included in the earliest Mongolian law code, the *jasaq* of Chinggis Qan.[8]

While they clung tenaciously to some culinary traditions, over time the Mongols began to borrow and adapt to their own tastes and needs the diverse foodways of their numerous sedentary subjects.[9] When Friar Carpini attended Güyüg's enthronement in 1246 the only food mentioned at the celebratory feast is salted and unsalted meat in broth, certainly standard Mongolian fare.[10] When, however, Rubruck arrived in the imperial city of Qara Qorum, less than a decade later, he found the food, although short in supply, to be somewhat more diversified: millet with butter, boiled dough, sour milk, unleavened bread, cooking oil, wine, mead, vinegar, and a variety of fruits and nuts, including almonds, grapes, and dried plums.[11]

While improved, for people from agricultural societies Mongolian imperial cooking still seemed undistinguished, if not downright primitive. This, however, changed during Qubilai's reign when the eastern Mongolian court, the seat of the nominal qaghan, was transferred from the steppe to North China with its vast agricultural resources and rich culinary traditions. This is what Marco Polo encountered during his stay at the court. He describes in some detail and with evident astonishment the "great hall" which held thousands for sumptuous feasts. The qaghan, a most generous host, provided his fortunate guests with a wide range of drinks: wine, spiced drinks, mares' milk (kumys) and camels' milk.[12]

But of the food which is brought to the tables [he continues] I will tell you nothing, because each must believe that in so magnificent a court it is there in great and lavish abundance of every sort; that he [the qaghan] has dishes and viands many and various of different flesh of animals and birds, wild and domestic, and of fish, when it is the season for this and when he pleases, prepared in various and different ways most delicately as befits his magnificence and his dignity.[13]

Such productions, most certainly, had moved beyond the rough fare of the steppe and had achieved the status of haute cuisine. While specifics are lacking, except in the matter of drinks, it is apparent that the Yuan court now strove to provide for the discriminating tastes of the qaghan's diverse retainers and guests, and that this required ingredients and cooking skills from all over Eurasia.

[8] Rashīd/Alizade, vol. II, pt. 1, pp. 184–85, and Rashīd/Boyle, pp. 77–78. See also Jūzjānī/Lees, p. 397, and Jūzjānī/Raverty, vol. II, p. 1146, on Chaghadai's prohibition on slaughtering sheep in the Muslim fashion.

[9] For the persistence of conflict over modes of slaughtering animals, which arose again in Qubilai's day, see *YS*, ch. 10, pp. 217–18; *YTC*, ch. 57, pp. 11a–b; Rashīd/Karīmī, vol. I, p. 654; Rashīd/Boyle, pp. 293–94; Pelliot, *Notes*, vol. I, pp. 77–78; and Paul Ratchnevsky, "Rašīd al-Dīn über die Mohammedaner-Verfolgungen in China unter Qubilai," *CAJ* 14 (1970), 163–80.

[10] *Mongol Mission*, p. 63.

[11] Rubruck/Jackson, pp. 204 and 207, and *Mongol Mission*, pp. 172 and 174.

[12] Marco Polo, pp. 209 and 218. [13] *Ibid.*, p. 220.

This tremendous undertaking, which so exemplifies the cosmopolitanism of the Mongolian court, was in the hands of a Director of Imperial Household Provisions (*Hsüan-hui shih*), which office, it will be recalled, was held during the years of Marco Polo's stay in China by our constant companion, Bolad. And if Marco Polo is any judge, Bolad set a fine table, one that befitted Qubilai's "magnificence and dignity."

Naturally, Bolad did not actually cook, like some mess sergeant, for the throngs in the great hall; rather he presided over a Chinese-style Bureau (*Hsüan-hui yuan*) which had grown out of the older office of *ba'urchi* but which was now much expanded in terms of personnel and functions. As it evolved in Qubilai's reign the Bureau was most immediately responsible for the emperor's food and drink, staging the imperial banquets, and feeding on a daily basis the large household staff, the guards and servants. The Bureau was also in charge of a vast network of subsidiary agencies, most located in North China, that produced or procured for the court all the required foodstuffs. These included offices dedicated to brewing and wine making, granaries, storehouses for produce, agricultural colonies, offices overseeing fuel supplies, fodder, the imperial herds, and, finally, hunting superintendencies providing game for the imperial table.[14] The Bureau became the primary, but by no means the only, conduit for foreign, primarily Muslim, culinary influence in China, and, as we shall see, Bolad likely had a hand in these exchanges.

The cuisine of the central Islamic lands, which drew on many culinary traditions and a wide variety of ingredients from Asia and Africa, had, nevertheless, some defining characteristics: the centrality of bread; absence of pork; importance of sweets, sugar and honey; and the wide use of dairy products.[15] That cooking was a serious matter in Muslim culture, one worthy of intellectual attention, is reflected in the fact that al-Nadīm, writing in the tenth century, lists ten cookbooks in his survey of Islamic literature, all now unfortunately lost.[16] By the thirteenth century, certainly, Muslim cookery had become the most international of the world's cuisines; by this date Muslim chefs could be found from Spain to China, where they exercised a measure of influence on local cooking and eating.[17]

In China this influence is most strikingly manifest in the *Yin-shan cheng-yao*, or "Proper Essentials of Drink and Food," the imperial dietary compendium of the Yuan dynasty. The great importance of this work, and its full potential as a primary source on medieval Eurasian cuisine, medicine,

[14] *YS*, ch. 87, pp. 2200–6, and Farquhar, *Government*, pp. 73–82.

[15] For an overview, see S. D. Goitein, *A Mediterranean Society*, vol. IV: *Daily Life* (Berkeley: University of California Press, 1983), pp. 226–53, and Muhammad Manazir Ahsan, *Social Life under the Abbasids* (London and New York: Longman, 1979), pp. 76–164.

[16] Al-Nadīm, *Fihrist*, vol. II, p. 742.

[17] Peter Heine, "Kochen im Exil – Zur Geschichte der arabischen Küche," *Zeitschrift der deutschen morgenländischen Gesellschaft* 139 (1989), 318–27, and Ibn Baṭṭuṭah/Gibb, vol. IV, p. 903.

ethnobotany, and cultural exchange, is only now being recognized.[18] Presented to the throne in 1330 by Hu Ssu-hui, an official of the *Hsuan-hui yuan*, as a guide to good health and long life, the *Yin-shan cheng-yao* contains several hundred recipes and makes reference to innumerable ingredients.[19] The majority are therapeutic, designed for specific ills, while a minority are for pure culinary enjoyment. On the surface at least, the work appears to follow and conform to Chinese models on materia medica, but in fact there are various other cultural layers evident as well – Mongolian, Turkic, and Perso-Islamic.

This culinary cosmopolitanism hardly began with the presentation of this work. As its preface points out, "valuable food items" from "near and far" had long flowed into the Yuan court and the compilation of materials included in the *Yin-shan cheng-yao* had already begun in Qubilai's day.[20] Thus, Bolad may have contributed to its formative stages while in China and even afterward in Iran where he was exposed to West Asian dishes and dietary methods. There was nothing to prevent him from sending recipes to his old friends in China.

In any event, the *Yin-shan cheng-yao* exhibits a pronounced West Asian flavor. In Buell's analysis of this document these influences include the following:

- extensive use of wheat products and pasta[21]
- wide use of legumes, particularly chickpeas
- heavy use of nuts, particularly walnuts and pistachios
- use of certain vegetables such as eggplant
- importance of sugars and syrups as ingredients
- use of spices of West Asian provenance.

These tendencies are well reflected in a recipe of *mu-ssu-ta-chi* puree, that is, mastic (Arabic *mastakī*): flavored mutton on a bed of pulverized chickpeas, or hummus.[22]

[18] Laufer, *Sino-Iranica*, pp. 236, 252, etc., used this work occasionally and indirectly. The first Western scholar to point out its full potential was L. Carrington Goodrich, "Some Bibliographical Notes on Eastern Asiatic Botany," *JAOS* 60 (1940), 258–60. The appearance of a modern, punctuated edition in simplified characters, Hu Ssu-hui, *Yin-shan cheng-yao* (Peking: Chung-kuo shang-yeh ch'u pan-she, 1988), attests to its enduring interest.

[19] My discussion relies on the pioneering work of Françoise Sabban, "Court Cuisine in Fourteenth Century Imperial China: Some Culinary Aspects of Hu Sihui's *Yinshan zhengyao*," *Food and Foodways* 1 (1986), 161–96, and Paul D. Buell, "The *Yin-shan cheng-yao*, A Sino-Uighur Dietary: Synopsis, Problems, Prospects," in Paul U. Unschuld, ed., *Approaches to Traditional Chinese Medical Literature* (Dordrecht, Boston and New York: Kluwer Academic Publishers, 1989), pp. 109–17.

[20] For a complete translation of the preface, see Paul U. Unschuld, *Medicine in China: A History of Pharmaceutics* (Berkeley: University of California Press, 1986), pp. 215–16. See also Buell, "The *Yin-shan cheng-yao*," p. 110.

[21] Compare the comments of Marco Polo, p. 244.

[22] Buell, "The *Yin-shan cheng-yao*," pp. 120–22, and Paul D. Buell, "Pleasing the Palate of the Qan: Changing Foodways of the Imperial Mongols," *Mongolian Studies* 13 (1990), 69–73.

In addition to these general trends there are various specific ingredients that reveal West Asian influence.[23] In the following sampling of Arabic-Persian words found in this text I have followed for the most part the lead of Lao and Franke, who first identified, explained, and reconstructed these terms. In each case, I have added a few notes and emendations of my own, with particular reference to the Arabic and Persian sources.

ch'u-chün-ta-erh: Persian, *chugunder*, "white sugar beet" (*Beta vulgaris*). Under the form *chughundar*, also known as *salq*, "beet," this plant is frequently mentioned by Rashīd al-Dīn, who reports that it was widely grown in Iran.[24]

pa-tan: Persian, *bādām*, "almond." Widespread in Iran in two varieties, a bitter and a sweet, the latter being the more popular, according to Rashīd al-Dīn.[25]

pai na-pa: Turkic, *nabad*, "sugar." A more accurate derivation, I believe, is the Persian *nabāt*, "fine sugar" or "rock candy." The initial character *pai*, "white," is not part of the transcription, as Franke correctly notes. Thus, the term means "white refined sugar." Damascus, an early thirteenth-century Persian geography notes, produced a quality "white sugar [*nabāt-i safīd*]."[26] Rashīd al-Dīn briefly describes its manufacture. He also notes that the best sugar cane comes from Shustar in Khūzistān, and from Baghdad and Wāsiṭ in Mesopotamia.[27] This is interesting, since Marco Polo relates that in Vuguen (Yung-chun, north of Zaitun) there was a manufactory of sugar that was under the direction of "people from the regions Babilonie" who taught the locals "to refine it with the ashes of certain trees."[28] This enterprise was likely connected with the *Sha-t'ang chü*, "Sugar Office," established in 1276 as an agency of the *Hsuan-hui yuan* "to manage the production of granulated sugar."[29] Thus, imperial chefs had ready access to high-quality West Asian sugar when their recipes called for it.

pi-ssu-ta: Persian, *pistah*, "pistachio." Also known as *fustuq*; widely grown and consumed in Iran, according to Rashīd al-Dīn.[30]

shih-lo: Persian, *zhīrah* or *zīrah*, "cumin seed." Here the meaning is "cumin," not "caraway seed" since Rashīd al-Dīn states in his agricultural manual: "as for *zīrah*, they say *kumān* in Arabic."[31] One of the main centers of production was Kirmān; in fact, the product became so identified with this region that "presenting cumin seeds to Kirmān" was the Persian equivalent of "taking coals to Newcastle."[32]

[23] Lao Yan-shuan, "Notes on non-Chinese Terms in the Yüan Imperial Dietary Compendium *Yin-shan cheng-yao*," *Bulletin of the Institute of History and Philology, Academia Sinica* 34 (1969), 399–416, and Herbert Franke, "Additional Notes on non-Chinese Terms in the Yuan Imperial Dietary Compendium *Yin-shan cheng-yao*," *Zentralasiatische Studien* 4 (1970), 8–15.

[24] Rashīd al-Dīn, *Āthār va Aḥyā'*, pp. 99, 153, 192, and 197–98. [25] *Ibid.*, pp. 21–23.

[26] Smirnova, *'Ajā'ib al-dunyā*, p. 504, Persian text and p. 201, Russian translation.

[27] Rashīd al-Dīn, *Āthār va Aḥyā'*, pp. 182–83. [28] Marco Polo, p. 347.

[29] *YS*, ch. 87, p. 2204. [30] Rashīd al-Dīn, *Āthār va Aḥyā'*, pp. 28–29. [31] *Ibid.*, pp. 161.

[32] Juvaynī/Qazvīnī, vol. I, p. 16, and Juvaynī/Boyle, vol. I, p. 22.

tsa-fu-lan: Arabo-Persian, *za'farān*, "saffron." Discussed by Rashīd al-Dīn at length, who says it was widely grown in Iran.[33] Saffron had, of course, been known in China well before the Mongols. In T'ang times saffron was in use, but as an incense or perfume. It is only in Yuan times that it is used as a food flavoring following West Asian practice.[34] This preference can be seen in the Baghdad cookbook of 1226, which includes no fewer than twenty-one recipes calling for saffron.[35]

Foreign terms such as these are not, however, the only indicators of foreign influence on the court cuisine of the Yuan. The use of certain vegetables, even those with Chinese names, tells us something of the transcontinental cultural currents of the era. The eggplant (*Solanum melongena* L.) is a case in point. Domesticated in South or Southeast Asia, it then spread into South China by the fourth century AD and somewhat later moved north. It reached the Arabs and Persians sometime before the rise of Islam and later diffused throughout the Mediterranean Basin and Africa.[36] In West Asia it quickly established itself as a mainstay, often as a substitute for meat. Its uses, manner of preparation, and presentation are numerous in West Asian cuisine.[37] Under the influence of its popularity in the West, eggplant entered the kitchens of the Yuan court. This may again be a case of a new variety gaining favor in China, for it is fairly clear that the indigenous variety of Southeast Asia was the smaller, oval white variety, while the West Asian eggplant was the larger and elongated type with dark purple skin.[38] In any event, the introduction of a new variety well accounts for popularization of the plant in North China and for the fact that the Mongolian name for eggplant is *badingqa*, which is derived from the Persian *bādinjān*, not the Chinese name, *ch'ieh*.[39]

The *Yin-shan cheng-yao* also has a recipe calling for the use of Hui-hui *hsiao-yu*. This is not Muslim "fat" as sometimes assumed but rather "lesser oil," some kind of vegetable oil.[40] Moreover, there is every reason to believe that this was a cooking oil made in China by West Asians. One of the principal suppliers of oil (*yu*) as well as wheat flour (*mai-mien*) to the imperial court and the summer capital at Shang-tu was the Hung-chou Agricultural Superintendency (*Chung-t'ien t'i-chü-ssu*). This again was a subordinate agency of the *Hsuan-hui yuan* and, most significantly, we know that Hung-chou, about 180 km west of Peking, was also the seat of a large Muslim artisan

[33] Rashīd al-Dīn, *Āthār va Aḥyā'*, pp. 203–5.
[34] Laufer, *Sino-Iranica*, pp. 310–12, and Schafer, *Golden Peaches*, pp. 124–26.
[35] A. J. Arberry, trans., "A Baghdad Cookery-Book," *Islamic Culture* 13 (1939), 21–47 and 189–214.
[36] Simoons, *Food in China*, pp. 169–70, and Watson, *Agricultural Innovation*, pp. 70–71.
[37] Arberry, "Baghdad Cookery-Book," 34, 37, 38, 39, 191, 200, 203, 205, and 206, and Peter Heine, *Kulinarische Studien: Untersuchungen zur Kochkunst im arabisch-islamischen Mittelalter, mit Rezepten* (Wiesbaden: Harrassowitz, 1988), pp. 124–25.
[38] See the comments of Li Chih-ch'ang, *Hsi-yü chi*, p. 346, and Li Chih-ch'ang, *Travels of an Alchemist*, p. 106, who encountered "Western" eggplants in Samarqand in 1220.
[39] Mostaert, *Le matériel mongol*, vol. I, p. 38.
[40] See Sabban, "Court Cuisine," 171.

colony established in the early 1220s shortly after the Mongols' conquest of the eastern Islamic lands.[41] Consequently, like the "sugar of Vuguen," the "Muslim oil" used in the imperial kitchens had an impeccable pedigree.

So, too, did the wine served at the emperor's table. The *Yin-shan cheng-yao*, while counseling moderation in all things, has an extensive section on alcoholic beverages, including the distilled variety. Here, however, discussion will be limited to grape wine, another "Western" introduction which tells us something of the growing sophistication of the Mongols' tastes and their accommodation to those of their diverse servitors.

The grape (*Vitis vinifera*), as Laufer long ago demonstrated, was one of the few Western plants actually brought back by Chang Ch'ien, the famed envoy and explorer of the Former Han. For some time thereafter it remained an exotic. In the T'ang, a most cosmopolitan age, there is evidence of growing popularity of grape wine, the introduction of new Western varieties, and domestic production.[42] This was repeated in the Yuan, which saw another revival of interest in grape wine. Some came as "tribute" from Westerners (*Hsi-fan*), especially the Uighurs whose capital Qara Qocho, a center of viticulture, was famous for its fine wines.[43] But some was produced domestically. One such source was Hsin-ma-lin, Rashīd al-Dīn's Sīmalī, northwest of Peking, which was home to a colony of Muslim artisans; throughout the thirteenth century, according to the testimony of both the Chinese and Persian sources, these colonists, mainly from Samarqand, grew grapes and made wine for the imperial court.[44]

Unfortunately, in gauging the extent of East Asian influence on Islamic and Persian cuisine we have no document equivalent to the *Yin-shan cheng-yao*, no recipes, and no menus. We do, however, have the writings of Rashīd al-Dīn, which allow us to judge his knowledge of Chinese cookery and this in turn provides a basis for assessing, at least in general terms, some hypotheses on the changing foodways in Iran during the Mongolian era.

To begin with the most obvious source of his information, Rashīd al-Dīn had direct and continuous access to Bolad, the former Director of Imperial Household Provisions. True, there is no text that says they discussed these matters, but as friends and colleagues, frequently thrown together on state and social occasions, it is hard to imagine that the subject of food, cuisine, and the management of the imperial kitchen never came up in conversation. Another source was Rashīd al-Dīn's Chinese cook. In the foundation deed for the Rabʿ-i

41 *YS*, ch. 87, pp. 2203 and 2206, and ch. 120, p. 2964, and Farquhar, *Government*, pp. 76–77 and 81.

42 Laufer, *Sino-Iranica*, pp. 220 ff., and Schafer, *Golden Peaches*, pp. 141–45.

43 *YS*, ch. 34, p. 755; Rashīd/Karīmī, vol. I, p. 648; Rashīd/Boyle, p. 286; Marco Polo, p. 156; and D. I. Tikhonov, *Khoziaistvo i obshchestvennyi stroi uigurskogo gosudarstva, X–XIV vv.* (Moscow and Leningrad: Nauka, 1966), pp. 71–73.

44 Rashīd/Karīmī, vol. I, p. 641; Rashīd/Boyle, p. 276; and *YS*, ch. 19, p. 419. For a history of this colony, see Paul Pelliot, "Une ville musulmane dans Chine du Nord sous les Mongols," *Journal Asiatique* 211 (1927), 261–79.

Rashīdī in Tabrīz there is a *ghulam* (slave) listed who is identified as "so-and-so [his personal name is undecipherable] of China, a cook [——— Khitāʿī, *bāūrchī*]."[45]

From such sources, Rashīd al-Dīn must have derived his extensive knowledge of Chinese specialty dishes. In his agricultural manual, under the general heading "water lily" (*nīlūfar*), Rashīd al-Dīn writes that:

> there are other types which are like the *nīlūfar* but are not. In the country of China [he continues] they are numerous and its name is *līnk khū* and they have a seed which is black, each one the dimension of a sebesten [a plum-like fruit] and the inhabitants of China open them up and eat their marrow.

Rashīd al-Dīn here describes the lotus root (*Nelumbium speciosum* W. Nd.) and his information is quite correct. The Chinese call this plant by two names, *lien* = *līnk* and *ho* = *khū*; further, the seeds are black and a desirable food. He is also correct when he states that "its root is white and strong" and that "the inhabitants of China frequently eat it fried." His statement that the flower of the lotus root "is bigger than the *nīlūfar*, sweeter smelling and better" leaves the strong impression that his information came from Chinese in Iran, someone like his own cook, who could compare, on the basis of firsthand experience, the qualities of the Chinese lotus root with that of the Persian water lily.[46]

While colleagues and retainers were the most accessible and immediate sources, Rashīd al-Dīn could and did obtain information on Chinese cuisine from the local Chinese community. In his discussion of beans (*mash*) and lentils (*ʾadas*), Rashīd al-Dīn relates that "in the country of China, they take the starch [*nishāstah*] from them [beans and lentils] and prepare *kūkā lāshah* from it; and here [in Iran] the Chinese [*khitāyān*] also make it."[47] As is well known, the Chinese consume starch mainly in the form of noodles, some of which are made of various kinds of bean flour.[48] This particular dish, while Chinese in origin, is given a Mongolian name, *kūkā lāshah*, which in a variant form, *kūkā lākhīshah*, is registered in the fourteenth-century Rasūlid *Hexaglot*, and twice defined there by the Arabic *al-iṭriyyah*, "vermicelli." The Mongolian original is *köke lakhsha*, or "blue vermicelli."[49]

Just as many West Asian foodways reached China through Turkic and

[45] Rashīd al-Dīn, *Vaqfnāmah*, p. 152. Togan, "The Composition of the History of the Mongols," 71, reads the name as Sulī.

[46] Rashīd al-Dīn, *Āthār va Aḥyāʾ*, pp. 202–3. On the Persian water lily, a specialty of Balkh, see Thaʿālibī, *Book of Curious and Entertaining Information*, pp. 136 and 116. On the lotus root as food and medicine, see Simoons, *Food in China*, pp. 112–15, and G. A. Stuart, *Chinese Materia Medica: Vegetable Kingdom*, repr. (Taipei: Southern Materials Center, 1987), pp. 278–81.

[47] Rashīd al-Dīn, *Āthār va Aḥyāʾ*, p. 160.

[48] E. N. Anderson, "Food and Health at the Mongol Court," in Edward H. Kaplan and Donald W. Whisenhunt, eds., *Opuscula Altaica: Essays Offered in Honor of Henry Schwarz* (Bellingham, Wash.: Center for East Asian Studies, Western Washington University, 1994), p. 27.

[49] Golden, *Hexaglot*, 187C21, p. 80 and 192C8, p. 137.

Mongolian mediation, there are many instances of the reverse.[50] Rashīd al-Dīn knows Chinese rice wine under the name *tarāsūn*, the Mongolian *darasun*, "wine."[51] And, more interestingly, chopsticks became known in the Islamic world under their Turkic name *shököl/shögü*. This is recorded in the *Hexaglot* in the form *shūkū* and defined in Arabic as "two pieces of wood with which one eats macaroni."[52]

Thus, through several different channels Rashīd al-Dīn was well acquainted with Chinese cuisine and its ingredients. The presence of Chinese communities in Iran who continued to prepare the food of their homeland certainly raises the possibility of influence on the local food culture. Indeed, Bert Fragner has recently argued that a dramatic shift in Iranian cuisine did take place in the period of Mongolian domination. He notes that in Iran rice has never been the staff of life as it is in the typical rice cultures of India, Southeast Asia and China, but a prestige food prepared in ways quite different from and more complicated than those practiced in East Asia. This, he suggests, became an important part of Persian cuisine in the Il-qan period when Chinese influence flowed west and rice became an important dish closely identified with the ruling class.[53]

To test this hypothesis several issues must be examined in greater depth. First, how important was rice in Persian cuisine in the pre-Mongolian era? Laufer, citing early Chinese accounts that assert there was no rice in Iran, argued that it was only introduced there after the Arab conquest and was certainly not a staple.[54] His views, however, require substantial modification.

On the basis of current archaeological and botanical evidence, rice (*Oryza sativa* L.) was first domesticated in the region of the lower Yangtze at the end of the sixth millennium BC, spread to Southeast and South Asia in the third millennium and from there, after a delay of several millennia, expanded westward into Iran and the Mediterranean world in the period before Islam and quite possibly even before Christianity.[55] The suggested chronology is affirmed by the fact that Middle Persian does have a well-attested word for rice, *brinj*,

[50] This issue is explored at length by Paul D. Buell, "Mongol Empire and Turkicization: The Evidence of Food and Foodways," in Amitai-Preiss and Morgan, *Mongol Empire*, pp. 200–23.

[51] Rashīd al-Dīn, *Āthār va Aḥyā'*, pp. 146–47.

[52] Golden, *Hexaglot*, 190C13, p. 112, and Peter B. Golden, "Chopsticks and Pasta in Medieval Turkic Cuisine," *Rocznik Orientalistyczny* 44 (1994), 73–74.

[53] Bert Fragner, "From the Caucasus to the Roof of the World: A Culinary Adventure," in Sami Zubaida and Richard Tapper, eds., *Culinary Cultures of the Middle East* (London and New York: I. B. Tauris, 1994), pp. 56–60.

[54] Laufer, *Sino-Iranica*, pp. 372–73. See, for example, Roy Andrew Miller, trans., *Accounts of Western Nations in the History of the Northern Chou Dynasty* (Berkeley: University of California Press, 1959), p. 15, which states emphatically that Persia (Po-ssu) had no rice.

[55] See Watson, *Agricultural Innovation*, pp. 15–19, and most recently, Ian C. Glover and Charles F. W. Higham, "New Evidence for Early Rice Cultivation in South, South East and East Asia," in David R. Harris, ed., *The Origins and Spread of Agriculture and Pastoralism in Eurasia* (Washington, D.C.: Smithsonian Institution Press, 1996), pp. 413–41 and especially 417–19 and 435.

and supported further by the historical researches of Canard and Petrushevskii, who independently came to the conclusion that rice entered Iran, as Rashīd al-Dīn himself believed, long before the Muslim era, if only on a limited basis.[56] While its popularity did increase over time and while rice achieved a place in West Asian cuisine before the Mongols, as witness a recipe for a kind of rice pilaf in the Baghdad cookbook of 1226, this does not preclude or fatally undermine Fragner's hypothesis.[57] The Mongolian presence may well have given a new and forceful impetus to an existing trend. There is, I believe, much evidence – direct and circumstantial – that sustains his argument in this slightly modified form.

General support for this hypothesis can be found in the fact that Hülegü and his immediate successors were all born and reared in the East and brought the tastes of Mongolia and China with them to Iran. It is most relevant in this regard to record that Qara Qorum, the center of Mongolian court life down to 1259, was an artificial creation in a steppe environment which could not support itself from local resources and had, perforce, to be supplied with wagon-loads of food and drink, including rice wine, from China.[58] Further, the core of the Hülegüid army, as well as the court officials, were also from cultures long accustomed to rice. The Uighurs, for example, who served in large numbers in Iran, grew and consumed much rice in their homeland in Turfan and it was the Uighurs in all likelihood who first brought chopsticks to West Asia.[59]

Even Ghazan, who was born in Iran, seems to have inherited the tastes of East Asia through his family. He had, after all, a Chinese wetnurse, a Chinese tutor, and a wife, although Mongolian, who was raised at the court in Peking.[60] It is not surprising that Ghazan took a keen personal interest in developing and diversifying Iranian rice cultivation. This emerges from Rashīd al-Dīn's treatment of rice in his agricultural manual. To begin with, he recognizes that "there are various varieties of rice, particularly in India, North and South China [which] have many types which no one in this kingdom [Iran] has seen." He then continues, noting that "there is a small [-grained] rice [*birinj-i kuchak*] which the notables [*ākābir*] in India eat." Consequently, this variety was sown in Iran during Ghazan's reign and "by way of an experiment," Rashīd al-Dīn says, "we boiled it several times" with the result in the

[56] D. N. MacKenzie, *A Concise Pahlavi Dictionary* (London: Oxford University Press, 1990), p. 19; M. Canard, "Le riz dans le Proche Orient aux premiers siècles de l'Islam," *Arabica* VI/2 (1959), 113–31; and Petrushevskii, *Zemledelie*, pp. 185–87.

[57] Arberry, "Baghdad Cookery-Book," 199.

[58] Rashīd/Karīmī, vol. I, p. 622; Rashīd/Boyle, p. 253; Rubruck/Jackson, pp. 162, 172, 178, and 202; and *Mongol Mission*, pp. 144, 149, 154, and 171.

[59] Tikhonov, *Khoziaistvo i obshchestvennyi stroi uigurskogo gosudarstva*, p. 71. On the Uighur presence in the West, see A. Sh. Kadyrbaev, "Uighury v Irane i na Blizhnem Vostoke v epokhu mongol'skogo gosudarstva," in *Voprosy istorii i kul'tury Uigurov* (Alma Ata: Nauka, 1987), pp. 41–51.

[60] Rashīd/Jahn II, pp. 3–4, 8, 13, and 39.

author's opinion that it "has the best taste and smell of all the known [types of] rice and is readily digestible."[61]

The effort to introduce this particular variety failed in the long run, but the essential point here is that under Ghazan rice production was encouraged and its consumption was explicitly associated with elite status and behavior, and that Ghazan's chief cook, Rashīd al-Dīn, from whose hand he took his daily meals, was a party to the enterprise and a self-proclaimed connoisseur of fine rices. In this way the common fare of the rice cultures of the East might well have become, as Fragner argues, the haute cuisine of the ruling elite of the West.

As I have already mentioned in the Introduction, the long-term effects of these cultural transfers is often very elusive. In the case of cuisine there is a considerable difference of opinion regarding the "Mongolian" impact on the foodways of their sedentary subjects. Kriukov, Maliavin, and Sofronov, in their ethnohistory of China, argue that:

> the century of Mongolian domination did not have a substantial influence on the traditional Chinese dietary regime. Therefore, the character of Chinese cuisine in the Ming, about which we are able to judge from the historical–archeological sources, is directly linked in its specifics to the pre-Mongolian period.[62]

This is a view which others share; Mote, for instance, concludes that the Mongols were generally conservative in matters of food, and kept to their own fare which had little impact on the Chinese.[63] On the other hand, the recent works of Saban, Buell, and Anderson posit quite different views in which Mongolian, Turkic, and Perso-Islamic cuisine exert considerable influence in China.[64]

To some extent, these differing assessments turn on what one means by "substantial" or "considerable." Further, there is the equally vexing question of timing. Let us take tea, for example. If tea drinking had become widespread in West Asia in the immediate aftermath of the Mongolian conquests, a connection between the two events would certainly be made. However, since tea drinking came much later, such a connection seems doubtful and is hardly likely to be raised. Nevertheless, the history of tea consumption in Iran is meaningfully linked to the transcontinental exchanges of the Mongolian era. As Rashīd al-Dīn's comments on the subject make clear (see above, p. 120) in his day tea was a medicine, taken for specific ills, and other evidence suggests it was a commodity that continued to be imported into Iran from the East

[61] Rashīd al-Dīn, *Āthār va Aḥyā'*, pp. 147–48.

[62] M. V. Kriukov, V. V. Maliavin, and M. V. Sofronov, *Etnicheskaia istoriia Kitaitsov na rubezhe srednevekov'ia i novogo vremia* (Moscow: Nauka, 1987), p. 116.

[63] Frederick W. Mote, "Yuan and Ming," in K. C. Chang, ed., *Food in Chinese Culture: Anthropological and Historical Perspectives* (New Haven, Conn.: Yale University Press, 1977), pp. 203–10.

[64] See, for example, Anderson, "Food and Health at the Mongol Court," 35–39.

after the fall of the Mongolian Empire.[65] Consequently, when it first became a popular social drink in the early Ṣafavid period, tea was hardly an alien commodity but one which had been demonstrated to the locals in a positive if limited way for centuries.[66] This, of course, fits nicely into larger patterns of cultural diffusion and social acceptance. Many distant and exotic goods, most particularly stimulants and spices, made their initial penetration into new cultural zones as prized medicines. While it may surprise many today, this is even true of tobacco, which entered the Old World as a promoter of good health and a cure for many maladies.[67]

A further problem in establishing borrowing and determining the degree of influence is that alien cultural wares are seldom accepted as originally presented; they are adapted, modified, and accepted piecemeal. Such syncretism, a major mechanism of cultural transmission, is readily seen in cuisine. A good example can be found in the *Shih-lin kuang-chi*, a houshold encyclopedia first compiled during the Chin and reissued in the Yuan. This work contains a dish called Muslim (Hui-hui) dumpling soup that consists of mutton broth, dumplings of glutinous rice flour, honey, cheese, pine nuts, walnuts and "Muslim" peas, the common or garden pea (*Pisum sativum* L.).[68] This is most definitely a fusion cuisine, a kind of *nouvelle* Jürchen which draws on a number of distinct traditions for ingredients and inspiration: mutton broth and cheese from the Mongols; rice flour from the Chinese; pine nuts from the peoples of Manchuria;[69] and honey, walnuts, and Muslim peas from West Asia. But even this formulation is not without its ambiguities. Peas, honey, and walnuts were widely used in Muslim cookery in the thirteenth century, but none of these ingredients were "new" to the Chinese.[70] Walnuts, for instance, entered China in the fourth century AD and enjoyed a certain popularity during the T'ang.[71] What is really new here, of course, is the combination of ingredients and the exotic name of the dish.

Despite the difficulties of measuring influence, the evidence favors the

[65] The early sixteenth-century Persian traveler ʿAlī Akbar notes that in China tea, *chāī*, was both a food and a medicinal herb decocted with some kind of liquid. ʿAlī Akbar Khitāʾī, *Khitāi-nāmah*, ed. by Iraj Afshār (Tehran: Asian Cultural Documentation Center for UNESCO, 1979), pp. 58, 155, and 163. Further, the Persian–Chinese vocabulary of the Ming registers tea (*ch'a*) along with many other trade goods. See Liu Ying-sheng, "Hui-hui kuan tsa-tzu yü Hui-hui kuan i-yü yen-chiu," *Yuan shih chi pei-fang min-tsu shih yen-chiu ch'i-k'an* 12–13 (1989–90), 156.

[66] On the changing fortunes of tea consumption in Iran, see Rudi Matthee, "From Coffee to Tea: Shifting Patterns of Consumption in Qajar Iran," *Journal of World History* 7 (1996), 199–230.

[67] Jordan Goodman, *Tobacco in History: The Cultures of Dependence* (London and New York: Routledge, 1994), pp. 19–55.

[68] See Herbert Franke, "Chinese Texts on the Jurchen: A Translation of the Jurchen Monograph in the *San-ch'ao pei-men hui-pen*," *Zentralasiatische Studien* 9 (1975), 172 and 177.

[69] See David Curtis Wright, trans., *The Ambassadors' Records: Eleventh Century Reports of Sung Ambassadors to the Liao* (Papers on Inner Asia 29; Bloomington, Ind.: Research Institute for Inner Asian Studies, Indiana University, 1998), p. 74.

[70] Heine, *Kulinarische Studien*, pp. 55, 92–93, and 126–27, and Arberry, "Baghdad Cookery-Book," 35, 36, 39, 40, 41, etc.

[71] Laufer, *Sino-Iranica*, pp. 254–72.

conclusion that the period of the Mongolian Empire saw real changes in the cuisines of China and Iran, some substantial and visible, and some small-scale and subtle. This evidence is by no means limited to the eating habits of the Yuan and the Il-qan courts, as reflected in the *Yin-shan cheng-yao* and the writings of Rashīd al-Dīn; equally persuasive are the data concerning the channels of contact and diffusion. Because of the tradition of bureaucratic record keeping in China, we can sometimes trace culinary influences back to their sources, in many cases Muslim communities in China producing West Asian style sugar or wine or cooking oil. Therefore, to explain foreign elements or changes in Chinese cookery, we do not have to rely upon the "trickle-down effect" of the haute cuisine prepared at the courts. Out in the North Chinese countryside there were Muslim agricultural colonies growing and processing these "West Asian" ingredients and products in near proximity to their Chinese neighbors. In other words, the centers of diffusion were now *within* China itself. The same is true of Iran. It, too, had its Chinese officials, troops, and, most importantly, its Chinese agriculturalists dispersed in the countryside – Marv, Khūi, and Tabrīz – to serve as centers of diffusion for East Asian crops and dishes.

Finally, the literary sources, while pointing up important connections and possibilities, can only take us so far. Ethnobotanical and ethnological studies are also needed. To cite but one obvious example, a careful ethnohistorical study of the agricultural practices and eating habits of the once Chinese town of Khūi in Azerbaijan might yield some most informative results. So, too, might a similar investigation of the one-time Muslim center of Hung-chou in North China.

SIXTEEN

Medicine

The Mongols of the imperial era possessed an extensive repertoire of medical practices, cures, and materia medica; as in all folk traditions, their healing techniques were rooted in both empirical knowledge and spiritual–magical belief. Interestingly, Rashīd al-Dīn tells us that certain tribes had greater skill in this field than others, particularly the peoples of southern Siberia, who, he says, "well understand Mongolian medicines and well apply Mongolian cures."[1] Some of their medicines are known by name, *qajir*, for example, but nothing is known of their composition or character.[2] In addition to their folk medicines, the Mongols also tried to harness the curative powers of mineral springs and the viscera of freshly killed animals which, if properly applied, were thought to heal various maladies and wounds.[3] In later centuries at least, bloodletting was also an important part of their medical repertoire.[4]

When they acquired empire and held sway over a vast territory and a multitude of peoples, the Mongolian ruling elite had access, of course, to the major medical systems of Eurasia – Chinese, Korean, Tibetan, Indian, Uighur, Muslim, and Nestorian Christian.[5] Chinggisid princes soon acquired their personal physicians who traveled with them on administrative rounds and military campaigns. Qubilai, who suffered from gout, had a large contingent of healers in his traveling camp (*orda*).[6] In some cases these medical retainers were simply conscripted like soldiers and artisans. In China, for which we have

[1] Rashīd/Alizade, vol. I, pt. 1, p. 239.

[2] *Ibid.*, p. 305. The Mongolian term derives from the Turkic *qajir*, "fierce," in the sense, apparently, of "potent [medicine]." See *DTS*, p. 407.

[3] Nicholas Poppe, "An Essay in Mongolian on Medicinal Waters," *Asia Major* 6 (1957), 99–105, and Francis W. Cleaves, "A Medical Practice of the Mongols in the Thirteenth Century," *HJAS* 17 (1954), 428–44.

[4] Menggen Bayar, "Unique Features of Bloodletting Treatment in Traditional Mongolian Medicine," *Mongolian Society Newsletter*, 13 (Feb., 1993), 46–52.

[5] See the survey of Leonardo Olschki, *Marco Polo's Asia* (Berkeley: University of California Press, 1960), pp. 414–32. Nothing like a medical history of Inner Asia yet exists, but see the preliminary remarks of Ruth I. Meserve, "Western Medical Reports on Central Eurasia," in Arpád Berta, ed., *Historical and Linguistic Interaction between Inner Asia and Europe* (University of Szeged, 1997), pp. 179–93.

[6] Marco Polo, pp. 231 and 233; Rashīd/Karīmī, vol. I, p. 658; and Rashīd/Boyle, pp. 298–99.

the most detailed information, the whole populace was classified by ethnicity and occupation, of which physician was a recognized and important category.[7] Others, however, did not have to be coerced but voluntarily sought fame and fortune at Mongolian courts, such as the "certain Lombard leech and chirurgeon" who showed up in China at the very beginning of the fourteenth century.[8] But whether coopted or attracted into service, these numerous court physicians, along with their diagnostic techniques, therapies, and medicines, were frequently moved about the empire. Consequently, healers of all types and backgrounds were regularly thrown together at Mongolian courts of the East and West.

To distinguish these healers from the native shamans, the Mongols called their foreign doctors *otochi*. Borrowed from the Uighur *otachi*, "physician," the Chinese sources of the era define this term as *tai-i*, "court physician."[9] The Mongols' term for "medicine," "drugs," and "herbs," *em*, was also borrowed from Turkic.[10] Indeed, the principal feature that distinguished the *otochi* from the shaman was that the former used herbs to treat illness while the latter relied mainly on spiritual means.[11] This is why in recent centuries Mongols associated "advanced medicine" with herbal remedies and why Westerners, like the Russian explorer Przhevalskii, who collected botanical specimens on their travels through Mongolia, were immediately identified by the locals as skilled healers.[12]

The first of these *otochi* to be transported across cultural boundaries were the Chinese physicians who accompanied the Mongolian armies into western Turkestan in 1219. Chinggis Qan's second son, Chaghadai, whose territory was Transoxania, had several Chinese doctors attached to his household.[13] When Hülegü came west in the mid-1250s he, too, had Chinese physicians (*iṭibbāʿ-i khitāī*) in his train.[14] These doctors were in attendance throughout his reign and during his final illness in early 1265 they treated the Il-qan with purgatives. His condition, however, worsened and he soon died.[15]

Arghun, Hülegü's grandson, although born and reared in the West, also favored East Asian medicine. During his final illness in 1291 extreme measures were taken: his physicians, variously described as Indians or Uighurs, fed him

[7] Ōshima Ritsuko, "The *Chiang-hu* in the Yuan," *Acta Asiatica* 45 (1983), 69–70.

[8] Yule, *Cathay*, vol. III, p. 49, and *Mongol Mission*, p. 226.

[9] Mostaert, *Le matériel mongol*, vol. I, p. 83, and *DTS*, p. 373.

[10] Mostaert, *Le matériel mongol*, vol. I, p. 54, and *DTS*, p. 171.

[11] This distinction is clearly drawn by Yūsuf Khāṣṣ Ḥājib, *Wisdom of Royal Glory* (*Kutadgu Bilig*): *A Turko-Islamic Mirror for Princes*, trans. by Robert Dankoff (University of Chicago Press, 1983), p. 181.

[12] N. Prejevalsky [Przhevalskii], *Mongolia, the Tangut Country and the Solitudes of Northern Tibet*, trans. by E. Delmar Morgan, repr. (New Delhi: Asian Educational Services, 1991), vol. I, p. 149.

[13] Li Chih-ch'ang, *Hsi-yü chi*, pp. 351–53; Li Chih-ch'ang, *Travels of an Alchemist*, p. 110; Rashīd/Karīmī, vol. I, p. 548; and Rashīd/Boyle, p. 154.

[14] Rashīd al-Dīn, *Chinageschichte*, folio 392r, *tafel* 1, Persian text, and p. 21, German translation.

[15] Rashīd/Karīmī, vol. II, p. 736.

several potions of cinnabar (*sīmāb-i adviyah*) which in all likelihood killed him.[16] Whatever the ethnicity of the attending physicians, cinnabar or mercury sulfide was a medicine closely identified with China, where it was widely used as an elixir of life. Generations of Taoist alchemists experimented with mercury with disastrous results; between the Han and T'ang large numbers of practitioners and their high-born patients, including a number of emperors, died of lead poisoning by ingesting cinnabar (*tan*).[17] Despite its lethal reputation, cinnabar retained a place in the materia medica of Asia and claimed yet further victims.

Ghazan, as well, made use of Chinese medicine. When he was afflicted with ophthalmia (*ramad*) for a second time and the local (Muslim) doctors proved unable to ameliorate the condition, he repaired to Tabrīz in October of 1303 where he underwent treatment at the hands of Chinese physicians who "cauterized his august person in two places." Ghazan, however, was weakened by the procedure and was unable to sit on a horse.[18]

This is clearly a form of moxibustion, common in East Asian medicine. Like acupuncture, moxibustion rests on a theory of channels and collaterals, or trunks and branches, along which flow *ch'i* or "influences" that condition and control the health of the human body. In this system of channels and collaterals there are certain points where stimulus can be applied to assist healing in specific parts of the body. In acupuncture needles are utilized and in moxibustion heat is applied in the form of the dried leaves of the tree *artemisia moxa*. These are ground into powder and formed into cones or cylinders and then applied with an insulator such as ginger or salt to one of the innumerable points where the moxa cone is allowed to burn slowly, giving off heat that stimulates the *ch'i* in a specific channel. In the case of Ghazan, there are in fact a variety of moxa points designated for ailments of the eye, most of which are located on the face or head but some of which are found on the extremities.[19]

There is, then, good evidence that Chinese medicine continued to enjoy an honorable place at the Il-qan court into the fourteenth century. After all, Ghazan himself was familiar with the basic principles of Chinese medicine and knew the properties of their drugs.[20] In part this can be attributed to Mongolian tradition and preference but it was also a product of Rashīd al-Dīn's open-mindedness and catholic interests.

Rashīd, it will be recalled, first entered Mongolian service as a cook/dietitian and doctor.[21] He was so identified with this profession that to his contemporaries he was Rashīd the Physician (*Ṭabīb*). He used his wealth and political

[16] Rashīd/Jahn I, p. 88, and Mu'īn al-Dīn Naṭanzī, *Muntakhab al-tavarīkh-i mu'īnī*, p. 149.

[17] See Joseph Needham, "Elixir Poisoning in Medieval China," in his *Clerks and Craftsmen in China and the West* (Cambridge University Press, 1970), pp. 316–39.

[18] Rashīd/Jahn II, p. 150.

[19] Dana Heroldova, *Acupuncture and Moxibustion* (Prague: Academia, 1968), pt. I, pp. 81–86, 101, 107–9, 119, 140–42, and 177–79.

[20] Rashīd/Jahn II, p. 172.

[21] Abū Bakr al-Ahrī, *Tarīkh-i Shaikh Uwais*, p. 146, Persian text, and p. 48, English translation.

influence to further, in various ways, his chosen profession. Most spectacularly, he built in Ghazan's time the Rabʿ-i Rashīdī, a suburb of Tabrīz, that became a center for scholars of the most diverse interests and origins, which made the Il-qan capital one of the leading cultural clearing houses of medieval Eurasia.[22] His quarter included a House of Healing that was both a hospital and a medical training facility.[23] And even if we discard the claims put forth in the *Correspondence* attributed to Rashīd al-Dīn that at this hospital he had physicians from China and other foreign lands teach their specialities to local "interns," there can be no doubt that he had extensive exposure to East Asian medicine and that he avidly sought out its secrets.

We know, for instance, that during Ghazan's reign the Chinese masters who arrived in Iran, Lītājī and K.msūn, were conversant with the various Chinese sciences, including medicine (*ṭībb*), and that they brought with them "books from China."[24] While there is no indication of their titles, we know of several Chinese medical works that appear in Persian translation. In the digest of his own literary output, Rashīd al-Dīn includes a section on Chinese books first translated into Persian and then into Arabic. The first was on the theoretical and practical medicine of the people of China, the second on the folk remedies in use in China "including those used by us and those unknown to us," and the third, a volume on the folk remedies utilized by the Mongols.[25] We hear no more of the Mongolian material but some of the Chinese medical literature has survived in the *Tanksūq-nāmah īl-khānī*, the "Treasure Book of the Il-qans."[26]

The single extant manuscript of this work, discovered in the Aya Sophia, was copied in Tabrīz in 1313 by a certain Muḥammad ibn Maḥmūd al-Kirmanī.[27] As it has come down to us, the work contains a long introduction by Rashīd al-Dīn, Persian translations of Chinese medical tracts, with illustrations, and a Persian commentary and explanations by one Safīʿ al-Dīn. In the opinion of Rall the translation was a cooperative enterprise in which a Chinese physician explained difficult passages to the Persians, presumably

[22] See Karl Jahn, "Tabris, ein mittelalterliches Kulturzentrum zwischen Ost und West," *Anzeiger der phil.-hist. Klasse der österreichischen Akademie der Wissenschaften* 11 (1968), 201–11.

[23] Donald N. Wilber and M. Minovi, "Notes on the Rabʿ-i Rashīdī," *Bulletin of the American Institute for Iranian Art and Archeology* 5 (1938), 247–54, especially 242 and 252, and A. I. Falina, "Rashīd al-Dīn – Vrach i estestvoispytatel," *Pis'mennye pamiatniki Vostoka, 1971* (Moscow: Nauka, 1974), pp. 127–32.

[24] Rashīd al-Dīn, *Chinageschichte*, folio 393r, *tafel* 4, Persian text, and p. 23, German translation.

[25] Rashīd/Quatremère, pp. CXXXVIII and CLX, and Muginov, "Persidskaia unikal'naia rukopis," p. 374.

[26] Rashīd al-Dīn, *Tanksūq-nāmah yā ṭibb ahl-i Khitā*, ed. by Mujtabā Mīnuvī (University of Tehran, 1972). This is the second work bearing this title; the first, a book on mineralogy and precious stones by Naṣīr al-Dīn Ṭūsī (1201–74), was dedicated to Hülegü. See O. F. Akimushkin, "Novye postupleniia persidskikh rukopisei v rukopisnyi otdel Instituta Narodov Azii AN SSSR," in *Ellinisticheskii Blizhnii Vostok, Vizantiia i Iran* (Moscow: Nauka, 1967), pp. 147–48.

[27] Abdulhak Adnan, "Sur le Tanksukname-i-Ilhani dar Ulum-u-Funun-i-khatai," *Isis* 32 (1940), 44–47.

Safīʿ al-Dīn and Rashīd al-Dīn, who then wrote them down. In any event, it is evident that the Persian translator and commentator was extremely well informed on Chinese medical concepts and literature. The principal Chinese work translated is ascribed to Vāng Shū khū (Wang Shu-ho [180–270]), the author of the *Mai-ching*, "Classic of Pulse." In fact, however, the work actually translated is the *Mai-chüeh*, "Secrets of the Pulse," a composite work dating from the Sung or Yuan eras. The confusion is not the fault of the Persians but goes back to Chinese misconceptions about the authorship of the *Mai-chüeh*. Also mentioned in the *Tanksūq-nāmah* is a Chinese work called the *Nām-līng*; this is probably a reference to the *Nan-ching*, "Classic of Difficulty," which also deals with sphygmology or pulse diagnosis.[28]

Additionally, there are some illustrations taken from yet another Chinese medical work on human physiology. Chinese understanding of human anatomy was based on the *Yellow Emperor's Classic of Internal Medicine*, China's *Canon*, dating to the third century BC. There is, however, no explicit reference to human dissection until the eleventh century. Then, in the early twelfth century, the Sung physician Yang Chieh compiled the *Ts'un-hsin huan-chung t'u*, "Illustrations of Internal Organs and Circulatory Vessels," based on the dissection of executed criminals. Pictures of human viscera in the *Tanksūq-nāmah* go back to Yang Chieh's work but are reproduced from drawings added to the Yuan edition of an older, traditional medical treatise called the *Hua T'o nei chao-t'u*, "Hua T'o's Illuminating Illustrations of Internal Medicine."[29]

Taken as a whole, it is quite obvious that the branch of Chinese medical knowledge most admired in Iran was pulse diagnosis. To be sure, medieval Muslim medicine concerned itself with the movement of the blood and with the pulse; Ibn Sina even wrote a tract on this subject.[30] Nevertheless, there is ample evidence to suggest that the decision to translate the *Mai-chüeh* was a by-product of conscious and strongly held preferences of the Mongolian elite.

Pulse taking as a diagnostic technique is very ancient in China. By the fifth century BC, if not before, it had become a standard practice in the art of healing. The technique was later elaborated and systematized in the *Nei-ching* and in the *Nan-ching*, a work sometimes ascribed to Pien Ch'iao, a physician of the fourth century BC, but now recognized as a work of the first century

[28] On the authorship, translation, and contents of the *Tanksūq-nāmah*, see Jutta Rall, "Zur persischen Übersetzung eines *Mo-chüeh*, eines chinesischen medizinischen Textes," *Oriens Extremus* 7 (1960), 152–57, and Mujtabā Mīnuvī, "Tanksūq-nāmah-i Rashīd al-Dīn," in S. H. Naṣr, ed., *Majmuʿah-i khatābah-ha-i taḥqīqī dar bārah-i Rashīd al-Dīn* (University of Tehran, 1971), pp. 307–17.

[29] Miyasita Saburō, "A Link in the Westward Transmission of Chinese Anatomy in the Later Middle Ages," *Isis* 58 (1967), 486–90.

[30] Manfred Ullman, *Islamic Medicine* (Edinburgh University Press, 1978), pp. 64–69; William E. Gohlman, trans., *The Life of Ibn Sina* (Albany: State University of New York Press, 1974), p. 97; and Ernest A. Wallis Budge, trans., *Syriac Book of Medicines: Syrian Anatomy, Pathology and Therapeutics in the Early Middle Ages*, repr. (Amsterdam: APA-Philo Press, 1976), vol. I, pp. 138, 248, 287, and 290.

AD, by an unknown author.[31] The first tract exclusively devoted to the subject is the *Mai-ching* of Wang Shu-ho, who, as already noted, was mistakenly credited with the *Mai-chüeh*. For all these practitioners, the pulse, heartbeat, and blood flow were interconnected; health depended on the monitoring and manipulation of these flows through the human body.[32]

By the Mongolian era diagnosis by pulse was commonplace among the Chinese and works like the *Mai-ching*, of which there is a Yuan edition, were held in high esteem.[33] The Mongols, too, soon placed great reliance on and made wide use of this diagnostic technique. In the spring of 1241, Ögödei, Chinggis Qan's third son and successor, became seriously ill and his "pulse [*mai*] became irregular." Yeh-lü Ch'u-ts'ai, one of his chief advisers, recommended amnesty for All-Under-Heaven. The emperor complied with his wish and as soon as the proclamation was issued his "physicians [*i-che*] felt his pulse and it had come back to life [i.e., returned to normal]."[34] For the Mongols, as well as for the Chinese, physical well-being and the moral order were closely linked.

A dozen years later, Rubruck, who visited Qara Qorum in the reign of Möngke, speaks highly of the Chinese physicians he met there, especially their use of herbs and their diagnosis through reading the pulse.[35] The preeminent status of this branch of medicine was further strengthened in Qubilai's reign when, sometime in the 1270s, the emperor ordered the Uighur scholar An-ts'ung to translate the *Nan-ching* into Mongolian.[36] Finally, under his successor, Temür, its priority in medical training received the force of law. According to contemporary administrative documents, the Imperial Academy of Medicine (*T'ai-i yuan*), which was charged with supervising medical schools, establishing curriculum, and certifying graduates, in 1305 ordered that all medical students were to be examined on ten subjects: the first two listed were pulse diagnosis for adults and pulse diagnosis for children. Among the texts recommended were the *Nan-ching* and the *Mai-chüeh*.[37] Rashīd al-Dīn's inclusion of the latter in the *Tanksūq-nāmah* was hardly a matter of chance or mere availability; rather, Mongolian priorities of long standing, first established by the eastern court, were transmitted to the Il-qans, who willingly followed the Yuan precedent.

The flow of West Asian medicine eastward in the thirteenth century is

[31] Paul U. Unschuld, "Terminological Problems Encountered and Experiences Gained in the Process of Editing a Commentated *Nan-ching* Edition," in Unschuld, ed., *Approaches to Traditional Chinese Medical Literature*, pp. 97–100.

[32] For an overview, see Ma Kanwen, "Diagnosis by Pulse Feeling in Chinese Traditional Medicine," in *Ancient China's Technology and Science*, pp. 358–68.

[33] R. C. Rudolph, "Medical Matters in an Early Fourteenth Century Chinese Diary," *Journal of the History of Medicine and Allied Sciences* 2 (1947), 304–5, and K. T. Wu, "Chinese Printing under Four Alien Dynasties," *HJAS* 13 (1950), 479.

[34] *YS*, ch. 146, p. 3463, and *YWL*, ch. 57, p. 20b.

[35] *Mongol Mission*, p. 144, and Rubruck/Jackson, pp. 161–62.

[36] K'o Shao-min, *Hsin Yuan shih* (Erh-shih-wu-shih ed.), ch. 192, p. 1b, and Fuchs, "Analecta zur mongolischen Uebersetzungsliteratur," 42–43.

[37] *YTC*, ch. 32, pp. 3a and 4a–b; *T'ung-chih t'iao-ko*, ch. 21, pp. 261–62; and Ratchnevsky, *Un code des Yuan*, vol. II, pp. 48–49.

closely linked to the presence of Eastern Christian and, more particularly, Nestorian communities in central Asia and China, communities that were well established, connected by local and regional networks, and which exercised considerable political influence. The movement of the Eastern Christians began with the Christological controversies of the third and fourth centuries, was accelerated by Sasanian persecution in the fifth and sixth centuries, and reached one of its early milestones with the construction of the famous stelae at Sian in the late eighth century. Nestorian influence also extended into the steppe. In Chinggis Qan's day many of the nomadic tribes of western and southern Mongolia – the Kereyid, Naiman, and Önggüd – were firm adherents of this creed and even the Tatars in the far northeast were at least touched by Nestorian influence.[38] Among the settled population of Inner Asia there were large pockets of Nestorians in Semirechie, the Tarim Basin, and Uighurstan, as well as numerous communities scattered throughout China.[39] Moreover, the centers were in contact with one another and with their ecclesiastical leaders in West Asia.[40] Under these favorable circumstances the Nestorians flourished and only fell into decline in the aftermath of the empire.[41]

Of equal importance, Nestorians in the East were closely associated with the medical profession. A considerable body of Syriac medical literature, some in the original and some in translation, has been recovered in central Asia.[42] This is hardly surprising, because Eastern Christians were an important fixture in West Asian medicine. Although the relationship between Eastern Christian and Muslim medicine is complex, often misrepresented, and not as direct as once thought, there is no doubt that the Nestorians were a vital conduit of the Galenic tradition to the Arabs. Even the extensive and long-lived mythology surrounding the origins of Islamic medicine at the Christian medical school at Jundi Shapur only served to add luster to the Nestorian physicians operating in Muslim society.[43] At the time of the Mongols' expansion,

[38] Louis Hambis, "Deux noms chrétiens chez les Tatars," *Journal Asiatique* 241 (1953), 473–75.

[39] Marco Polo mentions many of these in passing. See Marco Polo, pp. 143, 146, 151, 178–79, 181, 183, 263, 264, 277, 314, and 323.

[40] On their ecclesiastical ties, see Budge, *Monks of Ḳūblāi Khān*, pp. 136, 146, and 152, and Marco Polo, p. 100.

[41] On the spread of the Nestorians eastward, see A. B. Nikitin, "Khristianstvo v Tsentral'noi Azii (drevnost i srednevekov'e)," in B. A. Litvinskii, ed., *Vostochnoi Turkistan i Sredniaia Aziia: Istoriia, kul'tura, sviazi* (Moscow: Nauka, 1984), pp. 121–37. On their decline in the aftermath of the Mongols, see I. P. Petrushevskii, "K istorii Khristianstva v Srednei Azii," *Palestinskii sbornik*, vyp. 15(78) (1966), 141–47.

[42] P. Zieme, "Zu den nestorianisch-türkischen Turfantexten," in G. Hazai and P. Zieme, eds., *Sprache, Geschichte und Kultur der altaischen Völker* (Berlin: Akademie-Verlag, 1974), p. 665, and Nicolas Sims-Williams, "Sogdian and Turkish Christians in the Turfan and Tun-huang Manuscripts," in Alfredo Cadonna, ed., *Turfan and Tun-huang: The Texts* (Florence: Leo S. Olschki Editore, 1992), p. 51.

[43] For the traditional view, see Allen D. Whipple, *The Role of the Nestorians and Muslims in the History of Medicine* (Princeton University Press, 1967), pp. 20–23. For a more critical assessment which sees the relationship between Nestorian and Muslim medicine as interactive, see Michael W. Dols, "The Origins of the Islamic Hospital: Myth and Reality," *Bulletin of the History of Medicine* 61 (1987), 367–90.

Eastern Christian doctors were not only important figures in their own communities but continued to serve as court physicians to prominent Muslim rulers.[44] One of the centers was Edessa, which produced famous practitioners and a continuing medical literature in Syriac.[45]

Although the case has sometimes been overstated, it is quite evident that the Nestorians' position and influence in the early Mongolian Empire was all out of proportion to their numbers.[46] Their influence was exercised in numerous ways. Initially, marriage alliances led to the influx of Nestorians in the Chinggisid extended family. To cite but one case, Doquz Qatun, the principal wife of Hülegü and a political force in the early Il-qan state, was a devout Christian, the granddaughter of the Kereyid leader Ong-qan.[47] More visible as time went on were the Eastern Christians who held high office at the imperial court: Chinqai, the chief adviser of Ögödei; Qadaq, the atabeg (tutor) of Güyüg; and Bulghai, the senior administrative officer under Möngke, were all Nestorians.[48] The Christian cause was furthered by the large numbers of Uighurs in Chinggisid service, many of whom were Nestorians. So pervasive were Christian Uighurs at the court that Latin Christians such as Carpini mistakenly believed that Uighurs were all "of the Nestorian Sect" when in fact many were Buddhists and Manichaeans.[49] Indeed, Nestorian Christians of various ethnic backgrounds, always well connected at the Yuan court, were the bane of Catholic missionaries in the East throughout the thirteenth and fourteenth centuries. Such complaints are heard from Rubruck, John of Montecorvino, and others.[50]

Consequently, when Nestorians from West Asia went east to seek their fortune, they typically found a warm reception from their fellow communicants and from the Mongolian court. One of the first to do so was the church elder and physician Simeon, a native of Rum Qal'a on the upper Euphrates who journeyed to Mongolia in the late 1230s and early 1240s. Utilizing his medical skills, he successfully ingratiated himself with the "Qaghan," at this time Ögödei, and received the honorific Rabban Ata, a hybrid term from the Syriac *rabban*, "teacher," and the Turkic *ata*, "father." Simeon used his high standing at court to obtain a decree ending the Mongolian forces' harassment of the Christian population of Transcaucasia. He then returned home, where he used his political connections to improve the plight of his coreligionists. He built churches, converted "Tartars" to the faith, and gave protection to

44 Budge, *Monks of Ḳūblāi Khān*, pp. 152 and 153.

45 Bar Hebraeus, pp. 391–92.

46 See, for example, L. N. Gumilev, *Searches for an Imaginary Kingdom: The Legend of the Kingdom of Prester John* (Cambridge University Press, 1987), pp. 169–218, who pushes the evidence to the limits and sometimes well beyond.

47 Vardan, "Historical Compilation," 217.

48 Juvaynī/Qazvīnī, vol. I, pp. 213–14, and Juvaynī/Boyle, vol. I, p. 259. See also Rashīd/Karīmī, vol. I, p. 573, and Rashīd/Boyle, p. 188.

49 *Mongol Mission*, p. 20.

50 Yule, *Cathay*, vol. III, pp. 46–48 and 101–2; *Mongol Mission*, pp. 144–45 and 177–79; and Rubruck/Jackson, pp. 163–64 and 211–14. For an extended discussion, see Paul Pelliot, *Recherches sur les chrétiens d'Asie centrale et d'Extrême-Orient* (Paris: Imprimerie nationale, 1973), pp. 242–88.

Christian communities in Muslim-dominated areas such as Tabrīz and Nakhchivān. He was highly regarded by the local Mongolian commanders and he conducted extensive and profitable trade operations throughout the region with their support and capital. His later history is uncertain but he might be identified with the Rabban Simeon who joined Hülegü's service as a physician; if so, he continued to prosper in his medical and commercial ventures until 1290 when he was killed in the course of a political purge.[51] In any event, while Simeon did not himself remain long in the East, he paved the way for another Nestorian physician, Jesus (ʿIsā) the Interpreter, who did.

Unfortunately, little is known of ʿIsā's early life; his Chinese biography indicates he was born around 1227 in Fu-lin, the Chinese transcription of Hrom or Rum.[52] In this case, however, Rum should not be understood to mean the Eastern Roman Empire, Byzantium, but those areas such as Syria and Upper Mesopotamia that had large Christian populations. Our ʿIsā may be identical with the ʿIsā mentioned by Bar Hebraeus. He records:

At this time [mid-1240s] ʿIsā, the physician of Edessa, who was the disciple of Hasrān the physician, was famous in Melitene. This man went from Melitene to Cilicia [Lesser Armenia] and lived in the service of the king [Het'um, r. 1226–69] and he built the foundations of a wonderful church in the name of Saint Mār Bar-Sāwmā.[53]

While uncertainty remains, several points, beyond the obvious similarity of names and professions, favor this identification. First, both Edessa (Al-Ruhā) and Melitene (Malaṭiyyah) were major Christian centers in Upper Mesopotamia, an area reasonably associated with the Chinese notion of Fu-lin.[54] Second, Bar Hebraeus' ʿIsā takes up residence in Cilicia just before his patron and king, Hetʾum, sent his brother, Smbat the Constable, to see Güyüg in the year 1247.[55] This is just about the time our ʿIsā shows up in Mongolia.

Whatever the truth of the matter, the ʿIsā (Ai-hsieh) of the Chinese sources first took service with the Mongols in the reign of Güyüg, 1247–49. According to his biography, "Because of common religious belief, a certain Rabban Ata [Lieh-pien A-ta] who had come to know Ting-tsung [Güyüg] recommended his abilities [to the emperor and] he was summoned to serve the throne." From this passage, it is evident that after Rabban Ata returned home he sent word east regarding ʿIsā's skills and ʿIsā was then "offered" a position and induced to come to Mongolia. The skills that attracted Güyüg's attention are clearly

[51] Kirakos, *Istoriia*, pp. 174–75 and 181; Galstian, *Armianskie istochniki*, p. 41; Bar Hebraeus, p. 437; and Simon de Saint Quentin, *Histoire des Tartares*, ed. by Jean Richard (Paris: Libraire orientaliste, 1965), p. 30. For a detailed biographical study, see Paul Pelliot, *Les Mongols et la papauté* (Paris: Librairie August Picard, 1923), vol. II, pp. 29–66.

[52] Ch'eng Chü-fu, *Ch'eng hsüeh-lou wen-chi*, ch. 5, p. 4b.

[53] Bar Hebraeus, pp. 409–10.

[54] Guy Le Strange, *The Lands of the Eastern Caliphate* (London: Frank Cass and Co., 1966), pp. 103–4 and 120.

[55] On this embassy, see Galstian, *Armianskie istochniki*, pp. 64–66 and 71, and Kirakos, *Istoriia*, p. 222.

spelled out in the same source: "Regarding the various languages of the Western Region [Hsi-yü], their astronomy [*hsing-li*] and medicine [*i-yao*], there were none he did not study and practice."[56] No languages are specified but it is most likely that as an educated Nestorian Christian from Upper Mesopotamia, he knew Syriac, Greek and Arabic, to which he presumably added Armenian from his tour in Cilicia, Mongolian from his service at the Chinggisid capital of Qara Qorum, and later on Chinese from his long stay in Peking. Nor would it be surprising if he acquired some Persian along the way.

During his time in Mongolia ʿIsā met and impressed Qubilai with his plain speaking and multiple talents. When Qubilai became emperor and moved his political base to North China, ʿIsā accompanied him at the latter's suggestion. There he established around 1263 an Office of Western Medicine, *Hsi-yü i-yao ssu*, also known as the Medical Bureau at the Capital, *Ching-shih i-yao yuan*. In 1273 this organization's name was changed to the *Kuang-hui ssu*, literally "Broadening Benevolence Office," but more usually identified as the "Muslim Medical Office."[57]

This office was administratively subordinated to the Imperial Academy of Medicine, *T'ai-i yuan* and "was charged with the preparation of Muslim [Hui-hui] medicine for imperial use and with mixing medicine to relieve the members of the imperial guard [*keshig*] and the orphaned and poor in the capital."[58] ʿIsā remained the head of this organization for an undetermined number of years. He, of course, left for Iran with Bolad in the mid-1280s and was back in China by 1287, when he received his appointment to the Imperial Library Directorate.[59] He lived on until 1308 and following his death, according to his Chinese biography, Ai-hsieh (ʿIsā) was made "Prince of Rum [Fu-lin *wang*]" and his wife Sa-la (Sarah), also deceased, was made consort (*fu-jen*) to the Prince of Rum.[60]

In all probability, he was succeeded as superintendent of the *Kuang-hui ssu* first by his third son, Hei-ssu (Jesse?), and then by his fifth son, Lu-ho (Luke).[61] His eldest son, Yeh-li-ya (Elijah), also continued the family tradition of combining knowledge of languages and medicine. He was an interpreter (*ch'ieh-li-ma-ch'ih*) in the Imperial Library Directorate and on several occasions in the fourteenth century he was placed in charge of the Imperial Academy of Medicine. The dates of his first term are not known but his second tenure began around 1328 and he remained in office until August 1330 when he was beheaded for sedition and practicing magic.[62]

This seems to have ended ʿIsā's family's domination of Western medicine in Yuan China, but in 1334 the Superintendent of *Kuang-hui ssu* was a certain

[56] Ch'eng Chü-fu, *Ch'eng hsüeh-lou wen-chi*, ch. 5, p. 3a.
[57] *Ibid.*, pp. 4a–b; *YS*, ch. 8, p. 147 and ch. 134, p. 3249; and Moule, *Christians in China*, p. 228.
[58] *YS*, ch. 88, p. 2221.
[59] Ch'eng Chü-fu, *Ch'eng hsüeh-lou wen-chi*, ch. 5, p. 4b.
[60] *Ibid.*, pp. 3b, 4a and 5b.
[61] *YS*, ch. 134, p. 3250, and Moule, *Christians in China*, p. 229.
[62] *MSC*, ch. 3, p. 17b (p. 106); *YS*, ch. 32, p. 715, ch. 34, pp. 750 and 761; and Moule, *Christians in China*, pp. 231–32.

Nieh-chih-erh, who is described as a *yeh-li-k'o-wen*, the Chinese transcription of the Mongolian *erke'ün*, "Christian."[63] Thus, Western medicine in Yuan China, often characterized as "Muslim" (Hui-hui), was almost always in the hands of Nestorians, a situation that Western travelers found worthy of note. Odoric of Pordenone, speaking of the 1320s, says "of the leeches to take charge of the royal person there be four hundred idolaters [Chinese], eight Christians and one Saracen."[64] The numbers for each do not have to be accepted as they stand but the proportions seem about right. To some extent this duplicated and perpetuated the situation in West Asia, where Nestorians had long played a prominent and recognized role in the medical professions, particularly as court physicians.

To the best of my knowledge, there is no direct evidence that West Asian medical works were translated into Chinese during the Yuan. There was, however, at least one book on medicine of Western provenance in China. This is included in the Imperial Library Directorate's catalog of 1273 under the transcription *t'e-pi*, which answers to the Arabo-Persian *ṭibb/ṭabb*, "medicine." The work is defined there as an *i-ching*, "medical classic" in thirteen *pu*, "sections."[65] There is no way of knowing which particular title is intended, but Ibn Sina's *Qānūn fī al-ṭibb*, "The Canon on Medicine," nicely fits the Chinese *i-ching*. Moreover, in the thirteenth and fourteenth centuries Ibn Sina was held in high regard by physicians in West Asia. The chronicler Bar Hebraeus, also a physician, extols his virtues and even translated one of his works from Arabic into Syriac.[66] It seems plausible, therefore, to suggest that "Western" physicians would be inclined to use the *Qānūn* of Ibn Sina, the great synthesizer of Hellenistic and West Asian medical traditions, to represent the achievements of their profession in China.

These court physicians traveled with their medical literature, their diagnostic and therapeutic techniques, and of course with their medicines. The Mongols, as already noted, had their own herbal remedies and from the days of Chinggis Qan they took an active interest in the pharmacology of others. Rubruck remarks with admiration on the skills of the Chinese herbalists serving the imperial family at Qara Qorum.[67] By the time of Qubilai this concern with foreign medicines had been systematized. Sometime in the 1270s the emperor ordered the Uighur An-ts'ung to translate, in addition to the *Nan-ching*, a Chinese materia medica (*pen-ts'ao*) into Mongolian.[68] And in 1285 the court ordered the historiographer Sa-li-man (Sarman/Sarban) and the

[63] Yang Yü, *Beiträge zur Kulturgeschichte Chinas unter der Mongolenherrschaft: Das Shan-kü sin-hua des Yang Yü*, trans. by Herbert Franke (Wiesbaden: Franz Steiner, 1956), p. 34, and Moule, *Christians in China*, p. 234. On the word *erke'ün*, see Pelliot, *Notes*, vol. I, p. 49.

[64] Odoric of Pordenone, *The Eastern Parts of the World Described*, in Yule, *Cathay*, vol. II, p. 226.

[65] *MSC*, ch. 7, p. 14a (p. 209), and Kōdō Tasaka, p. 112.

[66] Bar Hebraeus, pp. XXXIV and 196–98.

[67] *Mongol Mission*, p. 144, and Rubruck/Jackson, pp. 161–62.

[68] K'o Shao-min, *Hsin Yuan shih*, ch. 192, p. 1b, and Fuchs, "Analecta zur mongolischen Uebersetzungsliteratur," 42–43.

Chinese Grand Academician (*Ta-hsüeh-shih*) Hsü Kuo-chen "to assemble the professors of the medical schools of each circuit [*lu*] to revise and collate the pharmacologies [*pen-ts'ao*]."[69]

This avid interest in Chinese materia medica the Mongols took with them when they went west. In many instances, however, these drugs and medicines of East Asian provenance traveled to the West long before the Mongols. Chinese rhubarb (*Rheum palmatum* L. and *Rheum officianale* Baillon) will serve as a case in point. Called "big-yellow" (*ta-huang*) in Chinese, the dried root of this plant, native to Kansu and northern Tibet, was highly regarded as a cathartic and astringent. In the course of the tenth and eleventh centuries it became a trade good in the West and an increasingly important item in Muslim pharmacology. The demand was sufficiently strong that a formula was devised for "improving Persian rhubarb [*Rheum ribes*]," that is, passing it off as "Chinese."[70]

While "big-yellow" never achieved the fame in China, its native land, that it enjoyed in the West, its purgative properties were well understood by Chinese physicians and herbalists.[71] The Mongols, too, soon came to appreciate rhubarb's curative powers. These were demonstrated to them in 1226 during the campaign against the Tanguts. After the fall of Ling-wu, a town in Kansu, the military commanders, according to the Chinese sources, seized textiles, valuables, and young maidens, while the famed statesman Yeh-lü Ch'u-ts'ai "took only some books and two camel[loads] of rhubarb [*ta-huang*]." When soon thereafter an epidemic broke out among the Mongolian troops Yeh-lü Ch'u-ts'ai's rhubarb was credited with saving thousands of lives.[72] Marco Polo was well aware that the "province of Tangut" produced "the very finest rhubarb" and that from there merchants "carry it . . . through all the world."[73]

Cubebs (*Piper cubeba* L.) also traveled west ahead of the Mongols and were initially in demand as a spice.[74] As time passed, their medical properties came to be appreciated. The plant's unripened berries were dried, then pounded and used in the treatment of a number of maladies. Although cubebs are native to Java and Sumatra, by Sung times they were also grown in South China, a variety known as *kabābah-i sīnī*, "Chinese cubeb" in West Asia.[75] Another product from the south, found, according to Rashīd al-Dīn, "on the frontiers

69 *YS*, ch. 13, p. 271.

70 U. I. Karimov, "Slovar meditsinskikh terminov Abu Mansura al-Kumri," in P. G. Bulgakova and U. I, Karimov, eds., *Materialy po istorii i istorii nauki i kul'tury narodov Srednei Azii* (Tashkent: Fan, 1991), pp. 141–42 and 154 note 26; Ibn Ridwān, *Le livre de la méthode du médicin*, trans. by Jacques Gran'Henry (Louvain-la-Neuve: Université catholique de Louvain, 1979), vol. I, p. 75; and S. D. Goitein, *Letters of Medieval Jewish Traders* (Princeton University Press, 1973), p. 295.

71 Laufer, *Sino-Iranica*, pp. 547–51, and Unschuld, *Medicine in China: A History of Pharmaceutics*, pp. 154–55 and 191.

72 *YWL*, ch. 57, p. 12a.

73 Marco Polo, p. 158.

74 Goitein, *Mediterranean Society*, vol. IV, p. 230.

75 Bertold Laufer, "Vidanga and Cubebs," *TP* 16 (1915), 282–88, especially 286.

of China" was white pepper (*falfal-i safīd*). This, we are further informed, was in great demand by Persian physicians as an ingredient in "the best theriaca [*tiryāq-i fārūq*] and many other electuaries [*ma'ajīn*]."[76] Chinese, or at least East Asian, materia medica was by this time a commonplace and an integral part of Persian pharmacology.

Cinnamon (*Cinnamomum cassia*), another "spice" indigenous to India, Southeast Asia, and China, was also coveted for its medicinal value. Made from the bark of a variety of laurel tree, cinnamon was early on also used in perfumes and only later was it regarded as a condiment. Trade in this commodity is ancient: it is mentioned in the Old Testament and widely discussed in the classical sources.[77] Although widely used in compound medicines in West Asia well before the Mongol era, there was considerable confusion regarding its place of origin. Initially called *dar-sīnī* in Persian, it was slowly realized that much of the trade was in Indian cinnamon and to distinguish the common South Asian product from the more highly regarded Chinese variety, the latter was renamed *dar-sīnī-sīnī*, "Chinese, Chinese cinnamon."[78]

While the nomenclature was confusing, it would have been most difficult to pass off inferior grades of cinnamon to Rashīd al-Dīn since, through his contacts with Chinese physicians and his familiarity with Chinese crops, he possessed a detailed knowledge of the varieties of cassia. To begin with, he knows the Chinese name for cinnamon – *kuei-p'i*. His agricultural manual records this name in the form *kūī sī*, in which the latter element is clearly a mistake for *pī*, graphically very similar. Moreover, he directly compares the different varieties available. One kind, he says, is "called bark [*qirfah*] and is found in some provinces of India and in some provinces of China as well." "But," he adds, "the bark of China [Chīn] is better." Further on, he alludes to another type, *dar-chīnī-khaṣṣ* or "imperial cinnamon," which he says grows in China and is used in theriaca.[79]

Besides basic ingredients, there were also prepared remedies that came from China. One of the most famous, *shāh-ṣīnī*, literally "Chinese sovereign," was a headache medicine made from the juice of a Chinese plant; its precise composition is unknown but from Rashīd al-Dīn's *History of India* we know that *shah-chīnī* was frequently prepared, or more accurately, "brewed," by the inhabitants of the borderlands between Tibet and southwest China where the air was deemed to be particularly unhealthy.[80]

Finally, while commercial channels supplied, at elevated prices, some of the demand for East Asian medicines, the Il-qan court had another source.[81] According to the *Yuan shih*, *sub anno* 1331, "The envoy of the imperial prince

[76] Rashīd al-Dīn, *Āthār va Aḥyā'*, p. 81. [77] Casson, *Ancient Trade and Society*, pp. 225–39.
[78] Samarqandī, *Medical Formulary*, pp. 57 and 171 note 13; Budge, *Syriac Book of Medicines*, p. 351; and Laufer, *Sino-Iranica*, pp. 541–45. [79] Rashīd al-Dīn, *Āthār va Aḥyā'*, p. 89.
[80] Rashīd al-Dīn, *Indiengeschichte*, folio 336r, *tafel* 16, Persian text, and p. 39, German translation. [81] On the international "drug" traffic of the era, see Rashīd/Jahn II, p. 173.

Abū Saʿīd [Pu-sai-yin] returned to the Western Region to announce that [the Yuan court] repaid the tribute which they had presented with materia medica [*yao-wu*] of [equal] value."[82] This indicates that on occasion the two courts exchanged substantial amounts of medicine.

The Yuan court's sustained interest in materia medica from the West lends weight to this conclusion. Qubilai, for example, in 1273 "dispatched envoys with 100,000 ounces of gold to imperial prince Abaqa [A-pu-ha] in order to purchase drugs in Ceylon [Shih-tzu *kuo*]."[83] The amount of gold sent for purchases may be an exaggeration or a misprint, but there is no reason to doubt that the Yuan court received much medicine from abroad, particularly West Asia. To "manage Muslim medicines" they established two Muslim Pharmaceutical Bureaus (Hui-hui *yao-wu yuan*), one at Ta-tu, the capital, and one at Shang-tu, the summer residence. Created in 1292, the two bureaus were later placed under the control of the *Kuang-hui ssu* in 1322.[84]

Through these organizations several kinds of West Asian medicines were introduced or reintroduced into China. Mastic, the resin of the *Pistacia lentisus* L., is first mentioned in the Yuan period. It is found as a food flavoring in the *Yin-shan cheng-yao* in the form *ma-ssu-ta-chi*. This goes back to the Arabic *mastakī/mastakā*, which itself is a borrowing from the Greek "to chew." This substance was widely used in West Asian medicine, both Muslim and Nestorian, for the treatment of various ailments but mainly as a stomachic.[85] Another Yuan introduction is the emetic nux vomica, the seed of the fruit of the strychnine tree (*Strychnos nux vomica* L.), which grows in Yemen. Its Arabic name is *jauz al-raqa'* or *jauz al-qaī*; the Persian is *kuchūlab*, which gave rise to the Chinese form *huo-shih-la*. According to Laufer, this substance is first mentioned by the Chinese in the fourteenth century.[86]

One of the reintroductions of the Yuan era is theriaca, a compound medicine with a lengthy history in the West. This complicated and varying recipe, consisting mainly of herbal ingredients, first emerged in the Hellenistic age as an antidote to animal and insect venom. In later centuries it became an antidote for all kinds of poisons and finally a cureall, a sovereign remedy for a variety of diseases.[87] From the Greek world it passed into Arabic and Persian in the form *tiryāq* and into Syriac as *tiryāḳē* and soon established

[82] *YS*, ch. 35, p. 792.

[83] *YS*, ch. 8, p. 148. On the medicines of Ceylon, see John de Marignolli, *Recollections of Eastern Travel*, in Yule, *Cathay*, vol. III, pp. 234–35.

[84] *YS*, ch. 88, p. 2221, and Farquhar, *Government*, pp. 134–35. See also T'ao Tsung-i, *Cho-keng lu* (Chin-tai mi-shu ed.), ch. 21, p. 18b, which mentions a Muslim Pharmaceutical Office (*chü*).

[85] Laufer, *Sino-Iranica*, pp. 252–53; Samarqandī, *Medical Formulary*, pp. 65 and 179 note 63; R. Dozy, *Supplément aux dictionnaires arabes*, repr. (Beirut: Librairie du Liban, n.d.), vol. II, p. 605; and Budge, *Syriac Book of Medicines*, pp. 51, 53, and 719.

[86] Laufer, *Sino-Iranica*, pp. 448–49; Samarqandī, *Medical Formulary*, pp. 108 and 217–18; and Budge, *Syriac Book of Medicines*, pp. 151 and 717.

[87] See Gilbert Watson, *Theriac and Mithridatium: Study in Therapeutics* (London: Wellcome Historical Medical Library, 1966).

itself as a mainstay of West Asian pharmacology.[88] China was first introduced to theriaca (*ti-yeh-chia*) during the T'ang and the reaction was mixed: some thought it an animal drug of little effectiveness while others deemed it useful.[89]

In the Mongolian era, theriaca was still widely used in West Asia and considered an indispensable component of the Muslim/Eastern Christian pharmaceutical kit. Successful makers of theriaca could even gain a local and fleeting fame like the certain Tāj Būlghārī, a "compounder of *thīryākī*," who, Bar Hebraeus recounts, died in the year 1240.[90] In Yuan China this substance is first mentioned in 1320 when "Muslim imperial physicians offered a medicine [to the court] called theriaca [*ta-li-ya*]." The Emperor Shidebala (r. 1320–23), obviously pleased, "granted them 150,000 strings of cash."[91] Twelve years later, in 1332, the *Yuan shih* reports that "Imperial Prince Abū Saʿīd sent an envoy with a tribute of 88 catties [Chinese pounds] of theriaca [*ta-li-ya*]." Again the throne was pleased and sent 3,300 ingots to Iran as a return gift.[92] The Mongolian interest in theriaca might well be related to its reputation as an antidote to all toxins, since poisoning at the hands of rivals was both a real and perceived threat among the Chinggisid princes. This, perhaps, is why Ghazan formulated his own special and "salutary" antidote, called *tiryāq-i Ghāzānī* in his honor.[93]

Last, there is the electuary sherbet which traveled east. Heavily used as a refreshing, restorative drink for envoys in the Il-qan realm, it was often a vehicle for the ingestion of other medicines and therefore an important tool for West Asian physicians.[94] First introduced into China during Yuan times, this drink is mentioned in the *Yin-shan cheng-yao* in the form *she-erh-pieh*, which goes back to the Arabo-Persian *sharbat*.[95] The earliest sherbet makers (*she-li-pa-ch'ih*) in China were Nestorians from Samarqand. In Qubilai's day the holder of the office of *sherbetchi* was Mar Sarghis (Ma Hsieh-li-chi-ssu). This was the Marsarchis whom Marco Polo met in Cinghianfu (Chen-chiang) on the Lower Yangtze, where the Nestorian had been sent as a *darughachi* in the late 1270s and where he built several Christian churches and monasteries.[96] It is interesting that when he later became embroiled in a case of tax arrears, ʿIsā (Ai-hsieh) intervened in the official investigation on behalf of his coreligionist.[97]

[88] Martin Levey, *Early Arabic Pharmacology: An Introduction Based on Ancient and Medieval Sources* (Leiden: E. J. Brill, 1973), pp. 70, 83, 87, and 135, and Budge, *Syriac Book of Medicines*, pp. 409, 432, 446, 451, and 726.
[89] Unschuld, *Medicine in China: A History of Pharmaceuticals*, p. 47, and Schafer, *Golden Peaches*, p. 184. [90] Bar Hebraeus, p. 405. [91] *YS*, ch. 27, p. 604.
[92] *YS*, ch. 37, p. 812. [93] Rashīd/Jahn II, p. 173. [94] *Ibid.*, p. 326.
[95] Buell, "The *Yin-shan cheng-yao*," p. 121.
[96] Moule, *Christians in China*, pp. 147–48; Marco Polo, p. 323; and Louis Ligeti, "Les sept monastères nestoriens de Mar Sargis," *AOASH* 26 (1972), 169–78.
[97] *T'ung-chih t'iao-ko*, ch. 29, p. 331, and Pelliot, *Notes*, vol. II, p. 775.

As a *sherbetchi*, Mar Sarghis made a wide variety of drinks, usually consisting of sugar, honey, the fresh juice of berries or citrus, and rosewater, a distillate of steeped rose petals. By the time he was in office, he could draw upon the sugar manufactured in China by the inhabitants of West Asia and upon the Baghdadi lemons (*li-mu*/*līmū*) specially grown in Kuangtung. In other words, it was possible to make "authentic" sherbet in East Asia because the basic ingredients, like the sherbet maker himself, had all been transported to China.

The long-term consequence of all this transcontinental to-ing and fro-ing of medical personnel is difficult to assess. Western medicine had reached parts of East Asia centuries before the Mongols and even had a perceptible impact in Tibet, where many court physicians were Muslims and other representatives of the Greek school of medicine. A Tibetan version of the Hippocratic oath testifies to their presence and influence.[98] In China, Muslim physicians were surely in the major ports of the south from the ninth century onward and under the Mongols, as we have seen, there was an influx of West Asian physicians in the north. Yet, despite these many points of contact, the Chinese do not seem to have borrowed much. Needham's judgment that Hellenistic, Muslim and Eastern Christian medicine had "no perceptible influence" in China, while true on some levels, needs to be explored in greater depth.[99] More specifically, why were the Chinese so resistant to the Galenic medical system?

Most obviously, there was professional rivalry and distrust of the foreign ways. This is manifested in Chinese comments on Western medical practice which place emphasis on the bizarre and the fantastic – amputated tongues that grow back and "small crabs" surgically removed from foreheads.[100] The Chinese therefore tended to view "Muslim" physicians, whether in China or on their home ground, with a certain skepticism and a suspicion that they were charlatans who ran "medicine shows."[101]

On a deeper level, borrowing was inhibited by the fundamental theoretical differences between the Chinese and Galenic systems of medicine. The latter, of course, was based on the humoral system, while the Chinese was intimately tied to the concepts of *yin-yang* and the Five Phases or Agencies (*wu-hsing*). Thus, for a Chinese to embrace the Galenic system would entail a drastic cosmological reorientation, a break with the native cultural tradition, since *yin-yang* and *wu-hsing* permeated all aspects of Chinese thought.

98 Christopher I. Beckwith, "The Introduction of Greek Medicine into Tibet in the Seventh and Eighth Centuries," *JAOS* 99 (1979), 297–313.

99 Joseph Needham, "The Unity of Science: Asia's Indispensable Contribution," in his *Clerks and Craftsmen*, pp. 17–18.

100 T'ao Tsung-i, *Cho-keng lu*, ch. 22, pp. 15a–b; Yang Yü, *Beiträge zur Kulturgeschichte Chinas*, p. 34; and Moule, *Christians in China*, p. 234.

101 Morris Rossabi, trans., "A Translation of Ch'en Ch'eng's *Hsi-yü fan-ku-chih*," *Ming Studies* 17 (1983), 52.

These ideological constraints, while real enough, should not be construed as some kind of unyielding or universal conservatism intrinsic to Chinese medicine as a whole. In fact, Chinese medical practice did change in substantial ways during the period of Mongolian domination. After all, this was the time of the "Four Great Schools of Medicine," which began in the Chin and flourished throughout the Yuan. Each school, while sharing certain basic assumptions, had its own preferred diagnostic and therapeutic techniques.[102] Clearly, there was no monolithic, unitary Chinese medical establishment opposing change in principle.

There is evidence of change as well in the Chinese pharmacology of the period. Herbalists and physicians made a major effort to create an applied pharmacology that linked practice with theory. Their endeavor, whether or not it succeeded in achieving its own goals, produced new treatments and new medicines even though its practitioners worked largely from inherited tradition.[103]

Besides the ongoing evolution of theory and practice there was a change in the social bases of the medical profession. In the course of the Yuan, medicine became a more popular career track. It became more acceptable in part because the profession successfully pointed out the social and ethical similarities between the practice of medicine and Confucianism. This was done, for instance, in the new preface specially prepared for the 1327 reprint of the *Mai-ching*. The result was that by the end of the Yuan Confucian literati, gentlemen, became doctors in increasing numbers.[104]

The changes sketched above may seem at first glance to be largely an internal Chinese matter, unconnected with outside "influence." Such a view, however, may be misleading. In the study of cultural contact there is, I believe, a strong predilection to envision change largely in terms of the direct borrowing of alien cultural traits. But borrowing is not the only, nor necessarily the most important, mechanism of change in such circumstances. When confronted with foreign culture, particularly when imposed from outside, the locals tend to reformulate, repackage and reaffirm what they consider to be the inherited tradition. Naturally, in so doing, they do not preserve a "pure" form of their culture but mold it, that is, change it, in these new conditions.

In our particular case, it seems to me that the dramatically new social, political, and cultural landscape of the Yuan, with all its foreign ways and officials,

102 K. Chimin Wong and Wu Lien-teh, *History of Chinese Medicine*, 2nd edn, repr. (Taipei: Southern Materials Center, 1985), pp. 98–104, and Jutta Rall, *Die Viergrossen Medizinschulen der Mongolenzeit* (Wiesbaden: Franz Steiner, 1920), pp. 38–95.

103 Ulrike Unschuld, "Traditional Chinese Pharmacology: An Analysis of its Development in the Thirteenth Century," *Isis* 68 (1977), 224–48, and Miyasita Saburō, "Malaria (*yao*) in Chinese Medicine during the Chin and Yuan Periods," *Acta Asiatica* 36 (1979), 104–8.

104 Paul U. Unschuld, *Medical Ethics in Imperial China: A Study in Historical Anthropology* (Berkeley: University of California Press, 1979), p. 53, and Robert P. Hymes, "Not Quite Gentlemen? Doctors in Sung and Yuan," *Chinese Science* 8 (1987), 9–76, especially 65–66.

might well have helped shape the evolution of the Chinese medicine of the period. To cite but one example, the Mongols, from the outset of their imperial enterprise, demonstrated a decided preference for individuals with specialized skills. These they coopted by the thousands and set to work on behalf of the Mongolian courts. Confucian scholars, by way of contrast, were generalists and usually proud of it. Not surprisingly, Mongolian rulers were only sporadically sympathetic to the literati and often by-passed them in favor of clerks and translators whom they promoted to high office. Therefore, without intending to do so, the Mongols, by importing many foreign physicians who enjoyed considerable standing in their homeland and at the Yuan court, may have encouraged Chinese gentlemen to become doctors. Since it is clear that during the Yuan many Chinese adopted Mongolian customs to advance their careers, it seems likely that some might have willingly accepted Mongolian notions of prestige occupations and, as was certainly the case with the Chinese physicians of the Yuan, justified this shift of attitude and social practice in purely Chinese, Confucian terms.[105] Consequently, change of this nature, although inspired by foreign models and stimuli, is sometimes difficult to detect because it tends to be carefully domesticated or, in other words, disguised.

In Iran we confront a similar situation. As is true of China, there is little evidence that Muslim or Eastern Christian physicians abandoned or altered the inherited, Galenic theory of medicine. But while there is no major discontinuity in "Muslim" medical history in consequence of the Mongolian occupation, this does not rule out more subtle change in the form of foreign-inspired reassessment of the established repertoire of diagnostic and therapeutic techniques. For example, although pulse taking had a secure place in West Asian medicine before the Mongols, the exposure to Chinese concepts of pulse diagnosis may have served to elevate or even undermine the technique in later Muslim medical practice. Only future research can provide answers to this and many other questions on the Chinese legacy in West Asian medicine. And even if these investigations demonstrate that there were no such influences, the effort will not have been in vain since such successful resistance will tell us something important as well.

The one area where some borrowing is detectable is in pharmacology. The reputation of Chinese rhubarb was solidified during the Mongolian era and thereafter spread from West Asia into Europe where it became the preferred stomachic down to the beginning of the twentieth century.[106] The fact that Chardin, in his day, observed the use of Chinese rhubarb as a purgative for horses in Iran reveals something of the Mongols' role in this long-term transmission of a dried root from the frontiers of Tibet.[107] Further, it should be noted that practically all the medicines of Chinese or Far Eastern origin avail-

105 For a survey, see Henry Serruys, "Remains of Mongol Customs in China during the Early Ming," *MS* 16 (1957), 137–90.

106 Clifford M. Foust, *Rhubarb: The Wondrous Drug* (Princeton University Press, 1992), pp. 3–17.

107 Sir John Chardin, *Travels in Persia*, repr. (New York: Dover Publications, 1988), p. 142.

able to the Il-qan court were still available and actively used in Egypt in the twentieth century.[108]

In light of this high regard for Chinese materia medica in Iran, it is not at all surprising that Rashīd al-Dīn used his connections to gain access to Chinese pharmacological literature. In his preface to the *Tanksūq-nāmah* he records that he had translated from Chinese a book dealing with "medicines from herbs, minerals, trees, animals, fish and [. . .?]"[109] No author or title is given but this work must be sought among the *pen-ts'ao*,[110] which will be difficult because by Yuan times there was already a large corpus of Chinese literature on materia medica. And under the Mongols new works were added and old works reissued: for example, the *Ching-shih cheng-lei ta-kuan pen-ts'ao*, "Materia Medica of the Ta-kuan Period, Annotated and Arranged by Types, Based upon the Classics and Histories," a comprehensive and composite treatise compiled at the very end of the eleventh century by T'ang Shen-wei and then reworked by Ai Ch'eng a few years later, was first published in 1108 and subsequently reprinted during the Southern Sung (1211), Chin (1214), and Yuan (1302). Its monograph section is divided into numerous chapters grouped by drug origin: minerals, herbs, trees, humans, quadrupeds, fowl, fish, fruit, rice (grain), and vegetables.[111] This accords in a rough way with the organization of the work Rashīd al-Dīn had translated, particularly if we combine separate sections such as humans, quadrupeds, and fowl into a single entry "animals/living creatures [*halvān*]." However, since these ten categories were conventional, it is impossible to narrow the range of possibilities without further data.

In China, too, materia medica was borrowed. Besides the Yuan introductions such as nux vomica, a case can be made for a Mongolian "popularization" of previously marginal, little-regarded medicines. The poppy, for example, was cultivated in China since T'ang times but opium only appears as a therapeutic drug in Chinese medical literature of the Ming period.[112] This may be related to the Mongol court's enthusiasm for the theriaca supplied by their Muslim physicians, since one of its key constituents from the outset was opium.[113]

Continuing Chinese interest in West Asian drugs is confirmed by early Ming translations of Muslim medical literature. One such work, the *Hui-hui i-shu*, "Book of Muslim Medicine," incorporated into the great Ming encyclopedia, *Yung-lo ta-tien*, contained seven chapters on medical prescriptions (*yao-fang*).

[108] M. A. Ducros, *Essai sur le droguier populaire arabe de l'Inspectorat des Pharmacies* (Cairo: Imprimerie de l'institut français d'archéologie orientale, 1930), pp. 61, 72–73, and 111–12.

[109] Rashīd al-Dīn, *Tanksūq-nāmah*, p. 15. I am unable to identify the last word, which Karl Jahn, "Some Ideas of Rashīd al-Dīn on Chinese Culture," 140, translates as "jellyfish."

[110] Initially, I believed that this was a translation of an agricultural manual rather than a medical treatise. The comments of Soucek, "The Role of Landscape in Iranian Painting," pp. 89–90, have persuaded me otherwise.

[111] Unschuld, *Medicine in China: A History of Pharmaceuticals*, pp. 72–77. [112] *Ibid.*, p. 158.

[113] Watson, *Theriaca and Mithridatium*, pp. 13, 38, 41, 47, 53, 56, 73, 88, and 94–100.

Another, the *Hui-hui yao-fang*, "Muslim Medical Prescriptions," was apparently compiled from various Persian sources and contains the names of many drugs and plants, the majority in Chinese transcription or translation, but some in the Persian script. This rare work, in four volumes, is now housed in the library of Peking University.[114]

[114] Paul Pelliot, "Le Hōǰa et le Sayyid Ḥusain de l'histoire des Ming," *TP* 38 (1948), note 31, and Huang Shijian and Ibrahim Feng Jin-yuan, "Persian Language and Literature in China," *Encyclopedia Iranica* (Costa Mesa, Calif.: Mazda Publishers, 1992), vol. V, pp. 447 and 449.

SEVENTEEN

Astronomy

The Mongols of the imperial era had a system of calendrical reckoning, their own names for constellations, and a folk cosmology, but the formalized astronomy of systematic observation, star charts, and mathematically derived tables comes late, the early eighteenth century, as a by-product of the Tibetan, Indian, and Chinese influence that accompanied the Mongols' conversion to lamaist Buddhism.[1] Despite the lack of a native scientific astronomy, the early Mongols evinced an avid and sustained interest in the study of the heavens. This is manifest in their restoration of existing observatories such as Ögödei's repair of the astronomical facilities in the Chin capital in 1236, and the construction of entirely new centers such as the one at Marāghah undertaken by Hülegü, a subject discussed below.[2] Astronomers, too, were highly prized by the Mongols, as the following anecdote reveals. In the aftermath of the Mongolian defeat at ʿAin Jālūt in 1260, Hülegü in anger ordered that all the subjects of the Egyptian monarch in his territory be put to the sword. One seized for this purpose was a certain Mūhai who signalled to his captors that he was an astronomer and was immediately spared as a matter of standard operating procedure needing no other justification or explanation.[3]

This intense concern for astronomy and astronomers led, inevitably, to the movement of scientists, instruments, and technical literature across the Eurasian continent and most particularly between China and Iran. As was true of the physicians, Chinese astronomers accompanied the Mongolian armies that invaded West Turkestan in 1219. When Ch'ang Ch'un arrived in Samarqand in 1222 the Chinese population of the city came out to greet him and on one occasion, his biographer records, they had an astronomer (*suan-li-che*) with them. From a later passage in the same source we learn that this individual, in charge of the observatory, was surnamed Li.[4] Unfortunately, there is no further information on this person or his activities.

When Hülegü came to Iran in the 1250s he brought, among other specialists, Chinese astronomers (*munajjimān*). One of their number, according to

[1] See L. S. Baranovskaia, "Iz istorii mongol'skoi astronomii," *Trudy instituta istorii estestvoznaniia i tekhniki* 5 (1955), 321–30. [2] *YS*, ch. 2, p. 34. [3] Bar Hebraeus, p. 438.

[4] Li Chih-ch'ang, *Hsi-yü chi*, pp. 328–29 and 331, and Li Chih-ch'ang, *Travels of an Alchemist*, pp. 94–95 and 97.

Rashīd al-Dīn, was a certain Fūm.njī who bore the honorific *sīnksink*. The latter term, which Rashīd correctly equates with the Arabic *ʿarif*, a "wise man" or "master," particularly of some specific branch of knowledge, answers to the Chinese *hsien-sheng*, "teacher" or "master."[5] While the form of his honorific is certain, the same cannot be said of his personal name: Needham thought it represented Fu Meng-chi and more recently two Chinese scholars have restored it as Fu Man-tzu.[6] In neither case, however, has Rashīd's Fūm.njī been successfully identified with a historical personage. My own search through various indices has also failed to turn up any likely candidates. Consequently, we have limited data on this intriguing figure or on the other Chinese astronomers who accompanied Hülegü to the West: we simply do not know how many came with him, how long they stayed in Iran, or if any ever returned to China. We do know, however, that reinforcements to the ranks of the Chinese astronomers came under Ghazan when two Chinese scholars, the aforementioned Lītājī and K.msūn, specializing in history, medicine, and astronomy (*ʿilm-i nujūm*), arrived bringing books from their native land.[7] In any event, since Rashīd al-Dīn says Hülegü was accompanied by astronomers (*munajjimān*), one of whom was Fūm.njī, presumably their leader, we can safely state that there were at least four, and possibly more, Chinese astronomers serving in Iran during the Mongolian era.

Interest in astronomy, widespread among the Chinggisids, was evident among the Il-qans from the advent of their state. When Lammasar (north of Qazvin), a fortress of the Ismaʿīlīs, fell in 1256, Hülegü authorized the removal and preservation of the non-heretical works in their library and various kinds of astronomical instruments including a "mount [*kurāsī*], armillary sphere [*zāt al-ḥalaq*], complete and partial astrolabes [*usṭurlab-hā*]."[8] His attraction to this field of knowledge seems on the whole quite genuine. Writing in the fourteenth century, Qāshānī asserts that Hülegü "loved science [*ḥikmat*] and was infatuated with astronomy [*nujūm*] and geometry [*handasīyyat*]. Consequently," the chronicler continues, "scientists from East and West congregated at his court and his contemporaries were fascinated by different branches of learning, geometry, and mathematics."[9] Even more persuasive of his interest in such matters is his role in the founding of Marāghah.

Taken and devastated by the Mongols in 1220, Marāghah was selected for the site of a major observatory which was laid out around 1260. From the beginning Hülegü took a personal interest in its progress and in late 1264 made a special trip there to press for the rapid completion of the observatory.[10]

[5] Rashīd al-Dīn, *Chinageschichte*, folio 392r–v, *tafeln* 2–3, Persian text, and pp. 21–22, German translation.

[6] Needham, *SCC*, vol. I, p. 218, and Chou Liang-hsiao and Ku Chü-ying, *Yuan-tai shih* (Shanghai: Jen-min ch'u-pan-she, 1993), p. 830.

[7] Rashīd al-Dīn, *Chinageschichte*, folio 393r, *tafel* 4, Persian text, and p. 23, German translation.

[8] Juvaynī/Qazvīnī, vol. III, pp. 269–70, and Juvaynī/Boyle, vol. II, p. 719.

[9] Qāshānī/Hambly, pp. 106–7.

[10] Juvaynī/Qazvīnī, vol. I, p. 116; Juvaynī/Boyle, vol. I, p. 148; and Rashīd/Karīmī, vol. II, p. 734.

Built on a leveled-off hill to the south of Tabrīz, the complex contained numerous buildings, a library, and an astronomical observatory equipped with various instruments, a quadrant, armillary sphere, etc. Funded in part by *vaqf* revenues, the observatory also served as a training center for astronomers.[11] Its first director, Naṣīr al-Dīn Ṭūsī, and his associates also received generous stipends and "shares."[12] Often seen as the apex of Islamic observatories, Marāghah had a long life because Hülegü's successors maintained some interest in its work.[13] When its operations ceased is not known precisely but it was still active when Öljeitü visited the site in 1304.[14]

Assembled at Marāghah were scientific works in diverse languages and scientists from many parts of Eurasia. All the educational and scientific work at the observatory was under the direction of the famed mathematician and astronomer Naṣīr al-Dīn Ṭūsī, whom Hülegü "rescued" from the Isma'īlīs.[15] And, most important from our perspective, Hülegü ordered Ṭūsī to collaborate with the Chinese astronomers he had brought from the East. More particularly, Ṭūsī and his Chinese colleague Fūm.njī were to teach one another their respective astronomical traditions and techniques. Ṭūsī, according to Rashīd al-Dīn, rapidly mastered Chinese astronomy.[16]

The major by-product of this compelled collaboration was the famous *Zīj-i Īl-khānī*, "Astronomical Tables of the Il-qans." According to the Persian sources the *Zīj* was compiled by a team of Muslim scholars, which included, in addition to Ṭūsī, Mu'ayyād al-Dīn 'Arūḍī, Fakhr al-Dīn Akhlāṭī, and Najm al-Dīn Qazvīnī.[17] No Chinese are named but it is clear that Fūm.njī and associates were deeply involved in the project.[18] This is evident from Ṭūsī's extensive knowledge of the Chinese calendrical system. In the treatment of this system the *Zīj* makes extensive use of Chinese technical vocabulary. For example, the three cycles of the sexagenary system are properly called "upper beginning [*shāng v.n*, Chinese *shang-yuan*]," "middle beginning [*jūng v.n*, Chinese *chung-yuan*]," and "lower beginning [*khā v.n*, Chinese *hsia-yuan*]." A longer period of time is called a *v.n*, which answers to the Chinese *wan*, "10,000." Further, the *Zīj* gives the Chinese names for the ten celestial stems and twelve earthly branches that make up the sexagenary cycle. For example, the year 1203 is designated as *kūī khāī*, the Chinese *kuei-hai*.[19]

The purpose of the Chinese material was the preparation of conversion

[11] The best history of Marāghah is Sayili, *The Observatory in Islam*, pp. 187–223.
[12] Rashīd/Jahn I, p. 8. [13] *Ibid.*, p. 75. [14] Qāshānī/Hambly, p. 41.
[15] Bar Hebraeus, pp. 2 and 451.
[16] Rashīd al-Dīn, *Chinageschichte*, folio 392r, *tafel* 2, Persian text, and p. 22, German translation.
[17] Ḥamd-Allāh Mustawfī Qazvīnī, *The Ta'rīkh-i Guzīdah or "Select History,"* ed. by E. G. Browne and R. A. Nicholson (Leiden: E. J. Brill, and London: Luzac, 1913), pt. II, p. 143.
[18] The introduction to the *Zīj* notes that Ṭusī assembled scholars and books from many lands to prepare the tables. See John A. Boyle, tr., "The Longer Introduction to the *Zīj-i Ilkhānī* of Naṣir-ad-dīn Ṭūsī," *Journal of Semitic Studies* 8 (1963), 246–47.
[19] Rashīd al-Dīn, *Chinageschichte*, folio 393v, *tafel* 5, Persian text, and pp. 22–23, German translation, and Boyle, "The Longer Introduction to the *Zīj-i Ilkhānī*," p. 248, Persian text, and pp. 250–51, English translation.

tables to equate dates between different calendrical systems in use in the empire. The Mongols, naturally, had their own measures of time. The divisions of the day were specific to the Mongols' nomadic culture, but the measurement of the month, season, and year was shared with others, Uighurs and Chinese.[20] Their shared luni-solar calendar contained twelve numbered months, intercalated to conform to the solar year, divided into four seasonal segments of three months each. The year was indicated on the basis of the twelve-year animal cycle, the origin of which is still debated, though most assume a Chinese prototype.[21] Thus, a typical Mongolian date, this one taken from a Yuan tax immunity, reads: "Our edict was written on the twenty-eighth [day] of the first autumn month, Year of the Tiger."[22]

Such dates had to be converted into the calendrical systems of various subject peoples. These systems were based on differing principles of computation and were quite numerous, especially in West Asia. Bar Hebraeus, in the space of a single page of his chronicle, written in the 1280s, uses no fewer than three distinct chronological systems![23] Thus the *Zīj*, in addition to tables on the sun, moon, the five planets, and fixed stars, contains conversion tables for the calendars of the Greeks, Arabs, Chinese, Jews, Christians, and Persians.[24] In the *Zīj*, Ṭūsī, by way of illustration, converts the date 1203 of the twelve-year animal cycle into the appropriate Chinese, Eastern Christian, Muslim, and Persian dates. The latter was the so-called Yazdigird era based upon the Sasanian ruler who ascended the throne in 632. This era continued in use after the Islamic conquest side by side with the *Hijrī* era and is still used by the Zoroastrians today.[25]

These conversion tables were obviously extremely useful for administrative purposes since Mongolian chancelleries received and issued documents in different languages and dated according to different calendrical systems. Such tables were also useful for historians, such as Rashīd al-Dīn, who compiled their works from diverse sources. Not surprisingly, the *Collected Chronicles* contains numerous dates given in the twelve-year animal cycle and the *Hijrī* era, as, for example, in the extended discussion of Chinggis Qan's age. Most certainly Rashīd al-Dīn used the *Zīj* to make these conversions. And even after

20 Choi Luvsanjav, "Customary Ways of Measuring Time and Time Periods in Mongolia," *Journal of the Anglo-Mongolian Society* 1/1 (1974), 7–16.

21 Peter A. Boodberg, "Marginalia to the Histories of the Northern Dynasties," *HJAS* 3 (1938), 243–53, and Louis Bazin, *Les systèmes chronologiques dans le monde Turc ancien* (Budapest: Akadémiai Kiadó, and Paris: Editions du CNRS, 1991), pp. 117 ff.

22 Nicolas Poppe, *The Mongolian Monuments in hP'ags-pa Script*, 2nd edn, trans. and ed. by John R. Krueger (Wiesbaden: Otto Harrassowitz, 1957), p. 49, Mongolian text, and p. 50, English translation.

23 Bar Hebraeus, p. 375.

24 Raymond Mercier, "The Greek 'Persian Syntaxis' and the *Zīj-i Ilkhānī*," *Archives Internationales d'Histoire des Sciences* 34 (1984), 33–60, and Benno van Dalen, E. S. Kennedy, and Mustafa Saiyid, "The Chinese-Uighur Calendar in Ṭūsī's *Zīj-i Ilkhānī*," *Zeitschrift für Geschichte der arabisch-islamischen Wissenschaften* 11 (1997), 111–51.

25 Boyle, "Longer Introduction to the *Zīj-i Ilkhānī*," p. 248, Persian text, and 250–51, English translation; S. H. Taqizadeh, "Various Eras and Calendars used in the Countries of Islam," *BSOAS* 9 (1939), 917–18; and François de Blois, "The Persian Calendar," *Iran* 34 (1996), 39.

Rashīd al-Dīn and the collapse of the Mongolian regime in West Asia, the twelve-year animal cycle continued in use in Iran for some time.[26]

The movement of West Asian astronomers to China was equally intense, and because of the richness of the records, the activities of these students of the heavens sent east are much better known than those of their counterparts in Iran.

So far as we know, the first contact between Chinese and Muslim astronomers came during the Mongols' campaign in Turkestan, 1219–22. As already noted, the astronomer Li headed an observatory in Samarqand which must have entailed collaboration with Muslims. Yeh-lü Ch'u-ts'ai, the sinicized Qitan, also accompanied Chinggis Qan on this campaign, and while most famous as the chief "Chinese" adviser of the early qaghans, it is quite apparent from his biography that he initially ingratiated himself with his Mongolian masters through his skills as an astronomer and prognosticator. During the campaigning against Khwārazm he frequently interpreted meteorological and astronomical phenomena – summer snow, eclipses, and a comet – for Chinggis Qan. The Mongols thought of his astrological work as a supplement to and check on their own methods of divining, as the following passage shows:

> Thereupon, on the eve of each military operation, [the emperor], without fail, ordered his excellency [Yeh-lü Ch'u-ts'ai] to foretell its good or bad fortune. The emperor also burnt the shoulder blade of a sheep to verify it [i.e., Yeh-lü Ch'u-ts'ai's prognostication].[27]

During his lengthy sojourn in the eastern Islamic world, he obviously met and came to admire Muslim astronomers and their work. This is brought out in a long passage in his biography:

> [Yeh-lü Ch'u-ts'ai] said that in the calendar of the Western Region [Hsi-yü], the five planets are more closely [calculated] than in China. Then there was compiled the *ma-ta-pa* calendar. The foregoing is the name of a Muslim [Hui-ho] calendar. Moreover as [the period of] the solar eclipse and movement of the stars [in the Muslim calendar] do not correspond to the Chinese and since errors gradually accumulated in the *Ta Ming* calendar, [Yeh-lü Ch'u-ts'ai] consequently corrected the *I-wei yuan* calendar compiled by his eminence Wen Hsien and disseminated [this revised calendar] to the world.[28]

Though obscurities and uncertainties remain, this passage can plausibly be interpreted in the following manner. Impressed by the accuracy of Muslim astronomical calculations, Yeh-lü Ch'u-ts'ai used one of their calendars or tables, the *Ma-ta-pa* (a term whose meaning is yet to be determined),[29] to

[26] Rashīd/Karīmī, vol. I, p. 417, and Charles Melville, "The Chinese Uighur Animal Calendar in Persian Historiography of the Mongol Period," *Iran* 32 (1994), 83–98.

[27] *YWL*, ch. 57, pp. 11a–b, and *YS*, ch. 146, p. 3456. See also Igor de Rachewiltz, "Yeh-lü Ch'u-ts'ai (1189–1243): Buddhist Idealist and Confucian Statesman," in Wright and Twitchett, *Confucian Personalities*, pp. 194–95.

[28] *YWL*, ch. 57, p. 22b.

[29] One suggestion, which seems implausible to me, is that *Ma-ta-pa* represents the Arabic *muqtabas* "quotation," "that which is quoted." See Yabuuti Kiyosi, "Astronomical Tables in China from the Wutai to the Ch'ing Dynasties," *Japanese Studies in the History of Science* 2 (1963), 98.

revise Chinese calendars. He first considered and rejected the *Ta-Ming* calendar, used by the Chin dynasty between 1137 and 1181, as too inaccurate and then decided on the *I-wei yuan* calendar of 1180, another product of the Chin dynasty, this one authored by Wen Hsien, who was Yeh-lü Ch'u-ts'ai's father.[30] The resulting revision, we learn from another source, was called the *Hsi-cheng keng-wu-yuan*, "The Western Campaign Calendar of the Keng-wu year." And although this calendar, which began with 1210, the *Keng-wu* year, was never officially promulgated or adopted, it was used by the Mongolian court.[31] This is evident from the testimony of Hsü T'ing, the Sung ambassador to the Mongols in 1237, who reports that he encountered a calendar in use in Mongolian territory that upon inquiry was identified as Yeh-lü Ch'u-ts'ai's. This calendar, he pointedly emphasizes, was one that Yeh-lü Ch'u-ts'ai "compiled by himself, printed by himself, and promulgated by himself."[32] Clearly, the Qitan was making every effort to gain acceptance for his calendar, revised with the aid of Muslim calculations, and to promote its use even if on an unofficial or informal basis. This represents the first, indirect phase of the penetration of West Asian astronomy into China; the next was inaugurated by the arrival of ʿIsā *kelemechi* in the East.

So far as we know, ʿIsā, who reached Mongolia in the reign of Güyüg, 1247–49, was the first West Asian astronomer to take up service at the court of the Grand Qans. During Möngke's reign ʿIsā fashioned a close relationship with Qubilai and when the latter became emperor he established, at ʿIsā's suggestion, the Office of Western Astronomy (Hsi-yü *hsing-li ssu*) in 1263, and placed ʿIsā in charge of its affairs.[33] What this office did is not spelled out in the sources. Nor is there any indication of its personnel. It seems most likely that this office was for the most part engaged in astrological prognostication in the Near Eastern tradition. In any event, it is only in connection with the Muslim astronomers who arrived after ʿIsā that we begin to get good information on the kinds of instruments and techniques that West Asians utilized in the astronomical observations in China.

Muslim astronomers seem to have reached Mongolia during the 1250s. There was, for example, a certain Ḥusām al-Dīn who served at Möngke's court and then returned west with Hülegü.[34] It was, however, Jamāl al-Dīn who initiated the third, and certainly the most significant phase in the history of West Asian astronomy in Yuan China. Because of the confusion surrounding his appearance in China, particularly the mistaken belief that he was sent from Marāghah to the Yuan court in 1267, the sources relating to his early career will be cited in full.

From the Persian end, Rashīd al-Dīn is the only source to mention Jamāl al-Dīn and does so in connection with Möngke's desire to recruit Naṣīr al-Dīn Ṭūsī for service in the East. The passage in question reads as follows:

[30] On this calendar, see *YS*, ch. 53, p. 1186. [31] *YS*, ch. 52, p. 1120.
[32] P'eng Ta-ya and Hsü T'ing, *Hei-ta shih-lüeh*, in Wang, *Meng-ku shih-liao*, p. 481.
[33] Ch'eng Chü-fu, *Ch'eng hsüeh-lou wen-chi*, ch. 5, pp. 4a–b; *YS*, ch. 134, p. 3249; and Moule, *Christians in China*, p. 228. [34] Rashīd/Karīmī, vol. II, p. 706.

[Möngke, owing to] his great wisdom and high mindedness, insisted that during his august reign an observatory [*raṣad*] be built. He commanded Jamāl al-Dīn Muḥammad ibn Ṭāhir ibn Muḥammad al-Zaydī of Bukhara to attend to this important matter [but] some of the work upon it was [too] complicated.

After Jamāl al-Dīn's failure, Möngke turned, Rashīd al-Dīn continues, to another astronomer:

The fame and attainments of Kwājah Naṣīr al-Dīn, like the wind, spread over the face of the earth. Möngke Qaghan at the time he said goodbye to [his] brother [Hülegü] ordered that when the Assassins' fortresses were subdued, Khwājah Naṣīr al-Dīn be sent to court. But at the time, since Möngke Qaghan was occupied with the subjugation of the country of Manzī [South China] and the seat of government [was so] far, Hülegü ordered that he [Ṭūsī] also construct an observatory here [i.e., Marāghah].[35]

The principal Chinese reference comes from the *Yuan shih*:

When Shih-tsu [Qubilai] was the heir apparent [during Möngke's reign] he issued an order to summon Muslim [Hui-hui] astronomers. Jamāl al-Dīn [Cha-ma-la-ting] and others, offering their skills, took service. There was [as yet] no government office [for them]. In the eighth year of the *Chih-yuan* period [1271] there was established for the first time the Astronomical Observatory [*Ssu t'ien-t'ai*].[36]

Comparing these two accounts, it is apparent that Jamāl al-Dīn was already in the East and in contact with Qubilai in the 1250s. Consequently, at the time he presented his terrestrial globe and other astronomical instruments to the Yuan court in 1267, he had been a resident of China for some years; he was not a recent arrival from Marāghah on a mission from Hülegü or Abaqa.

The statement in the *Yuan shih* that there was no government office for Muslim astronomers until 1271 also requires comment and explanation. First of all, this statement seemingly contradicts the fact that Qubilai in 1260 had established the Astronomical Observatory.[37] This, however, was the Chinese (Han-erh) observatory; what Qubilai founded in 1271 was the Muslim (Hui-hui) Astronomical Observatory with Jamāl al-Dīn as Intendant (*t'i-tien*).[38] This, however, does not solve all the apparent contradictions because there is also the question of the Office of Western Astronomy in existence since 1263. For unexplained reasons this office was not considered an appropriate institutional setting for Jamāl al-Dīn and his associates. Further, what became of the Office of Western Astronomy is not at all clear. It may have been abolished or, more likely, transformed into the Muslim (Hui-hui) Astronomical Observatory in 1271.

In any event, the institutional history of West Asian/Muslim astronomy in the Yuan after 1271, while complicated, is reasonably clear. In 1273 the Chinese Astronomical Observatory was placed under the control of the Imperial Library Directorate. So, too, was its Muslim counterpart which was charged with "observing the heavens and making calendars."[39] The next year,

35 *Ibid.*, p. 718. 36 *YS*, ch. 90, p. 2297. 37 *Ibid.*, p. 2297. 38 *YS*, ch. 7, p. 136.
39 *YS*, ch. 90, p. 2297.

1274, the Chinese and Muslim observatories were "joined into a single observatory" on the recommendation of Bolad and Liu Ping-chung.[40] Also on Bolad's recommendation, Jamāl al-Dīn took up a post in the Imperial Library Directorate and for a time, it appears, he even headed this agency.[41]

In 1288 the two observatories were separated and made independent. In 1312 the name of the Muslim Astronomical Observatory was changed to the Institute of Muslim Astronomy (Hui-hui *ssu-t'ien chien*). Three years later, although still independent, the institute's affairs were made subject to inspection and review by the Imperial Library Directorate. It says something about the importance of the Muslim Institute of Astronomy that Bayan the Merkid, the powerful chief chancellor of the Yuan, became its honorary inspector (*t'i-t'iao*) in the 1330s.[42]

Although ʿIsā *kelemechi*'s son Elijah (Yeh-li-ya) at some unspecified date headed one of the two astronomical observatories, control over the Muslim observatory and its successor, the institute, were for the most part in Muslim hands.[43] Following Jamāl al-Dīn, whose date of death is unknown, a certain Shāms al-Dīn (Shan-ssu-ting) was placed in charge of the Imperial Library Directorate and the Muslim Astronomical Observatory in 1301 and was still its head in 1310.[44] This may be the same Shāms al-Dīn, a native of Qundūz, a town in Khurāsān, mentioned by Rashīd al-Dīn as a servitor of Temür Qaghan.[45] Shāms al-Dīn was still active in 1320, at least as the head of the directorate and as a Grand Instructor (*ta ssu-t'u*).[46] His successor, it appears, was one Mīr Muḥammad (Mi-erh Mo-ho-ma), who directed the Muslim Institute of Astronomy in 1333.[47]

Some kind of West Asian astronomical observatory thus existed in the Yuan from 1263 to the dynasty's fall in 1368, that is, for over one hundred years. The high point of their activity was undoubtedly the era of Jamāl al-Dīn.

Because of his visibility, reputation, and his real contributions, all elements of West Asian mathematics and astronomy found in the Yuan have been attributed to him. It has even been suggested, for example, that a Muslim magical square unearthed in Sian in 1956 was brought east by Jamal al-Dīn. Such squares, a type of mathematical recreation, developed quite early in China and thereafter spread throughout Eurasia, reaching Iran in the pre-Mongolian era.[48] Thus, whatever Jamāl al-Dīn's role in its transport, the Sian square was merely a reintroduction, a variation on something quite familiar to the Chinese.

[40] *MSC*, ch. 7, pp. 1b–2a (pp. 184–85).
[41] *MSC*, ch. 1, pp. 2a–b (pp. 23–24), and ch. 9, p. 1a (p. 245).
[42] Yang Yü, *Beiträge zur Kulturgeschichte Chinas*, p. 72.
[43] Ch'eng Chü-fu, *Ch'eng hsüeh-lou wen-chi*, ch. 5, p. 4b.
[44] *MSC*, ch. 9, p. 1b (p. 246) and 16a (p. 255).
[45] Rashīd/Karīmī, vol. 1, p. 679, and Rashīd/Boyle, p. 330.
[46] *YS*, ch. 26, p. 592.
[47] *MSC*, ch. 9, p. 16b (p. 256).
[48] Ho Peng-yoke, "Magic Squares in East and West," *Papers on Far Eastern History* 8 (1973), 127–29.

Table 3 *The names of astronomical instruments*

Chinese transcription	Arabo-Persian name	Type of instrument
tsa-t'u ha-la-chi	*ẓāt al-ḥalaq*	armillary sphere
tsa-t'u shuo-pa-tai	*ẓāt al-shu'batai[n]*	long ruler or triquetrum
lu-ha-ma-i miao-wa-chih	*rukhāmah-i mu'vajj*	sundial for unequal hours
lu-ha-ma-i mu-ssu-t'a-yü	*rukhāmah-i mustavī*	sundial for equal hours
k'u-lai-i sa-ma	*kurah-i samā'*	celestial globe
k'u-lai-i a-erh-tzu	*kurah-i arẓ*	terrestrial globe
wu-su-tu-erh-la-pu	*usṭurlāb*	astrolabe

More certainly, and more importantly, in 1267 this man of the Western Region "compiled and presented to the throne 'The Ten Thousand Year Calendar' [*Wan-nien li*]. The emperor," this passage continues somewhat cryptically, "to some extent promulgated it."[49] Nothing further is said of this calendar in the Yuan sources but data from the early Ming, assembled by Kōdō Tasaka, indicate that the calendar in question was based on observations and calculations in the Western style, that is, utilizing the twelve zodiacal constellations and dividing the heaven into 360 degrees.[50]

At the same time, Jamāl al-Dīn prepared and presented to the throne models of astronomical instruments (*i-hsiang*). Thanks to the efforts of various scholars, these can now be identified with some confidence (see table 3).[51] In addition to these models there were three astronomical instruments in the possession of the Northern Observatory of the Imperial Library Directorate in 1273: an instrument for measuring the shadow of the sun (gnomon?), a small celestial globe, and some compasses.[52]

Another facet of West Asian astronomy transported to China, perhaps in the hands of Jamāl al-Dīn himself, was the collection of Muslim scientific books housed in the Northern Observatory.[53] There are listed four works in mathematics including Euclid (Wu-hu-lieh-ti, Uqlīdis in Arabic) in fifteen sections (*pu*). This selection is not too surprising, given his fame and importance in Muslim science and learning. When, for example, Rashīd al-Dīn wishes to praise Möngke's intellectual attainments he says the qaghan solved some of the problems of Euclid.[54] More to the point, Naṣīr al-Dīn Ṭūsī composed several works on Euclid, including an "edition" of the *Elements*, or more accurately, a reworking of Euclid on the basis of an Arabic translation which is in

49 *YS*, ch. 52, p. 1120. 50 Kōdō Tasaka, 120–21.

51 *YS*, ch. 48, pp. 998–99. We owe the identification of these terms and instruments to Kōdō Tasaka, 76–99; Needham, *SCC*, vol. II, pp. 373–74; and Willy Hartner, "The Astronomical Instruments of Cha-ma-lu-ting, their Identification, and their Relations with the Instruments of the Observatory of Marāgha," *Isis* 41 (1950), 184–94.

52 *MSC*, ch. 7, p. 14b (p. 210), and Kōdō Tasaka, 117–18.

53 *MSC*, ch. 7, pp. 13b–14b (pp. 208–10), and Kōdō Tasaka, 103–6, 108–10, and 115–17.

54 Rashīd/Karīmī, vol. II, p. 718. Cf. the comments of Abū'l Fidā, *Memoirs*, p. 31.

fifteen sections like that in Jamāl al-Dīn's possession as head of the Northern Observatory.[55]

Of the four volumes on astronomy proper, one was the *Almagest* of Ptolemy (Chinese *mai-che-ssu-ti* and Arabic *Majistī*), again not a surprising choice, since commentaries (*taḥīr*) on Ptolemy by Ṭūsī and others were central to Muslim astronomical debate and development.[56] Further, there was one book on calendars called a *chi-ch'ih*, which answers to the Arabic *Zīj*: in this case perhaps an early draft of Naṣīr al-Dīn Ṭūsī's *Zīj-i Il-khānī* which was finished just a few years before his death in 1274. There is also listed a single volume on the construction of astronomical instruments and another on astrology.

Lastly, the inventory of 1273 contains a volume of "history," *ta'rīkh*, Chinese *t'ieh-li-hei*. In principle, this could be any Arabic or Persian historical work from Ṭabarī to Juvaynī, as Kōdō indicates.[57] In my opinion, however, there is a much more likely possibility, one suggested by its Chinese annotation: "Summary of the names of eras and names of states [*t'ung nien-hao kuo-ming*]."[58] This neatly describes the contents of al-Bīrūnī's work *Al-Athār al-baqiyah 'an al-Qurūn al-khaliyah*, or "Surviving Traces from Bygone Eras," which treats the different eras, and chronological and calendrical systems used by various ancient peoples and states. Al-Bīrūnī (973–1050), an astronomer, mathematician, calendrical specialist, and geographer, would have been the kind of "historian" someone such as Jamāl al-Dīn would likely favor and use, particularly since his observatory was responsible for calendars.

While most Western astronomers worked for the court, there is at least one instance of a Muslim astronomer in the service of an imperial prince. This may not be unique but it is the only documented case. The princely line in question consisted of the descendants of A'urughchi, the seventh son of Qubilai, Rashīd al-Dīn's Ūqruqchī, who was allotted the province of Tibet. When he died his eldest son Temür Buqa inherited his rights over northern Tibet.[59] He was in turn succeeded by Chosbal, his second son, who bore a Tibetan name. *Doqubal, a son of the latter, was next in line, followed by Pu-na-la.[60] The latter, based at Ho Chou in Kansu at the time of the fall of the Yuan, surrendered in 1370 to Ming forces with his "Tibetan" following. Subsequently sent to Nanking, he made a favorable impression on the Hung-wu emperor and was appointed commandant of the Wu-ching commandery near his old base of Ho Chou. In 1373 he died and his son Darmarādza, who

[55] Ali A. Al-Daffa and John J. Stroyls, *Studies in the Exact Sciences in Medieval Islam* (Dhahran: University of Petroleum and Minerals, and Chichester: John Wiley, 1984), pp. 31–32; Bar Hebraeus, pp. XXIII, XXXVI, and 451; and H. Suter, *Die Mathematiker und Astronomen der Araber und Ihre Werke*, repr. (New York: Johnson Reprint Corp., 1972), p. 151.

[56] Ṭūsī's work was completed ca. 1247. See George Saliba, "The Role of the *Almagest* Commentaries in Medieval Arabic Astronomy: A Preliminary Survey of Ṭūsī's Redaction of Ptolemy's *Almagest*," *Archives Internationales d'Histoire des Sciences* 37 (1987), 3–20.

[57] Kōdō Tasaka, 112–14. [58] *MSC*, ch. 7, p. 14a (p. 209).

[59] Rashīd/Karīmī, vol. I, p. 614, and Rashīd/Boyle, p. 244.

[60] Louis Hambis, *Le chapitre CVIII du Yuan che*: *Les fiefs attribués aux membres de la famille impériale et aux ministres de la cour mongole* (Leiden: E. J. Brill, 1954), vol. I, p. 142.

took up his office and titles, is mentioned several times in 1376 and then the family disappears from view.[61]

This family, princes of Chen-hsi and Wu-ching, had, it appears, a special right to dispatch military and political missions to central Tibet. Chosbal, a great-grandson of Qubilai, was particularly active in this regard, confirming in office powerful religious and lay leaders in the early decades of the fourteenth century. His grandson, Pu-na-la, in 1353 visited the famous monastery of Za-lu and took religious instruction from Bu-stan, a renowned scholar and historian. This Pu-na-la, according to the Tibetan sources, was named Prajnā, Baradnā in Arabic transcription, which is certainly the Mongolian form of Prajna. The Chinese form of his name therefore involves an inversion of characters which should properly read Pu-la-na.[62]

It is this Prajnā, with his wide interests in Tibetan history and Buddhist doctrine, who also supported Muslim astronomy. In 1366, Abū Muḥammad ʿAṭā ibn Aḥmad ibn Muḥammad Khwājah al-Sanjufīnī, a native of Samarqand, compiled a set of astronomical tables (*zīj*) for his patron, Prajnā. The forty-two tables, written in Arabic, include astrological calculations, lists of the Chinese names of the fixed stars transcribed into the Arabic alphabet, material on spherical astronomy and the planets, and tables for the prediction of solar and lunar eclipses and the appearance of the new moon, a matter of particular importance to Muslims. Interestingly, the title of the tables on lunar and solar positions states that they were computed according to "Jamālī observations," an apparent reference to Jamāl al-Dīn (Cha-ma-la-ting).[63]

Besides the many Chinese calendrical and astronomical terms in Arabic transcription, this manuscript has numerous Mongolian glosses. For the most part, these are word-by-word translations of the table headings in which many Arabic technical terms are simply transcribed into the Mongolian–Uighur alphabet. To add an even more cosmopolitan flavor to this important cultural document, there are a few Tibetan glosses in the form of transcriptions of the Arabic and Persian names for the months.[64]

Most certainly, then, there was in the Mongolian era extensive contact

[61] Henry Serruys, "The Mongols of Kansu during the Ming," *Mélanges Chinois et Bouddiques* 11 (1952–55), 231–33 and 237–39.

[62] On this family, their role in the governance of Tibet, and the forms of their names, see Petech, *Central Tibet and the Mongols*, pp. 42–43, 76–77, 79, 91, and 115, and Luciano Petech, "Princely Houses of the Yuan Period Connected with Tibet," in Tadeusz Skorupski, ed., *Indo-Tibetan Studies: Papers in Honor and Appreciation of Professor David L. Snellgrove's Contribution to Indo-Tibetan Studies* (Tring, England: Institute of Buddhist Studies, 1990), pp. 262–69.

[63] E. S. Kennedy, "Eclipse Predictions in Arabic Astronomical Tables Prepared for the Mongol Viceroy of Tibet," *Zeitschrift für Geschichte der arabisch-islamischen Wissenschaften* 4 (1987–88), 60–80, and E. S. Kennedy and Jan Hogendijk, "Two Tables from an Arabic Astronomical Handbook for the Mongol Viceroy of Tibet," in Erle Leichty *et al.*, eds., *A Scientific Humanist: Studies in Memory of Abraham Sachs* (Philadelphia: The University Museum, 1988), pp. 233–42.

[64] Herbert Franke, "Mittelmongolische Glossen in einer arabischen astronomischen Handschrift von 1366," *Oriens* 31 (1988), 98–103.

between Chinese and Muslim astronomers all across Eurasia – in China, Tibet, central Asia, and Transcaucasia – but was there exchange and borrowing? This, as usual, is not easily answered; clearly, there is no general formula that accurately describes the situation. It is best, therefore, to look at specifics.

To begin with the Muslim scientific literature deposited in the Imperial Library Directorate, there is no indication that these works had any appreciable influence on Chinese astronomy or mathematics. Further, during the Yuan at least, there is no evidence to suggest that they were translated in part or in whole into Chinese. They seem to have formed the working library of Jamāl al-Dīn and his West Asian associates who made their calculations and observations along traditional Hellenistic and Islamic lines. In short, these works were not intended to "inform" Chinese scientists and so far as we know no Chinese scholar of the period showed any interest in them.[65]

As regards instrumentation, it has been suggested by Needham that among Kuo Shou-ching's instruments there was an equatorial mounting. This he believes was stimulated in part by a Muslim and European instrument known as a *torquedum*. Kuo's version was called the "simplified instrument" in Chinese because it eliminated the ecliptic components and retained, following Chinese tradition, the system of equatorial coordinates. This, Needham and others have argued, anticipates Tycho Brahe and the equatorial mountings of modern telescopes.[66]

On the whole, however, Needham detects little of Muslim influence on Chinese astronomy either in instrumentation, system of coordinates, methods of computation, or the Ptolemaic planetary model. He does leave open the possibility of Muslim influence on Chinese techniques of calendar computation.[67] But, even here, there is not much evidence in hand to make such a case. The official calendar of the Yuan was the *Shou-shih li*, "Calendar for Fixing the Seasons." This was compiled by Kuo Shou-ching with the aid of a large team of observers and specialists. The calendar was promulgated in 1281 and remained the official calendar of China until the end of the Ming. The consensus opinion of historians of Chinese science is that this calendar betrays no obvious foreign influence and appears to have been compiled on the basis of traditional Chinese methods.[68]

While I cannot address these issues on a technical level, it is certainly beyond dispute that the Ming dynasty, which followed the Mongols, exhibited a lively and sustained interest in Muslim astronomy, astrology, and calendars. The legacy was therefore mainly institutional rather than scientific or technological.

In the first place, the Ming continued the Institute of Muslim Astronomy

[65] Cf. the discussion of Peter M. Engelfriet, *Euclid in China* (Leiden: E. J. Brill, 1998), pp. 73–75.

[66] Joseph Needham, "The Peking Observatory in AD 1280 and the Development of the Equatorial Mounting," *Vistas in Astronomy* 1 (1955), 67–83. See also the comments of M. C. Johnson, "Greek, Moslem and Chinese Instrument Designs in the Surviving Mongol Equatorials of 1279 AD," *Isis* 32 (1940), 27–43.

[67] Needham, *SCC*, vol. III, pp. 372–82.

[68] Ho Peng-yoke, "Kuo Shou-ching," in de Rachewiltz *et al.*, *In the Service of the Khan*, pp. 285–93, and Yabuuti, "Astronomical Tables in China," 96–97.

(Hui-hui *ssu-t'ien chien*) which they transferred to their southern capital, Nanking. It was formally abolished as a separate entity in 1398, but its personnel remained in service and came to dominate the Ming Astronomical Institute (*T'ai-shih chien*).[69] Throughout the life of the dynasty Muslim astronomers made observations on eclipses, occultations, sun spots, etc., and used their findings to determine auspicious days. They also continued to compile a Muslim calendar (Hui-hui *li*). This was never officially promulgated but ran concurrently with the Chinese calendar. The court's interest in "Western" calendars continued until the end of the dynasty, when the Jesuits demonstrated that their predictions were the more reliable. Following the Manchu conquest of China in 1644 they added a "Western" (now meaning European) section to their Institute of Astronomy.[70]

The Ming court also supported the translation of Muslim scientific works into Chinese. The Hung-wu emperor (1368–99) authorized the translation of a Muslim calendar called the Hui-hui *li-fa*. This was undertaken by a certain Mashāīkh (Ma-sha-i-hei), a native of Samarqand who came to China toward the end of the Yuan era. What he and his associates translated was not the standard Muslim lunar calendar but rather one based on the Old Persian solar calendar. Interestingly, Naṣīr al-Dīn Ṭūsī's *Zij* contained conversion tables for this calendar which, as already noted, began in 632, the Yazdigird era. Further, Mashāīkh and his collaborators also translated, probably from the Persian, a composite work on astrology which was given the Chinese title *Ming t'ien wen-shu*, "The Ming Book Interpreting Heaven." This was ascribed to the "early Arabs" but many of the concepts are much older, going back to the Hellenistic era and even to ancient Mesopotamia. The preface attributes this work to a certain Kuo-shih-ya-erh, most likely Kūshyār ibn Labbān, a Persian scholar of the late tenth century who authored several works on astronomy/astrology. Since the original of the text was found in Peking during the early Ming, one might speculate that astrological material of this nature reached China in the first instance through the mediation of someone like ʿIsā *kelemechi*, who by background and training was an heir to such ancient traditions. This translation was followed by another, entitled *Ch'i-cheng t'ui-pu* in Chinese, which outlines methods of calculating the movements of the "Seven Planets," that is, the five visible planets together with the sun and the moon. The original of this treatise, as yet unidentified, was presented to the Ming court in 1385 by a Muslim who had recently arrived from the Western Region.[71]

[69] Serruys, "Remains of Mongol Customs," 146.

[70] On Ming Astronomy, see Ho Peng-yoke, "The Astronomical Bureau in Ming China," *Journal of Asian History* 3 (1969), 137–57, and Willard J. Peterson, "Calendar Reform Prior to the Arrival of Missionaries at the Ming Court," *Ming Studies* 21 (1986), 45–61.

[71] Kōdō Tasaka, 120–58; Pelliot, "Le Hōja et le Sayyid Ḥusain," 232–35, note 311; Yabuuti Kiyosi, "Islamic Astronomy in China," *Actes du dixième congrès international d'histoire des sciences* (Paris: Hermann, 1964), 555–57; Yabuuti Kiyosi, "The Influence of Islamic Astronomy in China," in David A. King and George Saliba, eds., *From a Different Equant: A Volume of Studies in the History of Science in the Ancient and Medieval Near East in Honor of E. S. Kennedy* (New York: New York Academy of Sciences, 1987), pp. 550–55.

Yet despite these translations, there is still no suggestion that Muslim astronomy had any substantial impact on the Chinese. This was due in some measure to the court's desire to keep separate the methods of observation and computation so that the results of one could be checked against the results of the other, a practice first noticed by Mateo Ricci.[72] This, in fact, was a venerable tradition in China. During the T'ang dynasty, Indian astronomers brought new techniques – Indian numerals and tables – but this had no effect on the Chinese. Such innovations in the T'ang and the Yuan remained the property of the foreigners; the Chinese continued to make observations and calculations according to their own traditions. In other words, the Chinese willingly made use of the *findings* of foreign astronomers, which they then plugged into their own cosmological system, but they rarely made use of the *methods* by which they achieved their results. Foreigners were welcome to predict specific heavenly events so long as Chinese could define their import.[73]

On the other side of Eurasia, the situation is somewhat similar. Despite exposure to Chinese astronomy, Muslim practitioners seem little changed by the experience. Recent research on the work of Ṭūsī and the "Marāghah School" indicates that they focused their attention on the inherited tradition, Ptolemy, and the other Hellenistic astronomers. Most impressively, while adhering to the geocentric theory, they criticized and revised, sometimes drastically, the Ptolemaic system, particularly his planetary model. These revisions were so extensive and innovative as to constitute, in the opinion of some, a scientific revolution that, in astronomy at least, anticipates and perhaps influences Copernicus.[74] Moreover, this fundamental reworking of Ptolemy went well beyond Marāghah geographically and chronologically.[75] It is of course possible that alternative cosmological views supplied by the Chinese astronomers at Marāghah provided some kind of stimulus for this sustained challenge to the reigning paradigm. But this is a question others who are qualified to do so will have to take up.

The only area where there is a visible and long-lasting Chinese legacy in Muslim astronomy is in calendar making. Like their counterparts in Ming China, Muslim astronomers continued their interest in the Chinese calendrical practice. For example, the *Zīj-i khāqānī* of Jamshīd al-Kashī of 1413

[72] Matthew [Mateo] Ricci, *China in the Sixteenth Century: The Journals of Matthew Ricci, 1583–1610* (New York: Random House, 1953), pp. 31–32.

[73] Yabuuti Kiyosi, "Indian and Arabian Astronomy in China," in *Silver Jubilee Volume of the Zinbun Kagaku-Kenkyusyo Kyoto University*, pp. 589 and 595; Nathan Sivin, "Chinese Archaeoastronomy: Between Two Worlds," in A. F. Aveni, ed., *World Archaeoastronomy* (Cambridge University Press, 1989), p. 56; and Mary W. Helms, *Ulysses' Sail: An Ethnographic Odyssey of Power, Knowledge and Geographical Distance* (Princeton University Press, 1988), pp. 106–7.

[74] George Saliba, "The Role of Maragha in the Development of Islamic Astronomy: A Scientific Revolution before the Renaissance," *Revue de Synthèse* 1 (1987), 361–73, and George Saliba, "The Astronomical Tradition of Maragha: A Historical Survey and Prospects for Future Research," *Arabic Sciences and Philosophy: A Historical Journal* 1 (1991), 67–99.

[75] Ahmad Dallal, "A Non-Ptolemaic Lunar Model from Fourteenth Century Central Asia," *Arabic Sciences and Philosophy: A Historical Journal* 2 (1992), 237–43.

describes in detail the luni-solar calendar of the Chinese. He uses much Chinese terminology and gives figures for the length of the solar year and the length of a mean lunation that go back to Chinese standards. His data go back to Ṭūsī's *Zīj*, whose tables on the Chinese–Uighur calendar were continuously reproduced in the eastern Islamic world until the end of the sixteenth century.[76]

We can close with an examination of the Mongols' attitude toward calendars and timekeeping. First of all, and most obviously, the Mongols, once they acquired sedentary subjects, needed accurate calendars for purposes of administration, particularly dating documents. Additionally, they needed precise conversion tables for all of the different chronological systems of their subject peoples: Chinese, Muslim, etc.

But calendars have other and possibly more important functions: timekeeping always has ritual and cosmological implications. Any astronomical irregularity, any miscalculation of a cosmic event such as an eclipse, undermined the emperor's connectedness to the cosmos and thus his legitimacy and mandate to rule.[77] This Chinese notion was taken over by the Mongols, who conducted their own set of rituals tied to their own cosmological beliefs.

Further, calendars were important symbols of sovereignty over which rulers, Chinese, Muslim, and Mongol, claimed an exclusive monopoly, such as the right to mint coins.[78] For the Mongols, the acceptance of their calendar and their court dress became by the middle decades of the thirteenth century the basic criterion for submission.[79]

Astronomers were therefore managers of time, specialists who determined the proper moment to begin and end all kinds of activity – economic, military, ritual, and spiritual. And implicit in all this is the perceived ability of astronomers to foretell the future. To the Mongols, this was perhaps their most important attribute. And this in turn explains why the Chinggisids surrounded themselves with large numbers of specialists who claimed the power to read the heavens. So close and so visible was this association that Roger Bacon concluded that the Mongols' "success must be due to the wonderful works of science by which means they have tread the world underfoot." Their extensive conquests, he continues, were not achieved by force of arms alone and "hence they must have succeeded by means of science and especially by means of astronomy by which they profess to be ruled and directed in all things."[80] This intriguing subject – the intimate connection between astronomy, calendar making, prognostication, and the Mongols' political culture – will be addressed more fully in the concluding section.

[76] E. S. Kennedy, "The Chinese–Uighur Calendar as Described in the Islamic Sources," *Isis* 55 (1964), 435–43. One of the later reproductions is found in Abū'l Faẓl, *ʿAin-i Akbarī*, vol. II, p. 19–21.

[77] Howard J. Wechsler, *Offerings of Jade and Silk: Ritual and Symbol in the Legitimation of the T'ang Dynasty* (New Haven, Conn.: Yale University Press, 1985), pp. 212–15.

[78] David Landes, *Revolution in Time* (Cambridge, Mass.: Harvard University Press, 1983), p. 33.

[79] *YWL*, ch. 24, p. 19a.

[80] Roger Bacon, *Opus Majus*, trans. by Robert Belle Burke (New York: Russell and Russell, 1962), p. 416.

EIGHTEEN

Printing

The Chinese priority in paper making and printing, as in the case of gunpowder, is well established. The earliest specimens of paper date to the second century BC and following improvements in the second century AD this new writing material came into wide use in China, gradually replacing bamboo, wood slips, and silk in subsequent centuries.[1] According to a tradition well known in Islam, knowledge of paper making reached Samarqand following the Battle of Talas, 751, when Chinese prisoners of war taught the technique to the locals.[2] There was likely a ready market for the new product since Chinese paper had been exported to Samarqand as early as 680.[3] In any event, there was a paper mill in Baghdad by the end of the eighth century and the technology steadily diffused west into North Africa and finally to Europe in the twelfth century.[4]

The history of printing in China, at least in general outline if not in technical detail, is also well known, thanks to the labors of many scholars over the last century. The first plausible literary references to the process of block printing go back to the seventh century AD. The first extant specimens of printing date to the eighth century and the first nearly complete book, the *Diamond Sutra* of 868, was recovered at Tunhuang. A few years later printed calendars appear. During the Sung dynasty (960–1279) there was a rapid expansion of printing and the formation of a publishing business. The central government, local authorities, and private presses all produced numerous titles on a multitude of subjects.

The technology began with xylography, texts incised on wood blocks. Around 1050 we have the first experiments with movable type. Made of earthenware, this type was occasionally used down to the Yuan period. Wood type was also tried. In the Yuan this method was used to publish Wang Chen's *Nung shu*, "Book of Agriculture," in 1313. Metal type, in the development of which the Koreans played an important role, arose in the thirteenth century but was not perfected or widely used until after the Mongolian era. These methods,

1 Tsien Tsuen-hsiun, *Paper and Printing*, in Needham, *SCC*, vol. V, part 1, pp. 23–52.
2 Tha'ālībī, *Book of Curious and Entertaining Information*, p. 140.
3 Laufer, *Sino-Iranica*, pp. 557–59.
4 Tsien, in Needham, *SCC*, vol. V, pt. 1, pp. 293–303.

although representing a major technological breakthrough, never replaced block printing in China until recent times because of the nature of the Chinese literary language with its thousands of distinctive characters.[5]

As Thomas Carter, one of the pioneers in the field of Asian print history, correctly notes, besides the Chinese, the Mongols early on encountered and conquered many other peoples who regularly used printing, particularly in East Turkestan.[6] After China, this was one of the very earliest centers of printing: a Sanskrit Buddhist text was block printed there in the ninth century. In total, printed texts in seventeen different languages have been recovered from Turfan alone. Further, it should not be forgotten that the Mongols' immediate predecessors in North and West China, the Qitans, Jürchens, and Tanguts, all printed their special writing systems. The Tangut royal house sponsored the publication of Buddhist works, printed in movable wood type in the twelfth century and their near relatives, the Tibetans, at some later date combined block printing with movable type.[7] Finally, one of the earliest specimens of movable type is a safe conduct in Uighur dating to ca. 1300.[8]

Given the rich and varied printing milieu they entered, it is hardly surprising that the Mongols soon adopted the technology themselves and that they later helped to demonstrate the method to peoples further afield. The first such demonstration, a most dramatic and visible one, was the introduction of Chinese paper money, *ch'ao*, into Iran in 1294 during the reign of Geikhatu. The reasons for this experiment are variously given in the sources, but the desire to amass precious metals in the treasury and the bankruptcy of Geikhatu's regime owing to extravagance, corruption, and mismanagement were key factors. But whatever the exact motives, when Ṣadr al-Dīn and others of Geikhatu's advisers proposed this idea, Bolad was summoned to explain the Chinese monetary system. He responded, according to Rashīd al-Dīn, in the following manner:

> *Chāw* is paper which has the sovereign's seal [*tamgha*] on it and it circulates throughout Khitāī in place of minted coins and the ready money there are ingots [*balish*] and it is received by the imperial treasury.[9]

From other of Rashīd al-Dīn's writings it is evident that Bolad also informed the court that *chāw* was made of mulberry paper and that since it continuously passed from hand to hand it soon wore out. The tattered notes were then

[5] My account follows the most recent synthesis, that by Tsien, in *ibid.*, pp. 132–72, 194–222, and 325–31.

[6] Thomas Francis Carter, *The Invention of Printing in China and its Spread Westward*, 2nd edn, rev. by L. Carrington Goodrich (New York: Ronald Press, 1955), pp. 140–48.

[7] L. Carrington Goodrich, "Movable Type Printing: Two Notes," *JAOS* 99 (1974), 476–77, and Richard P. Palmieri, "Tibetan Xylography and the Question of Movable Type," *Technology and Culture* 32 (1991), 82–90.

[8] For an overview of early printing along the inland frontiers of China, see A. P. Terent'ev-Katanskii, *S Vostoka na zapad: Iz istorii knigi i knigopechataniia v stranakh Tsentral'noi Azii VIII–XIII vekov* (Moscow: Glavnaia redaktsiia vostochnoi literatury, 1990), pp. 131–37.

[9] Rashīd/Jahn I, p. 87.

turned in to the *dīvān* and exchanged for new ones on a one-to-one basis. The old bills, Rashīd relates, were destroyed by fire and a replacement of the same denomination was issued.[10]

Following Bolad's explanation the decision was taken to try the paper money. In the summer of 1294 the first *chāw* was issued; from literary description these bills were oblong, and bore Chinese characters, Muslim formulas, and the name and seal of the Il-qan. And like their Chinese prototypes the bills proclaimed the death penalty for forging or counterfeiting. The denominations ran from a half dirham to ten dinars. The paper money was launched in Tabrīz in September and, in anticipation of trouble, the Il-qan decreed summary execution for anyone refusing to accept the bills. But despite the dire threats, the *chāw* immediately produced commercial chaos, a boycott, and overt resistance. In the face of this universal public rejection of paper money, the *chāw* was withdrawn from circulation and destroyed. No examples have ever been found.[11]

Since Bolad was the primary source of information, we need to take a closer look at his knowledge of *ch'ao*. Not unexpectedly, he, as a long-time resident of China, had personal experience with the monetary system and with the bills themselves. Indeed, in January of 1281, just before Bolad left for Iran, Qubilai "transferred paper money [*ch'ao*], gold and silver to Bolad [Po-lo] to be handed over to needy people."[12] In other words, *ch'ao* passed through Bolad's hands on this, and no doubt on many other occasions, and it is almost certain that specimens of Chinese paper money were available in Iran at the time *chāw* was produced.

What, then, was the nature of the bills Bolad encountered and used in China? Paper money was of course an old institution in China and the Mongols quickly adopted it. On a limited basis paper currency circulated under Ögödei and Möngke, but its widespread use did not begin until the reign of Qubilai. Bills of the *chung-t'ung* era, 1260–64, were issued in 1261 and continued until 1276 at least. Those of the *chih-yuan* era, 1264–94, were first issued in 1287, at which time the newly issued *ch'ao* was exchanged for the old. These bills, backed by either silk or precious metals (Bolad's *balish*), were issued in denominations of 10, 20, 50, 100, 200, 300, 500, 1,000, and 2,000. They constituted a universal currency used throughout the Yuan realm and readily accepted there as legal tender.[13] While *chih-yuan* issues may have reached Iran by 1294, Bolad's personal experience with paper money in China was thus

[10] Rashīd al-Dīn, *Āthār va Aḥyā'*, p. 37.

[11] For full details, see Karl Jahn, "Paper Currency in Iran: A Contribution to the Cultural and Economic History of Iran in the Mongol Period," *Journal of Asian History* 4 (1970), 101–35. For a complete translation of Rashīd al-Dīn's account of this experiment, see Bernard Lewis, ed. and trans., *Islam*, vol. II: *Religion and Society* (New York: Walker and Co., 1974), pp. 170–72.

[12] *YS*, ch. 11, p. 229.

[13] Nancy Shatzman Steinhardt, "Currency Issues of Yuan China," *Bulletin of Sung Yuan Studies* 16 (1980), 63–68.

largely confined to the *chung-t'ung* bills, since he began his embassy to the Il-qans sometime after 1283.

A few details on the production of *ch'ao* in China are reported in the sources. According to the *Yuan shih*, paper money was printed by wood blocks until 1275, when they shifted to bronze (*t'ung*).[14] One such bronze plate has survived, as have a very few specimens of *chung-t'ung* and *chih-yuan* bills.[15]

From the timing of this shift it is apparent that Bolad was probably familiar with both methods of printing *ch'ao*. For our immediate purposes, however, the more important question is how *chāw* was produced in Iran. In describing the preparation of paper money, Rashīd al-Dīn uses a number of terms: Geikhatu orders "that they complete [*tamūm kunand*] it rapidly"; amīrs are sent to Tabrīz "for the issuance [*ba-jihat-i ijrā'*] of *chāw*"; and when they arrived there the amīrs "arranged for [*tartīb kardand*] much *chāw*."[16] There is, then, in this wording no hint of the underlying technology, no reference to "stamping," much less to "printing."

It is certain, however, that *chāw* was produced by block printing, since no other method was possible or feasible. Moreover, Rashīd al-Dīn was fully informed about the Chinese technique. In the introduction to his *History of China* he describes in detail the procedure: first, he says, they copy a page of a book on plates (*lawḥ-hā*); second, the transfer is corrected by scholars; third, engravers cut out the characters; fourth, each block is numbered and placed in a bag secured with a seal; last, whenever someone desires a copy "they bring out the plates of the book and, as [in minting] gold money, they impress the plates on leaves of paper [*awraq-i kāghaẓ*]."[17] Elsewhere in his writings Rashīd al-Dīn records that the plates are of wood and that the paper was made from the bark of mulberry bushes.[18]

These passages, it deserves to be stressed, constituted, in their own day, and for some time thereafter, the fullest and most detailed statements about the methods of Chinese printing in any language, including Chinese![19] Naturally, the origin of Rashīd's very accurate information is of interest. While in neither case does he cite a source, we can confidently invoke Bolad once again. Not only did he inform the Il-qan court about *ch'ao*, but the Chinese sources indicate that he was an enthusiastic supporter of printing. In 1273 Bolad, as Grand Supervisor of Agriculture, and Liu Ping-chung memorialized the

[14] *YS*, ch. 93, p. 2370, and Schurmann, *Economic Structure*, p. 139.

[15] L. Carrington Goodrich, "A Bronze Block for the Printing of Chinese Paper Currency," *American Numismatic Society Museum Notes* 4 (1950), 127–30; V. N. Kazin, "K istorii Khara-khoto," *Trudy gosudarstvennogo Ermitazha* 5 (1961), 282–83; and Rintchen, "A propos du papier-monnaie mongol," *AOASH* 4 (1954), 159 and 163.

[16] Rashīd/Jahn I, p. 87.

[17] Rashīd al-Dīn, *Die Chinageschichte*, folio 393r, *tafel* 4, Persian text, and p. 24, German translation. For a full English translation, taken from the history of Banākatī, *Tārīkh*, pp. 338–39, who repeats Rashīd's description word for word, see Browne, *Literary History of Persia*, vol. III, pp. 102–3.

[18] Rashīd al-Dīn, *Tanksūq-nāmah*, pp. 36–37, and Jahn, "Some Ideas of Rashīd al-Dīn on Chinese Culture," 145–46.

[19] Tsien, in Needham, *SCC*, vol. V, pt. 1, pp. 306–7.

throne with a recommendation "to establish a drafting office [*hsing wen-shu*], attached to the Imperial Library Directorate to engrave and print [*yin*] government documents." The emperor approved and in addition to administrative personnel the office employed four proofreaders, one recorder, forty engravers (*tiao-tzu chiang*), thirty-nine workmen (*chiang*) and sixteen printers (*yin-chiang*).[20] Here we have all the necessary personnel – copyists, proofreaders, engravers and printers – to carry out the tasks outlined in Rashīd al-Dīn's account of Chinese printing. Even the security measures noted by the Persian historian can be ascribed to Bolad, who on one occasion investigated, with two Chinese colleagues, Chang Tso-ch'eng and Chao Shih-lang, the unauthorized tampering with printed material in the Imperial Library Directorate.[21] It is evident, therefore, that Rashīd al-Dīn's account of Chinese printing derives from Bolad and that the methods of production and security procedures he describes are more closely associated with government-sponsored publications than with private, commercial presses.

These two pieces of evidence, the issuance of *chāw* in Iran and Rashīd's accurate depiction of Chinese printing, have often been cited in discussions of the westward migration of printing technology. This, of course, is a highly controversial matter that is still being debated. Was the development of printing in Europe an independent invention or was it indebted to Chinese precedent and practice? If Chinese influence was indeed exerted, what were its chronology and conduits? Why were the obvious benefits of printing apparently ignored in the Muslim world? I cannot pretend that these complex issues are in any way resolved here; rather, I hope that the following brief review of the long debate will serve to cast some additional light on Sino-Islamic cultural relations in the Mongolian era.

Advocates of the Chinese pedigree of Gutenberg's invention, such as Carter and Tsien, have indicated various ways Chinese influence might have been exerted in Europe: first, the direct transmission of Chinese techniques of typography to Europe through channels yet to be demonstrated; and, second, various indirect means, such as paper money, playing cards, or the transmission of Chinese books to Europe. In these latter cases, some degree of Muslim mediation is asserted or assumed.[22]

The first possibility, direct transmission between China and Europe, is beyond my competence and not strictly relevant to the theme of this book. The others, however, do bear on our subject and require brief comment. To my mind the experiment with *chāw* is an unlikely vehicle for technological transfer since it was so limited in space and time. While it is possible that the many Western travelers who commented on *ch'ao* brought back samples from China, the *chāw* of Iran is not a link in the chain of transmission. Nor does it

[20] *MSC*, ch. 7, pp. 15a–b (pp. 211–12), and Wu, "Chinese Printing under Four Alien Dynasties," 461. [21] *MSC*, ch. 6, p. 1a (p. 169).

[22] Carter, *Invention of Printing*, pp. 241–42, and Tsien, in Needham, *SCC*, vol. V, pt. 1, pp. 303–19.

seem plausible to argue that Muslims picked up printing from the Chinese and later diffused this technology to Europe. As Carter long ago acknowledged, block printing in West Asia long predates the arrival of the Mongols, but he argued that Chinese influence best accounts for the emergence of this technology in ninth-century Egypt.[23] One problem with this hypothesis is chronological: somehow Chinese printing in its formative stages influences Egyptian developments thousands of miles away. Moreover, recent research convincingly argues that block printing in the Arab world was independent of the Chinese. For the most part, early Muslim printing took the form of amulets, usually quotes from the Qur'an designed to ward off evil. The printing blocks, from all indications, were made of molded or cast metal, most probably tin, and not the wood blocks that the Chinese preferred. This technology, whether native or not, died out around 1400, largely because the purveyors of printed amulets were often confidence tricksters associated with the Banū Sāsān, the Muslim underworld. In Bulliet's opinion, this is why this indigenous technology was so isolated from Muslim society at large.[24]

Further, there is the suggestion that playing cards from China stimulated printing in Europe. If so, it is not likely that the Muslim world served as an intermediary; the earliest playing cards in Islam, dating to the twelfth and fifteenth centuries, are all hand painted and seem to be the prototypes for early Italian and Spanish cards. The Muslim cards may have been inspired by printed Chinese models but they hardly transmitted the original technology.[25]

Finally, there is the claim that so large was the number of printed books in China during the Mongol period that Western travelers must have encountered them frequently and brought a few specimens home. The subsequent discussion of Chinese books in Europe provided an incentive to invention, a process called stimulus diffusion. This interesting and promising avenue of research, while not strictly part of our inquiry, will be examined in greater depth because it opens another, admittedly small, window on Chinese–Iranian relations.

This argument rests on several premises, the first of which is that there were many books to be encountered in Yuan China. This is undoubtedly true. During the Sung, private printing became big business. Their presses published all kinds of works, introduced punctuated editions, produced a substantial number of reprints, and engaged in what amounts to copyright disputes.[26] Under the Yuan the same pattern persisted. Government and private presses turned out an impressive volume of works: classics, dynastic

[23] Carter, *Invention of Printing*, pp. 176–81.

[24] Richard W. Bulliet, "Medieval Arabic *Ṭarsh*: A Forgotten Chapter in the History of Printing," *JAOS* 107 (1987), 427–38.

[25] L. A. Mayer, *Mamluk Playing Cards*, ed. by R. Ettinghausen and O. Kurz (Leiden: E. J. Brill, 1971), pp. 6 and 10.

[26] K. K. Flug, *Istoriia kitaiskoi pechatnoi knigi Sunskoi epokhi X–XIII vv* (Moscow and Leningrad: Izdatel'stvo akademii nauk SSSR, 1959), pp. 112–32.

histories, encyclopedias, textbooks, literary collections, medical works, and Buddhist canon.[27] Some students think the quality of printing declined in the Yuan, but whatever the aesthetic judgment, it is numbers that count in matters of technological transfer and all the evidence sustains the view that the Mongols patronized and encouraged printing on a large scale.

While the basic technology unquestionably came from the Chinese, an analysis of the Mongolian word stock relating to printing and bookmaking strongly suggests the Uighurs, and to a lesser degree the Tibetans, were primarily responsible for introducing their Chinggisid overlords to this medium.[28] One of the earliest of the Mongols' printing enterprises was the publication of the Taoist canon in the reign of Ögödei. A bilingual Chinese–Mongolian inscription, executed in the name of Töregene, Ögödei's wife, testifies to their interest and support.[29] This, moreover, was not an isolated phenomenon; the Mongolian government quickly founded a number of active printing centers in North China. In 1236, at the suggestion of Yeh-lü Ch'u-ts'ai, the Mongolian court established an Office of Literature (*Ching-chi-so*) at P'ing-yang in Shansi and a Compilation Office (*Pien-hsiu-so*) at Yen-ching. In 1266 the Office of Literature was transferred to the new capital, Ta-tu, and the next year renamed the Hung-Wen Academy (*yuan*).[30] The above-named offices were thus the predecessors to the Imperial Library Directorate, founded in 1273, which became one of the major government printing offices in the Yuan.

Granted, therefore, that many Chinese books were printed under Mongolian auspices, and further, that some may have reached Europe, the question of whether such a medium really provides a viable vehicle for technological transfer still has to be addressed. The first to do so was George Macartney, the British envoy to Ch'ing China in 1793–94. With great perspicacity he notes in his journal that European printing comes 150 years after Marco Polo and then adds tellingly "that such [Chinese] books as he [i.e., Marco Polo] may have seen these he mistook for manuscripts, and indeed to the eye of a stranger they have much of that appearance."[31] In other words, Chinese printed books are unlikely to have enlightened Europeans; rather, they would have confused and bewildered them, and effectively distracted attention from the underlying technology.

[27] Wu, "Chinese Printing under Four Alien Dynasties," pp. 454–501 and 515–16; Frederich W. Mote, Hung-lam Chu, and Pao-chen Ch'en, "The High Point of Printing in the Sung and Yuan Dynasties," *Gest Library Journal* 2/2 (1988), 97–132; and Kenneth Ch'en, "Notes on the Sung and Yuan Tripitaka," *HJAS* 14 (1951), 213–14.

[28] András Róna-Tas, "Some Notes on the Terminology of Mongolian Writing," *AOASH* 18 (1965), 136–39, and Kara, *Knigi mongol'skikh kochevnikov*, p. 114.

[29] Francis W. Cleaves, "The Sino-Mongolian Inscription of 1240," *HJAS* 23 (1960–61), 65, and Igor de Rachewiltz, "Some Remarks on Töregene's Edict of 1240," *Papers on Far Eastern History* 23 (1981), 43–53.

[30] *YS*, ch. 2, p. 34, ch. 6, pp. 112 and 114, and ch. 146, p. 3459.

[31] George Macartney, *An Embassy to China*, ed. by J. L. Cranmer-Byng (London: Longmans, 1962), p. 270.

In my opinion, a more promising, or at least more plausible vehicle, are books printed in alphabetic languages. And here it is crucial to recognize that under the Mongols the printing of alphabetic writing systems, including their own in both the Uighur and hPags-pa scripts, was commonplace. One Buddhist work was block printed (*tamgha laghulju*) in 1,000 copies at Peking.[32] Fragments of other printed texts, religious and secular, have been recovered on Yuan territory.[33]

Examples of printing in alphabet scripts were therefore readily available to Western travelers in Mongol China, but did they actually see and acquire them? Most obviously, as many have pointed out, European travelers commented frequently on paper money. Marco Polo, for example, describes Qubilai's *ch'ao* at some length, noting correctly that it was made of the bark of mulberry "trees."[34] What is less well understood is that Marco Polo encountered and discussed printing in another form. Speaking of the Chinese, Muslim, and Christian astrologers at the Mongolian court, he records a source of their income:

> And so they will *make many* little pamphlets in which they write everything which shall happen in each month that year; which pamphlets are called *tacuini*. And they sell one of these pamphlets for one groat to any who wishes to buy that he may know what may happen that year. And those who shall be found to have spoken more truly will be held more perfect masters in the art and obtain greater honor.

Marco Polo continues that anyone planning any action always consults these astrologers' works, saying "see in your *books* how the sky stands just now."[35]

The term *tacuini* used by Marco Polo to describe these pamphlets is revealing in itself; this is the Arabic *taqwīm*, "almanac" or "calendar," which appears in medieval Latin texts in the form *tacuinum* and is used there as "table." In Latin translations of Arabic works *taqwīm* is rendered as *dispositio per tabellas*.[36] From Marco Polo's data we can fairly conclude that *tacuini* were produced in vast numbers, that they were printed, and that, taking into account the cultural backgrounds of their authors/compilers, they were published in several different languages and scripts.

These conclusions are sustained by other sources of information. Large sections of a Mongolian calendar from Turfan, block printed on paper, and dating to 1324, testify to the linguistic diversity of printed *tacuini*. This

32 Francis W. Cleaves, "The *Bodistw-a Čari-a Awatar-un Tayilbur* of 1312 by Čosgi Odsir," *HJAS* 17 (1954), 86.

33 N. Ts. Munkuyev, "Two Mongolian Printed Fragments from Khara Khoto," in Ligeti, *Mongolian Studies*, pp. 341–49, and G. J. Ramstedt, "A Fragment of Mongolian 'Quadratic' Script," in C. G. Mannerheim, *Across Asia from West to East*, repr. (Oosterhout: Anthropological Publications, 1969), vol. II, pp. 3–5.

34 Marco Polo, p. 238.

35 *Ibid.*, p. 252. Italics mine.

36 Dozy, *Supplément aux dictionnaires arabes*, vol. II, p. 435, and George Sarton, "*Tacuinum, taqwīm*," *Isis* 10 (1928), 490–93.

particular example, in the Uighur script, is based on a Chinese original which gives a listing of activities which may or may not be propitious on a given day.[37] The Chinese sources also provide helpful information on the issuance of these pamphlets. According to the *Yuan shih* the Academy of Calendrical Studies (*T'ai-shih yuan*), established sometime before 1278, compiled and published almanacs and calendars for public consumption. A special officer, Administrator for Calendar Printing (*Yin-li kuan-kou*), oversaw their productions. By the year 1328, some 3,123,185 calendars were sold annually, of which, intriguingly, 5,257 were Muslim (Hui-hui) calendars.[38] If these *taqwīm* were, as one might reasonably assume, published in a Hui-hui language, most likely Persian, then it means that the Arabic script was widely printed in Yuan China.[39]

Obviously, considering the total volume of publication in China at this period, it is more likely that some printed works found their way to the West, particularly in the form of calendars and almanacs in alphabetic scripts. These, to my mind, provide much better vehicles for technological transfer than playing cards, paper money, or Chinese books. However, until the case is proven, the independent invention of printing in Europe must be considered a viable hypothesis.

While linkage between Chinese and European printing remains elusive, this is not true of Iran: the technology was described and applied there but without discernible consequence. We must therefore turn to the question of the Muslim rejection of Chinese-style printing technology.

So far as I can determine, only one individual in the Muslim West, Rashīd al-Dīn, fully appreciated the value and potential of printing. He describes Chinese block printing with great admiration and, incidentally, he at no time betrays any knowledge of the indigenous Arabic tradition. Indeed, he seems to consider this technology one of the wonders of the age and a major proof of the high level of Chinese civilization. And he even sees great merit in paper money. To him, its utility is beyond description; it is a kind of philosopher's stone whose value is immeasurable and for this reason he greatly laments that "*jāw*" cannot be brought into circulation in Iran.[40] In these sentiments, however, Rashīd al-Dīn was quite alone.

Chroniclers contemporary to Rashīd al-Dīn, whether Arabs, Armenians, or Syriac Christians, all recorded the experiment, all thought it outlandish, and all emphasized its disruptive nature, disastrous consequences, and ignomin-

[37] Herbert Franke, "Mittelmongolische Kalenderfragmente aus Turfan," *Bayerische Akademie der Wissenschaften, philosophisch-historische Klasse, Sitzungsberichte* 2 (1964), 9–11 and 33–35.

[38] *YS*, ch. 88, p. 2219, and ch. 94, p. 2404.

[39] That "Hui-hui writing" means Persian in Yuan texts has been convincingly demonstrated by Huang Shijian, "The Persian Language in China during the Yuan Dynasty," *Papers on Far Eastern History* 34 (1986), 83–95.

[40] Rashīd al-Dīn, *Tanksūq-nāmah*, p. 38, and Jahn, "Some Ideas of Rashīd al-Dīn on Chinese Culture," 146.

ious end.[41] Later Persian historians also record the introduction but again as a bizarre episode that was a complete failure in the end.[42] By all available measures this experiment with paper money left a long-lasting and indelible impression on the Muslim East. When, for instance, Giyāth al-Dīn, whose account of a Temürid embassy to China in 1419–22 is included in Ḥāfiẓ-i Abrū's chronicle, relates the Ming emperor's gift of *ch'ao* to court performers, the Chinese term is simply transcribed *chāw* without further explanation.[43] Clearly, the fifteenth-century author expected his audience to understand this word.

From these data it is possible to argue that the dramatic and traumatic context of its introduction undermined the technology's chances of acceptance. Or, to put it another way, the underlying technology was overwhelmed and even obscured by the very concept of *paper* money, the major vehicle of its introduction. To a certain extent this is probably true, but the explanation is not entirely satisfactory. There were, in addition, more basic sources of opposition to printing. Certainly the Muslim world exhibited an active and sustained opposition to movable type technologies emanating from Europe in the fifteenth century and later. This opposition, based on social, religious, and political considerations, lasted well into the eighteenth century.[44] Only then were presses of European origin introduced into the Ottoman Empire and only in the next century did printing become widespread in the Arab world and Iran. This long-term reluctance, the disinterest in European typography, and the failure to exploit the indigenous printing traditions of Egypt certainly argue for some kind of fundamental structural or ideological antipathy to this particular technology that goes far beyond the circumstances of its foreign introduction, however unpleasant.[45]

[41] See for example, Bar Hebraeus, pp. 496–97; Orbelian, *Histoire de la Sioune*, p. 259; and Walter J. Fischel, "On the Iranian Paper Currency *al-chāw* of the Mongol Period," *JRAS* (1939), 601–3, who analyzes the report of the Iraqi chronicler Ibn al-Fuwaṭī on the failed attempt to introduce *chāw* into Baghdad.

[42] Abū Bakr al-Ahrī, *Tarīkh-i Shaikh Uwais*, p. 141, Persian text, and p. 44, English translation.

[43] Ḥāfiẓ-i Abrū, *Persian Embassy to China*, p. 77, Persian text and English translation.

[44] Bernard Lewis, *The Muslim Discovery of Europe* (New York: W. W. Norton, 1982), p. 50, and Toby E. Huff, *The Rise of Early Modern Science* (Cambridge University Press, 1993), pp. 224–26.

[45] Recent discussions of this opposition include Gy. Káldy-Nagy, "The Beginnings of Arabic-Letter Printing in the Muslim World," in Gy. Káldy-Nagy, ed., *The Muslim East: Studies in Honor of Julius Germanus* (Budapest: Loránd Eötvös University, 1974), pp. 201–11, and J. S. Szyliowicz, "Functional Perspectives on Technology: The Case of the Printing Press in the Ottoman Empire," *Archivum Ottomanicum* 11 (1986–88), 249–59. One further possibility to consider is resistance by the scribal class, who feared loss of jobs. See the comments of J. Ovington, *A Voyage to Surat in the Year 1689*, ed. by H. G. Rawlinson (Oxford University Press, 1929), pp. 149–50, on the attitudes toward printing of Hindu "scrivans" in Mughal India.

PART V

Analysis and conclusions

NINETEEN

Models and methods

The issue explored in the concluding sections is the nomads as cultural mediators. Inner Asia, of course, has long been recognized as a zone of cultural transmission, but the nomads' role in such transfer is typically couched in purely political and logistical terms: the nomads create a *pax*, thus permitting secure travel and trade across the continent. As we have already seen, the nomads' role in East–West exchange is in fact far more intimate and complex than is usually acknowledged. However, to come to grips with this matter, we need first to look more closely at the nature of cross-cultural contact and exchange.

In the early days of European anthropology the study of contact between cultures was cast in terms of diffusion, which was viewed as change by simple addition. New traits in the form of ideas, commodities, or technologies were borrowed from an outside "donor" culture, thereby transforming, in some measure, the "receptor" culture. Moreover, it was fashionable to assume that humans were so unimaginative that innovation was rare and diffusion therefore the main engine of history. In its more strident forms this theory led to fanciful reconstructions of world cultural history based upon transcontinental and intercontinental cultural transfers from a single center of innovation, usually identified as ancient Egypt.

In the course of the first half of the twentieth century there emerged a much more sophisticated and subtle understanding of intercultural relations, a school of thought generally called acculturation studies.[1] This school profitably switched the emphasis from the fact of diffusion to the act of borrowing; this involved a detailed look at the entire context of contact, and its cultural and social dynamics. On the most general level, there is the question of the typology of the cultures in contact, and their levels of complexity, the sources of their world view, and their openness to innovation. More specifically, investigation of these phenomena soon revealed, among other things, that only part of the cultural inventory is displayed in contact situations, never "full

[1] The classic statement of the principles of this school is Bernard J. Siegel *et al.*, "Acculturation: An Explanatory Formula," *American Anthropologist* 56 (1954), 973–1000.

representation." What part is represented is of course conditioned by the nature and purposes of the contact. In other words, contact entails "intercultural role playing": the projection, sometimes quite stereotypically, of self-images judged appropriate to the occasion. Those experienced in role playing often function as "contact specialists" – merchants, for example, who initiate and broker intercultural transmission. Thus, sedentary peoples negotiating surrender to Chinggisid armies regularly selected for their "peace delegations" individuals from those vocations – merchants, weavers, musicians, etc. – they felt the Mongols most admired and whose skills the Mongols most desired.[2]

It is important to take into consideration as well that even the most traditionalist societies were hardly homogeneous and that they always contained individuals or strata whose attitudes toward foreign introductions differed widely. Russia at the time of Peter the Great affords a striking example: some elements of that society were fanatically opposed to all innovation while others enthusiastically embraced all things foreign. Therefore, to comprehend why some traits are borrowed and others rejected one needs to inquire closely into the internal structure and dynamics of the receptor culture.

Finally, from the ethnographic study of contact, it became apparent as well that borrowing inevitably induces change on several levels, since the alien cultural elements transmitted undergo substantial transformation during the process of borrowing. Further, it was realized that rejection of alien cultural wares often produced a reaffirmation of inherited tradition or nativistic reactions, both of which constitute forms of change.

While acculturation studies represent a major advance on the old-line diffusionist school, problems remain for someone evaluating East–West exchange under the Mongols. First of all, their methods, models, and theories are normally based upon formulations in which only two cultures interact with one another. Such one-on-one exchanges are of course common and have attracted most attention. Glick's classic work on Christian–Muslim relations in Spain is a case in point that demonstrates how much can be gained from a detailed historical examination of two cultures in intensive contact.[3] There is indeed a most interesting precedent for such an approach: perhaps the very first model of acculturation is the theory of Ibn Khaldūn that nomadic conquerors of sedentary societies become assimilated in the course of three or four generations.[4] Whatever the merits of his hypothesis, it does not address the issue of long-distance, transcontinental exchanges initiated and mediated by the nomads of Inner Asia. Mediation of this sort is also frequent in cultural transfer. Not surprisingly, exchanges of this nature are far more complex, and more difficult to disentangle and explain. Because of intermediaries, bor-

[2] For examples, see Sayf, *Ta'rīkh-i nāmah-i Harāt*, pp. 81 and 106–7, and Bar Hebraeus, p. 443.

[3] Thomas F. Glick, *Islamic and Christian Spain in the Early Middle Ages* (Princeton University Press, 1979), pp. 217 ff.

[4] Ibn Khaldūn, *The Muqaddimah*, trans. by Franz Rosenthal (New York: Pantheon Books, 1958), vol. I, pp. 278–82 and 343–51.

rowed traits are refashioned by several cultures in succession, making their origins and routes of diffusion hard to trace. The issue is further confused by the tendency of many societies, and China in particular, to disguise and domesticate foreign, mediated borrowings by means of invented traditions and popular etymologies.[5]

A second problem is that too often theories of acculturation equate political and economic superiority with cultural dominance. There are many examples to the contrary. As Braudel points out, England emerged in the eighteenth century as the premier political power but France retained and even extended its cultural influence.[6] This is true of Roman cultural reliance on the Greeks and Achaemenid dependence on Mesopotamia. Consequently, it is no anomaly that the Mongols of the thirteenth and fourteenth centuries were certainly dominant in the political and military spheres but hardly in the cultural.

The reason for such blind spots and omissions is that the study of cultural transmission and acculturation has, for the most part, focused on instances where an expansive, colonizing society, usually European in origin, introduces or imposes its own culture on a subjugated "native" population. Thus the conquerors and cultural "donors" were one and the same people. This, however, was not true in the history of East–West cultural contacts as a whole. The Mongols, with some exceptions, were not primarily engaged in transmitting their own ethnic culture to their diverse sedentary subjects; rather, they functioned as a medium through which various elements of the agriculturally based civilizations of East and West were exchanged over long distances. They were, in sum, agents, not donors. The Mongols and other nomads were, however, often instrumental in selecting which particular traits were diffused in either direction. And, of course, when a trait from one cultural zone of the empire was introduced into another through Mongolian agency, there was as well a secondary selection process, which Foster, in another historical context, has termed "screening."[7] Consequently, the diffusion of material and spiritual culture across Eurasia was rarely a "two sphere problem," but rather a "three or four sphere problem," since the Mongols were appropriating and sharing out the cultures of their numerous subjects: Chinese, Persians, Uighurs, Syriac Christians, and others.

It should also be noted that acculturation studies peaked in the period 1920–50 and thereafter there was a decline of interest in intercultural communication. This trend has been reversed in the last decade and new theoretical perspectives have been developed that shed much light on long-distance cultural exchange. One of the most influential and productive approaches has

[5] See, for example, Schuyler Cammann, "Notes on the Origin of Chinese K'o-ssu Tapestry," *Artibus Asiae* 11 (1948), 90–110, especially 92–95, and M. N. Krechetova, "Tkani 'kesy' vremeni Sun (X–XIII vv.) v Ermitazhe," *Trudy gosudarstvennogo Ermitazha* 10 (1969), 237–48.

[6] Fernand Braudel, *Civilization and Capitalism*, vol. II: *The Perspective of the World* (New York: Harper and Row, 1979), pp. 67–68.

[7] George M. Foster, *Culture and Conquest: America's Spanish Heritage* (Chicago: Quadrangle Books, 1960), pp. 10–20.

been pioneered by Mary Helms, who has concentrated her attention on the nature of artisanship and the ethnography of distance.[8]

This brief preamble to my discussion of the social and cultural dynamics of East–West exchange is, I wish to stress, intended only as a means of identifying those individuals and schools which have provided me with the models and methodologies from which I fashioned my analytical framework. Since I am not a theoretician, I have sought guidance in many directions and am therefore indebted to all who have addressed the issue of contact and exchange, from traditional diffusionists such as Laufer to acculturationists such as Herskovits,[9] as well as to the more recent contributions of anthropologists and archeologists working on "interregional interaction."[10]

Lastly, it must also be stated that in contrast to the study of exchange in non-literate or archeological cultures, which has generated most of the models and methods in the field, investigations of contact between historical societies have tended to be more concerned with specifics and less prone to generalization. Certainly in one important respect the historian's task is much easier. In our case, for instance, the basic facts about cultural transmission in the Mongolian Empire are not in dispute. The chronology of contact is well known and even the names, ethnic affiliations, and occupations of the chief agents of transmission are firmly established. And it is to this vital and unusually well-documented issue of agency that we now turn our attention.

8 Her work will be discussed at greater length below.

9 To my mind, one of the best introductions to the study of cultural contact and exchange is contained in the relevant chapters of Melville J. Herskovits' textbook, *Man and His Work: The Science of Cultural Anthropology* (New York: Alfred A. Knopf, 1951), pp. 459–621. For a more succinct discussion, see Ralph Linton, *The Tree of Culture* (New York: Alfred A. Knopf, 1955), pp. 41–49.

10 For discussions of recent research with extensive bibliographies, see Edward M. Schortman and Patricia A. Urban, "Current Trends in Interaction Research," in Edward M. Schortman and Patricia A. Urban, eds., *Resources, Power and Interregional Interaction* (New York and London: Plenum Press, 1992), pp. 235–55, and Per Hage, Frank Harary, and David Krackhardt, "A Test of Communication and Cultural Similarity in Polynesian Prehistory," *Current Anthropology* 39 (1998), 699–703.

TWENTY

Agency

In this discussion of agency we will begin with specifics and then move to more general considerations: that is, we will look first at the historical evidence and second at the ethnological.

The argument that the Mongols were the prime movers in this exchange rests on a firm evidentiary foundation. As we have seen, Mongolian rulers ordered and patronized many exchanges, and one of the chief conduits of exchange and the key cultural broker of the era was an ethnic Mongol, Bolad Aqa. Further, and far more persuasive, it was the Chinggisids who created, consciously or unconsciously, innumerable opportunities for cross-cultural and transcontinental contact. To put it another way, the major carriers of foreign cultural wares from one end of Eurasia to the other were for the most part acting as agents of the empire; these included diplomats, military personnel, administrators, technologists, artisans, scholars, merchants, and hostages, just to name the most obvious.

What traveled across the continent did so in large part because it brought comfort, prestige, economic profit, or political advantage to the Mongolian elite. The chronology of these exchanges affirms such a conclusion, since the periodization of contact can be tied to datable "events," transitional moments in the history of the Mongolian Empire.[1] Three such moments are readily discernible in the historical record. First, the invasion of Turkestan, 1219–24, which saw the Mongols' conquest of the eastern Islamic world. The invaders brought with them large numbers of Chinese specialists and scholars and deported en masse Muslims to East Asia. Second, Hülegü's attack on the Isma'īlīs and ʿAbbāsids, 1255–59, brought a fresh contingent of East Asians to Iran – artisans, scholars, soldiers, and scientists. He and his immediate successors reciprocated by sending various specialists to China. Third is the embassy of Bolad to Iran in the mid-1280s. As we traced in detail, he formed

[1] For a more generalized periodization which subsumes the Mongolian Empire as one phase of a larger "age of transregional nomadic empires," ca. 1000–1500, see Jerry H. Bentley, "Cross-Cultural Interaction and Periodization in World History," *American Historical Review* 10 (1996), 766–69.

an intimate partnership with Rashīd al-Dīn that resulted in many further cultural transfers.

The breakup of the empire in 1260 no doubt inhibited exchange in the sense that political fragmentation and civil war made communication more difficult; none the less, cultural transfers of various types continued well into the fourteenth century because of the special relationship between the Yuan and Il-qan courts. The reasons why so much of the exchange flowed along this particular axis deserve closer scrutiny.

First, and most obviously, specific historical and political circumstances connected with the formation of the Il-qan state made them allies in a civil war. As such they continued, following the precedent of Chinggis Qan's immediate successors, sharing resources – troops, war matériel, scientific personnel, technology, and intelligence – as a means of mutual support in the face of common foes.[2] Most often these grants of assistance were permanent, but occasionally they were in the form of loans.[3]

The continuance of this aid was not, however, merely a matter of politics. The Il-qans and the Yuan dynasty controlled cultural resources that could be traded. Indeed, while their enemies, the Chaghadai Qanate and the Golden Horde, were anomalous polities without recognizable territorial precedent or cultural cohesion, the Il-qans and the Yuan continued well-defined, historically established imperial traditions of great antiquity: the Yuan was a close equivalent of the Han and T'ang, and the Hülegüid state resembled the Achaemenid, Sasanian and ʿAbbāsid in its cultural and geographical configuration.[4] Moreover, the rulers of the Il-qans and the Yuan shared to a large extent the same ecological zones as their sedentary subjects and consequently their economic, social, and political structures were integrated with their subjects.[5] This meant the two regimes faced similar challenges and possessed similar resources; consequently, they experienced similar problems and adopted similar cultural policies and attitudes that fueled exchange.

The result, of course, was that much East Asian culture was demonstrated in the West, and many West Asian traditions were displayed in China. Demonstration or display should not, however, be equated with exchange and borrowing. Not all opportunities were exploited; in some cases, moreover, they were firmly rejected. To understand this it must be borne in mind that it was the Mongolian rulers who promoted and patronized these cultural

[2] See the comments of Juvaynī, Juvaynī/Qazvīnī, vol. I, p. 32, and Juvaynī/Boyle, vol. I, p. 43.

[3] Rashīd/Alizade, vol. I, pt. 1, pp. 523–24.

[4] Cf. the comments of V. V. Bartol'd, "Retsenziia na knigu: *The Tarikh-i Rashidi of Mirza Muhammad Haidar*," in his *Sochineniia*, vol. VIII, p. 66; Bert G. Fragner, "Iran under Ilkhanid Rule in a World Historical Perspective," in Aigle, *Iran*, pp. 127–29; and R. G. Kempiners, Jr., "Vaṣṣāf's *Tajziyat al-amṣar va tazjiyat al-aʿsār* as a Source for the History of the Chaghadayid Khanate," *Journal of Asian History* 22 (1988), 169–70.

[5] Anatolii M. Khazanov, "The Early State among the Eurasian Nomads," in Henri J. M. Claessen and Peter Skalnik, eds., *The Study of the State* (The Hague: Mouton, 1981), pp. 155–75, especially pp. 169–73.

exchanges, and not, with the notable exception of Rashīd al-Dīn, local scholars. The latter with some consistency ignored or resented the appearance of learned men from foreign parts on their "turf." Beyond general cultural conservatism their behavior may be ascribed to several factors: first, there was too much, too soon; they were force-fed and simply could not absorb the alien tradition; second, the promoters were outsiders and conquerors and their specialists became identified with the enemy; and, third, locals felt threatened by the intruders' skills and knowledge: jobs were at stake.

Whatever the full explanation, there is certainly evidence that local scholars clung to the inherited tradition, especially in the more theoretical sciences and disciplines. Qāshānī, in his chronicle, provides for each year a brief obituary section and all the scientists included there are extolled for their mastery of Greek and Islamic philosophy and learning.[6] Knowledge of Chinese science, well demonstrated by this time, is never mentioned as an accomplishment. In this, Muslim scholars were following an older tradition that made the Greek philosophers "the most respected among people of knowledge."[7] That prestige survived the Mongolian conquest and the provision of scientific alternatives. This in part is a consequence of the fact that new technology spreads as "a matter of economic calculus," while alien science, always linked to world views, "runs afoul" of the core cultural beliefs and norms of the receiving culture.[8]

This reluctance is more sharply manifested in China, perhaps because of the large number of Muslim administrators and tax collectors in Yuan service who became the visible instruments of the exploitation of the Chinese populace. The focal point of this resentment, Qubilai's financial adviser Aḥmad (A-ha-ma), was considered an "evil minister" (*chien-ch'en*) by the Confucians and thoroughly hated by the public.[9] This translated into Chinese suspicion of everything Muslim and deep-seated anti-Islamic attitudes on the popular level.[10] Such views, naturally, help to inhibit borrowing from West Asia because of the distasteful associations.

In considering Mongolian motives for fostering such exchange, whether successful or not, reasons of state must be brought into our calculations. New military technologies and printing were essential tools of conquest and administration. The Mongols acquired technologies in one cultural zone and deployed them in another to further imperial expansion and control. The reasons for these transfers are self-evident but what of food, medicine, and the like?

[6] Qāshānī/Hambly, pp. 76, 108, and 198.

[7] Saʿīd al-Andalusī, *Science in the Medieval World: Book of the Categories of Nations*, trans. by Semaʿan I. Salem and Alok Kumar (Austin: University of Texas Press, 1991), p. 21.

[8] E. L. Jones, *Growth Recurring: Economic Change in World History* (Oxford University Press, 1988), p. 68.

[9] *YS*, ch. 205, pp. 4558 ff., and Marco Polo, p. 215.

[10] Herbert Franke, "Eine mittelalterliche chinesische Satire auf die Mohammedaner," in Hoernerbach, *Der Orient in der Forschung*, pp. 202–8.

To start with the latter, it is apparent that West Asian physicians in China and their Chinese counterparts in Iran were not treating the native population at large but for the most part restricted their practice to court circles and foreigners in residence. It is a well-established sociological principle that even within a given medical tradition new procedures and cures are slow to gain acceptance and are often rejected or shunned by the patients themselves, the ostensible beneficiaries.[11] Not unexpectedly, initial resistance to clearly alien procedures is even more intense. Even in today's world these questions of "cultural comfort" are important in making medical decisions, particularly among Chinese and Japanese in the West who retain high levels of confidence in their ethnic medical tradition.[12] To some extent, therefore, the Mongolian courts of China and Iran were providing medical services that were culturally acceptable to their many foreign servitors.

The same, I believe, can be said of food and drink. On one level the Mongols constructed an internationalized court cuisine of diverse elements that was a palpable and edible manifestation of the Mongols' great "reach," one that validated their claims of universal empire.[13] At the same time, this food service catered to foreigners' tastes and preferences. A case in point is Möngke's famous "drinking fountain" constructed in Qara Qorum, an elaborate automaton that dispensed the favorite alcoholic beverages – grape wine, kumys, mead, and rice wine – of the whole of Eurasia.[14] Here was a bar anyone could step up to with confidence.

This is not to argue that the Mongolian courts in China and Iran created separate cultural enclaves for the exclusive use of their foreign-born underlings, such as the hill stations of the British Raj which recreated patches of England in the subcontinent, but they did make a sustained effort to provide their diverse officialdom with some of the sights, sounds, smells, and tastes of home. This, of course, was designed to encourage the loyalty of their numerous *gästarbeiter* and to help them retain their ethnic identities. Thus there was a kind of multiplier effect at work here in which the recruitment of one group of outsider specialists led to the recruitment of a second group who could tend to the cultural needs of the first.

The exchanges in historiography can also be approached under the same rubric: reasons of state. The Mongols of China and Iran found themselves with common military enemies who openly questioned their legitimacy. One response to this challenge was a search for historical validation: the collection of records concerning the founding fathers whose words, even after death,

[11] See Bernard J. Stern, *Social Factors in Medical Progress* (New York: Columbia University Press, 1927), pp. 60–65.

[12] See articles in the *New York Times*, January 27, 1990, p. 29, and September 29, 1990, pp. 1 and 28.

[13] Anderson, "Food and Health at the Mongol Court," pp. 37–39.

[14] For a detailed discussion of its technical and symbolic characteristics, see Leonardo Olschki, *Guillaume Boucher: A French Artist at the Court of the Khans*, repr. (New York: Greenwood Press, 1969), pp. 45–106.

carried great authority. As the *Secret History* reveals, "old words [*ötögüs üges*]" and "ancient words [*qa'uchin üges*]" carried substantial force for the Mongols in the thirteenth century; not surprisingly, at a later date Chinggis Qan's words were thought to be divinely inspired.[15] These, of course, had to be preserved and were frequently invoked (and reinterpreted) in the course of policy debates and political disputes. Even Ghazan, a convert to Islam, prided himself on his knowledge of old Mongolian tradition and based his claims of rulership on historical arguments.[16] While these arguments were designed to reassure followers and subjects rather than convince enemies, they were of necessity embedded in the histories of many different peoples. Since the political fate of Yuan China was now important in Iran, so too were its antecedents, its history, its legitimacy.

Rashīd al-Dīn's *Collected Chronicles* therefore reflect both the transcontinental political tensions and the universal political pretensions of the Mongolian Empire, itself an echo or perhaps the culmination of Chinese and ancient Near Eastern claims of universalism.[17]

The next matter to be addressed is why the Mongols, the intermediaries, were so open to outside influence. Marco Polo, among others, was well aware that the Mongols were subject to the culture of conquered peoples, both Muslim and Chinese.[18] This is because nomads not only need the economic products of sedentary societies, but their cultural resources as well, especially during phases of conquest and state formation.[19] As Service has argued, expansive societies, leaving their own physical and cultural environment and entering into a substantially different milieu, are of necessity more open to innovation and thus more adaptive.[20] In our case, the Mongols, well adapted to their own environment, were culturally conservative at home but open and flexible in conquest, skillfully picking and choosing institutions and technologies from subject peoples that facilitated further military expansion and successful exploitation of their new economic base. In other words, compared to their principal sedentary opponents, the Mongols in the early phases of the empire were the most innovative polity in the sense of their willingness to learn from others and their skill at cultural adaptation. Free from the parochialism and bias generated by high cultures and scholastic intellectual traditions, particularly in the realm of science and religion, the Mongols, despite

[15] *SH*/Cleaves, sect. 78, p. 24 and sect. 260, p. 201; *SH*/de Rachewiltz, sect. 78, p. 30 and sect. 260, p. 156; Jūzjānī/Lees, pp. 373–74; and Jūzjānī/Raverty, vol. II, pp. 1077–78.

[16] Rashīd/Jahn II, pp. 171 and 177.

[17] On Mongolian universalism and its antecedents, see E. Voegelin, "The Mongol Orders of Submission to the European Powers," *Byzantium* 15 (1940–41), 378–413, and Garth Fowden, *Empire to Commonwealth: Consequences of Monotheism in Late Antiquity* (Princeton University Press, 1993), pp. 3–11.

[18] Marco Polo, pp. 174–75.

[19] Anatolii Khazanov, "Ecological Limitations of Nomadism in the Eurasian Steppe and their Social and Cultural Implications," *Asian and African Studies* 24 (1990), 10–15.

[20] Elman R. Service, *Origins of the State and Civilization: The Process of Cultural Evolution* (New York: Norton and Co., 1975), pp. 319–22.

the disinclination of their subjects, became the chief promoters of cultural change and exchange.

Matters, however, run deeper than this. The fundamental structure and characteristics of Mongolian society promoted, indeed required, such exchange. Nomads by nature are generalists; the entire culture by and large is encapsulated in the individual. This is probably true of all subsistence economies, even agricultural, in which the population, for sound ecological reasons, is thinly dispersed over large tracts of territory.[21] Mongolian society exhibited little occupational specialization and the division of labor, beyond that produced by age and gender, was weakly developed. There were in fact only a few specialists in Mongolian society who had withdrawn from subsistence activities and made a living selling one particular service – shamans, bards, and perhaps metalsmiths.[22] This lack of specialization is revealed in the evolution of the early Mongolian state: in 1188, 1203, and again in 1206 when Chinggis Qan formed and then reorganized his household establishment/imperial guard, all the positions enumerated required only those skills – herding, cooking, etc. – traditional to nomadic life. Each individual appointed to a specific office could have taken over the duties of any other office without major difficulty. Before 1206 the only functionary whose knowledge was not part of the pool of skills common to all nomads was the shaman, the office held by Teb Tenggeri.

The situation, of course, is very different in developed agrarian societies. Their level of specialization is infinitely higher and so is the degree of social complexity. Such specialization is already evident in early stages of Near Eastern history, and it grew steadily over time.[23] By the thirteenth century, a civilization like that of China had hundreds if not thousands of specialists.

The need for specialists to administer sedentary societies is clearly noted in the *Secret History* when Chinggis Qan recognizes that the "customs and laws of cities" were unknown to the Mongols.[24] Faced with new cultural requirements that could not be met from internal sources, the Mongols' solution was not to convert themselves into such specialists but to acquire them from the sedentary world. The Mongols began this process by coopting as the need arose military men to aid conquest and administrative experts to help them rule.[25] Thereafter, their attention turned to various cultural specialists like Yeh-lü Ch'u-ts'ai, who was intensely recruited because he possessed ritual and

[21] Ernest Gellner, *State and Society in Soviet Thought* (Oxford: Blackwell, 1988), p. 95, and Ester Boserup, "Environment, Population and Technology in Primitive Societies," in Donald Worster, ed., *The Ends of the Earth: Perspectives on Modern Environmental History* (Cambridge University Press, 1988), pp. 34–35.

[22] For hints of the latter, see *SH*/Cleaves, sect. 97, p. 33 and sect. 211, p. 153, and *SH*/de Rachewiltz, sect. 97, pp. 37–38 and sect. 211, p. 121.

[23] Hans J. Nissen, *The Early History of the Ancient East* (University of Chicago Press, 1988), pp. 43 ff.

[24] *SH*/Cleaves, sect. 263, pp. 203–4, and *SH*/de Rachewiltz, sect. 263, p. 157.

[25] See Igor de Rachewiltz, "Personnel and Personalities in North China in the Early Mongol Era," *Journal of the Economic and Social History of the Orient* 9 (1966), 88–144.

scientific knowledge.[26] In time, the search for talent became increasingly systematic and sophisticated. Special commissioners (*shih-che*) brought out scholars, physicians, and artisans before cities were plundered.[27] Eventually, census rolls were compiled and the population identified and to some degree organized by occupational categories.

It is important as well that the Mongols favored sedentary peoples with specific skills – technicians, engineers, or mathematicians – over those who were generalists such as Confucian scholars known for classical learning.[28] The Mongols also preferred "outsiders" without local connections and networks. To this end, naturally, the Mongols made heavy use of foreigners as well as people from the lower strata of society.[29] In either case, recruits with such backgrounds were more likely to remain loyal to the Chinggisids and less likely to identify with local elites.

Once formed, pools of outside specialists possessing military, managerial, technical, and ritual skills were shared out and loaned among the empire's ruling strata. In some instances the qaghan distributed these experts to show his generosity and thus his majesty. In other cases they were distributed on the basis of reciprocity, in which the giver expects the recipient to respond in like fashion at some future date. In either case, the Mongolian elite was conforming to nomadic cultural norms, in which displays of generosity and reciprocity are highly valued and critical to the successful functioning of pastoral society.

Many exchanges, therefore, flowed naturally from nomadic conquest on a continental scale. The Mongols did not see themselves as creators of a unified world culture, a mission sometimes attributed to Alexander the Great.[30] On the contrary, cultural diversity and confrontation were ingredients in their success, not cultural unity. Internationalism, like nationalism, is a modern ideological construct.

What the Mongols did fashion was a culture created for and bounded by the state.[31] To put it another way, the culture of the Mongolian Empire was not coterminous with the culture of the Mongolian people; indeed, it was not an ethnic culture at all but one rapidly constructed out of diverse material for

[26] de Rachewiltz, "The *Hsi-yü lu* by Yeh-lü Ch'u-ts'ai," 18; *YWL*, ch. 50, p. 11a; and *YS*, ch. 146, p. 3455.

[27] Erich Haenisch, *Zum Untergang zweier Reiche: Berichte von Augenzeugen aus den Jahren 1232–33 und 1368–70* (Wiesbaden: Franz Steiner, 1969), p. 11v, Chinese text, and p. 25, German translation.

[28] See the comments of Hok-lam Chan, "Liu Ping-chung (1216–74)," 137–39.

[29] Juvaynī complains bitterly about the upstarts and parvenus rapidly promoted in the Mongols' administration in Khurāsān. See Juvaynī/Qazvīnī, vol. I, pp. 4–5, and Juvaynī/Boyle, vol. I, pp. 7–8.

[30] W. W. Tarn, "Alexander the Great and the Unity of Mankind," *Proceedings of the British Academy* 9 (1933), 147–48.

[31] Cf. the comments of Mark G. Kramarovsky, "The Culture of the Golden Horde and the Problem of the 'Mongol Legacy'," in Gary Seaman and Daniel Marks, eds., *Rulers from the Steppe: State Formation on the Eurasian Periphery* (Los Angeles: Ethnographics Press, 1991), p. 256.

the needs of the new polity. It was therefore highly syncretic and "state bound." The term "state culture," it seems to me, is more appropriate in this context than the more familiar "court culture." For our purposes the latter is too narrow, since court culture is primarily concerned with the comfort, pleasure, and majesty of the ruling house, whereas state culture, which subsumes court culture, had a much wider responsibility: the governance of the realm. This creation, however artificial, well served Mongolian political interests because their state culture displaced or at least neutralized the traditional ruling elites in China and Iran and consequently weakened temporarily the great tradition that validated local structures of authority. In providing an alternative, state-bound culture, the Mongols created new contacts, confrontations, and opportunities for exchange. Naturally, because its existence was so closely linked to the state, when the empire disintegrated so did many elements of its state culture, most particularly the long-distance exchange of specialist personnel. Mongolian practice was not entirely unprecedented – the Türk after all had their Sogdians and the Qitans their Uighurs – but the scale on which the Mongols operated, the sheer magnitude of their enterprise, was unique in world history before European maritime expansion.

While this state culture, in its elaboration and implementation, had as one of its principal goals political control and the mobilization of resources, men, money, and material, there was another dimension to the Mongols' accumulation of "power" that has received far less attention. Beyond and beside its "practical ends" the Mongols' state culture strove to mobilize and monopolize the spiritual forces of the realm. This included those found in the natural world, those controlled by ancestors, the charisma of former dynasties and, most important for our purposes, those possessed by ritual specialists, artisans, and scholars.[32] Among these latter, the most noticeable are the clergy of all faiths, whom the Mongols endeavored to coopt with patronage and tax immunities, a policy which began with the Taoists.[33] In this instance it is clear that the Mongols wished to harness the clerics' spiritual power and communications networks for the benefit of the empire. This explains the Mongols' intense interest in diverse religious teachings and traditions, why they staged doctrinal debates, and why adherents of many sects always came away from court with the feeling that the qaghan was really "one of them."[34] Somewhat less evident is the spiritual power ascribed to other skilled specialists, scholars, and artisans.

To a degree, the accumulation of talented individuals was a display designed

[32] For a survey, see Thomas T. Allsen, "Spiritual Geography and Political Legitimacy in the Eastern Steppe," in Henri J. M. Claessen and Jarich G. Oosten, eds., *Ideology and the Formation of Early States* (Leiden: E. J. Brill, 1996), pp. 116–35.

[33] Yao Tao-chung, "Ch'iu Ch'u-chi and Chinggis Khan," *HJAS* 46 (1986), 201–19.

[34] Wm. Theodore de Bary, "Introduction," in Hok-lam Chan and Wm. Theodore de Bary, eds., *Yuan Thought: Chinese Thought and Religion under the Mongols* (New York: Columbia University Press, 1982), p. 18, comments correctly on the sincerity of the Mongols' religious interests.

to create an aura of majesty, and Mongolian rulers played this game. Qubilai, for instance, when he dispatched the elder Polos home in the 1260s, did so with a request to the Pope to send back "wise men of learning" and those who know "the seven arts."[35] This tactic certainly helped his image because he was well known in West Asia where, as Bar Hebraeus says, he was a "just and wise king" who "honored the men of books and learned men, and the physicians *of all nations*."[36] Such persons, because they are literate, enjoy prestige in their own communities, and communicate with one another over time and space, are marvelous press agents, easily purchased, like intellectuals everywhere, with favor and coin.

This, however, was only one facet of the attraction of skilled specialists to premodern rulers. In several recent studies, Mary W. Helms has drawn attention to the meaning of distance and human talent in many traditional societies. Skill in the various crafts, she argues, involves transforming raw material into cultural wares, and this transformation, in preindustrial societies, is not viewed as mere mechanical manipulation but as a mystical and supernatural process performed by specially gifted individuals commanding technical skill *and* spiritual force. Thus, besides the factor of prestige commonly associated with the capacity to collect talented people for service at court, the ruler is also exercising control over the spiritual power of his realm. Further, the ability to attract or forcibly acquire raw materials, finished goods, or talented people from great distances enhances a kingly reputation and augments authority because what is distant is mysterious and what is mysterious in traditional societies always contains spiritual power. Wise men, possessed of esoteric knowledge, typically come from afar.[37] As Thomas Roe so elegantly phrased it almost 400 years ago,"wonder [is] in the distance [and] remotenes is the greatnes."[38]

The Yuan court was obviously conscious that their success, or good fortune, and their glory, or majesty, were closely linked to the many foreigners in their service. This is expressed succinctly by Ch'eng Chü-fu, writing in the early fourteenth century:

> I venture to say that all those who founded empires in the past, had, as the cornerstone [of their success], the ability to obtain the services of worthy men. Our [Yuan] Dynasty, with supernatural military power and benevolent leniency, has brought order to the four seas [the World]. Loyal, virtuous, brave and talented men from a multitude of places and myriad countries all willingly enter the emperor's service. Each passing generation adds to their luster.[39]

Ch'eng's initial assertion that this practice was common among earlier empires is fully borne out by the historical record. Darius, the Achaemenid

[35] Marco Polo, p. 79. [36] Bar Hebraeus, p. 439. My italics.

[37] Mary W. Helms, *Craft and the Kingly Ideal: Art, Trade and Power* (Austin: University of Texas Press, 1993), pp. 13–27 and 69–87, and Helms, *Ulysses' Sail*, pp. 3–19 and 94–110.

[38] Thomas Roe, *The Embassy of Sir Thomas Roe to the Court of the Great Mogul, 1615–1619*, ed. by William Foster (London: Hakluyt Society, 1899), vol. I, p. 122.

[39] Ch'eng Chü-fu, *Ch'eng hsüeh-lou wen-chi*, ch. 5, p. 5a.

emperor (521–481 BC), boasts in one of his inscriptions that his winter capital of Susa was made of building materials from Lebanon, Sardis, Bactria, Sogdia, Egypt, Ethiopia, Sind, and Elam, while the artisans and artists came from Ionia, Sardis, Media, Egypt, and Babylonia.[40] A runic Turkic book from ninth-century Tunhuang contains similar sentiments: "After having ascended the throne, a khan built a royal camp [*ordu*]. His realm remained [firm]. The good and skillful men in all quarters of the world, having assembled [there] rejoice and adorn [his court]." This, the passage concludes, "is a good omen."[41] The latter, admittedly, is not an official proclamation like that of Darius but a statement in a book of omens, which indicates that such notions were carried in the folk traditions as well as in imperial ideologies.

This tradition, however communicated over time, survived the Mongols. Temür, like his Chinggisid predecessors, collected artisans and other individuals of talent wherever he campaigned. And like Darius of old, he too advertised his possession of and control over skilled individuals. Clavijo, the Spanish ambassador who was in Samarqand in 1405, relates that in honor of a grandson's marriage, all artisans of that city, the royal capital, were ordered to appear in Temür's encampment in the suburbs. "The whole Horde [*ordu*]," he says, "was filled with them, each craft and trade being allotted a street where the men of the same, each separately and in due order, displayed their art. Further," he continues, "in every craft there was set up an exhibition or separate show to display their skill at the matter in hand, and these shows perambulated throughout the whole Horde for the entertainment of the people."[42]

The antiquity and longevity of this notion is quite impressive: it was a common feature of the political culture of Eurasia for at least 2,000 years. Consequently, all premodern empires, that of the Mongols included, were inevitably mechanisms of intercultural exchange.

[40] Roland G. Kent, *Old Persian: Grammar, Texts, Lexicon*, 2nd edn (New Haven, Conn.: American Oriental Society, 1953), p. 144.

[41] Talat Tekin, *Irk Bitiq: The Book of Omens* (Wiesbaden: Otto Harrassowitz, 1993), p. 17.

[42] Ruy González Clavijo, *Embassy to Tamerlane, 1403–1406*, trans. by Guy Le Strange (New York: Harper Brothers, 1928), pp. 134, 248–49, 286, and 287.

TWENTY ONE

Filtering

The Mongols' propensity to borrow from subject peoples, while certainly extensive, was neither unbounded nor open-ended. The state culture they fashioned consisted of three basic components: the indigenous traditions and institutions of conquered peoples, foreign traditions imported by the Chinggisids and, finally, the Mongols' own social and cultural norms. This component is usually downplayed, but should not be overlooked in the study of Mongolian governance or of trans-Eurasian cultural exchange. The long-established cultural categories of the Mongols and their closest allies, such as the Uighurs, acted as filtering devices that selected what was to be appropriated, apportioned, and transmitted. Like all peoples, the Mongols tended to select those items which were compatible with their native traditions, a process that placed some restrictions on borrowing but in the main was quite flexible. Even in the realm of high literary culture and science the Mongols found functional equivalents that complemented rather than displaced elements of their own culture.

In this chapter we will explore the filtering mechanisms at work in the Mongols' appropriation of medicine, astronomy, geography, and cartography from sedentary cultures. These disciplines, at least in terms of goals, were quite compatible with the practice of shamanism; their methods differed radically but in their quests for cures, for knowledge of the future, for charting the powers of nature, the Mongols found ready analogies in their own cultural schema. To understand the reasons for these equations, we must first look into the types and functions of Mongolian shamans of the thirteenth century.

While there is some ambiguity in the Turkic and Mongolian terminology for healers, sorcerers, and prognosticators, a basic categorization is possible.[1] In the Mongol case we have guidance from the *Secret History*. In 1231 when Ögödei fell ill, we are told that he was tended by *bö'e* and *tölgechin*.[2] In the Chinese interlinear translation of this passage *bö'e* is equated with *shih-kung*,

[1] For a brief overview of the terms, see Judith Szalontai-Dmitrieva, "The Etymology of the Chuvash Word *Yumśa*, 'Sorcerer'," in András Róna-Tas, ed., *Chuvash Studies* (Wiesbaden: Otto Harrassowitz, 1982), pp. 171–77.

[2] *SH*/Cleaves, sect. 272, pp. 211–12, and *SH*/de Rachewiltz, sect. 272, p. 163.

which can be rendered as "medical master," and *tölgechin* with *pu-jen*, "diviner" or "soothsayer."[3] As Roná-Tas rightly concludes, *bö'e* is the generic term for shaman, while *tölgechin* designates the more specialized diviner. The difference between the two is substantial: the *bö'e*/shaman conducts his business by means of spiritual quests or trips, and the *tölgechin*/diviner through a search for signs provided by burnt bones, bird flights, dreams, or even dice.[4]

Of the two, the *bö'e* enjoyed the higher status in Mongolian culture, but both were extensively used by all segments of the populace. They of course treated the sick, but are most often encountered divining.[5] Their ability to foretell the future was greatly prized and a crucial element in Mongolian political culture. Future events, the rise of Chinggis Qan, the outcome of battles were divined by anomalies of nature, reading stalks and, most frequently, by scapulmancy: reading cracks on the burnt shoulder blades of sheep.[6] Chinggis Qan himself, according to Muslim tradition, read sheep bones during his campaigns in India.[7] Indeed, government business at large was conducted by such methods. In the testimony of Rubruck, policy initiatives and the placement of new encampments were in the hands of diviners.[8]

At one point, early in his career, Chinggis Qan had a chief shaman, Kököchü, or Teb Tenggeri, who "revealed secrets and future events" and who reported "heavenly foretokens" about future political developments.[9] He soon ran foul of the Mongol leader because of interference in family matters. He was killed in 1206 and there seems to have been no replacement; very likely Chinggis Qan and his successors preferred second opinions, alternative visions of the future.

At first glance, this apparent reliance on divination may seem surprising for so successful a political enterprise. But this is a modernist misunderstanding. In Moore's words, divination has a "positive latent function, that is, even though magic fails to achieve its manifest ends, except by accident or coincidence, it serves its practitioners and/or their society in other critically important ways."[10] These other ways have been clearly delineated by Park: first,

[3] B. I. Pankratova, ed., *Iuan-chao bi-shi (Sekretnaia istoriia Mongolov)* (Moscow: Izdatel'stvo vostochnoi literatury, 1962), sect. 272, p. 566.

[4] András Roná-Tas, "Dream, Magic Power and Divination in the Altaic World," *AOASH* 25 (1972), 232–33.

[5] On their medical functions, see Juvaynī/Qazvīnī, vol. I, pp. 43–44, and Juvaynī/Boyle, vol. I, p. 59.

[6] *SH*/Cleaves, sect. 121, pp. 52–53 and sect. 207, p. 147; *SH*/de Rachewiltz, sect. 121, pp. 50–51 and sect. 207, p. 118; Marco Polo, pp. 165–66; Chao Hung, *Meng-ta pei-lu*, in Wang, *Meng-ku chih-liao*, p. 453; and P'eng Ta-ya and Hsü T'ing, *Hei-ta shih-lüeh*, pp. 485 and 506.

[7] Jūzjānī/Lees, pp. 355 and 374, and Jūzjānī/Raverty, vol. II, pp. 1046–47 and 1078.

[8] *Mongol Mission*, pp. 121 and 141, and Rubruck/Jackson, pp. 121 and 156. Peter Munday, traveling in India, says the same thing about the court of Shāh Jahān (r. 1628–57). See *The Travels of Peter Munday in Europe and Asia, 1608–1667*, ed. by Sir Richard Carrol Temple, repr. (Nendeln, Liechtenstein: Kraus, 1967), vol. II, pp. 194–95.

[9] Rashīd/Alizade, vol. I, pt. 1, pp. 418–19; *SH*/Cleaves, sect. 244, p. 177; and *SH*/de Rachewiltz, sect. 244, p. 139.

[10] Omar Khayyam Moore, "Divination – A New Perspective," *American Anthropologist* 59 (1957), 69.

divination in "situations of problematical action," lends the indicated act "a peculiar but effective type of legitimation"; second, the diviner "removes agency," the responsibility for decisions, and places it upon the heavens; and, third, divination helps establish consensus and is therefore "closely related to the problem of controlling and channelling public opinion and belief."[11]

From this perspective divination emerges as a complex phenomenon with a variety of functions and we should not therefore assume that Mongolian strategy and political decision making were determined by chance, by a throw of the dice. Divination was simply part of the careful preparations which preceded all campaigns, a ceremony in which victory was prophesied and success publicly proclaimed, all of which helped to encourage consensus, build confidence, and boost morale. The decisions themselves were made on a number of grounds. This is clear from the fact that the Mongols always took multiple readings so always had "policy options." In short, the various prognosticators in Mongolian service divined the intentions of their masters, not future events.

Given the importance of such input, diviners were heavily recruited and many were accumulated at the imperial court. When the qaghan moved on his annual rounds, so did his team of futurologists.[12] Their organization in the early empire is noted in the sources. According to the *Yuan shih*, among the officials attached to the imperial guard (*kesig*) were those in charge of "medicines [*i-yao*], divination [*pu*] and invocations [*chu*]."[13] We even know the names of two such officials; the same source relates that in 1252 Möngke "appointed A-hu-ch'a to superintend sacrifices, healers [*i-wu*] and diviners [*pu-shih*]; Alaq Buqa [A-la Pu-hua] assisted him."[14] The terminology used in this text is interesting: *i-wu* means "medical shaman" and *pu-shih*, encountered in the *Secret History*, means literally "diviner by stalks." If we had the Mongolian version of Möngke's *Veritable Records*, prepared by Sarman and associates, *i-wu* would certainly translate *bö'e* and *pu-jen*, *tölgechin*. But were the subordinates of A-hu-ch'a and Alaq Buqa just Mongolian practitioners of shamanism? From a number of sources the answer is clearly no: this bureau supervised Mongolian shamans, Nestorian doctors, Chinese pulse specialists, and Muslim astronomers. Rubruck, among others, testifies to this fact. During his stay in Qara Qorum he encountered the soothsayers, *divini*, at Möngke's court. Some, he relates, "are skilled in astronomy . . . and they foretell the eclipse of the sun and moon."[15] These certainly were not traditional shamans, but astronomers recruited from sedentary cultures. In this particular instance, it might well have included ʿIsā *kelemechi*.

The Mongols' reidentification of astronomers with shamans and diviners is well attested in the contemporary sources. In one passage Juvaynī starts out speaking of the *qām*, the Turkic *qam*, "shaman," and ends up saying that the

[11] George K. Park, "Divination and its Social Contexts," in John Middleton, ed., *Magic, Witchcraft, and Curing* (Austin: University of Texas Press, 1989), pp. 235, 236, and 241–42.
[12] Marco Polo, p. 233. [13] *YS*, ch. 99, p. 2524. [14] *YS*, ch. 3, p. 46.
[15] *Mongol Mission*, p. 197, and Rubruck/Jackson, p. 240.

Mongolian princes will conclude no business until their "astronomers [*munajjimān*]" have passed on it.[16] Bar Hebraeus, in his turn, explicitly states that the Mongols equated Chinese prognosticators with the *kāmāyē*.[17] Other sources, too, pair diviners and astronomers/astrologers, and note that both were the constant companions of the Chinggisids.[18] Astronomy, astrology, scapulmancy, geomancy, divining by stalks, and casting diagrams from the *Book of Changes* (*I-ching*)[19] were all forms of spiritual intelligence, were viewed by the Mongols as compatible and complementary enterprises, and were organized accordingly.

What appealed to the Mongols about astronomers was their ability to predict heavenly portents. This is hardly surprising for adherents of the Tengri religion. After all, they had received a political mandate from Heaven, Tengri, to rule the world and were naturally intensely interested in further guidance. Such signposts came in the form of comets, phases of the moon, various meteorological phenomena – "thunders," "tempests," "thunderbolts," and "lightnings," and, most impressively, eclipses.[20] Indeed, the Mongols' initial recruitment of Chinese and Muslim astronomers around 1220 was linked directly to competitions in predicting lunar eclipses.[21]

Henceforth, large numbers of astrologers, of diverse cultural backgrounds, were recruited for service at the court and set to work, along with sorcerers, charmers, necromancers, and diviners, to foretell the future.[22] Astronomers in actuality performed the very same services as shamans: they determined auspicious days to launch campaigns or to enthrone a new ruler.[23] Astronomers (*munajjimān*) selected the day of Möngke's elevation – Naṣīr al-Dīn Ṭūsī chose the date of Abaqa's – while the timing of Güyüg's enthronement was determined by the *qam*.[24]

Some of the results of their deliberations were in the public domain and some were carefully guarded state secrets. Astronomers/astrologers produced intelligence that was not to be shared, even within the imperial family. ʿIsā once refused an empress access to secret astronomical documents. And Marāghah, the major observatory in northwest Iran, was in a "prohibited area," Mongolian *qorigh*.[25]

16 Juvaynī/Qazvīnī, vol. I, pp. 43–44, and Juvaynī/Boyle, vol. I, p. 59.

17 Bar Hebraeus, pp. 355–56. 18 Marco Polo, p. 249.

19 See Janet Rinaker Ten Broeck and Yiu Tung, "A Taoist Inscription of the Yuan Dynasty: *The Tao-chiao pei*," *TP* 40 (1950), 108–9.

20 Grigor of Akancʿ, "History of the Nation of Archers," 351; Roux, *La religion des Turcs et des Mongols*, pp. 130–31; and Marco Polo, p. 252.

21 *YWL*, ch. 51, p. 11b, and *YS*, ch. 146, p. 3456.

22 Marco Polo, pp. 188–89 and 252. On their organization under the Yuan, see Elizabeth Endicott-West, "Notes on Shamans, Fortunetellers and *Ying-yang* Practitioners and Civil Administration in Yuan China," in Amitai-Preiss and Morgan, *Mongol Empire*, pp. 224–39.

23 Marco Polo, p. 196.

24 Juvaynī/Qazvīnī, vol. I, pp. 206–7 and vol. III, pp. 29–30; Juvaynī/Boyle, vol. I, p. 251 and vol. II, pp. 567–68; Rashīd/Karīmī, vol. I, pp. 584–85; Rashīd/Boyle, p. 205; and Rashīd/Jahn I, p. 7.

25 *YS*, ch. 134, p. 3250; Moule, *Christians in China*, p. 229; and Qāshānī/Hambly, p. 41. The Persian text has *qūrngh*, an obvious copyist's error for *qūrīgh*.

It should occasion no surprise, therefore, that Roger Bacon persuaded himself that the Mongols' success could be attributed to their employment of legions of learned astronomers.

In matters of health, the Mongols also filtered sedentary medicine through traditional shamanic beliefs. This can be illustrated by the Mongols' attraction to Chinese pulse lore, or sphygmology.

For the Chinese, one of the key concepts underlying medical practice was that of *ch'i*, sometimes translated as "influence." In their conceptualization *ch'i* was an emanation arising from the natural environment and its interaction with the human body was the chief determinant of health. *Ch'i* and blood circulated through the body and well-being depended upon monitoring this flow and adapting lifestyles to this "system of influences."[26] One of the diagnostic means of tracking flows was pulse taking, which developed in China into a special branch of medicine.

Among the Turkic and Mongolian nomads there was an analogous and widespread belief that the blood was one of the major seats of the soul, that is, the life force was closely associated with the circulatory system.[27] This notion was no doubt reinforced by the Mongols' empirical knowledge of the circulation of the blood, derived from their method of slaughtering animals, which entailed opening the chest and stopping the heart to retain all blood within the carcass.[28]

This belief explains why the medieval Mongols, following earlier steppe tradition, always executed kinsmen and powerful enemies by bloodless means, usually strangulation or suffocation. If properly dispatched and the corpse properly disposed, the life force of the deceased foe could bring benefit to his executioner from the beyond.[29] If, on the other hand, royal blood was spilled on the ground, it could, in Marco Polo's phrase, "make lamentations in the air" and induce misfortune.[30] Thus, the Mongols' concern for the numinous force carried in the blood predisposed them to look upon Chinese pulse diagnosis as a critical means of gauging and treating physical health as well as spiritual well-being. Over time, Mongols began to equate medical examination with monitoring the pulse, in the Chinese fashion, of both wrists.[31]

The Mongols' reinterpretation of *ch'i* as a life force in the blood led to the preference for Chinese pulse diagnosis and explains as well the selection of Chinese medical literature translated in Rashīd al-Dīn's *Tanksūq-nāmah*.

[26] Paul U. Unschuld, *Medicine in China: A History of Ideas* (Berkeley: University of California Press, 1985), pp. 67–76.

[27] See Jean-Paul Roux, *La mort chez les peuples altaiques anciens et médiévaux d'après les documents écrits* (Paris: Adrien-Maisonneuve, 1963), pp. 75 ff.

[28] Pelliot, *Notes*, vol. I, pp. 77–78, and Régis-Evariste Huc and Joseph Gabet, *Travels in Tartary, Thibet and China* (New York and London: Harper and Bros., 1928), vol. I, pp. 274–75.

[29] For examples of bloodless execution, see, among many others, *SH*/Cleaves, sect. 201, p. 140; Bar Hebraeus, p. 431; and Clavijo, *Embassy to Tamerlane*, p. 251.

[30] Marco Polo, pp. 199–200.

[31] James Gilmore, *Among the Mongols*, repr. (New York: Praeger, 1970), p. 181, and Huc and Gabet, *Travels in Tartary*, vol. I, p. 87.

In the Mongols' marked attraction to, and support for, geographical and cartographical scholarship there were similar cultural forces at work. As pastoralists, the Mongols were extremely sensitive to the land. Knowledge of routes, topography, hydrology, and seasonal changes in climate and vegetation was central to their successful adaptation to a demanding environment. As conquerors, they were interested in geographical intelligence. Mongolian envoys to foreign lands were charged, in the words of Rubruck, with taking "stock of the routes, the terrain, the towns and castles, and the people and their weapons."[32] And once subdued and incorporated into the empire, geographical data on conquered lands had great administrative value. In the 1270s the Yuan court ordered that final decisions on the placement of garrisons in the south be deliberated by "people versed in military affairs and knowledgeable in geography [*ti-li*]."[33] A few years later the court sponsored an expedition to explore the sources of the Yellow River and the lines of communications to their dependency, Tibet. As a result, the expedition acquired a good knowledge of the upper course of the Yellow River and produced a quality map of the region based on Tibetan sources.[34]

The Mongols' concern for landscape, however, went far beyond such mundane considerations. For them and their fellow nomads potent spiritual forces inhered in the earth, water, and stones, which influenced in substantial ways all human affairs.[35] When Ögödei became ill in 1231 during the campaign against the Chin, the Mongolian shamans attributed this to "the lords and rulers of the land [*qajar*] and rivers [*usun*] of the Kitat," that is, to spiritual forces of the Chinese landscape which were seen as defending themselves against the Mongolian onslaught.[36] This concern for the spirits of the land was manifested in various ways. The Mongols, for example, went to great lengths to properly site their capital, Qara Qorum, in the same region as the imperial city of the Türk qaghanate and Uighur empire because they believed that there inhered in that particular locale a special good fortune, a charisma (Turkic *qut*) that would favor their own political enterprise.[37] Such considerations are exhibited as well by the Mongol practice of siting and orienting buildings, including those at Qara Qorum, by means of bowshots.[38]

The consequence of these native traditions was that the Mongols were most interested in foreign geomantic traditions and techniques. In the Yuan, the Chi-hsun Academy, founded in 1281 and subordinated to the Han-lin

[32] *Mongol Mission*, p. 159, and Rubruck/Jackson, p. 186.
[33] *YS*, ch. 99, p. 2545, and Hsiao, *Military*, p. 118.
[34] Herbert Franke, "The Exploration of the Yellow River Sources under Emperor Qubilai in 1281," in G. Gnoli and L. Lanciotti, eds., *Orientalia Iosephi Tucci Memoriae Dicata* (Rome: Istituto Italiano per il Medio ed Estremo Oriente, 1985), vol. I, pp. 401–16. The map is preserved in T'ao Tsung-i, *Cho-keng lu*, ch. 22, pp. 2b–3a.
[35] Roux, *La religion des Turcs et des Mongols*, pp. 132–44.
[36] *SH*/Cleaves, sect. 272, p. 212, and *SH*/de Rachewiltz, sect. 272, p. 163.
[37] See Allsen, "Spiritual Geography and Political Legitimacy," pp. 125–27.
[38] Hok-lam Chan, "Siting by Bowshot: A Mongolian Custom and its Sociopolitical and Cultural Implications," *Asia Major* 4/2 (1991), 53–78.

Academy, had as one of its duties the regulation of practitioners of geomancy (*yin-yang chi-ssu*).[39] And the Imperial Library Directorate, it is relevant to note, housed "calendars, maps, registers, as well as prohibited books on geomancy."[40] Naturally, Chinese geomantic techniques were highly prized at the Yuan court, but so too were Muslim ones. Though less famous than the Chinese *feng-shui*, "wind and water," the Islamic world also developed a system of geomancy. Called the science of sand (*ʿilm al-raml*) in Arabic, it had a respectable place in Muslim learning and seems to have flourished in the thirteenth century. Naṣīr al-Dīn Ṭūsī was a major figure in the field and this may well have added to his luster in the eyes of Mongolian courts East and West.[41] There is even a Muslim work on geomancy in the Imperial Library Directorate; transcribed as *Mi-a* (Arabic *miyah*, "waters"?), it is described as a book that "distinguishes wind and water," that is, methods of selecting sites by *feng-shui*.[42]

Qubilai himself seems to have been a practitioner of some form of geomancy. According to one of Bayan's biographies, the Southern Sung succumbed because "Shih-tsu succeeded to the fortune [*yün*], stroked the map [*tu*], and put forth a most excellent strategy."[43] In this terse passage Qubilai (Shih-tsu) inherits Chinggis Qan's charisma (Mongolian *su*), and makes use of a map to successfully subdue the enemy. Here the map clearly represents the country, and if one can, like Qubilai, smooth the map, soothe it, one can pacify the country and its landscape, which, as we have already seen, could mount its own kind of resistance, a spiritual resistance that had to be quelled by equivalent means.

As the case of geography and cartography nicely demonstrates, the Mongols of the imperial era never considered empirical and esoteric knowledge or practical and magical means as mutually exclusive opposites; on the contrary, in combination they possessed a kind of synergy that induced good fortune and worldly success.

39 *YS*, ch. 87, p. 2192. 40 *YS*, ch. 90, p. 2296, and Farquhar, *Government*, p. 137.

41 Emilie Savage-Smith and Marion B. Smith, *Islamic Geomancy and a Thirteenth-Century Divinatory Device* (Malibu, Calif.: Undena Publications, 1980), pp. 1–14.

42 *MSC*, ch. 7, p. 14a (p. 209), and Kōdō Tasaka, 113–14.

43 *YWL*, ch. 24, p. 11a, and Cleaves, "Biography of Bayan of the Bārin," 275.

TWENTY TWO

Summation

Inner Asia has long been seen as a zone of contact and transmission, a lengthy conveyor belt on which commercial and cultural wares traveled between the major civilizations of Eurasia. On the basis of the evidence presented here, the following conclusions seem warranted on the nomads' essential but largely unacknowledged role in this cultural traffic.

In the first place, the very act of creating a state in the steppe always stimulated the transcontinental circulation of prestige goods, especially textiles, because such luxuries were in fact necessities in the political culture of the Mongols and other nomads.[1]

Second, while the state-bound culture of the empire had as its primary objective the control and exploitation of the Mongols' sedentary subjects, its secondary effect was the creation of numerous opportunities for cross-cultural contact, comparison, and exchange.

Third, the selection of the various components that entered into this syncretic state culture was determined by Mongolian cultural, social, and aesthetic norms as mediated, of course, by the conditions of conquest and pressing political interest.

Fourth, the Chinggisids viewed human talent and skill as a form of booty, to be "shared out" among the family just like land, herd animals, and material goods. The various Chinggisid branches, dispersed throughout Eurasia, competed for these specialists who were vital to their efforts to tap into the economic and cultural wealth of the settled zones of the empire.

Fifth, the Mongols and other nomads, while normally included in the analysis of the political context of trans-Eurasian exchange, are typically left out of the cultural equation. Here the great sedentary civilizations are placed at center stage.[2] This is particularly apparent when scientific transfers are under

[1] Allsen, *Commodity and Exchange*, pp. 103–4.

[2] See, for example, Adshead, *China in World History*, p. 24, and Karl Jahn, "Wissenschaftliche Kontakte zwischen Iran und China in der Mongolenzeit," *Anzeiger der phil.-hist. Klasse der österreichischen Akademie der Wissenschaften* 106 (1969), 199–211.

consideration.[3] But, as we have seen, the filtering mechanism of Mongolian culture was quite capable of valuing and transmitting the great scientific achievements of East and West Asia. In a word, Muslim astronomers came to China because the Mongols wanted second opinions on the reading of heavenly signs and portents, not because they or their Chinese counterparts wanted scientific exchange.

Sixth, under Mongolian auspices many new products, commodities, technologies, and ideologies, as well as human, animal, and plant populations, circulated throughout the vast Eurasian continent. Much that was so introduced and demonstrated was ignored or rejected, but some was adopted and adapted, and, perhaps most importantly, many persistent, powerful, and consequential images of distant places and cultures were formed, reinforced, and disseminated. The Mongolian Empire functioned, therefore, as the principal cultural clearing house for the Old World for well over a century. And when it declined and disintegrated, it was gradually replaced by maritime Europe which in time came to perform similar offices for the Old World and the New.[4]

In sum, pastoral nomads were the chief initiators, promoters, and agents of this exchange, and their cultural preferences, as articulated in the form of imperial policy, go far to explain what passed between East and West in the Mongolian era.

[3] Joseph Needham, "Central Asia and the History of Science and Technology," in his *Clerks and Craftsmen*, p. 30. For a rare and welcome contrary opinion that argues for nomadic contributions, see Ruth I. Meserve, "On Medieval and Early Modern Science and Technology in Central Eurasia," in Michael Gervers and Wayne Schlepp, eds., *Cultural Contact, History and Ethnicity in Inner Asia* (Toronto: Joint Centre for Asia Pacific Studies, 1996), pp. 49–70.

[4] Cf. the comments of Gregory G. Guzman, "Were the Barbarians a Negative or Positive Factor in Ancient and Medieval History?" *The Historian* 50 (1988), 568–70.

Bibliography

Aboul Ghāzī Bēhādour Khān, *Histoire des Mongols et des Tatares*, trans. by Petr I. Desmaisons, repr., Amsterdam: Philo Press, 1970.

Abū'l Faẓl, *The 'Ain-i Akbarī*, trans. by H. Blochmann and H. S. Jarret, repr., Delhi: Atlantic Publishers, 1979, vols. I and II.

Abū'l-Fidā, *The Memoirs of a Syrian Prince*, trans. by P. M. Holt, Wiesbaden: Franz Steiner, 1983.

Adnan, Abdulhak, "Sur le Tanksukname-i-Ilhani dar Ulum-u-Funun-i Khatai," *Isis* 32 (1940), 44–47.

Adshead, S. A. M., *China in World History*, London: Macmillan, 1988.

Ahmad, S. Maqbul, "Cartography of al-Sharīf al-Īdrīsī," in Harley and Woodward, *History of Cartography*, vol. II, bk. 1, pp. 156–74.

Al-Ahrī, Abū Bakr, *Ta'rīkh-i Shaikh Uwais, an Important Source for the History of Adharbaijān*, ed. and trans. by H. B. Van Loon, 's-Gravenhage: Mouton, 1954.

Ahsan, Muhammad Manazir, *Social Life under the Abbasids*, London and New York: Longman, 1979.

Aigle, Denise, ed., *L'Iran face à la domination Mongol*, Tehran: Institut français de recherche en Iran, 1997.

Akimushkin, O. F., "Novye postupleniia persidskikh rukopisei v rukopisnyi otdel Instituta Narodov Azii AN SSSR," in *Ellinisticheskii Blizhnii Vostok, Vizantiia i Iran*, Moscow: Nauka, 1967, pp. 144–56.

'Alī Akbar Khitā'ī, *Khitāi-nāmah*, ed. by Iraj Afshār, Tehran: Asian Cultural Documentation Center for UNESCO, 1979.

Allsen, Thomas T., *Commodity and Exchange in the Mongol Empire: A Cultural History of Islamic Textiles*, Cambridge University Press, 1997.

Mongol Imperialism: The Policies of the Grand Qan Möngke in China, Russia and the Islamic Lands, 1251–1259, Berkeley: University of California Press, 1987.

"Notes on Chinese Titles in Mongol Iran," *Mongolian Studies* 14 (1991), 27–39.

"The Princes of the Left Hand: An Introduction to the History of the *Ulus* of Orda in the Thirteenth and Early Fourteenth Centuries," *AEMA* 5 (1985–87), 5–40.

"The *Rasūlid* Hexaglot in its Eurasian Cultural Context," in Golden, *Hexaglot*, pp. 25–49.

"Spiritual Geography and Political Legitimacy in the Eastern Steppe," in Henri J. M. Claessen and Jarich G. Oosten, eds., *Ideology and the Formation of Early States*, Leiden: E. J. Brill, 1996, pp. 116–35.

Amano Motonosuke, "Dry Farming and the *Ch'i-min yao-shu*," in *Silver Jubilee Volume of the Zinbun-Kagaku-Kenkyusyo Kyoto University*, pp. 451–65.

"On *Nung-sang chi-yao*," *Tōhōgaku* 30 (1965), English summary, 6–7.

Amitai-Preiss, Nitzan and Reuven Amitai-Preiss, "Two Notes on the Protocol on Hülegü's Coinage," *Israel Numismatic Journal* 10 (1988–89), 117–28.

Amitai-Preiss, Reuven, "Evidence for the Early Use of the Title *īlkhān* among the Mongols," *JRAS* 1 (1991), 353–61.

"An Exchange of Letters in Arabic between Abaγa Ilkhān and Sultan Baybars," *CAJ* 38 (1994), 11–33.

"Ghazan, Islam and Mongol Tradition: A View from the Mamlūk Sultanate," *BSOAS* 54 (1996), 1–10.

"New Material from the Mamlūk Sources for the Biography of Rashīd al-Dīn," *Oxford Studies in Islamic Art* 12 (1996), 23–37.

Amitai-Preiss, Reuven and David O. Morgan, eds., *The Mongol Empire and its Legacy*, Leiden: Brill, 1999.

Ananias of Širak, *The Geography of Ananias of Širak*, trans. by Robert Hewsen, Wiesbaden: Ludwig Reichert, 1992.

Ancient China's Technology and Science, Peking: Foreign Language Press, 1983.

Anderson, E. N., "Food and Health at the Mongol Court," in Edward H. Kaplan and Donald W. Whisenhunt, eds., *Opuscula Altaica: Essays Offered in Honor of Henry Schwarz*, Bellingham, Wash.: Center for East Asian Studies, Western Washington University, 1994, pp. 17–43.

Arberry, A. J., trans., "A Baghdad Cookery-Book," *Islamic Culture* 13 (1939), 21–47 and 189–214.

Aubin, Jean, *Emirs mongols et vizirs persans dans les remous de l'acculturation*, Studia Iranica, vol. XV; Paris, 1995.

"Les princes d'Ormuz du XIIIe au XVe siècle," *Journal Asiatique* 241 (1953), 77–138.

Bacon, Roger, *Opus Majus*, trans. by Robert Belle Burke, New York: Russell and Russell, 1962.

Bailey, H. W., "Iranian Studies," *BSOAS* 6 (1932), 945–56.

Bakrān, Muḥammad ibn Najīb, *Dzhakhān name (Kniga o mire)*, ed. by Iu. E. Borshchevskii, Moscow: Izdatel'stvo vostochnoi literatury, 1960.

Jahān-nāmah, Tehran: Ibn-i Sīnā, 1963.

Banākatī, *Ta'rīkh-i Banākatī*, ed. by Jaʿfar Shiʿār, Tehran: Chāpkhānah-i Bahram, 1969.

Bar Hebraeus, *The Chronography of Gregory Abū'l-Faraj . . . commonly known as Bar Hebraeus*, trans. by Ernest A. Wallis Budge, London: Oxford University Press, 1932, vol. I.

Baranovskaia, L. S., "Iz istorii mongol'skoi astronomii," *Trudy instituta istorii estestvoznaniia i tekhniki* 5 (1955), 321–30.

Bartol'd, V. V., "Evropeets XIII v. v Kitaiskikh uchenykh uchrezhdeniiakh (K voprosu pizantse Izole)," in his *Sochineniia*, vol. V, pp. 382–91.

"Otchet o komandirovke v Turkestan," in his *Sochineniia*, vol. VIII, pp. 119–210.

"Persidskaia nadpis na stene anniskoi mechete Munuche," in his *Sochineniia*, vol. IV, pp. 313–38.

"Retsensiia na knigu: The Tarikh-i Rashidi of Mirza Muhammad Haidar," in his *Sochineniia*, vol. VIII, pp. 63–73.

Sochineniia, Moscow: Nauka, 1963–77, 9 vols.

de Bary, Wm. Theodore, "Introduction," in Hok-lam Chan and Wm. Theodore de Bary, eds., *Yuan Thought: Chinese Thought and Religion under the Mongols*, New York: Columbia University Press, 1982, pp. 1–25.

Bayani, Chirine, "*L'histoire secrète des Mongols* – une des sources de *Jāme-al-tawārīkh* de Rachīd ad-Dīn," *Acta Orientalia* (Copenhagen) 37 (1976), 201–12.

Bayar, Menggen, "Unique Features of Bloodletting Treatment in Traditional Mongolian Medicine," *Mongolian Society Newsletter* 13 (Feb., 1993), 41–52.

Bazin, Louis, *Les systèmes chronologiques dans le monde Turc ancien*, Budapest: Akadémiai Kiadó, and Paris: Editions du CNRS, 1991.

Beckwith, Christopher I., "The Introduction of Greek Medicine into Tibet in the Seventh and Eighth Centuries," *JAOS* 99 (1979), 297–313.

Bentley, Jerry H., "Cross-Cultural Interaction and Periodization in World History," *American Historical Review* 10 (1996), 749–70.

Blair, Sheila S., "The Coins of the Later Ilkhanids: A Typological Analysis," *Journal of the Economic and Social History of the Orient* 26 (1983), 295–317.

"The Inscription from the Tomb Tower at Bastām: An Analysis of Ilkhanid Epigraphy," in C. Adle, ed., *Art et société dans le monde iranien*, Paris: ADPF, 1982, pp. 263–86.

de Blois, François, "The Persian Calendar," *Iran* 34 (1996), 39–54.

Bold, Bat-Ochir, "The Quantity of Livestock Owned by the Mongols in the Thirteenth Century," *JRAS* 8 (1998), 237–46.

Boodberg, Peter A., "Marginalia to the Histories of the Northern Dynasties," *HJAS* 3 (1938), 223–53.

Boserup, Ester, "Environment, Population and Technology in Primitive Societies," in Donald Worster, ed., *The Ends of the Earth: Perspectives in Modern Environmental History*, Cambridge University Press, 1988, pp. 23–38.

Bowie, Theodore, ed., *East–West in Art*, Bloomington, Ind.: Indiana University Press, 1966.

Boyle, John A., "The Death of the Last ʿAbbāsid Caliph: A Contemporary Muslim Account," *Journal of Semitic Studies* 6 (1961), 145–61.

"The Last Barbarian Invaders: The Impact of the Mongolian Conquests upon East and West," *Memoirs and Proceedings of the Manchester Literary and Philosophical Society* 112 (1970), 1–15. Reprinted in his *The Mongolian World Empire, 1206–1370*, London: Variorum Reprints, 1977, art. no. I.

"The Longer Introduction to the *Zīj-i Ilkhānī* of Naṣir-ad-dīn Ṭūsī," *Journal of Semitic Studies* 8 (1963), 244–54.

"Rashīd al-Dīn: The First World Historian," *Iran* 9 (1971), 19–26.

"Sites and Localities Connected with the History of the Mongol Empire," *The Second International Congress of Mongolists*, Ulan Bator, n.p., 1973, vol. I, pp. 75–80.

Braudel, Fernand, *Civilization and Capitalism*, vol. II: *The Perspective of the World*, New York: Harper and Row, 1979.

Bray, Francesca, *Agriculture*, in Needham, *SCC*, vol. VI, pt. 2.

Bretschneider, Emil, *Medieval Researches from Eastern Asiatic Sources*, London: Routledge and Kegan Paul, 1967, 2 vols.

Brosset, M., trans., *Histoire de la Géorgie*, pt. 1: *Histoire ancienne, jusqu'en 1469 de JC*, St. Petersburg: Académie des sciences, 1850.

Browne, Edward G., *A Literary History of Persia*, vol. III: *The Tartar Domination (1265–1502)*, Cambridge University Press, 1969.

Budge, Ernest A. Wallis, trans., *The Monks of Ḳūblāi Khan*, London: Religious Tract Society, 1928.

Syriac Book of Medicines: *Syrian Anatomy, Pathology and Therapeutics in the Early Middle Ages*, repr., Amsterdam: APA-Philo Press, 1976, vol. I.

Buell, Paul D., "Mongol Empire and Turkicization: The Evidence of Food and Foodways," in Amitai-Preiss and Morgan, *Mongol Empire*, pp. 200–23.

"Pleasing the Palate of Qan: Changing Foodways of the Imperial Mongols," *Mongolian Studies* 13 (1990), 57–81.

"Sino-Khitan Administration in Mongol Bukhara," *Journal of Asian History* 13 (1979), 121–51.

"The *Yin-shan cheng-yao*. A Sino-Uighur Dietary: Synopsis, Problems, Prospects," in Unschuld, *Approaches to Traditional Chinese Medical Literature*, pp. 109–27.

Bulliet, Richard W., "Medieval Arabic *Ṭarsh*: A Forgotten Chapter in the History of Printing," *JAOS* 107 (1987), 427–38.

Cahen, Claude, "Notes pour une histoire de l'agriculture dans les pays musulmans médiévaux," *Journal of the Economic and Social History of the Orient* 14 (1971), 63–68.

Cammann, Schuyler, "Notes on the Origin of Chinese K'o-ssu Tapestry," *Artibus Asiae* 11 (1948), 90–110.

Canard, M., "Le riz dans le Proche Orient aux premiers siècles de l'Islam," *Arabica* 6/2 (1959), 113–31.

Carter, Thomas Francis, *The Invention of Printing in China and Its Spread Westward*, 2nd edn, rev. by L. Carrington Goodrich, New York: Ronald Press, 1955.

Casson, Lionel, *Ancient Trade and Society*, Detroit: Wayne State University Press, 1984.

Chan, Hok-lam, "Chinese Official Historiography at the Yuan Court: The Composition of the Liao, Chin, and Sung Histories," in John D. Langlois, ed., *China under Mongol Rule*, Princeton University Press, 1981, pp. 56–106.

"Liu Ping-chung (1216–74): A Buddhist–Taoist Statesman at the Court of Khubilai Khan," *TP* 53 (1967), 98–146.

"Prolegomena to the *Ju-nan i-shih*: A Memoir on the Last Chin Court under the Mongol Siege of 1234," *Sung Studies Newsletter* 10, supplement 1 (1974), 2–19.

"Siting by Bowshot: A Mongolian Custom and its Sociopolitical and Cultural Implications," *Asia Major* 4/2 (1991), 53–78.

"Wang O's Contribution to the History of the Chin Dynasty," in Chan Ping-leung, ed., *Essays in Commemoration of the Golden Jubilee of the Fung Ping Shan Library, 1932–1982*, Hong Kong University Press, 1982, pp. 345–75.

Chao Hung, *Meng-ta pei-lu*, in Wang, *Meng-ku shih-liao*.

Chardin, Sir John, *Travels in Persia*, repr., New York: Dover Publications, 1988.

Chau Ju-kua, *His Work on Chinese and Arab Trade in the Twelfth and Thirteenth Centuries, entitled Chu-fan-chi*, trans. by Friedrich Hirth and W. W. Rockhill, repr., Taipei: Literature House, 1965.

Chavannes, Edouard, *Documents sur les Tou-kiue (Turks) occidentaux*, repr., Taipei: Ch'eng wen, 1969.

Ch'en, Kenneth, "Notes on the Sung and Yuan Tripitaka," *HJAS* 14 (1951), 208–14.

Chen, Paul Heng-chao, *Chinese Legal Tradition under the Mongols: The Code of 1291 as Reconstructed*, Princeton University Press, 1979.

Ch'en Yuan, *Western and Central Asians in China under the Yuan*, trans. by Ch'ien Hsing-hai and L. Carrington Goodrich, Los Angeles: Monumenta Serica and the University of California, 1966.

Ch'eng Chü-fu, *Ch'eng hsüeh-lou wen-chi*, Yuan-tai chen-pen wen-chi hui-k'an ed.; Taipei, 1970.

Ch'ien Ta-hsin, *Pu-Yuan shih i-wen chih*, Shih-hsüeh ts'ung-shu ed.; Taipei, 1964.

Chin shih, Peking: Chung-hua shu-chü, 1975.

Chou Liang-hsiao, "Yuan-tai t'ou-hsia fen-feng chih-tu ch'u-t'an," *Yuan shih lun-ts'ung* 2 (1983), 53–76.

Chou Liang-hsiao and Ku Chü-ying, *Yuan-tai shih*, Shanghai: Jen-min ch'u-pan-she, 1993.

Chung, Kei Won and George F. Hourani, "Arab Geographers on Korea," *JAOS* 58 (1938), 658–61.

Clark, Hugh R., "Muslims and Hindus in the Culture and Morphology of Quanzhou from the Tenth to Thirteenth Century," *Journal of World History* 6 (1995), 49–74.

Clavijo, Ruy González, *Embassy to Tamerlane, 1403–1406*, trans. by Guy Le Strange, New York: Harper Brothers, 1928.

Cleaves, Francis W., "*Aqa minu*," *HJAS* 24 (1962–63), 64–81.

"Biography of Bayan of the Barīn in the *Yuan-shih*," *HJAS* 19 (1956), 185–303.

"The *Bodisatw-a Čari-a Awatar-un Tayilbur* of 1312 by Čosgi Odsir," *HJAS* 17 (1954), 1–129.

"A Chinese Source Bearing on Marco Polo's Departure from China and a Persian Source on His Arrival in Persia," *HJAS* 36 (1976), 181–203.

"A Medical Practice of the Mongols in the Thirteenth Century," *HJAS* 17 (1954), 428–44.

"The Memorial for Presenting the *Yuan shih*," *Asia Major* 1 (1988), 59–69.

"The Mongolian Documents in the Musée de Téhéran," *HJAS* 16 (1953), 1–107.

"The Sino-Mongolian Inscription of 1240," *HJAS* 23 (1960–61), 62–75.

"The Sino-Mongolian Inscription of 1362 in Memory of Prince Hindu," *HJAS* 12 (1949), 1–133.

Comnena, Anna, *The Alexiad*, trans. by E. R. A. Sewter, New York: Penguin Books, 1985.

Crosby, Alfred W., *The Columbian Exchange: Biological and Cultural Consequences of 1492*, Westport, Conn.: Greenwood Press, 1972.

Al-Daffa, Ali A. and John J. Stroyls, *Studies in the Exact Sciences in Medieval Islam*, Dhahran: University of Petroleum and Minerals, and Chichester: John Wiley, 1984.

Van Dalen, Benno, E. S. Kennedy, and Mustafa Saiyid, "The Chinese–Uighur Calendar in Ṭūsī's *Zīj-i Ilkhānī*," *Zeitschrift für Geschichte der arabisch-islamischen Wissenschaften* 11 (1997), 111–51.

Dallal, Ahmad, "A Non-Ptolemaic Lunar Model from Fourteenth Century Central Asia," *Arabic Sciences and Philosophy: A Historical Journal* 2 (1992), 237–43.

Davis, Richard L., *Wind against the Mountain: Crises of Politics and Culture in Thirteenth Century China*, Cambridge, Mass.: Harvard University Press, 1998.

Dawson, Christopher, ed., *The Mongol Mission: Narratives and Letters of the*

Franciscan Missionaries in Mongolia and China in the Thirteenth and Fourteenth Centuries, New York: Sheed and Ward, 1955.

Deng, Gang, *Chinese Maritime Activities and Socioeconomic Development c. 2100 BC–1900 AD*, Westport, Conn.: Greenwood Press, 1997.

Dien, Albert E., "The *Sa-pao* Problem Reexamined," *JAOS* 82 (1962), 335–46.

Doerfer, Gerhard, "Mongolica aus Ardabīl," *Zentralasiatische Studien* 9 (1975), 187–263.

Türkische und mongolische Elemente im Neupersischen, Wiesbaden: Franz Steiner, 1963, vol. I.

Dols, Michael W., "The Origins of the Islamic Hospital: Myth and Reality," *Bulletin of the History of Medicine* 61 (1987), 367–90.

Dozy, R., *Supplément aux dictionnaires arabes*, repr., Beirut: Librairie du Liban, n.d., vol. II.

Ducros, M. A., *Essai sur le droguier populaire arabe de l'Inspectorat des Pharmacies*, Cairo: Imprimerie de l'institut français d'archéologie orientale, 1930.

Dupree, Louis, "From Whence Cometh Pasta," in Peter Snoy, ed., *Ethnologie und Geschichte: Festschrift für Karl Jettmar*, Wiesbaden: Franz Steiner, 1983, pp. 128–34.

Eberhard, Wolfram, "Die Kultur der alten Zentral- und West-asiatischen Völker nach chinesischen Quellen," *Zeitschrift für Ethnologie* 73 (1941), 215–75.

Ecsedy, I., "Early Persian Envoys in the Chinese Courts (5th–6th Centuries A.D.)," in J. Harmatta, ed., *Studies in the Sources on the History of Pre-Islamic Central Asia*, Budapest: Akadémiai Kaidó, 1979, 153–62.

"A Middle Persian–Chinese Epitaph from the Region of Ch'ang-an (Hsian) from 874," *Acta Antiqua Academiae Scientiarum Hungaricae* 19 (1971), 149–58.

Elliot, H. M. and John Dowson, trans., *The History of India as Told by its Own Historians*, repr., New York: AMS Press, 1966, vol. III.

Endicott-West, Elizabeth, *Mongolian Rule in China: Local Administration in the Yuan Dynasty*, Cambridge, Mass.: Harvard University Press, 1989.

"Notes on Shamans, Fortunetellers and *Ying-yang* Practitioners and Civil Administration in Yuan China," in Amitai-Preiss and Morgan, *Mongol Empire*, pp. 224–39.

Engelfriet, Peter M., *Euclid in China*, Leiden: E. J. Brill, 1998.

Enoki, K., "Marco Polo and Japan," in *Oriente Poliano*, Rome: Istituto Italiano per il Medio ed Estremo Oriente, 1957, pp. 23–41.

Falina, A. I., "Rashīd al-Dīn – Vrach i estestvoispytatel," *Pis'mennye pamiatniki Vostoka, 1971*, Moscow: Nauka, 1974, pp. 127–32.

Farquhar, David M., *The Government of China under Mongolian Rule: A Reference Guide*, Stuttgart: Franz Steiner, 1990.

"The Official Seals and Ciphers of the Yuan Period," *MS* 25 (1966), 362–93.

Fedorov, M. N., "Klad serebrianykh khulaguidskikh monet iz Iuzhnogo Turkmenistana," in *Kul'tura Turkmenii v srednie veka*, Trudy Iu. TAKE, vol. XVII; Ashabad: Ylym, 1980, pp. 95–99.

Al-Feel, Muhammad Rashid, *The Historical Geography of Iraq between the Mongolian and Ottoman Conquests, 1258–1534*, Nejef: al-Adab Press, 1965, vol. I.

Ferenczy, Mary, "Chinese Historiographers' Views on Barbarian–Chinese Relations," *AOASH* 21 (1968), 353–62.

Fischel, Walter J., "On the Iranian Paper Currency *al-chāw* of the Mongol Period," *JRAS* (1939), 601–4.

Flug, K. K., *Istoriia kitaiskoi pechatnoi knigi Sunskoi epokhi X–XIII vv.*, Moscow and Leningrad: Izdatel'stvo akademii nauk SSSR, 1959.

Forte, Antonio, *The Hostage An Shigao and his Offspring*, Italian School of East Asian Studies, Occasional Papers 6; Kyoto, 1995.

Foster, George M., *Culture and Conquest: America's Spanish Heritage*, Chicago: Quadrangle Books, 1960.

Foust, Clifford M., *Rhubarb: The Wondrous Drug*, Princeton University Press, 1992.

Fowden, Garth, *Empire to Commonwealth: Consequences of Monotheism in Late Antiquity*, Princeton University Press, 1993.

Fragner, Bert, "From the Caucasus to the Roof of the World: A Culinary Adventure," in Sami Zubaida and Richard Tapper, eds., *Culinary Cultures of the Middle East*, London and New York: I. B. Tauris, 1994, pp. 49–62.

"Iran under Ilkhanid Rule in a World Historical Perspective," in Aigle, *Iran*, pp. 121–31.

Frank, André Gunder, "Bronze Age World System Cycles," *Current Anthropology* 34 (1993), 383–429.

Franke, Herbert, "Additional Notes on non-Chinese Terms in the Yuan Imperial Dietary Compendium *Yin-shan cheng-yao*," *Zentralasiatische Studien* 4 (1970), 8–15.

"Aḥmad (?–1282)," in de Rachewiltz *et al.*, *In the Service of the Khan*, pp. 539–57.

"Chia Ssu-tao (1213–75): A 'Bad Last Minister'?" in Wright and Twitchett, *Confucian Personalities*, pp. 217–34.

"Chinese Historiography under Mongol Rule: The Role of History in Acculturation," *Mongolian Studies* 1 (1974), 15–26.

"Chinese Texts on the Jurchen: A Translation of the Jurchen Monograph in the *San-ch'ao pei-men hui-pen*," *Zentralasiatische Studien* 9 (1975), 119–86.

"The Exploration of the Yellow River Sources under Emperor Qubilai in 1281," in G. Gnoli and L. Lanciotti, eds., *Orientalia Iosephi Tucci Memorial Dicata*, Rome: Istituto Italiano per il Medio ed Estremo Oriente, 1985, vol. I, pp. 401–16.

From Tribal Chieftain to Universal Emperor and God: The Legitimation of the Yuan Dynasty, Munich: Bayerische Akademie der Wissenschaften, 1978, heft 2.

"Eine mittelalterliche chinesische Satire auf die Mohammedaner," in Hoernerbach, *Der Orient in der Forschung*, pp. 202–8.

"Mittelmongolische Glossen in einer arabischen astronomischen Handschrift von 1366," *Oriens* 31 (1988), 93–118.

"Mittelmongolische Kalenderfragmente aus Turfan," *Bayerische Akademie der Wissenschaften, philosophisch-historische Klasse, Sitzungsberichte* 2 (1964), 5–45.

"Some Sinological Remarks on Rašīd al-Dīn's History of China," *Oriens* 4 (1951), 21–26.

Fuchs, Walter, "Analecta zur mongolischen Uebersetzungsliteratur der Yuan-Zeit," *MS* 11 (1946), 33–64.

"Drei neue Versionen der chinesischen Weltkarte von 1402," in Herbert Franke, ed., *Studia Sino-Altaica: Festschrift für Erich Haenisch*, Wiesbaden: Franz Steiner, 1961, pp. 75–77.

The "Mongol Atlas" of China by Chu Ssu-pen and the Kuang-yü-t'u, Peking: Fu Jen University, 1946.

"Was South Africa Already Known in the 13th Century?" *Imago Mundi* 9 (1953), 50–51.
"Zur technischen Organisation der Übersetzungen buddhischer Schriften ins Chinesische," *Asia Major* 6 (1930), 84–103.
Galstian, A. G., *Armianskie istochniki o Mongolakh*, Moscow: Izdatel'stvo vostochnoi literatury, 1962.
Gardner, Charles S., *Chinese Traditional Historiography*, Cambridge, Mass.: Harvard University Press, 1961.
Gazagnadou, Didier, "La lettre du gouverneur de Karak: A propos des relations entre Mamlouks et Mongols au XIIIe siècle," *Etudes Mongoles et Sibériennes* 18 (1987), 129–32.
Gellner, Ernest, *State and Society in Soviet Thought*, Oxford: Blackwell, 1988.
Gibb, H. A. R., "*Nā'ib*," *EI*, 2nd edn, vol. VII, pp. 915–16.
Gilmore, James, *Among the Mongols*, repr., New York: Praeger, 1970.
Glick, Thomas F., *Islamic and Christian Spain in the Early Middle Ages*, Princeton University Press, 1979.
Glover, Ian C. and Charles F. W. Higham, "New Evidence for Early Rice Cultivation in South, Southeast and East Asia," in David R. Harris, ed., *The Origins and Spread of Agriculture and Pastoralism in Eurasia*, Washington, D.C.: Smithsonian Institution Press, 1996, pp. 413–41.
Godard, André, "Historique du Masdjid-é Djum'a d'Isfahān," *Athar-é Irān* 1 (1936), 213–82.
Gohlman, William E., trans., *The Life of Ibn Sina*, Albany: State University of New York Press, 1974.
Goitein, S. D., *Letters of Medieval Jewish Traders*, Princeton University Press, 1973.
A Mediterranean Society, vol. IV: *Daily Life*, Berkeley: University of California Press, 1983.
Golden, Peter B., "Chopsticks and Pasta in Medieval Turkic Cuisine," *Rocznik Orientalistyczny* 44 (1994), 73–82.
Golden, Peter B., ed., *The King's Dictionary: The Rasūlid Hexaglot, Fourteenth Century Vocabularies in Arabic, Persian, Turkic, Greek, Armenian and Mongol*, Leiden: Brill, 2000.
Goodman, Jordan, *Tobacco in History: The Cultures of Dependence*, London and New York: Routledge, 1994.
Goodrich, L. Carrington, "A Bronze Block for the Printing of Chinese Paper Currency," *American Numismatic Society Museum Notes* 4 (1950), 127–30.
"The Connection between the Nautical Charts of the Arabs and those of the Chinese before the Days of the Portuguese Navigators," *Isis* 44 (1953), 99–100.
"Geographical Additions of the XIV and XV Centuries," *MS* 15 (1956), 203–12.
"Movable Type Printing: Two Notes," *JAOS* 99 (1974), 476–77.
"Some Bibliographical Notes on Eastern Asiatic Botany," *JAOS* 60 (1940), 258–60.
Grigor of Akanc', "History of the Nation of Archers," trans. by Robert P. Blake and Richard N. Frye, *HJAS* 12 (1949), 269–399.
Gumilev, L. N., *Searches for an Imaginary Kingdom: The Legend of the Kingdom of Prester John*, Cambridge University Press, 1987.
Guzman, Gregory G., "Were the Barbarians a Negative or Positive Factor in Ancient and Medieval History?," *The Historian* 50 (1988), 558–72.

Haenisch, Erich, "Kulturbilder aus Chinas Mongolenzeit," *Historische Zeitschrift* 164 (1941), 21–48.

Zum Untergang zweier Reiche: Berichte von Augenzeugen aus den Jahren 1232–33 und 1368–70, Wiesbaden: Franz Steiner, 1969.

Ḥāfiẓ-i Abrū, *A Persian Embassy to China*, trans. by K. M. Maitra, repr., New York: Paragon Book Corp., 1970.

Ẕayl jāmiʿ al-tavārīkh-i Rashīdī, ed. by Khānbābā Bayānī, Salsalat-i intishārāt-i anjuman-i aṣar millī, no. 88; Tehran, 1971.

Hage, Per, Frank Harary, and David Krackhardt, "A Test of Communication and Cultural Similarity in Polynesian Prehistory," *Current Anthropology* 39 (1998), 699–703.

Hambis, Louis, *Le chapitre CVIII du Yuan che: Les fiefs attribués aux membres de la famille impériale et aux ministres de la cour mongole*, Leiden: E. J. Brill, 1954, vol. I.

"Deux noms chrétiens chez les Tatars," *Journal Asiatique* 241 (1953), 473–75.

Ḥamd-Allāh Mustawfī Qazvīnī, *The Geographical Part of the Nuzhat al-Qulūb*, ed. by Guy le Strange, London: Luzac, 1915.

The Taʾrīkh-i Guzidah or "Select History," ed. by E. G. Browne and R. A. Nicholson, Leiden: E. J. Brill, and London: Luzac, 1913, pt. II.

Hamdani, Abbas, "Columbus and the Recovery of Jerusalem," *JAOS* 99 (1974), 39–48.

Harley, J. B. and David Woodward, eds., *The History of Cartography*, University of Chicago Press, 1992–94, vol. II, bk. 1 and bk. 2.

Harmatta, J., "Sino-Iranica," *Acta Antiqua Academiae Scientiarum Hungaricae* 19 (1971), 113–47.

Hartner, Willy, "The Astronomical Instruments of Cha-ma-lu-ting, their Identification and their Relations with the Instruments of the Observatory of Marāgha," *Isis* 41 (1950), 184–94.

Hartwell, Robert M., *Tribute Missions to China, 960–1126*, Philadelphia: n.p., 1983.

Hayton [Het'um], *La flor des estoires de la terre d'Orient*, in *Recueil des historiens des croisades, Documents arméniens*, Paris: Imprimerie nationale, 1906, vol. II.

Hedin, Sven, *Southern Tibet*, Stockholm: Lithographic Institute of the General Staff of the Swedish Army, 1922, vol. VIII.

Heine, Peter, "Kochen im Exil – Zur Geschichte der arabischen Küche," *Zeitschrift der deutschen morgenländischen Gesellschaft* 39 (1989), 318–27.

Kulinarische Studien: Untersuchungen zur Kochkunst im arabisch-islamischen Mittelalter mit Rezepten, Wiesbaden: Otto Harrassowitz, 1988.

Helms, Mary W., *Craft and the Kingly Ideal: Art, Trade and Power*, Austin: University of Texas Press, 1993.

Ulysses' Sail: An Ethnographic Odyssey of Power, Knowledge and Geographical Distance, Princeton University Press, 1988.

Herb, G. Henrik, "Mongolian Cartography," in Harley and Woodward, *History of Cartography*, vol. II, bk. 2, pp. 682–85.

Herbert, P. A., "From *Shuku* to *Tushukuan*: An Historical Overview of the Organization and Function of Libraries in China," *Papers on Far Eastern History* 22 (1980), 93–121.

Heroldova, Dana, *Acupuncture and Moxibustion*, Prague: Academia, 1968, pt. I.

Herskovits, Melville J., *Man and His Works: The Science of Cultural Anthropology*, New York: Alfred A. Knopf, 1951.

Ho Peng-yoke, "The Astronomical Bureau in Ming China," *Journal of Asian History* 3 (1969), 137–57.

"Kuo Shou-ching," in de Rachewiltz *et al.*, *In the Service of the Khan*, pp. 282–99.

"Magic Squares in East and West," *Papers on Far Eastern History* 8 (1973), 115–41.

Hoernerbach, Wilhelm, ed., *Der Orient in der Forschung: Festschrift für Otto Spies zum 5. April 1966*, Wiesbaden: Otto Harrassowitz, 1967.

Hoffman, Birgitt, "The Gates of Piety and Charity: Rashīd al-Dīn Faḍl Allāh as Founder of Pious Endowments," in Aigle, *Iran*, pp. 189–202.

Holt, Peter M., "The Ilkhān Aḥmad's Embassies to Qalāwūn: Two Contemporary Accounts," *BSOAS* 49 (1986), 128–32.

Horst, Heribert, "Eine Gesandtenschaft des Mamlūken al-Malik an-Naṣīr am Il-khān Hof in Persien," in Hoernerbach, *Der Orient in der Forschung*, pp. 348–70.

Die Staatsverwaltung des Grosselǧūgen und Horazmšahs (1038–1231): Eine Untersuchung nach Urkundenformularen der Zeit, Wiesbaden: Franz Steiner, 1964.

Hsiao Ch'i-ch'ing, *The Military Establishment of the Yuan Dynasty*, Cambridge, Mass.: Harvard University Press, 1978.

"Shuo Ta-ch'ao: Yuan-ch'ao chien-hao ch'ien Meng-ku te Han-wen kuo-hao," *Han-hsüeh yen-chiu* 3/1 (1985), 23–40.

"Yen Shih (1182–1240)," *Papers on Far Eastern History* 33 (1986), 113–27.

Hsin T'ang-shu, Peking: Chung-hua shu-chü, 1986.

Hsü Yu-jen, *Chih-cheng chi*, Ying-yin wen-yuan ko-ssu k'u-ch'üan shu ed.

Kuei-t'ang hsiao-kao, Ying-yin wen-yuan ko-ssu k'u-ch'üan shu ed.

Hu Ssu-hui, *Yin-shan cheng-yao*, Peking: Chung-kuo shang-yeh ch'u- pan-she, 1988.

Huang Chin, *Chin-hua Huang hsien-sheng wen-chi*, Ssu-pu ts'ung-k'an ed.

Huang Shijian, "The Persian Language in China during the Yuan Dynasty," *Papers on Far Eastern History* 34 (1986), 83–95.

Huang Shijian and Ibrahim Feng Jin-yuan, "Persian Language and Literature in China," *Encyclopedia Iranica*, Costa Mesa, Calif.: Mazda Publishers, 1992, vol. V, pp. 446–53.

Huber, H. W., "Wen T'ien-hsiang," in Herbert Franke, ed., *Sung Biographies*, Wiesbaden: Franz Steiner, 1976, vol. III, pp. 1187–1201.

Huc, Régis-Evariste and Joseph Gabet, *Travels in Tartary, Thibet and China*, New York and London: Harper and Bros., 1928, vol. I.

Hucker, Charles O., *The Censorial System of Ming China*, Stanford University Press, 1966.

A Dictionary of Official Titles in Imperial China, Stanford University Press, 1985.

"The Yuan Contribution to Censorial History," *Bulletin of the Institute of History and Philology, Academia Sinica*, extra vol., no. 4 (1960), 219–27.

Huff, Toby E., *The Rise of Early Modern Science*, Cambridge University Press, 1993.

Humphreys, R. Stephen, *Islamic History: A Framework for Inquiry*, Minneapolis: Bibliotheca Islamica, 1988.

Hung, William, "The Transmission of the Book Known as the *Secret History of the Mongols*," *HJAS* 14 (1951), 433–92.

Huzayyin, S. A., *Arabia and the Far East: Their Commercial and Cultural Relations in Graeco-Roman and Irano-Arabian Times*, Cairo: Publications de la société royale de géographie d'Egypte, 1942.

Hyer, Paul, "The Re-evaluation of Chinggis Khan: Its Role in the Sino-Soviet Dispute," *Asian Survey* 6 (1966), 696–705.

Hymes, Robert P., "Not Quite Gentlemen? Doctors in Sung and Yuan," *Chinese Science* 8 (1987), 9–76.

Ibn al-Athīr, *Al-Kamīl fī al-Ta'rīkh*, ed. by C. J. Thornberg, repr., Beirut: Dar Sader, 1966, vol. XII.

Ibn Baṭṭūṭah, *The Travels of Ibn Baṭṭūṭah*, trans. by H. A. R. Gibb, Cambridge University Press for the Hakluyt Society, 1958–94, 4 vols.

Ibn Khaldūn, *The Muqqaddimah*, trans. by Franz Rosenthal, New York: Pantheon Books, 1958, vol. I.

Ibn Ridwān, ʿAlī, *Le livre de la méthode du médicin*, trans. by Jacques Gran'Henry, Louvain-la-Neuve: Université catholique de Louvain, 1979, vol. I.

Ishida Mikinosuke, "Etudes sino-iraniennes, I: A propos du *Huo-siun-wou*," *Memoirs of the Research Department of Toyo Bunko* 6 (1932), 61–76.

Iskandar Munshī, *History of Shah ʿAbbas the Great*, trans. by Roger M. Savory, Boulder, Colo.: Westview Press, 1978, vol. II.

Jackson, Peter, "The Accession of Qubilai Qa'an: A Re-Examination," *Journal of the Anglo-Mongolian Society* 2/1 (1975), 1–10.

"The Dissolution of the Mongol Empire," *CAJ* 22 (1978), 186–243.

"From *Ulus* to Khanate: The Making of the Mongol States," in Amitai-Preiss and Morgan, *Mongol Empire*, pp. 12–37.

Jackson, Peter, trans. and David O. Morgan, ed., *The Mission of Friar William of Rubruck*, London: Hakluyt Society, 1990.

Jahn, Karl, "China in der islamischen Geschichtsschreibung," *Anzeiger der phil.-hist. Klasse der österreichischen Akademie der Wissenschaften* 108 (1971), 63–73.

"Kamālashri – Rashīd al-Dīn's Life and Teaching of Buddha," *CAJ* 2 (1956), 81–128.

"A Note on Kashmir and the Mongols," *CAJ* 2 (1956), 176–80.

"Paper Currency in Iran: A Contribution to the Cultural and Economic History of Iran in the Mongol Period," *Journal of Asian History* 4 (1970), 101–35.

"Rashīd al-Dīn as World Historian," in *Yadname-ye Jan Rypka*, Prague: Akademia, and The Hague: Mouton, 1967, pp. 79–87.

"Some Ideas of Rashīd al-Dīn on Chinese Culture," *CAJ* 14 (1970), 134–47.

"The Still Missing Works of Rashīd al-Dīn," *CAJ* 9 (1964), 113–22.

"Study of the Supplementary Persian Sources for the Mongol History of Iran," in Denis Sinor, ed., *Aspects of Altaic Civilization*, Bloomington: Indiana University, 1963, pp. 197–204.

"Tabris, ein mittelalterliches Kulturzentrum zwischen Ost und West," *Anzeiger der phil.-hist. Klasse der österreichischen Akademie der Wissenschaften* 11 (1968), 201–11.

"Wissenschaftliche Kontacte zwischen Iran und China in der Mongolenzeit," *Anzeiger der phil.-hist. Klasse der österreichischen Akademie der Wissenschaften* 106 (1969), 199–211.

Jakobi, Jürgen, "Agriculture between Literary Tradition and Firsthand Experience: The *Irshād al-Zirāʿa* of Qāsim b. Yūsuf Abū Nasrī Havarī," in Lisa Golembek and Maria Subtelny, eds., *Timurid Art and Culture: Iran and Central Asia in the Fifteenth Century*, Leiden: E. J. Brill, 1992, pp. 201–8.

James, David, *Qur'āns of the Mamluks*, New York: Thames and Hudson, 1988.

Du Jarric, Pierre, S.J., *Akbar and the Jesuits: An Account of Jesuit Missions to the Court of Akbar*, trans. by C. H. Payne, London: Routledge, 1926.

Jensen, Jørgen, "The World's Most Diligent Observer," *Asiatische Studien* 51 (1997), 719–28.

Johnson, Helen, "The Lemon in India," *JAOS* 57 (1937), 381–96.

Johnson, M. C., "Greek, Moslem and Chinese Instrument Designs in the Surviving Mongol Equatorials of 1279 AD," *Isis* 32 (1940), 27–43.

Jones, E. L., *Growth Recurring: Economic Change in World History*, Oxford University Press, 1988.

Juvaynī, ʿAṭā-Malik, *The History of the World Conqueror*, trans. by John A. Boyle, Cambridge, Mass.: Harvard University Press, 1958, 2 vols.

Taʾrīkh-i Jahāngushā, ed. by Mīrzā Muḥammad Qazvīnī, E. J. W. Gibb Memorial Series, vol. XVI; London: Luzac, 1912–37, 3 vols.

Jūzjānī, *Ṭabaqāt-i nāṣirī*, ed. by W. Nassau Lees, Bibliotheca Indica, vol. XLIV; Calcutta: College Press, 1864.

"*Ṭabaqāt-i nāṣirī*, trans. by H. G. Raverty, repr., New Delhi: Oriental Books Reprint Corp., 1970, 2 vols.

Kadyrbaev, A. Sh., "Uighury v Irane i na Blizhnem Vostoke v epokhu mongol'skogo gosudarstva," in *Voprosy istorii i kul'tury Uigurov*, Alma Ata: Nauka, 1987, pp. 41–51.

Kakabadze, S. S., *Gruzinskie dokumenty IX–XV vv.*, Moscow: Nauka, 1982.

Káldy-Nagy, Gy., "The Beginnings of Arabic-Letter Printing in the Muslim World," in Gy. Káldy-Nagy, ed., *The Muslim East: Studies in Honor of Julius Germanus*, Budapest: Loránd Eötvös University, 1974, pp. 201–11.

Kara, D. [György], *Knigi mongol'skikh kochevnikov*, Moscow: Glavnaia redaktsiia vostochnoi literatury, 1972.

Karimov, U. I., "Slovar meditsinskikh terminov Abu Mansura al-Kumri," in P. G. Bulgakova and U. I. Karimov, eds., *Materialy po istorii i istorii nauki i kul'tury narodov Srednei Azii*, Tashkent: Fan, 1991, pp. 112–55.

Kazin, V. N., "K istorii Khara-khoto," *Trudy gosudarstvennogo Ermitazha* 5 (1961), 273–85.

Kempiners, R. G., Jr., "Vaṣṣāf's *Tajziyat al-amṣar va tazjiyat al-aʿṣār* as a Source for the History of the Chaghadayid Khanate," *Journal of Asian History* 22 (1988), 160–92.

Kennedy, E. S., "The Chinese–Uighur Calendar as Described in the Islamic Sources," *Isis* 55 (1964), 435–43.

"Eclipse Predictions in Arabic Astronomical Tables Prepared for the Mongol Viceroy of Tibet," *Zeitschrift für Geschichte der arabisch-islamischen Wissenschaften* 4 (1987–88), 60–80.

Kennedy, E. S. and Jan Hogendijk, "Two Tables from an Arabic Astronomical Handbook for the Mongol Viceroy of Tibet," in Erle Leichty *et al.*, eds., *A Scientific Humanist: Studies in Memory of Abraham Sachs*, Philadelphia: The University Museum, 1988, pp. 233–42.

Kent, Roland G., *Old Persian: Grammar, Texts, Lexicon*, 2nd edn, New Haven, Conn.: American Oriental Society, 1953.

Khazanov, Anatoly M., "The Early State among the Eurasian Nomads," in Henri J. M. Claessen and Peter Skalnik, eds., *The Study of the State*, The Hague: Mouton, 1981, pp. 155–75.

"Ecological Limitations of Nomadism in the Eurasian Steppe and their Social and Cultural Implications," *Asian and African Studies* 24 (1990), 1–15.

Nomads and the Outside World, Cambridge University Press, 1984.
"The Origins of the [*sic*] Genghiz Khan's State: An Anthropological Approach," *Etnografia Polska* 24 (1980), 29–39.
Khorenats'i, Moses, *History of the Armenians*, trans. by Robert W. Thomson, Cambridge, Mass.: Harvard University Press, 1970.
Kirakos Gandzaketsi, *Istoriia Armenii*, trans. by L. A. Khanlarian, Moscow: Nauka, 1976.
K'o Shao-min, *Hsin Yuan shih*, Erh-shih-wu-shih ed.
Kramarovsky, Mark G., "The Culture of the Golden Horde and the Problem of the 'Mongol Legacy'," in Gary Seaman and Daniel Marks, eds., *Rulers from the Steppe: State Formation on the Eurasian Periphery*, Los Angeles: Ethnographics Press, 1991, pp. 255–73.
Krawulsky, Dorthea, *Iran – Das Reich der Īlkhāne: Eine topographische-historische Studie*, Wiesbaden: Ludwig Reichert, 1978.
Krechetova, M. N., "Tkani 'kesy' vremeni Sun (X–XIII vv.) v Ermitazhe," *Trudy gosudarstvennogo Ermitazha* 10 (1969), 237–48.
Kriukov, M. V., V. V. Maliavin, and M. V. Sofronov, *Ethnicheskaia istorii Kitaitsov na rubezhe srednevekov'ia i novogo vremia*, Moscow: Nauka, 1987.
Lambton, A. K. S., The *Āthār wa aḥyā'* of Rashīd al-Dīn and his Contribution as an Agronomist, Arboriculturalist, and Horticulturist," in Amitai-Preiss and Morgan, *Mongol Empire*, pp. 126–54.
Landes, David, *Revolution in Time*, Cambridge, Mass.: Harvard University Press, 1983.
Lane, Arthur and R. B. Serjeant, "Pottery and Glass Fragments from the Aden Littoral, with Historical Notes," *JRAS*, nos. 1–2 (1948) 108–33.
Lang, David M., *Studies in the Numismatic History of Georgia in Transcaucasia*, New York: American Numismatic Society, 1955.
Lao Yan-shuan, "Notes on non-Chinese Terms in the Yüan Imperial Dietary Compendium *Yin-shan cheng-yao*," *Bulletin of the Institute of History and Philology, Academia Sinica* 34 (1969), 399–416.
Laufer, Bertold, "Columbus and Cathay, and the Meaning of America to the Orientalist," *JAOS* 51 (1931), 87–103.
"History of the Finger Print System," *Annual Report of the Board of Regents of the Smithsonian Institution, 1912*, Washington, D.C.: Government Printing Office, 1913, pp. 631–52.
"The Lemon in China and Elsewhere," *JAOS* 54 (1934), 143–60.
Sino-Iranica: Chinese Contributions to the History of Civilization in Ancient Iran, repr., Taipei: Ch'eng-wen, 1967.
"Vidanga and Cubebs," *TP* 16 (1915), 282–88.
Le Strange, Guy, *The Lands of the Eastern Caliphate*, London: Frank Cass and Co., 1966.
Ledyard, Gari, "Cartography in Korea," in Harley and Woodward, *History of Cartography*, vol. II, bk. 2, pp. 235–345.
Lee, H. C., "A Report on a Recently Excavated Sung Ship at Quanzhou and a Consideration of its True Capacity," *Sung Studies* 11–12 (1975–76), 4–9.
Leslie, Donald Daniel, "The Identification of Chinese Cities in Arabic and Persian Sources," *Papers on Far Eastern History*, 26 (1982), 1–38.
"Moses, the Bamboo King," *East Asian History* 6 (1993), 75–90.
"Persian Temples in T'ang China," *MS* 35 (1981–83), 275–303.

Leslie, Donald Daniel and K. H. J. Gardiner, "Chinese Knowledge of Western Asia during the Han," *TP* 68 (1982), 254–308.

Lessing, Ferdinand D., *Mongolian–English Dictionary*, Bloomington, Ind.: Mongolia Society, 1973.

Levey, Martin, *Early Arabic Pharmacology: An Introduction Based on Ancient and Medieval Sources*, Leiden: E. J. Brill, 1973.

Lewis, Bernard, ed. and trans., *Islam*, vol. II: *Religion and Society*, New York: Walker and Co., 1974.

"The Mongols, the Turks and the Muslim Polity," in his *Islam in History: Ideas, Men and Events in the Middle East*, New York: Library Press, 1973, pp. 179–98.

The Muslim Discovery of Europe, New York: W. W. Norton, 1982.

Li Ch'ang-nien, *Tou-lei*, Peking: Chung-hua shu-chü, 1958.

Li Chih-ch'ang, *Hsi-yü chi*, in Wang, *Meng-ku shih-liao*.

The Travels of an Alchemist, trans. by Arthur Waley, London: Routledge and Kegan Paul, 1963.

Ligeti, Louis, ed., *Mongolian Studies*, Amsterdam: B. R. Grüner, 1970.

"Les sept monastères nestoriens de Mar Sargis," *AOASH* 26 (1972), 169–78.

Linton, Ralph, *The Tree of Culture*, New York: Alfred A. Knopf, 1955.

Liou Ho and Claudius Roux, *Aperçu bibliographique sur les anciens traités chinois de botanique, d'agriculture, de sericulture et de fungiculture*, Lyon: Bose Frères et Riou, 1927.

Liu Ying-sheng, "Hui-hui kuan tsa-tzu yü Hui-hui kuan i-yü yen-chiu," *Yuan shih chi pei-fang min-tsu shih yen-chiu ch'i-k'an* 12–13 (1989–90), 145–80.

Liu Yüeh-shen, *Shen-chai Liu hsien-sheng wen-chi*, Yuan-tai chen-pen wen-chi hui-k'an ed.

Lupprian, Karl-Ernst, *Die Beziehungen der Päpste zu islamischen und mongolischen Herrschern in 13. Jahrhundert, anhand ihres Briefwechsels*, Vatican: Biblioteca Apostolica Vaticana, 1981.

Luvsanjav, Choi, "Customary Ways of Measuring Time and Time Periods in Mongolia," *Journal of the Anglo-Mongolian Society* 1/1 (1974), 7–16.

Ma Kanwen, "Diagnosis by Pulse Feeling in Traditional Chinese Medicine, in *Ancient China's Technology and Science*, pp. 358–68.

Macartney, George, *An Embassy to China*, ed. by J. L. Cranmer-Byng, London: Longmans, 1962.

MacKenzie, D. N., *A Concise Pahlavi Dictionary*, London: Oxford University Press, 1990.

Maejima Shinji, "The Muslims in Ch'üan-chou at the End of the Yuan, Part I," *Memoirs of the Research Department of Toyo Bunko* 31 (1973), 27–52.

Mahler, Jane Gaston, "Art of the Silk Route," in Bowie, *East–West in Art*, pp. 70–83.

Maḥmūd Kāšγarī, *Compendium of the Turkic Dialects* (*Dīwan Luγāt at-Turk*), trans. by Robert Dankoff, Sources of Oriental Languages and Literature, vol. VII; Cambridge, Mass.: Harvard University Printing Office, 1982, 3 vols.

Mair, Victor H., "Old Sinitic *Myag, Old Persian Maguš and English Magician," *Early China* 15 (1990), 27–47.

Mangold, Gunter, *Das Militärwesen in China unter der Mongolenherrschaft*, Bamberg: aku Fotodruck, 1971.

Marco Polo, *The Description of the World*, trans. by A. C. Moule and Paul Pelliot, London: Routledge, 1938, vol. I.

Martinez, A. P., "The Third Portion of the History of Ǧāzān Xan in Rašīdu'd-Dīn's *Ta'rīx-e mobārak-e Ǧāzānī*," *AEMA* 6 (1986–88), 129–242.

Marvazī, *Sharaf al-Zamān Tāhir Marvazī on China, the Turks and India*, trans. by V. Minorsky, London: Royal Asiatic Society, 1942.

Matthee, Rudi, "From Coffee to Tea: Shifting Patterns of Consumption in Qajar Iran," *Journal of World History* 7 (1996), 199–230.

Mayer, L. A., *Mamluk Playing Cards*, ed. by R. Ettinghausen and O. Kurz, Leiden: E. J. Brill, 1971.

Mazahéri, Aly, *La vie quotidienne des Musulmans au Moyen Age*, Paris: Librairie Hachette, 1951.

McClure, Shannon, "Some Korean Maps," *Transactions of the Korean Branch of the Royal Asiatic Society* 50 (1975), 70–102.

McGovern, William M., *The Early Empires of Central Asia*, Chapel Hill: University of North Carolina Press, 1939.

Meisami, Julie Scott, trans., *The Sea of Precious Virtues* (*Baḥr al-Favā'id*): *A Medieval Islamic Mirror for Princes*, Salt Lake City: University of Utah Press, 1991.

Melikov, G. V., "Ustanovlenie vlasti mongol'skikh feodalov v Severo-Vostochnom Kitae," in Tikhvinskii, *Tataro-Mongoly*, pp. 62–84.

Melville, Charles, "Abū Sa'īd and the Revolt of the Amirs in 1319," in Aigle, *Iran*, pp. 89–120.

"The Chinese Uighur Animal Calendar in Persian Historiography of the Mongol Period," *Iran* 32 (1994), 83–98.

"The Ilkhān Öljeitü's Conquest of Gīlān (1307): Rumor and Reality," in Amitai-Preiss and Morgan, *Mongol Empire*, pp. 73–125.

"The Itineraries of Sultan Öljeitü," *Iran* 28 (1990), 55–70.

"Pādshāh-i Islām: The Conversion of Sulṭān Maḥmūd Ghāzān Khān," *Pembroke Papers* 1 (1990), 159–77.

Meng Ssu-ming, *Yuan-tai she-hui chieh-chi chih-tu*, Hong Kong: Lung-men shu-tien, 1967.

Menges, Karl H., "Rašidu'd-Dīn on China," *JAOS* 95 (1975), 95–98.

Mercier, Raymond, "The Greek 'Persian Syntaxis' and the *Zīj-i Ilkhānī*," *Archives Internationales d'Histoire des Sciences* 34 (1984), 33–60.

Meserve, Ruth I., "On Medieval and Early Modern Science and Technology in Central Eurasia," in Michael Gervers and Wayne Schlepp, eds., *Cultural Contact, History and Ethnicity in Inner Asia*, Toronto: Joint Centre for Asia Pacific Studies, 1996, pp. 49–70.

"Western Medical Reports on Central Eurasia," in Arpád Berta, ed., *Historical and Linguistic Interaction between Inner Asia and Europe*, University of Szeged, 1997, pp. 179–93.

Meyvaert, Paul, "An Unknown Letter of Hulagu, Il-khan of Persia, to King Louis of France," *Viator* 11 (1980), 245–61.

Miller, Roy Andrew, trans., *Accounts of Western Nations in the History of the Northern Chou Dynasty*, Berkeley: University of California Press, 1959.

Minorsky, Vladimir, *Persia in AD 1478–1490*, London: Royal Asiatic Society, 1957.

Minuvī, Mujtabā, "Tanksūq-nāmah-i Rashīd al-Dīn," in S. H. Naṣr, ed., *Majmu'ah-i khatābah-ha-i taḥqīqī dar bārah-i Rashīd al-Dīn*, University of Tehran, 1971, pp. 307–17.

Miyasita Saburō, "A Link in the Westward Transmission of Chinese Anatomy in the Later Middle Ages," *Isis* 58 (1967), 486–90.
"Malaria (*yao*) in Chinese Medicine during the Chin and Yuan Periods," *Acta Asiatica* 36 (1979), 90–112.
Moore, Omar Khayyam, "Divination – A New Perspective," *American Anthropologist* 59 (1957), 69–74.
Morgan, David O., "Rashīd al-Dīn," *EI*, 2nd edn, vol. VIII, pp. 443–44.
"Rashīd al-Dīn and Ghazan Khan," in Aigle, *Iran*, pp. 179–88.
Morton, A. H., "The Letters of Rashīd al-Dīn: Īlkhanīd Fact or Timurid Fiction?," in Amitai-Preiss and Morgan, *Mongol Empire*, pp. 155–99.
Mostaert, Antoine, *Le matériel mongol du Houa I I Iu de Houng-ou* (*1389*), ed. by Igor de Rachewiltz, Mélanges chinois et bouddhiques, vol. XVIII; Brussels: Institut belge des hautes études chinoises, 1977, vol. I.
Mostaert, Antoine and Francis W. Cleaves, *Les lettres de 1289 et 1305 des ilkhan Arγun et Öljeitü à Philippe le Bel*, Cambridge, Mass.: Harvard University Press, 1962.
"Trois documents mongols des Archives Secrètes Vaticanes," *HJAS* 15 (1952), 419–506.
Mote, Frederick W., "Yuan and Ming," in K. C. Chang, ed., *Food in Chinese Culture: Anthropological and Historical Perspectives*, New Haven, Conn.: Yale University Press, 1977, pp. 195–257.
Mote, Frederick W., Hung-lam Chu, and Pao-chen Ch'en, "The High Point of Printing in the Sung and Yuan Dynasties," *Gest Library Journal* 2/2 (1988), 97–132.
Moule, A. C., *Christians in China before the Year 1500*, London: Society for Promoting Christian Knowledge, 1930.
Quinsai with Other Notes on Marco Polo, Cambridge University Press, 1957.
Muginov, A. M., "Persidskaia unikal'naia rukopis Rashīd al-Dīna," *Uchenye zapiski instituta vostokovedeniia* 16 (1958), 352–75.
Muʿīn al-Dīn Naṭanzī, *Muntakhab al-tavārīkh-i muʿīni*, ed. by Jean Aubin, Tehran: Librairie Khayyam, 1957.
Mukhamadiev, A. G., *Bulgaro-Tatarskaia monetnaia sistema*, Moscow: Nauka, 1983.
Munday, Peter, *The Travels of Peter Munday in Europe and Asia, 1608–1667*, ed. by Sir Richard Carrol Temple, repr., Nendeln, Liechtenstein: Kraus, 1967, vol. II.
Munkuyev, N. Ts., "Two Mongolian Printed Fragments from Khara Khoto," in Ligeti, *Mongolian Studies*, pp. 341–57.
"Zametki o drevnikh mongolakh," in Tikhvinskii, *Tataro-Mongoly*, pp. 377–408.
Nadeliaev, V. M. *et al.*, eds., *Drevnetiurkskii slovar*, Leningrad: Nauka, 1969.
Al-Nadīm, *The Fihrist of al-Nadīm*, trans. by Bayard Dodge, New York: Columbia University Press, 1970, 2 vols.
Needham, Joseph, "Central Asia and the History of Science and Technology," in his *Clerks and Craftsmen*, pp. 30–39.
Clerks and Craftsmen in China and the West, Cambridge University Press, 1970.
"Elixir Poisoning in Medieval China," in his *Clerks and Craftsmen*, pp. 316–39.
"The Peking Observatory in AD 1280 and the Development of the Equatorial Mounting," *Vistas in Astronomy* 1 (1955), 67–83.
"The Unity of Science: Asia's Indispensable Contribution," in his *Clerks and Craftsmen*, pp. 14–29.

Needham, Joseph *et al.*, *Science and Civilization in China*, Cambridge University Press, 1954–.
Nikitin, A. B., "Khristianstvo v Tsentral'noi Azii (drevnost i srednevekov'e)," in B. A. Litvinskii, ed., *Vostochnoi Turkestan i Srednaia Aziia: Istoriia, kul'tura, sviazi*, Moscow: Nauka, 1984, pp. 121–37.
Nissen, Hans J., *The Early History of the Ancient East*, University of Chicago Press, 1988.
Nung-sang chi-yao, Ssu-pu pei-yao ed.
Okada, Hidehiro, "The Chinggis Khan Shrine and the *Secret History of the Mongols*," in Klaus Sagaster, ed., *Religious and Lay Symbolism in the Altaic World and Other Papers*, Wiesbaden: Otto Harrassowitz, 1989, pp. 284–92.
"Origins of the Dörben Oyirad," *Ural-Altaische Jahrbücher* 7 (1987), 181–211.
Olschki, Leonardo, *Guillaume Boucher: A French Artist at the Court of the Khans*, repr., New York: Greenwood Press, 1969.
Marco Polo's Asia, Berkeley: University of California Press, 1960.
"Poh-lo: Une question d'onomatologie chinoise," *Oriens* 3 (1950), 183–89.
Orbelian, Stephannos, *Histoire de la Sioune*, trans. by M. Brosset, St. Petersburg: Académie imperiale des sciences, 1864.
Ōshima Ritsuko, "The *Chiang-hu* in the Yuan," *Acta Asiatica* 45 (1983), 60–95.
Ovington, J., *A Voyage to Surat in the Year 1689*, ed. by H. G. Rawlinson, Oxford University Press, 1929.
Pakhomov, E. A., *Monety Gruzii*, Tbilisi: Izdatel'stvo "Metsniereba," 1970.
Palmieri, Richard P., "Tibetan Xylography and the Question of Movable Type," *Technology and Culture* 32 (1991), 82–90.
Pankratova, B. I., ed., *Iuan-chao bi-shi* (*Sekretnaia istoriia mongolov*), Moscow: Izdatel'stvo vostochnoi literatury, 1962.
Park, George K., "Divination and its Social Contexts," in John Middleton, ed., *Magic, Witchcraft, and Curing*, Austin: University of Texas Press, 1989.
Pellat, Ch., "Ǧāhiẓiana, I," *Arabica* 2 (1955), 153–65.
Pelliot, Paul, "Des artisans chinois à la capitale Abbasside en 751–762," *TP* 26 (1928), 110–12.
"Chrétiens d'Asie centrale et d'Extrême-Orient," *TP* 15 (1914), 623–44.
"Les grands voyages maritimes chinois au début du XVe siècle," *TP* 30 (1933), 237–452.
"Le Hōǰa et le Sayyid Ḥusain de l'histoire des Ming," *TP* 38 (1938), 81–292.
"Les influences iraniennes en Asie centrale et en Extrême Orient," *Revue Indochinois* 18 (1912), 1–15.
Les Mongols et la papauté, Paris: Librairie August Picard, 1923, vol. II.
"Note sur la carte des pays du Nord-Ouest dans le *King-che ta-tien*," *TP* 25 (1928), 98–100.
Notes on Marco Polo, Paris: Librairie Adrien-Maisonneuve, 1959–61, 2 vols.
Recherches sur les chrétiens d'Asie centrale et d'Extrême-Orient, Paris: Imprimerie nationale, 1973.
"Review of Charignon, *Le livre de Marco Polo*," *TP* 25 (1928), 156–69.
"Une ville musulmane dans Chine du Nord sous les Mongols," *Journal Asiatique* 211 (1927), 261–79.
Pelliot, Paul and Louis Hambis, *Histoire des campagnes de Gengis Khan*, Leiden: E. J. Brill, 1951.

P'eng Ta-ya and Hsü T'ing, *Hei-ta shih-lüeh*, in Wang, *Meng-ku shih-liao*.

Perlee, Kh., "On Some Place Names in the *Secret History*," *Mongolian Studies* 9 (1985–86), 83–102.

Petech, Luciano, *Central Tibet and the Mongols: The Yuan-Sa-skya Period in Tibetan History*, Rome: Istituto Italiano per il Medio ed Estremo Oriente, 1990.

"Princely Houses of the Yuan Period Connected with Tibet," in Tadeusz Skorupski, ed., *Indo-Tibetan Studies: Papers in Honor and Appreciation of Professor David L. Snellgrove's Contribution to Indo-Tibetan Studies*, Tring, England: Institute of Buddhist Studies, 1990, pp. 257–69.

Peterson, Willard J., "Calendar Reform Prior to the Arrival of Missionaries at the Ming Court," *Ming Studies* 21 (1986), 45–61.

Petrushevskii, I. P., "Feodal'noe khoziaistvo Rashīd al-Dīna," *Voprosy istorii* no. 4 (1951), 87–104.

"K istorii Khristianstva v Srednii Azii," *Palestinskii sbornik*, vyp. 15(78) (1966), 141–47.

"Persidskii traktat po agrotekhnike vremeni Gazan-khan," in *Materialy pervoi vsesoiuznoi nauchnoi konferentsii vostokovedov v. g. Tashkente*, Tashkent: Akademii nauk Uzbekskoi SSR, 1958, pp. 586–98.

"Rashīd al-Dīn's Conception of the State," *CAJ* 14 (1970), 148–62.

Zemledelie i agrarnye otnosheniia v Irane, XIII–XIV vekov, Moscow and Leningrad: Izdatel'stvo akademii nauk SSSR, 1960.

Pigulevskaia, N. V., *Kul'tura Siriitsev v srednie veka*, Moscow: Nauka, 1979.

Po-chu-lu Ch'ung, *Chü-t'an chi*, Ou-hsing ling-shih ed.

Poppe, Nicholas, "An Essay in Mongolian on Medicinal Waters," *Asia Major* 6 (1957), 99–105.

The Mongolian Monuments in hP'agspa Script, 2nd edn, trans. and ed. by John R. Krueger, Wiesbaden: Otto Harrassowitz, 1957.

"On Some Geographical Names in the *Jāmiʿ al-Tawārīx*," *HJAS* 19 (1956), 33–41.

Prejevalsky [Przhevalskii], N., *Mongolia, the Tangut Country and the Solitudes of Northern Tibet*, trans. by E. Delmar Morgan, repr., New Delhi: Asian Educational Services, 1991, vol. I.

Al-Qāshānī, Abū al-Qasīm, *Ta'rīkh-i Ūljaytū*, ed. by Mahin Hambly, Tehran: BTNK, 1969.

Quinn, Sholeh A., "The *Muʿizz al-ansāb* and the 'Shuʿab-i panjgānah' as Sources for the Chaghatayid Period of History: A Comparative Analysis," *CAJ* 33 (1989), 229–53.

de Rachewiltz, Igor, "An-t'ung," in de Rachewiltz *et al.*, *In the Service of the Khan*, pp. 539–57.

"The Dating of the *Secret History of the Mongols*," *MS* 24 (1965), 185–206.

"The *Hsi-yü lu* by Yeh-lü Ch'u-ts'ai," *MS* 21 (1962), 1–128.

Index to the Secret History of the Mongols, Indiana University Publications, Uralic and Altaic Series, vol. CXXI; Bloomington, 1972.

"Marco Polo Went to China," *Zentralasiatische Studien* 27 (1997), 34–92.

"The Mongols Rethink Their Early History," in *The East and the Meaning of History*, Rome: Bardi Editore, 1994, pp. 357–80.

"Personnel and Personalities in North China in the Early Mongol Era," *Journal of the Economic and Social History of the Orient* 9 (1966), 88–144.

"Some Remarks on Töregene's Edict of 1240," *Papers on Far Eastern History* 23 (1981), 38–63.

"Yeh-lü Ch'u-ts'ai (1189–1243): Buddhist Idealist and Confucian Statesman," in Wright and Twitchett, *Confucian Personalities*, pp. 189–216.
de Rachewiltz, Igor *et al.*, eds., *In The Service of the Khan: Eminent Personalities of the Early Mongol–Yuan Period (1200–1300)*, Wiesbaden: Harrassowitz, 1993.
Rall, Jutta, *Die Viergrossen Medizinschulen der Mongolenzeit*, Wiesbaden: Franz Steiner, 1970.
"Zur persischen Übersetzung eines *Mo-chüeh*, eines chinesischen medizinischen Textes," *Oriens Extremus* 7 (1960), 152–57.
Ramstedt, G. J., "A Fragment of Mongolian 'Quadratic' Script," in C. G. Mannerheim, *Across Asia from West to East*, repr., Oosterhout: Anthropological Publications, 1969, vol. II, pp. 1–5.
Raschid-eldin [Rashīd al-Dīn], *Histoire des Mongols de la Perse*, trans. and ed. by E. Quatremère, repr., Amsterdam: Oriental Press, 1968.
Rashīd al-Dīn, *Āthār va Aḥyā'*, ed. by M. Sutūdah and I. Afshār, Tehran University Press, 1989.
Die Chinageschichte des Rašīd al-Dīn, trans. by Karl Jahn, Vienna: Herman Böhlaus, 1971.
Die Indiengeschichte des Rašīd al-Dīn, trans. by Karl Jahn, Vienna: Verlag der österreichischen Akademie der Wissenschaften, 1980.
Jāmiʿ al-tavārīkh, ed. by A. A. Alizade, A. A. Romaskevich, and A. A. Khetagurov, Moscow: Nauka, 1968–80, vols. I and II.
Jāmiʿ al-tavārīkh, ed. by B. Karīmī, Tehran: Eqbal, 1959, 2 vols.
Mukātabāt-i Rashīdī, ed. by Muḥammad Shafīʿ, Lahore: Punjab Educational Press, 1947.
"Shuʿab-i panjgānah," ms., Topkapi Sarayi Museum, cat. no. 2932.
The Successors of Genghis Khan, trans. by John A. Boyle, New York: Columbia University Press, 1971.
Tanksūq-nāmah yā ṭibb ahl-i Khitā, ed. by Mujtabā Minuvī, University of Tehran, 1972.
Ta'rīkh-i mubārak-i Ghāzānī, ed. by Karl Jahn, London: Luzac, 1940.
Ta'rīkh-i mubārak-i Ghāzānī, ed. by Karl Jahn, 's-Gravenhage: Mouton, 1957.
Vaqfnāmah-i Rabʿ-i Rashīdī, ed. by M. Minuvī and I. Afshār, Tehran: Offset Press, 1972.
Ratchnevsky, Paul, *Un code des Yuan*, Paris: Collège de France, 1937–85, 4 vols.
"Rašīd al-Dīn über de Moḥammedaner-Verfolgungen in China unter Qubilai," *CAJ* 14 (1970), 163–80.
"Über den mongolischen Kult am Hofe der Grosskhane in China," in Ligeti, *Mongolian Studies*, pp. 417–43.
"Zum Ausdruck 't'ou-hsia' in der Mongolenzeit," in Walther Heissig, ed., *Collectanea Mongolica: Festschrift für Professor Dr. Rintchen zum 60. Geburtstag*, Wiesbaden: Otto Harrassowitz, 1966, pp. 173–91.
Rawson, Jessica, *Chinese Ornament: The Lotus and the Dragon*, London: British Museum Publications, 1984.
Reichert, Folker E., *Begegnungen mit China: Die Entdeckung Ostasiens im Mittelalter*, Sigmaringen: Jan Thorbecke, 1992.
Reischauer, Edwin O., *Ennin's Diary: The Record of a Pilgrimage to China in Search of the Law*, New York: Ronald Press, 1955.

Ricci, Matthew [Mateo], *China in the Sixteenth Century: The Journals of Matthew Ricci, 1583–1610*, New York: Random House, 1953.
Rintchen, "A propos du papier-monnaie mongol," *AOASH* 4 (1954), 159–64.
Roe, Thomas, *The Embassy of Sir Thomas Roe to the Court of the Great Mogul*, ed. by William Foster, London: Hakluyt Society, 1899, vol. I.
Röhrborn, Klaus, "Die islamische Weltgeschichte des Rašīduddīn als Quelle für den zentralasiatischen Buddhismus?," *Journal of Turkish Studies* 13 (1989), 129–33.
Roná-Tas, András, "Dream, Magic Power and Divination in the Altaic World," *AOASH* 25 (1972), 227–36.
"Some Notes on the Terminology of Mongolian Writing," *AOASH* 18 (1965), 114–47.
Rossabi, Morris, trans., "A Translation of Ch'en Ch'eng's *Hsi-yü fan-ku-chih*," *Ming Studies* 17 (1983), 49–59.
Roux, Jean Paul, *La mort chez les peuples altaiques anciens et médiévaux d'après les documents écrits*, Paris: Adrien-Maisonneuve, 1963.
La religion des Turcs et des Mongols, Paris: Payot, 1984.
Rudolph, R. C., "Medical Matters in an Early Fourteenth Century Chinese Diary," *Journal of the History of Medicine and Allied Sciences* 2 (1947), 299–306.
Ruska, J. "Cassionus Bassus Scholasticus und die arabischen Versionen der griechischen Landwirtschaft," *Der Islam* 5 (1914), 174–79.
Sabban, Françoise, "Court Cuisine in Fourteenth Century Imperial China: Some Culinary Aspects of Hu Sihui's *Yinshan zhengyao*," *Food and Foodways* 1 (1986), 161–96.
Sagaster, Klaus, trans., *Die Weisse Geschichte*, Wiesbaden: Otto Harrassowitz, 1976.
Saʿīd al-Andalusī, *Science in the Medieval World: Book of the Categories of Nations*, trans. by Semaʿan I. Salem and Alok Kumar, Austin: University of Texas Press, 1991.
Saliba, George, "The Astronomical Tradition of Maragha: A Historical Survey and Prospects for Future Research," *Arabic Sciences and Philosophy: A Historical Journal* 1 (1991), 67–99.
"The Role of the *Almagest* Commentaries in Medieval Arabic Astronomy: A Preliminary Survey of Ṭūsī's Redaction of Ptolemy's *Almagest*," *Archives Internationales d'Histoire des Sciences* 37 (1987), 3–20.
"The Role of Maragha in the Development of Islamic Astronomy: A Scientific Revolution before the Renaissance," *Revue de Synthèse* 1 (1987), 361–73.
Al-Samarqandī, *The Medical Formulary of al-Samarqandī*, ed. and trans. by Martin Levey and Noury al-Khaledy, Philadelphia: University of Pennsylvania Press, 1967.
Sanjian, Avedis K., *Colophons of Armenian Manuscripts: A Source for Middle Eastern History*, Cambridge, Mass.: Harvard University Press, 1969.
Sarianidi, V. I., "The Lapis Lazuli Route in the Ancient East," *Archaeology* 24/1 (1971), 12–15.
Sarton, George, "*Tacuinum, taqwīm*," *Isis* 10 (1928), 490–93.
Savage-Smith, Emilie, "Celestial Mapping," in Harley and Woodward, *History of Cartography*, vol. II, bk. 1, pp. 12–70.
Savage-Smith, Emilie and Marion B. Smith, *Islamic Geomancy and a Thirteenth-Century Divinatory Device*, Malibu, Calif.: Undena Publications, 1980.

Sayf ibn Muḥammad ibn Yaʿqub al-Havarī, *Taʾrīkh-i nāmah-i Harāt*, ed. by Muḥammad Zubayr al-Ṣiddīqī, Calcutta: Baptist Mission Press, 1944.

Sayili, Aydin, *The Observatory in Islam and its Place in the General History of the Observatory*, 2nd edn, Ankara: Türk Tavih Kurumu Basimevi, 1988.

Schafer, Edward H., *The Golden Peaches of Samarkand: A Study of T'ang Exotics*, Berkeley: University of California Press, 1963.

"Iranian Merchants in T'ang Dynasty Tales," in *Semitic and Oriental Studies: A Volume of Studies Presented to William Popper*, University of California Studies in Semitic Philology, vol. XI; Berkeley, 1951, 403–22.

Shore of Pearls, Berkeley: University of California Press, 1970.

Schortman, Edward M. and Patricia A. Urban, "Current Trends in Interaction Research," in Edward M. Schortman and Patricia A. Urban, eds., *Resources, Power and Interregional Interaction*, New York and London: Plenum Press, 1992, pp. 235–55.

Schreiber, Gerhard, "The History of the Former Yen Dynasty, Part II," *MS* 15 (1956), 1–141.

Schurmann, Herbert F., *The Economic Structure of the Yuan Dynasty*, Cambridge, Mass.: Harvard University Press, 1956.

The Secret History of the Mongols, trans. by Francis W. Cleaves, Cambridge, Mass.: Harvard University Press, 1982.

Seifeddini, M. A., *Monetnoe delo i denezhnoe obrashchenie v Azerbaidzhane XII–XV vv.*, Baku: Elm, 1978–81, 2 vols.

Serruys, Henry, "Mongol *Altun* 'Gold' = Imperial," *MS* 21 (1962), 357–78.

"The Mongols of Kansu during the Ming," *Mélanges Chinois et Bouddiques* 11 (1952–55), 215–346.

"Remains of Mongol Customs in China during the Early Ming," *MS* 16 (1957), 137–90.

Service, Elman R., *Origins of the State and Civilization: The Process of Cultural Evolution*, New York: Norton and Co., 1975.

Shakanova, Nurila Z., "The System of Nourishment among the Eurasian Nomads: The Kazakh Example," in Gary Seaman, ed., *Ecology and Empire: Nomads in the Cultural Evolution of the Old World*, Los Angeles: Ethnographics Press, 1989, pp. 111–17.

Shcheglova, O. P., *Katalog litografirovannykh knig na persidskom iazyke v sobranii LO IV AN SSSR*, Moscow: Nauka, 1975, vol. II.

Shelkovnikov, B. A., "Kitaiskaia keramike iz raskopok srednevekovykh gorodov i poseleni Zakavkaz'ia," *Sovetskaia arkheologiia* 21 (1954), 368–78.

Shen Chin-ting, "Introduction to Ancient Cultural Exchange between Iran and China," *Chinese Culture* 8 (1967), 49–61.

Sheng-wu ch'in-cheng lu, in Wang, *Meng-ku shih-liao*.

Shepherd, Dorothy G., "Iran between East and West," in Bowie, *East–West in Art*, pp. 84–105.

Shiba Yoshinobu, *Commerce and Society in Sung China*, trans. by Mark Elvin, Ann Arbor: University of Michigan Center for Chinese Studies, 1970.

Al-Shihabi, Mustafa, "Filāha," *EI*, 2nd edn, vol. II, pp. 899–901.

Shimo Hirotoshi, "Two Important Persian Sources of the Mongol Empire," *Etudes Mongoles et Sibériennes* 27 (1996), 222–23.

Shimo Satoko, "Three Manuscripts of the Mongol History of *Jāmiʿ al-tavārīkh*, with Special Reference to the History of the Tribes," *Etudes Mongoles et Sibériennes* 27 (1996), 225–28.

Shiu Iu-nin, "Lemons of Kwantung with a Discussion Concerning Origin," *Lingnan Science Journal* 12, supplement (1933), 271–94.

Siegel, Bernard J. *et al.*, "Acculturation: An Exploratory Formulation," *American Anthropologist* 56 (1954), 973–1000.

Silver Jubilee Volume of the Zinbun Kagaku-Kenkyusyo Kyoto University, Kyoto University, 1954.

Simon de Saint Quentin, *Histoire des Tartares*, ed. by Jean Richard, Paris: Libraire orientaliste, 1965.

Simoons, Frederick J., *Food in China: A Cultural and Historical Inquiry*, Boca Raton, Ann Arbor and Boston: CRC Press, 1991.

Sims-Williams, Nicolas, "Sogdian and Turkish Christians in Turfan and Tun-huang Manuscripts," in Alfredo Cadonna, ed., *Turfan and Tun-huang: The Texts*, Florence: Leo S. Olschki Editore, 1992, pp. 43–61.

Sivin, Nathan, "Chinese Archaeoastronomy: Between Two Worlds," in A. F. Aveni, ed., *World Archaeoastronomy*, Cambridge University Press, 1989, pp. 55–64.

Smirnova, L. P., trans. and ed., *'Ajā'ib al-dunyā*, Moscow: Nauka, 1993.

Smith, John Masson, "Mongol Campaign Rations: Milk, Marmots and Blood?," *Journal of Turkish Studies* 8 (1984), 223–28.

Soucek, Priscilla, "Role of Landscape in Iranian Painting to the 15th Century," in *Landscape and Style in Asia*, Percival David Foundation Colloquies in Art and Archaeology in Asia 9; London, 1980.

Sperling, Elliot, "Hülegü and Tibet," *AOASH* 45 (1990), 145–57.

Spuler, Bertold, *Die Mongolen in Iran*, 4th edn, Leiden: E. J. Brill, 1985.

Stein, Aurel, *Ancient Khotan*, Oxford University Press, 1907.

Innermost Asia: Detailed Report of Explorations in Central Asia, Kan-su and Eastern Iran, Oxford: Clarendon Press, 1928.

Steinhardt, Nancy Shatzman, "Currency Issues of Yuan China," *Bulletin of Sung Yuan Studies* 16 (1980), 59–81.

Stern, Bernard J., *Social Factors in Medical Progress*, New York: Columbia University Press, 1927.

Stuart, G. A., *Chinese Materia Medica: Vegetable Kingdom*, repr., Taipei: Southern Materials Center, 1987.

Su T'ien-chüeh, *Yuan wen-lei*, Taipei: Shih-chiai shu-chü ying-hsing, 1967.

Sudzuki Osamu, "The Silk Road and Alexander's Eastern Campaign," *Orient: Report of the Society for Near Eastern Studies in Japan* 11 (1975), 67–92.

Sun, K'o-k'uan, "Yü Chi and Southern Taoism during the Yuan," in John Langlois, ed., *China under Mongol Rule*, Princeton University Press, 1981, pp. 212–55.

Suter, H., *Die Mathematiker und Astronomen der Araben und Ihre Werke*, repr., New York: Johnson Reprint Corp., 1972.

Szalontai-Dmitrieva, Judith, "The Etymology of the Chuvash Word *Yumśa*, 'Sorcerer'," in András Roná-Tas, ed., *Chuvash Studies*, Wiesbaden: Otto Harrassowitz, 1982, pp. 171–77.

Szyliowicz, J. S., "Functional Perspectives on Technology: The Case of the Printing Press in the Ottoman Empire," *Archivum Ottomanicum* 11 (1986–88), 249–59.

Ta-Yuan sheng-cheng kuo-ch'ao tien-chang, repr. of the Yuan edn, Taipei: Kuo-li ku-kung po-wu yuan, 1976.

Tampoe, Moira, *Maritime Trade between China and the West: An Archaeological Study of the Ceramics from Shiraf (Persian Gulf), 8th to 15th Centuries*, Oxford, BAR Publications, 1989.

T'an Ch'i-hsiang, ed., *Chung-kuo li-shih ti-t'u chi*, vol. VII: *Yuan Ming-te ch'i*, Shanghai: Ti-t'u ch'u-pan-she, 1982.

T'ao Tsung-i, *Cho-keng lu*, Chin-tai mi-shu ed.

Taqizadeh, S. H., "Various Eras and Calendars Used in the Countries of Islam," *BSOAS* 9 (1939), 903–22.

Tarn, W. W., "Alexander the Great and the Unity of Mankind," *Proceedings of the British Academy* 9 (1933), 123–66.

Tasaka Kōdō, "An Aspect of Islam[ic] Culture Introduced into China," *Memoirs of the Research Department of Toyo Bunko* 16 (1957), 75–160.

Taylor, Romeyn, "Review of Rashīd al-Dīn, *Successors of Genghis Khan*," *Iranian Studies* 5 (1972), 189–92.

Teall, John L. "The Byzantine Agricultural Tradition," *Dumbarton Oaks Papers* 25 (1971), 33–59.

Tekin, Talat, *Irk Bitiq: The Book of Omens*, Wiesbaden: Harrassowitz, 1993.

Ten Broeck, Janet Rinaker, and Yiu Tung, "A Taoist Inscription of the Yuan Dynasty: *The Tao-chiao pei*, *TP* 40 (1950), 60–122.

Terent'ev-Katanskii, A. P., *S Vostoka na zapad: Iz istorii knigi i knigopechataniia v stranakh Tsentral'noi Azii VIII–XIII vekov*, Moscow: Glavnaia redaktsiia vostochnoi literatury, 1990.

Thaʿālibī, *The Book of Curious and Entertaining Information: The Laṭāʾif al-Maʿārif of Thaʿālibī*, trans. by C. E. Bosworth, Edinburgh University Press, 1968.

Thorley, J., "The Silk Trade between China and the Roman Empire at its Height, circa A.D. 90–130," *Greece and Rome*, 2nd series, 18 (1971), 71–80.

Tibbetts, Gerald R., "Later Cartographic Developments," in Harley and Woodward, *History of Cartography*, vol. II, bk. 1, pp. 137–55.

Tikhonov, D. I., *Khoziaistvo i obshchestvennyi stroi uighurskogo gosudarstva, X–XIV vv.*, Moscow and Leningrad: Nauka, 1966.

Tikhvinskii, S. L., ed., *Tataro-Mongoly v Azii i Evrope: Sbornik statei*, 2nd edn, Moscow: Nauka, 1977.

[Togan], Ahmet Zeki Validi, "Islam and the Science of Geography," *Islamic Culture* 8 (1934), 511–27.

Togan, Zeki Velidi, "The Composition of the History of the Mongols by Rashīd al-Dīn," *CAJ* 7 (1962), 60–72.

Tolmacheva, Marina, "The Medieval Arabic Geographers and the Beginnings of Modern Orientalism," *International Journal of Middle Eastern Studies* 27 (1995), 141–56.

Toussaint-Samat, Maguelonne, *A History of Food*, Oxford: Blackwell, 1992.

Ts'ai Mei-piao, *Yuan-tai pai-hua pei chi-lu*, Peking: K'o-hsüeh ch'u-pan-she, 1955.

Tsien Tsuen-hsuin, *Paper and Printing*, in Needham, *SCC*, vol. V, pt. 1.

T'u Chi, *Meng-wu-erh shih-chi*, Taipei: Shih-chieh shu-chü, 1962.

Tugusheva, L. Iu., trans., *Fragmenty uigurskoi versii biografii Siuan-tszana*, Moscow: Nauka, 1980.

T'ung-chih t'iao-ko, Hangchou: Che-chiang ku-chi ch'u-pan-she, 1986.

Turner, Howard R., *Science in Medieval Islam: An Illustrated Introduction*, Austin: University of Texas Press, 1995.

Twitchett, Denis, "Chinese Biographical Writing," in W. G. Beasley and E. G. Pulleyblank, eds., *Historians of China and Japan*, London: Oxford University Press, 1961, pp. 95–114.

Ullman, Manfred, *Islamic Medicine*, Edinburgh University Press, 1978.

Die Nature- und Geheimwissenschaften im Islam, Handbuch der Orientalistik, Ergänzungband VI.2; Leiden: E. J. Brill, 1972.

Al-ʿUmarī, Ibn Faḍl Allāh, *Das mongolische Weltreich: al-ʿUmarī's Darstellung der mongolischen Reiche in seinem Werk Masālik al-abṣār fī mamālik al-amṣār*, trans. by Klaus Lech, Wiesbaden: Otto Harrassowitz, 1968.

Unschuld, Paul U., ed., *Approaches to Traditional Chinese Medical Literature*, Dordrecht, Boston and New York: Kluwer Academic Publishers, 1989.

Medical Ethics in Imperial China: A Study in Historical Anthropology, Berkeley: University of California Press, 1979.

Medicine in China: A History of Ideas, Berkeley: University of California Press, 1985.

Medicine in China: A History of Pharmaceutics, Berkeley: University of California Press, 1986.

"Terminological Problems Encountered and Experiences Gained in the Process of Editing a Commentated *Nan-ching* Edition," in Unschuld, *Approaches to Traditional Chinese Medical Literature*, pp. 97–107.

Unschuld, Ulrike, "Traditional Chinese Pharmacology: An Analysis of its Development in the Thirteenth Century," *Isis* 68 (1977), 224–48.

Van Ess, Joseph, *Der Wesir und seine Gelehrten*, Wiesbaden: Franz Steiner, 1981.

Vardan Arewelcʿi, "The Historical Compilation of Vardan Arewelcʿi," trans. by Robert W. Thomson, *Dumbarton Oaks Papers*, 43 (1989), 125–226.

Varisco, Daniel Martin, "Medieval Agricultural Texts from Rasulid Yemen," *Manuscripts of the Middle East* 4 (1989), 150–54.

Vaṣṣāf al-Ḥaẓrat, *Taʾrīkh-i Vaṣṣāf*, Tehran: Ibn-i Sīnā, 1959.

Vesel, Živa, "Les traités d'agriculture en Iran," *Studia Iranica* 15 (1986), 99–108.

Voegelin, E., "The Mongol Orders of Submission to the European Powers," *Byzantium* 15 (1940–41), 378–413.

Voiret, Jean-Pierre, "China 'Objektiv' Gesehen: Marco Polo als Berichterstatter," *Asiatische Studien* 51 (1997), 805–21.

Wang Kuo-wei, ed., *Meng-ku shih-liao ssu-chung*, Taipei: Cheng-chung shu-chü, 1975.

Wang Shih-tien, *Mi-shu chih*, Taipei: Wei-wen tu-shu pan-she, 1976.

Watson, Andrew, *Agricultural Innovation in the Early Islamic World: The Diffusion of Crops and Techniques, 700–1100*, Cambridge University Press, 1983.

Watson, Gilbert, *Theriac and Mithridatium: A Study in Therapeutics*, London: Wellcome Historical Medical Library, 1966.

Watson, William, "Iran and China," in Ehsan Yarshater, ed., *The Cambridge History of Iran*, Cambridge University Press, 1983, vol. III/1, pp. 537–58.

Wechsler, Howard J., *Offerings of Jade and Silk: Ritual and Symbol in the Legitimation of the T'ang Dynasty*, New Haven, Conn.: Yale University Press, 1985.

Weiers, Michael, "Münzaufschriften auf Münzen mongolischer Il-khane aus dem Iran," *The Canada–Mongolia Review* 4/1 (1978), 41–62.

Wheatley, Paul, "Analecta Sino-Africana Recensa," in H. Neville Chittick and Robert I. Rotberg, eds., *East Africa and the Orient: Cultural Synthesis in Pre-Colonial Times*, New York: Africana Publishing Co., 1978, pp. 76–114.

"Geographical Notes on Some Commodities Involved in Sung Maritime Trade," *Journal of the Malayan Branch of the Royal Asiatic Society* 32/2 (1961), 5–140.

Whipple, Allen D., *The Role of the Nestorians and Muslims in the History of Medicine*, Princeton University Press, 1967.

Whitehouse, David and Andrew Williamson, "Sasanian Maritime Trade," *Iran* 11 (1973), 29–49.

Wilber, Donald N. and M. Minovi, "Notes on the Rabʿ-i Rashīdī," *Bulletin of the American Institute for Iranian Art and Archeology* 5 (1938), 247–54.

Wilkinson, Endymion, *The History of Imperial China: A Research Guide*, Cambridge, Mass.: Harvard University Press, 1973.

Wittfogel, Karl A. and Feng Chia-sheng, *History of Chinese Society, Liao (907–1125)*, Transactions of the American Philosophical Society, n.s., vol. XXXVI, Philadelphia, 1949.

Wong, K. Chimin and Wu Lien-teh, *History of Chinese Medicine*, 2nd edn, repr., Taipei: Southern Materials Center, 1985.

Woods, John E., "The Rise of Tīmurīd Historiography," *Journal of Near Eastern Studies* 46/2 (1987), 81–108.

Wright, Arthur R. and Denis Twitchett, eds., *Confucian Personalities*, Stanford University Press, 1962.

Wright, David Curtis, *The Ambassadors' Records: Eleventh Century Reports of Sung Ambassadors to the Liao*, Papers on Inner Asia 29; Bloomington: Research Institute for Inner Asian Studies, Indiana University, 1998.

Wu, K. T., "Chinese Printing under Four Alien Dynasties," *HJAS* 13 (1950), 447–523.

Wu Han, *Teng-hsia ch'i*, Peking: Hsin-chih san-lien shu-tien, 1961.

Wylie, A., *Notes on Chinese Literature*, Shanghai: Presbyterian Mission Press, 1922.

Yabuuti Kiyosi, "Astronomical Tables in China from the Wutai to the Ch'ing Dynasties," *Japanese Studies in the History of Science* 2 (1963), 94–100.

"Indian and Arabian Astronomy in China," in *Silver Jubilee Volume of the Zinbun Kagaku-Kenkyusyo Kyoto University*, pp. 585–603.

"The Influence of Islamic Astronomy in China," in David A. King and George Saliba, eds., *From a Different Equant: A Volume of Studies in the History of Science in the Ancient and Medieval Near East in Honor of E. S. Kennedy*, New York: New York Academy of Sciences, 1987, pp. 547–59.

"Islamic Astronomy in China," *Actes du dixième congrès international d'histoire des sciences*, Paris: Hermann, 1964, pp. 555–57.

Yang Chih-chiu and Ho Yung-chi, "Marco Polo Quits China," *HJAS* 9 (1945–47), 51.

Yang Hsüan-chih, *A Record of Buddhist Monasteries in Lo-yang*, trans. by Yi-t'ung Wang, Princeton University Press, 1984.

Yang Yü, *Beiträge zur Kulturgeschichte Chinas unter der Mongolenherrschaft: Das Shan-kü sin-hua des Yang Yü*, trans. by Herbert Franke, Wiesbaden: Franz Steiner, 1956.

Yao Tao-chung, "Ch'iu Ch'u-chi and Chinggis Khan," *HJAS* 46 (1986), 201–19.

Yazdī, Sharaf al-Dīn ʿAlī, *Ẓafar-nāmah*, ed. by M. ʿAbbasī, Tehran: Chap-i rangin, 1957, vol. I.

Yee, Cordell D. K., "Taking the World's Measure: Chinese Maps between Observation and Text," in Harley and Woodward, *History of Cartography*, vol. II, bk. 2, pp. 96–127.

Yuan Chüeh, *Ch'ing-jung chü-shih chi*, Ssu-pu ts'ung-k'an ed.

Yuan-shih, Peking: Chung-hua shu-chü, 1978.

Yule, Sir Henry, *Cathay and the Way Thither, Being a Collection of Medieval Notices of China*, repr., Taipei: Ch'eng-wen Publishing Company, 1966, 4 vols.

Yūsuf Khāṣṣ Ḥājib, *Wisdom of Royal Glory (Kutadgu Bilig): A Turko-Islamic Mirror for Princes*, trans. by Robert Dankoff, University of Chicago Press, 1983.

Zhang Zhishan, "Columbus and China," *MS* 41 (1993), 177–87.

Zhou Shide, "Shipbuilding," in *Ancient China's Technology and Science*, pp. 479–93.

Zhukovskaia, N. L., *Kategorii i simvolika traditsionnoi kul'tury Mongolov*, Moscow: Nauka, 1988.

Zieme, P., "Zu den nestorianisch-türkischen Turfantexten," in G. Hazai and P. Zieme, eds., *Sprache, Geschichte und Kultur der altaischen Völker*, Berlin: Akademie-Verlag, 1974, pp. 661–68.

Zuev, Iu. A., "*Dzhāmiʿ al-tavārīkh* Rashīd al-Dīna kak istochnik po rannei istorii Dzhalairov," *Pis'mennye pamiatniki vostoka, 1969*, Moscow: Nauka, 1972, pp. 178–85.

Index

Other titles in the series

Popular Culture in Medieval Cairo
BOAZ SHOSHAN 0 521 43209 X

Early Philosophical Shiism *The Ismaili Neoplatonism of Abū Yaʿqūb al-Sijistānī*
PAUL E. WALKER 0 521 44129 3

Indian Merchants and Eurasian Trade, 1600–1750
STEPHEN FREDERIC DALE 0 521 45460 3

Palestinian Peasants and Ottoman Officials *Rural Administration around Sixteenth-Century Jerusalem*
AMY SINGER 0 521 45238 4 hardback 0 521 47679 8 paperback

Arabic Historical Thought in the Classical Period
TARIF KHALIDI 0 521 46554 0 hardback 0 521 58938 X paperback

Mongols and Mamluks *The Mamluk–Īlkhānid War, 1260–1281*
REUVEN AMITAI-PREISS 0 521 46226 6

Hierarchy and Egalitarianism in Islamic Thought
LOUISE MARLOW 0 521 56430 1

The Politics of Households in Ottoman Egypt *The Rise of the Qazdağlis*
JANE HATHAWAY 0 521 57110 3

Commodity and Exchange in the Mongol Empire *A Cultural History of Islamic Textiles*
THOMAS T. ALLSEN 0 521 58301 2

State and Provincial Society in the Ottoman Empire *Mosul, 1540–1834*
DINA RIZK KHOURY 0 521 59060 4

The Mamluks in Egyptian Politics and Society
THOMAS PHILIPP AND ULRICH HAARMANN (eds.) 0 521 59115 5

The Delhi Sultanate *A Political and Military History*
PETER JACKSON 0 521 40477 0

European and Islamic Trade in the Early Ottoman State *The Merchants of Genoa and Turkey*
KATE FLEET 0 521 64221 3

Reinterpreting Islamic Historiography *Hārūn al-Rashīd and the Narrative of the ʿAbbāsid Caliphate*
TAYEB EL-HIBRI 0 521 65023 2

The Ottoman City between East and West *Aleppo, Izmir, and Istanbul*
EDHEM ELDEM, DANIEL GOFFMAN AND BRUCE MASTERS 0 521 64304 X

A Monetary History of the Ottoman Empire
ŞEVKET PAMUK 0 521 44197 8

The Politics of Trade in Safavid Iran *Silk for Silver, 1600–1730*
RUDOLPH P. MATTHEE 0 521 64131 4

The Idea of Idolatry and the Emergence of Islam *From Polemic to History*
G. R. HAWTING 0 521 65165 4

Classical Arabic Biography *The Heirs of the Prophets in the Age of al-Maʾmūn*
MICHAEL COOPERSON 0 521 66199 4

Empire and Elites after the Muslim Conquest *The Transformation of Northern Mesopotamia*
CHASE F. ROBINSON 0 521 78115 9

Poverty and Charity in Medieval Islam *Mamluk Egypt, 1250–1517*
ADAM SABRA 0 521 772915

Christians and Jews in the Ottoman Arab World *The Roots of Sectarianism*
BRUCE MASTERS 0 521 80333 0

9 780521 803359